Theology and Anthropology in the Book of Sirach

Septuagint and Cognate Studies

Wolfgang Kraus, General Editor

Editorial Board:
Robert Hiebert
Arie van der Kooij
Siegfried Kreuzer
Philippe Le Moigne

Number 73

SBL PRESS

Theology and Anthropology in the Book of Sirach

Edited by
Bonifatia Gesche, Christian Lustig, and Gabriel Rabo

SBL PRESS

S|B|L PRESS

Atlanta

Library of Congress Cataloging-in-Publication Data

Names: Gesche, Bonifatia, editor. | Lustig, Christian, editor. | Rabo, Gabriel, editor.
Title: Theology and anthropology in the Book of Sirach / edited by Sr. Bonifatia Gesche, Christian Lustig, Gabriel Rabo.
Description: SBL Press, 2019. | Series: Septuagint and cognate studies; 73 | Includes bibliographical references and index.
Identifiers: LCCN 2019043352 (print) | LCCN 2019043353 (ebook) | ISBN 9781628372670 (paperback) | ISBN 9780884144236 (hardcover) | ISBN 9780884144243 (ebook)
Subjects: Bible. LCSH: Bible. Ecclesiasticus—Criticism, interpretation, etc.
Classification: LCC BS1765.52 .T54 2019 (print) | LCC BS1765.52 (ebook) | DDC 229/.406—dc23
LC record available at https://lccn.loc.gov/2019043352
LC ebook record available at https://lccn.loc.gov/2019043353

Contents

God mixture male & female but many faces are the same

vi

Contents

Preface

This volume combines the papers of an international conference held at Eichstatt (6–8 October 2017) that focused on the theology and anthropology of the book of Ben Sira. The topic of this meeting arose from research on a project to present a polyglot synopsis of the book of Ben Sira covering the Hebrew, Syriac, Greek, and Latin traditions of the text with their German translations (see www.sirach-synopse.de). This project and also the conferences were, and still are, funded by the Deutsche Forschungsgemeinschaft (DFG). It was the second conference organized by the team engaged on the project. (For the first, see Gerhard Karner, Frank Ueberschaer und Burkard M. Zapff, eds., *Texte und Kontexte des Buches Sirach/Texte und Kontexte des Sirachbuches*, SCS 66 [Atlanta: SBL Press, 2017]).

The complicated and diverse ways in which the book of Sirach has been passed down result in a variety of ideas concerning theology and anthropology in the different text versions. The goal of the conference was to shed new light on the question of how the author, translators and editors understood central theological ideas and their concept of the human being as portrayed in the different versions.

The value and necessity of the synoptic work was demonstrated in a public lecture given by Markus Witte in which he examined the principles of the creation of humans and their relationship to God within each of the Hebrew, Greek and Latin traditions. This modus operandi makes it possible to detect views specific to each tradition on a range of subjects, for example, to pinpoint the explicit influence of Christian thought in both the Latin and Syriac texts. Undoubtedly, the particular view of each of the traditions bears the imprint of their social and cultural context.

The papers presented here address questions from different viewpoints in relation to the subject of the conference and so add up to an in-depth understanding of theological and anthropological issues in the book of Sirach. They make a significant contribution to the academic debate on Sirach in particular but also to the ongoing research into biblical wisdom literature in general.

We would like to thank the authors who have made available their contributions for the present volume. We are also grateful to the members of the editorial board who admitted the volume to the series Septuagint and Cognate Studies and to Nicole Tilford for her editorial assistance. We received valuable support from the academic assistants of the Chair of Old Testament Studies in Eichstätt, Josephin Kain and Angelika Nießlbeck, compiling the index.

Bonifatia Gesche, Christian Lustig, Gabriel Rabo

Vorwort

Dieser Band enthält die Beiträge einer internationalen Konferenz mit dem Themenschwerpunkt „Theologie und Anthropologie des Buches von Ben Sira", die vom 6. bis 8. Oktober 2017 in Eichstätt stattfand. Das Thema dieser Tagung entstand aus der Forschungsarbeit an einem Projekt mit dem Ziel, eine mehrsprachige Synopse für das Buch von Ben Sira zu erstellen, die die hebräische, syrische, griechischen und lateinischen Texttraditionen mit ihren jeweiligen deutschen Übersetzungen umfasst (www.sirach-synopse.de). Dieses Projekt und auch die Konferenz wurden und werden von der Deutschen Forschungsgemeinschaft (DFG) gefördert. Es war bereits die zweite Konferenz, die von den Mitgliedern des Projekts organisiert wurde (zur ersten s. Gerhard Karner, Frank Ueberschaer und Burkard M. Zapff, Hrsg., Texte und Kontexte des Buches Sirach/Texte und Kontexte des Sirachbuches, SBL.SCS 66, 2017).

Die komplizierte und vielschichtige Überlieferungsgeschichte des Buches Sirach führt zu teils heterogenen Vorstellungen hinsichtlich Theologie und Anthropologie in den jeweiligen Textversionen. Ziel der Konferenz war es, die Frage aufs Neue zu erörtern, wie Autor, Übersetzer und Redakteure die zentralen Themen der Theologie behandeln und welches Menschenbild ihren Bearbeitungen zugrundeliegt. Von besonderem Interesse war es zu zeigen, wie die verschiedenen Versionen diese Konzepte abbilden.

Wert und Notwendigkeit einer synoptischen Arbeit werden nicht zuletzt an dem öffentlichen Vortrag von Markus Witte deutlich. Er untersucht die Schöpfung des Menschen und dessen Beziehung zu Gott im Hinblick auf die verschiedenen Versionen. Dabei berücksichtigt er die hebräischen, syrischen, griechischen und lateinischen Traditionen.

Dieser Modus operandi ermöglicht es, die für die Versionen charakteristische Sicht auf eine ganze Reihe von Themen zu erkennen. So wird beispielsweise der explizite Einfluss christlicher Gedanken in einigen lateinischen und auch in den syrischen Versionen erkennbar. Zweifellos ist bei allen Traditionen einsichtig, dass ihre Anschauungen jeweils durch einen eigenen sozialen und kulturellen Kontext geprägt sind.

Die im vorliegenden Band zusammengestellten Vorträge behandeln Fragen zum Thema der Konferenz aus verschiedenen Blickwinkeln und bieten ein vertieftes Verständnis dieser Themen anhand des Buches Sirach. Sie leisten so einen wesentlichen Beitrag zur wissenschaftlichen Diskussion auf dem Gebiet der Sirachforschung im Besonderen und der biblischen Weisheitsliteratur im Allgemeinen.

Wir danken den Autorinnen und Autoren, die Ihre Beiträge für den vorliegenden Band zur Verfügung gestellt haben. Außerdem gilt unser Dank den Herausgebern für die Aufnahme des Bandes in die Reihe der Septuagint and Cognate Studies sowie Nicole Tilford für die Betreuung seitens des Verlags. Bei der Erstellung des Index haben wir von den Hilfskräften des Lehrstuhls für Alttestamentliche Wissenschaft in Eichstätt, Josephin Kain und Angelika Nießlbeck, wertvolle Unterstützung erhalten.

Bonifatia Gesche, Christian Lustig, Gabriel Rabo

Menschenbilder des Sirachbuches

Markus Witte

Zum Gedenken an Otto Kaiser
(30.11.1924–14.12.2017)

ABSTRACT: This essay interprets the book of Ben Sira as a history of human education and demonstrates that it reflects and constructs a variety of images of humanity. The number of these images becomes particularly evident when one considers the Hebrew (H), Greek (G), Syriac (S), and Latin (L) versions of the book and examines each in its own right and with regard to its unique context. Thus, the polyglot character of the book requires a polyglot presentation of its anthropology. A synoptic exegesis of key anthropological texts (Sir 4:10; 6:15–16[16–17]; 14:15–19; 18:13–14; 23:27; 33[36]:7–15; 39:11; 43:32–33; 50:22–24; and 50:28–29) exposes the differences between H, G, S, and L regarding the image of humanity. This approach also demonstrates the specific intertextual relations of the different versions to the Pentateuch, Prophets, Proverbs, Psalms, Job and the New Testament and thereby provides an outline of Ben Sira's own history of reception. The fundamental principles of the creation of humans and their relation to God, which all versions share, are examined for their anthropological differences under the following headings: life and death; wisdom and knowledge; the individual and society; family and gender; mercy and justice; freedom and dependence.

1. Weisheit und Anthropologie

Alttestamentliche Weisheit zielt auf Orientierung des Menschen in einer als ambivalent, häufig auch als chaotisch erfahrenen Welt.[1] Genaue Beob-

---

1. Folgende Ausgaben des Sirachbuches liegen den in diesem Beitrag gebotenen Übersetzungen zugrunde: Für H: Pancratius C. Beentjes, Hrsg., *The Book of Ben Sira*

2 Markus Witte

achtung und Erfahrung sollen dem Einzelnen wie der Gemeinschaft Wege zu einem gelingenden Leben zeigen. Schlagen sich solche lebensorientierenden Erkenntnisse zunächst in knappen Sentenzen nieder, so führt die systematische Sammlung von Einzelsprüchen und die Komposition von thematisch und stilistisch verwandten Spruchreihen zu ausgeführten Lehrreden.

Das im ersten Drittel des 2. Jh. v.Chr. entstandene Sirachbuch stellt literatur- und traditionsgeschichtlich—neben der um etwa fünf Generationen jüngeren Sapientia Salomonis—die reifste Frucht der israelitisch-jüdischen Weisheit dar. Mit seinen 51 Kapiteln ist es die umfangreichste alttestamentliche Weisheitsschrift. Hinsichtlich seiner langen Lehrreden, seiner Mischung von unterschiedlichen weisheitlichen und psalmistischen Gattungen, seinen übergreifenden Kompositionsstrukturen sowie seiner Verschmelzung genuin weisheitlicher Traditionen mit Elementen der geschichtlichen und prophetischen Überlieferungen Israels überragt es alle älteren israelitisch-jüdischen Weisheitsbücher. Wie diese ist das Sirachbuch Teil einer von Ägypten bis Mesopotamien nachweisbaren

---

in Hebrew. A Text Edition of All Extant Hebrew Manuscripts and a Synopsis of All Parallel Hebrew Ben Sira Texts, VTSup 68 (Leiden: Brill, 1997), für G: Joseph Ziegler, Hrsg., *Sapientia Iesu Filii Sirach*, 2., durchgesehene Auflage, Septuaginta. Vetus Testamentum Graecum Auctoritate Academiae Scientiarum Gottingensis editum XII,2 (Göttingen: Vandenhoeck & Ruprecht, 1980), für S: Núria Calduch-Benages, Joan Ferrer und Jan Liesen, Hrsg., *Wisdom of the Scribe. Diplomatic Edition of the Syriac Version of Ben Sira according to Codex Ambrosianus, with Translations in Spanish and English* (Estella: Editorial Verbo Divino, 2003), für L: Robert Weber und Roger Gryson, Hrsg., *Biblia Sacra iuxta Vulgatam*, 5. durchgesehene Auflage (Stuttgart: Deutsche Bibelgesellschaft, 2007). Daneben wurden berücksichtigt: Francesco Vattioni, Hrsg., *Ecclesiastico. Testo ebraico con apparato critico e versioni greca, latina e siriaca*, Pubblicazioni del Seminario di Semitistica, Testi 1 (Neapel: Istituto Orientale di Napoli, 1968); Zeeb Ben-Ḥayyim, Hrsg., *The Book of Ben Sira. Text, Concordance and an Analysis of the Vocabulary* (Jerusalem: The Academy of the Hebrew Language and the Shrine of the Book, 1973); Alfred Rahlfs, Hrsg., *Septuaginta. Id est Vetus Testamentum graece iuxta LXX interpretes*, editio altera quam recognovit et emendavit Robert Hanhart, duo volumina in uno (Stuttgart: Deutsche Bibelgesellschaft, 2006); *Liber Hiesu Filii Sirach cum praefationibus et variis capitulorum seriebus*, Biblia Sacra, iuxta latinam Vulgatam versionem ad codicum fidem iussu Pauli PP. VI cura et studio monachorum Abbatiae Pontificiae Sancti Hieronymi in Urbe Ordinis Sancti Benedicti edita XII (Rom: Typis Polyglottis Vaticanis, 1964) sowie Walter Thiele und Anthony J. Forte, Hrsg., *Sirach (Ecclesiasticus)*, Vetus Latina: Die Reste der altlateinischen Bibel XI,2 (Freiburg: Herder, 1987–).

Weisheitstradition und basiert gleichermaßen auf der grundsätzlichen Überzeugung einer vom Schöpfergott in diese Welt eingesenkten gerechten Weltordnung, die dem Menschen, der sich an ihr ausrichtet, ein glückliches Leben gewährt. Gleichzeitig integriert es Vorstellungen paganer griechischer, vor allem stoischer Philosophie und entwickelt eine eigene Theologie, die sich aus einer allgemeinen weisheitlichen Empirie und einer besonderen auf die Tora bezogenen und mittels der heiligen Schriften Israels und paganer Texte gedeuteten Offenbarung speist. In der Figur der kosmischen Weisheit, die sich am Jerusalemer Tempel niederlässt, in der Tora des Mose inkarniert und als Gottesfurcht verwirklicht, besitzt diese Theologie ihre sachliche Mitte. In der Komposition ausführlicher Mahnreden und in der schriftgelehrten Auseinandersetzung mit der eigenen Überlieferung hat diese Theologie ihre literarische Gestalt gefunden. Der die Weisheitsliteratur von ihren Anfängen an kennzeichnende anthropologische Grundzug ist im Sirachbuch voll entfaltet. So steht in seinem Zentrum die aus Ps 8 und Ps 144 bekannte Frage nach dem Wesen des Menschen, nach seiner Stellung in der Welt und nach seinem Handeln (Sir 18,8 [G]):

Was ist ein Mensch und was ist sein Nutzen?
Was ist sein Gutes und was ist sein Schlechtes?

Zwar wird man auch beim Sirachbuch noch nicht von einer Lehre vom Menschen im engeren Sinn sprechen, wohl aber von einer systematischen Reflexion menschlichen Lebens in unterschiedlichen Lebensbezügen und Lebensverhältnissen. Wie jede Reflexion menschlichen Lebens setzt auch das Nachdenken über den Menschen im Sirachbuch einerseits ein bestimmtes Menschenbild voraus und konstruiert andererseits ein solches. In jüngerer Zeit hat Oda Wischmeyer die grundsätzlichen Strukturen der Anthropologie des Sirachbuches herausgearbeitet.[2] So sei die Anthropologie Ben Siras erstens theologisch referentiell, insofern er den Menschen durchgehend im Blick auf seine Beziehung zu Gott betrachte und als ein dialogisches Wesen verstehe.[3] Diese Anthropologie sei zweitens exklusiv,

2. Oda Wischmeyer, „Theologie und Anthropologie im Sirachbuch", in *Ben Sira's God. Proceedings of the International Ben Sira Conference Durham—Ushaw College 2001*, hrsg. von Renate Egger-Wenzel, BZAW 321 (Berlin: de Gruyter, 2002), 18–33.

3. In diesem Punkt trifft sich Wischmeyers Definition mit der vor allem von Bernd Janowski im Schatten der grundlegenden Studie von Hans Walter Wolff

das heißt gruppen-, religions- und geschlechtsspezifisch, insofern zwar allgemein vom Menschen geredet werde, letztlich aber der jüdische schriftgelehrte Mann gemeint sei. Die Verbindung einer Schöpfungstheologie, wie sie für die Weisheit im Alten Testament und im Alten Orient grundlegend ist, mit einer sich an der Tora, den Bundesschlüssen, wie sie der Pentateuch beschreibt, und an der Geschichte Israels orientierten Theologie belegen diesen exklusiven Charakter. Drittens sei die Anthropologie des Sirachbuches prozessual, insofern es mit seinen Mahnungen zur Gottesfurcht und zu einem an den Zehn Geboten ausgerichteten Handeln auf die Selbsterziehung des Weisen ziele. Wischmeyer konnte in diesem Zusammenhang von einer „panethischen" Pragmatik sprechen, mittels derer zwar nicht der Tod, wohl aber die Sünde überwunden werden könne.[4] Meine Überlegungen zu Menschenbildern des Sirachbuches setzen an dem dritten Punkt von Wischmeyers Bestimmung der Anthropologie Ben Siras ein. Dabei sollen zwei Thesen entfaltet werden.

1. *Das Sirachbuch lässt sich als ein Buch der Menschwerdung lesen.* Anders gesagt: Das Sirachbuch stellt in seiner kompositionellen Anlage eine Art menschliche Bildungsgeschichte dar. Hintergrund dieser These ist die Beobachtung, dass die einzelnen Buchteile jeweils mit einer grundsätzlichen anthropologischen Reflexion enden. Den anthropologischen Schlüsseltexten in Sir 16,24–18,14; 33(36),7–15; 40,1–41,13 und 42,15–43,33, die in Wischmeyers strukturellen Überlegungen, aber auch in Otto Kaisers basalen Ausführungen zur Anthropologie Ben Siras im Mittelpunkt stehen,[5] sind damit weitere Texte zum Wesen, Werden und Handeln des Menschen zur Seite zu stellen.

(*Anthropologie des Alten Testaments* [München: Chr. Kaiser, 1973]) vertretenen These, die alttestamentliche Anthropologie kennzeichne durchgehend ein dialogischer Charakter (Bernd Janowski, „Mensch", *RGG4* 5:1057–1058; Janowski, „Der ganze Mensch. Zu den Koordinaten der alttestamentlichen Anthropologie", *ZTK* 113 [2016]: 1–28).

4. Wischmeyer, „Theologie", 30.

5. Otto Kaiser, „Der Mensch als Geschöpf Gottes. Aspekte der Anthropologie Ben Siras", in *Zwischen Athen und Jerusalem. Studien zur griechischen und biblischen Theologie, ihrer Eigenart und ihrem Verhältnis*, BZAW 320 (Berlin: de Gruyter, 2003), 224–46; Kaiser, „‚Was ist der Mensch und was ist sein Wert?' Beobachtungen zur Anthropologie des Jesus Sirach nach Sir 16,24–18,14", in *Gott, Mensch und Geschichte. Studien zum Verständnis des Menschen und seiner Geschichte in der klassischen, biblischen und nachbiblischen Literatur*, BZAW 413 (Berlin: de Gruyter, 2010), 290–304; Kaiser, „Die Furcht und die Liebe Gottes—Ein Versuch, die Ethik Ben Siras mit der des Apostels Paulus zu vergleichen", in *Gott, Mensch und Geschichte*, 305–340; Kaiser,

2. *Das Sirachbuch enthält, reflektiert und konstruiert nicht nur ein Menschenbild, sondern eine Vielzahl von Menschenbildern.* Damit meine ich, dass angesichts der Überlieferungs- und Kanonsgeschichte des Buches die unterschiedlichen hebräischen, griechischen, lateinischen und syrischen Textformen als selbständige und eigengewichtige anthropologische Zeugen wahrzunehmen sind. Ich bestreite nicht, dass sich mittels eines Vergleichs von H, G, L und S ein hebräischer Ausgangstext rekonstruieren lässt. Ein solcher textgeschichtlicher Zugang prägt die genannten Studien von Wischmeyer und Kaiser wie alle neueren Kommentare. Er hat in historischer und philologischer Hinsicht seine volle Berechtigung. Man muss sich aber bewusst sein, dass der von Ben Sira um 180 v.Chr. selbst verfasste Text nur annäherungsweise erreichbar ist und dass die Rezeptionsgeschichten des Buches auf den überlieferten Textformen basieren. Eine der überlieferungs- und wirkungsgeschichtlichen Komplexität des Buches gerecht werdende Darstellung seiner Anthropologie muss daher synoptisch geschehen. Das heißt die Unterschiede zwischen den hebräischen, griechischen, lateinischen und syrischen Textformen sind, auch wenn sie sich textgeschichtlich entweder auf eine divergierende Vorlage oder auf ein Missverständnis oder auf eine binnensprachliche Verschreibung zurückführen und als solche erklären lassen, jeweils inhaltlich zu gewichten, buchimmanent zu verorten sowie traditions- und zeitgeschichtlich zu bestimmen. Im Folgenden versuche ich am Beispiel ausgewählter Texte eine solche polyglotte Darstellung der Menschenbilder des Sirachbuches. Dabei orientiere ich mich weitgehend an der von Otto Kaiser vorgelegten Gliederung des Buches und unterstelle, dass die älteste erhaltene Vollversion, die zwischen 132 und 117 v.Chr. angefertigte griechische Übersetzung (G-I), abgesehen von der Blattvertauschung im Bereich der Kapitel 30–36, die Kompositionsstruktur repräsentiert, die auch für den bis heute nur fragmentarisch erhaltenen hebräischen Text anzunehmen ist.[6] Dementsprechend unterscheide ich die Abschnitte Sir 1,1–4,10; 4,11–6,17; 6,18–14,19; 14,20–18,14; 18,15–23,27(28); 24,1–33,15; 33,16–39,11;

„Göttliche Weisheit und menschliche Freiheit bei Ben Sira", in *Vom offenbaren und verborgenen Gott. Studien zur spätbiblischen Weisheit und Hermeneutik*, BZAW 392 (Berlin: de Gruyter, 2008), 43–59, Kaiser, „Die stoische Oikeiosis-Lehre und die Anthropologie des Jesus Sirach", in *Vom offenbaren und verborgenen Gott*, 60–77.

6. Cf. Otto Kaiser, *Weisheit für das Leben. Das Buch Jesus Sirach übersetzt und eingeleitet* (Stuttgart: Radius, 2005), 5.

39,12–43,33; 44,1–50,24 sowie den Buchschluss in 50,27–29 und werte jeweils die letzten Verse dieser Abschnitte anthropologisch aus.

2. Auf dem Weg zur Sohnschaft Gottes (Sir 4,10)

H^A	G	L	S
Sei wie ein Vater für die Waisen und anstelle des Ehemanns für die Witwen. Und Gott wird dich Sohn nennen und dir gnädig sein und dich aus der Grube retten.	Sei den Waisen wie ein Vater und anstelle des Ehemanns für ihre Mutter. Und du wirst sein wie ein Sohn des Höchsten, und er wird dich mehr lieben als deine Mutter.	(10) Beim Richten sei den Waisen gegenüber barmherzig wie ein Vater und anstelle des Ehemanns für die Mutter jener. (11) Und du wirst sein wie ein Sohn des Höchsten, gehorsam, und er wird sich deiner erbarmen mehr als eine Mutter.	Sei wie ein Vater für die Waisen und anstelle des Ehemanns für die Witwen, und du wirst für Gott wie ein Sohn sein, und er wird sich über dich erbarmen.

Die Abschlusssentenz des ersten Teils (Sir 1,1–4,10) spiegelt gleich drei Grundsätze der Anthropologie Ben Siras: erstens die Verpflichtung zu zwischenmenschlicher Gerechtigkeit, die sich gemäß einem im Alten Testament breit belegten Ethos im Einsatz für rechtlich und wirtschaftlich Benachteiligte auswirkt, zweitens die wesenhafte Bezogenheit des Menschen auf Gott und drittens die generelle Gefährdung und Verletzlichkeit menschlicher Existenz. Das Handeln des Menschen und seine Gottesbeziehung werden in einem unmittelbaren Zusammenhang gesehen, ohne dass ein Automatismus zwischen beiden konstruiert wird. Die Ankündigung der Gottessohnschaft beschreibt keine zwangsläufige Folge sittlich verantwortlichen Verhaltens, sondern soll zu diesem motivieren. So weiß Ben Sira als aufmerksamer Leser des Buches Hiob, dass auch ein vorbildliches Verhalten gegenüber Witwen und Waisen nicht vor der Erfahrung

---

7. Siehe dazu ausführlich Markus Witte, „Das Ethos der Barmherzigkeit in der jüdischen Weisheit der hellenistisch-römischen Zeit", in *Texte und Kontexte des Sirachbuches. Gesammelte Studien zu Ben Sira und zur frühjüdischen Weisheit*, FAT 98 (Tübingen: Mohr Siebeck, 2015), 225–43.

bewahrt, am Rande oder gar in der Grube des Todes zu sein (cf. Hi 29–31). Die Zusage der Gottessohnschaft an *den*, der Gerechtigkeit übt, überträgt ein Element der altorientalischen und hellenistischen Königsideologie auf den Einzelnen und weist diesem mittels Gerechtigkeit einen königlichen Rang zu, der sich in unmittelbarer Zugehörigkeit zu Gott ausdrückt (cf. 2 Sam 7,14; Ps 2,7).[8] Insofern in der Ben Sira vorgegebenen Tradition auch die Beziehung zwischen Israel und seinem Gott mit der Metapher der Sohnschaft ausgedrückt werden kann (cf. Ex 4,22; Hos 11,1),[9] hat die anthropologisch-ethische Sentenz Ben Siras auch einen heilsgeschichtlichen Aspekt: Durch sein gerechtes Handeln erweist sich der Einzelne als wahres Glied des Gottesvolkes. Das die Verheißung in H[A] beschließende Bild von der Errettung vor oder aus der Grube (ויציל משחת) bezieht sich wie seine Parallelen im Psalter und in den Proverbien wohl zunächst auf die Bewahrung vor Gefährdungen in diesem Leben, es ist aber offen für ein postmortales Verständnis.[10] Insofern Ben Sira sonst den Tod als absolute Grenze versteht und wie Kohelet oder die Grundschicht des Hiobbuches nicht von einer grundsätzlichen Überwindung des Todesgeschicks oder einer den Tod überdauernden Beziehung zu Gott auszugehen scheint,[11] erhebt sich die Frage nach der Ursprünglichkeit der Wendung ויציל משחת (V.10d).

Die griechische Version teilt die anthropologischen Grundsätze der hebräischen Fassung. Die ethische Mahnung des zweiten Kolons ist aber auf die *eine* Witwe und deren Kinder (τῇ μητρὶ αὐτῶν) konzentriert.[12] Ein Ausblick auf den Tod oder tödliche Gefährdung fehlt. Der relationale und funktionale Charakter der Gottessohnschaft des Gerechten besteht auch in G, insofern ein Vergleich formuliert wird. Gleichwohl zeigt sich die Tendenz zu einem stärker seinsmäßigen Verständnis. Mit der Wendung „Sohn des Höchsten" (υἱὸς ὑψίστου) erklingt zudem ein anderer Intertext als in H[A], namentlich Ps 82(81),6. Damit wird einerseits menschliches gerechtes Handeln als Entsprechung zu einem göttlichen Handeln cha-

---

8. Siehe dazu auch Pancratius C. Beentjes, „Sei den Waisen wie ein Vater und den Witwen wie ein Gatte"', in *„Happy the One who Meditates on Wisdom" (Sir. 14,20). Collected Essays on the Book of Ben Sira*, CBET 43 (Leuven: Peeters, 2006), 44–46.

9. Siehe weiterhin Jes 43,6; 45,11; 49,15.

10. Cf. Ps 16,10; 33,19; 56,14; 103,4; Prov 10,2; 11,4.

11. Cf. Sir 14,15–19; 17,28–30 (G); 40,1.11.

12. Darin mag sich eine verschärfte jüdische Sexualethik zur Zeit des griechischen Übersetzers widerspiegeln.

rakterisiert (cf. Ps 82[81]),2–4), andererseits der Gedanke des göttlichen Gerichts über die, die sich gegenüber den Armen und Elenden nicht als gerecht erweisen, eingespielt (cf. Ps 82[81],1.8). Gegenüber der Aussicht auf eine Errettung *vor* der Grube in H^A steht die Aussicht auf umfassende Gottesliebe. Der Ausdruck „er wird dich mehr lieben als deine Mutter" (ἀγαπήσει σε μᾶλλον ἢ μήτηρ σου) in V.10d beinhaltet den Gedanken der Gnade Gottes, den H^A bietet. Er verleiht der Sentenz aber eine höhere stilistische und theologische Dichte, als sie H^A aufweist. So werden nicht nur das Vatersein des Gerechten und die Vaterschaft Gottes korreliert (cf. Ps 103,13), sondern auch die Sorge des Gerechten um die Mutter der Waisen und die jede Mutterliebe übertreffende Liebe Gottes (cf. Jes 49,15; 66,13). Noch deutlicher als im hebräischen Text werden die wesenhafte Differenz zwischen Gott und Mensch und gleichzeitig die Aufgabe des Menschen, der göttlichen Liebe zu entsprechen, mithin der Auftrag der *imitatio dei*, unterstrichen (cf. Lk 6,35).[13] Ich werde auf dieses Motiv im Kontext von Sir 18,13–14 zurückkommen.

Die lateinische Version steht hier grundsätzlich der griechischen näher als der hebräischen, weist aber eigene Akzente und gegen G auch Übereinstimmungen mit H^A auf. Der Rat zum angemessenen Verhalten gegenüber Waisen und Witwen wird in eine gerichtliche Situation eingeordnet. Dies entspricht Normen der Tora (cf. Dtn 10,18; 24,17) und beispielsweise auch den paradigmatischen Unschuldserklärungen Hiobs in Hi 29,12–13 und 31,16–18, bedeutet aber gegenüber G und H^A eine Einschränkung der Maxime. Das angemessene Verhalten gegenüber den gesellschaftlich und ökonomisch Benachteiligten wird ausdrücklich als Barmherzigkeit *und* als Akt des Gehorsams (*obaudiens*)[14] gegenüber Gott gekennzeichnet. Die Reziprozität menschlichen und göttlichen Handelns und Verhaltens, hier verdeutlicht durch das Gegenüber der Wörter „barmherzig" (*misericors*, V.10a) und „sich erbarmen" (*misereor*, V.11b), wird dadurch unterstrichen. Für das Menschenbild des lateinischen Sirach ergibt sich hieraus, dass der Mensch eine Anlage zum Richten und Gerichtetwerden, zum Üben und zum Empfang von Barmherzigkeit sowie zum Gehorsam und Ungehorsam gegenüber Gott hat. Liest man Sir 4,10 (L) im Kontext der

---

13. Zur Aufnahme von Sir 4,10 (G) in Lk 6,35 siehe Rosario Pistone, „Blessing of the sage, prophecy of the scribe: from Ben Sira to Matthew", in *The Wisdom of Ben Sira. Studies on Tradition, Redaction, and Theology*, hrsg. von Angelo Passaro und Giuseppe Bellia, DCLS 1 (Berlin: de Gruyter, 2008), 310–11.

14. Var. *obaudieris/oboedieris*, cf. Gen 22,18; Dtn 30,20.

christlichen Bibel—und eine solche Lektüre ist für die lateinische Version des Sirachbuches auch entstehungsgeschichtlich anzunehmen—,[15] dann ist nicht ausgeschlossen, dass sich die besondere Betonung des Gehorsams in L vor dem Hintergrund des Motivs des vorbildhaften Gehorsams des Gottessohnes Jesus Christus erklärt (cf. Phil 2,8.12).

Die syrische Version bietet die kürzeste Fassung der Sentenz und die schwächste Form des Motivs der Gottessohnschaft des Barmherzigen. Dabei steht sie H^A am nächsten, enthält aber weder einen Ausblick auf die Todesgefahr wie H^A noch den Vergleich der Liebe Gottes mit der Liebe einer Mutter wie G und L. Dadurch liegt der Schwerpunkt ganz auf der Korrelation der Barmherzigkeit des Menschen mit der Barmherzigkeit Gottes.

3. Auf dem Weg zur wahren Freundschaft (Sir 6,15–16[16–17])

H^A	G	L	S
[15] Ein Beutel des Lebens ist ein treuer Freund, der, der Gott fürchtet, wird es erlangen.	[16] Ein treuer Freund ist ein Medikament des Lebens, und die, die den Herrn fürchten, werden ihn finden.	[16] Ein treuer Freund ist ein Medikament des Lebens und der Unsterblichkeit, und die, die den Herrn fürchten, werden jenen finden.	[16] Ein treuer Freund ist ein Medikament des Lebens, und wer Gott fürchtet, der ist so.
[16] Denn wie einer selbst ist, so ist sein Nächster, und wie sein Name ist,	[17] Wer den Herrn fürchtet, wird seine Freundschaft stärken, denn wie er	[17] Wer Gott fürchtet, wird gleichsam gute Freundschaft haben, denn gemäß	[17] Diejenigen, die Gott fürchten, werden ihre Freundschaft stärken, denn

15. Zum christlichen Hintergrund der lateinischen Sir-Version siehe bereits Rudolf Smend, *Die Weisheit des Jesus Sirach erklärt* (Berlin: Reimer, 1906), CXXIX, sowie Thierry Legrand, „La version latine de Ben Sira: état de la question, essai de classement thématiques des ‚additions"', in *The Texts and Versions of the Book of Ben Sira. Transmission and Interpretation*, hrsg. von Jean-Sébastien Rey und Jan Joosten, JSJSup 150 (Leiden: Brill, 2011), 234. Kritisch gegenüber christlichem Einfluss auf L ist Maurice Gilbert, „The Vetus Latina of Ecclesiasticus", in *Studies in the Book of Ben Sira*, hrsg. von Géza G. Xeravits und József Zsengellér, JSJSup 127 (Leiden: Brill, 2008), 1–9.

| so sind seine Taten. | selbst ist, so ist auch sein Nächster. | jenem wird jener Freund sein. | wie er ist, so sind seine Freunde, <und wie sein Name, so sind seine Werke.>[16] |

Freundschaft ist ein zentrales Thema des Sirachbuches.[17] Vielleicht deutlicher als in anderen Passagen zeigt sich hier der kulturgeschichtliche Ort Ben Siras, insofern sich in hellenistischer Zeit traditionelle politische und soziale Ordnungssysteme auch in Syrien-Palästina auflösen und sich der einzelne Mensch stärker als in früheren Zeiten als Individuum in einer räumlich immer größer und kulturell immer vielfältiger werdenden Welt erlebt. So ist es nicht überraschend, dass der zweite Teil der weisheitlichen Mahnungen Ben Siras mit einem Lobpreis der Freundschaft endet und diese der Gotteskindschaft als zweiter Stufe der Menschwerdung zur Seite stellt. Der „Beutel des Lebens" (צְרוֹר חַיִּם), der traditionell als Beutel, in den bei der Zählung von Vieh Zählsteine eingelegt wurden, verstanden wird,[18] der aber auch als ein versiegeltes Dokument, vergleichbar dem „Buch des Lebens" (ספר חיים), gedeutet werden kann,[19] taucht im Bereich der israelitisch-jüdischen Schriften nur in 1 Sam 25,29 und in den Lobliedern aus Qumran (1QH[a] X,22–23) auf.[20] In Sir 6,15–16 dient das Motiv—zumal vor dem Hintergrund von 1 Sam 25,29—der Betonung des Wertes eines wahren Freundes, der sich in lebensbedrohlichen Situa-

---

16. Diese Zeile findet sich nicht in allen syrischen Handschriften, aber im Codex Ambrosianus (7a1), cf. Calduch-Benages et al., *Wisdom of the Scribe*.

17. Siehe dazu ausführlich Friedrich V. Reiterer, Hrsg., *Freundschaft bei Ben Sira. Beiträge des Symposions zu Ben Sira Salzburg 1995*, BZAW 244 (Berlin: de Gruyter, 1996); Jeremy Corley, *Ben Sira's Teaching on Friendship*, BJS 316 (Providence: Brown Judaic Studies, 2002).

18. Cf. Hans Joachim Stoebe, *Das erste Buch Samuelis*, KAT 8/1 (Gütersloh: Gütersloher Verlagshaus, 1973), 450; Fritz Stolz, *Das erste und zweite Buch Samuel*, ZBK.AT 9 (Zürich: Theologischer Verlag, 1981), 161; Georg Hentschel, *1 Samuel*, NEchtB.AT 33 (Würzburg: Echter, 1994), 141.

19. Cf. Ps 69,29; cf. Ex 32,32; Dan 12,1, und *DCH* 7, s.v. צְרוֹר I.2.

20. Der Beleg in 4Q419 fragm. 8 i,2 ist zu fragmentarisch, als dass er sich hier auswerten ließe. Zu inschriftlichen Belegen aus der Spätantike siehe William Horbury und David Noy, *Jewish Inscriptions of Graeco-Roman Egypt* (Cambridge: Cambridge University Press, 1992), 204–205 (nr. 119), und Hans Peter Rüger, *Die Weisheitsschrift aus der Kairoer Geniza. Text, Übersetzung und philologischer Kommentar* (Tübingen: Mohr Siebeck, 1991), 93 (zu WKG III,14).

tionen, so wie Abigail, als Retter erweisen kann. Dass 1 Sam 25,29 hinter Sir 6,15–16 steht, ergibt sich auch aus der Gegenüberstellung von Name und Tat, in der eine Anspielung auf den aus 1 Sam 25 bekannten Nabal, den sprichwörtlichen Toren (נבל), gesehen werden kann.[21] Dass die Sentenz aber wohl noch auf mehr als einen verlässlichen Freund, nämlich auf den Gewinn des Lebens selbst und auf die Bewahrung vor dem Tod zielt, zeigen erstens die Formulierung „er wird *es* erlangen" (ישיגם), die sich nur auf den Erwerb des Lebens (חיים) beziehen kann,[22] und zweitens die Parallele in 1QHª X,22–23:

> Ich danke dir, Herr, dass du meine „Seele" [נפשי] in den Beutel des Lebens gelegt und mich vor allen Fallen der Grube beschützt hast. (cf. Sir [Hᴬ] 4,10d)

Charakteristisch für Sir 6 ist die Verbindung von Leben, Freundschaft und Gottesfurcht in V.15. Der Spiegelsatz in V.16 unterstreicht lediglich den weisheitlichen und empirisch nachvollziehbaren Grundsatz, dass eigenes Verhalten und Handeln auf das eigene Ergehen zurückwirken und dass es zwischen dem Wesen eines Menschen und seinen Taten eine Entsprechung gibt. In anthropologischer Hinsicht ergibt sich aus Sir 6,15–16, dass der Mensch auf Gemeinschaft hin angelegt ist und dass Gottesfurcht ein entscheidendes Lebensmittel ist. Letztere Vorstellung ist ein roter Faden im Sirachbuch.[23]

Die Versionen weisen charakteristische Differenzen auf. In G erscheint anstelle des möglicherweise aus der Handelssprache stammenden Bildes für den Wert eines treuen Freundes die in hellenistischen Mysterienkulten bekannte magisch-medizinisch geprägte Metapher vom „Medikament des Lebens" (φάρμακον ζωῆς).[24] Gegenüber Hᴬ wird die Bedeutung der

---

21. Zum Nachweis siehe Pancratius C. Beentjes, „„Ein Mensch ohne Freund ist wie eine linke Hand ohne die Rechte"", in *Happy the One who Meditates*, 73–74, und Corley, *Ben Sira's Teaching*, 52, 60, 63.

22. Zum Bezug des Plural-Suffixes auf das *rectum* siehe auch Dtn 9,4b sowie Georg Sauer, *Jesus Sirach / Ben Sira*, ATD. A 1 (Göttingen: Vandenhoeck & Ruprecht, 2000), 80.

23. Cf. Sir 6,37 (Hᴬ); 9,16; 10,22; 16,2; 32,12 (Hᴬ); 40,26–27; 50,29 (Hᴮ) und dazu den Klassiker von Josef Haspecker, *Gottesfurcht bei Jesus Sirach. Ihre religiöse Struktur und ihre literarische und doktrinäre Bedeutung*, AnBib 30 (Rom: Pontificio Istituto Biblico, 1967).

24. Siehe dazu Rudolf Bultmann, „ἀθανασία", *ThWNT* 3:24.

Freundschaft noch stärker betont, wenn nun denen, die Gott fürchten, nicht das Leben, sondern der treue Freund in Aussicht gestellt und die Gottesfurcht als Mittel, die Freundschaft zu stärken, qualifiziert wird. So ist eine gelingende Beziehung zwischen zwei Menschen Folge (und Motivation) einer intakten Gottesbeziehung. Dabei ist die Formulierung von G in V.16b („ihn", αὐτόν) und in V.17a („seine", αὐτοῦ) durchaus offen für einen Bezug auf Gott, und zwar in dem Sinn, dass derjenige, der Gott fürchtet, Gott selbst findet (cf. Am 5,6) und die Freundschaft zu Gott stärkt (cf. Sap 7,27). Damit wäre dann in den Lobpreis der menschlichen Freundschaft das Motiv der Gottesfreundschaft eingespielt, wie es alttestamentlich—auch bei Sirach—seinen exemplarischen Ausdruck in dem Gottesfreund Mose findet (cf. Sir 45,1 in Weiterführung von Ex 33,11 und Dtn 34,10) und im paganen Bereich als Ideal des Philosophen begegnet.[25] Das vierte Kolon, das dem dritten in H[A] entspricht, kehrt dann eindeutig wieder zu dem im ersten Kolon ausgedrückten Gedanken der zwischenmenschlichen Freundschaft zurück.[26]

In der lateinischen Version wird die in H[A] mittels der Metapher vom „Beutel des Lebens" nur angedeutete Vorstellung, dass Freundschaft eine Bedeutung über den Tod hinaus haben könnte, expliziert. Zwar teilt das lateinische Sirachbuch mit den hebräischen Fragmenten und dem griechischen Kurztext (G-I) die Überzeugung von der grundsätzlichen Sterblichkeit des Menschen (cf. 17,29: *non est inmortalis filius hominis*). Es leuchten aber immer wieder eschatologische Motive auf, denen zufolge eine Überwindung der Todesgrenze punktuell möglich erscheint.[27] Dazu zählt Sir 6,16 (L), was zugleich der einzige Beleg im lateinischen Sirach für

---

25. Cf. Jes 41,8; 2 Chr 20,7; Jak 2,23; Jub 30,20–21; Sib. Or. II,245; T. Ab. A 1,6; Apoc. Sedr. 9,1; CD-A III,2–3; 4Q252 frag. 1 II,8; Jes 51,2 (LXX); Dan 3,35 (LXX); Philo, *Mos.* 1,156; *Cher.* 49 sowie im paganen Bereich bei Plato, *Leg.* 716c–d; *Tim.* 53d; *Symp.* 193b; *Resp.* 621c; Epiktet, *diss. ab Arriano* 4,3,9—siehe dazu auch David Winston, *The Wisdom of Solomon. A New Translation with Introduction and Commentary*, AB 43 (New York: Doubleday, 1979), 188–189.

26. Johannes Chrysostomus zitiert Sir 6,16a im Rahmen der Auslegung von 1 Thess 2,8 (*In epistulam I ad Thessalonicenses* [PG 62:403,45]); zur Buße als φάρμακον ἀθανασίας siehe z.B. Johannes Chrysostomos, *De paenitentia* (PG 60:766,57).

27. Cf. Sir (L) 1,19; 3,10; 14,25; 15,8.16; 17,20; 18,22; 24,31; 27,9 u.v.a.; siehe dazu nach wie vor Conleth Kearns, *The Expanded Text of Ecclesiasticus. Its Teaching of the Future Life as a Clue to Its Origin*. Enlarged with A Biographical Sketch of Kearns by Gerard Norton. An Introduction to Kearns' Dissertation by Maurice Gilbert. Bibliographical Updates (1951–2010) by Núria Calduch-Benages, hrsg. von Pancratius C.

den Begriff inmortalitas ist.[28] Die traditions- und rezeptionsgeschichtliche Bedeutung der lateinischen Version wird noch deutlicher, wenn man im Hintergrund von V.16a die Wendung φάρμακον ἀθανασίας („Medikament der Unsterblichkeit") annimmt und damit einerseits unmittelbar eine Formulierung aus der Beschreibung der Heilung bringenden Wunder der Göttin Isis bei Diodor Siculus (1,25,6) vor sich hat, andererseits die Qualifikation der Eucharistie im Brief des Ignatius an die Epheser 20,2.[29] Wie schon bei Sir 4,10 erhält die lateinische Version von Sir 6,16–17 im Rahmen der christlichen Bibel eine besondere Nuance, insofern dieser Text offen ist für eine Identifikation des treuen Freundes mit dem johanneischen Christus, der sein Leben für seine Freunde gibt und ihnen damit das Leben in unmittelbarer Gottesgemeinschaft schenkt (Joh 15,13–17).[30]

S entspricht einerseits G und L (so in V.16a und 17a), andererseits H^A (so in V.17b). Ein eigenständiges anthropologisches Profil erhält S durch die Identifikation eines treuen Freundes mit einem, der Gott fürchtet (V.16b): Frömmigkeit ist somit ein Merkmal eines wahren Freundes. Die von Oda Wischmeyer als Kennzeichen der Anthropologie des Sirachbuches angesprochene Gruppen- und Religionsspezifik ist hier offensichtlich.[31]

4. Auf dem Weg durch das Leben (Sir 14,15–19)   *Life*

H^A	G	L	S
[16] Gib dem Bruder[32] und gib[33]	[16] Gib und empfange und lenke	[16] Gib und empfange und	[16] Gib und empfange und stärke deine

Give & receive   *nourish soul*

Beentjes, DCLS 11 (Berlin: de Gruyter, 2011), 87–88, 108–10, 123, 132–209; Legrand, „La version latine", 227.

28. Cf. außerhalb von Sir: Sap (Vg) 3,4; 4,1; 8,13.17; 15,3; 4 Esr (Vg) 7,13; 8,54.

29. Siehe dazu auch Bultmann, „ἀθανασία", ThWNT 3:24.

30. Zur Bezeichnung Jesu Christi als Medikament des Lebens in der altkirchlichen syrischen Literatur siehe Patrick W. Skehan und Alexander A. Di Lella, The Wisdom of Ben Sira. A New Translation with Notes, Introduction and Commentary, AB 39 (New York: Doubleday, 1987), 189.

31. Wischmeyer, „Theologie", 26–27.

32. אם wird häufig als Fehler für לקח angesehen (cf. G, L, S; Smend, Weisheit, 135; Jean-Sébastien Rey, „L'espérance post-mortem dans les différentes versions du Siracide", in The Texts and Versions of the Book of Ben Sira. Transmission and Interpretation, hrsg. von Jean-Sébastien Rey und Jan Joosten, JSJSup 150 [Leiden: Brill, 2011], 273–74; Pancratius C. Beentjes, „The Concept of ‚Brother' in the Book of Ben Sira, in „Happy the One who Meditates on Wisdom" (Sir. 14,20), 253: „the result of a

Markus Witte

und verwöhne dich selbst („deine Seele"), denn in der Scheol gibt es kein Suchen nach Vergnügen. Und alle Dinge, die schön sind zu tun vor Gott, tue.³⁴

[…]

¹⁹ Alle seine Taten werden gewiss vermodern, und das Werk seiner Hände wird ihm nachfolgen.

dich selbst („deine Seele") ab, denn im Hades gibt es kein Suchen nach Genuss.

[…]

¹⁹ Jedes vermodernde Werk schwindet dahin, und der, der es wirkt, wird mit ihm dahingehen.

rechtfertige deine Seele, ⁽¹⁷⁾ vor deinem Abgang tue Gerechtigkeit, weil es bei den Toten/in der Unterwelt kein Finden von Speise gibt.

[…]

⁽²⁰⁾ Jedes verdorbene Werk wird am Ende schwach werden, und der, der jenes wirkt, wird mit ihm dahingehen.

⁽²¹⁾ Und jedes auserlesene Werk wird gerechtfertigt werden, und der, der jenes tut, wird in jenem geehrt werden.

Seele, und jede Tat, die schön ist zu tun vor Gott, die tue.

[…]

¹⁹ Und alle seine Werke sind offenbar vor ihm³⁵, und das Werk seiner Hände geht mit ihm dahin.

---

dictation error") oder als Dittographie von לאחר aus 15 gestrichen (so Víctor Morla, *Los manuscritos hebreos de Ben Sira. Traducción y notas*, Asociación Biblica Española 59 [Estella: Verbo Divino, 2012], 131). Allerdings ist Hᴬ gut verständlich (cf. Josef Schreiner, *Jesus Sirach 1–24*, NEchtB 38 [Würzburg: Echter, 2002], 82–83; Sauer, *Jesus Sirach*, 126).

33. Nach Beentjes, „The Concept", 252, weisen ein Querstrich über dem ungewöhnlich punktierten תֵ und drei Punkte am Rand von Hᴬ darauf hin, dass der Schreiber das Wort ותין als sekundär betrachtete, womit er Recht haben könnte (cf. Sauer, *Jesus Sirach*, 126).

34. Die Segmentierung und damit der syntaktische Bezug der Zeile וכל דבר שיפה sind umstritten. Nach der Gliederung von Hᴬ bildet die Wendung לעשות לפני אלהים עשה zweites, zu תענוג paralleles Objekt zu לבקש. Doch sprechen die Poetologie und S dafür, in der Zeile ein eigenes Bikolon zu sehen, dessen erstes Kolon die Wörter וכל דבר שיפה לעשות umfasst (cf. Moshe Z. Segal, ספר בן־סירא השלם, 3. Auflage [Jerusalem: Bialik Foundation, 1972], 88).

35. Das heißt: Gott.

Auch der dritte Buchteil (Sir 6,18–14,19) endet mit einer Gegenüberstellung eines ethisch verantwortlichen Handelns und eines Ausblickes auf den Tod. So gipfeln die an Mahnungen Kohelets und an Ps 49 erinnernden Ratschläge zu einem sinnvollen Umgang mit Besitz, zur Fähigkeit, zu schenken und sich beschenken zu lassen, sowie zum Genuss des Augenblicks im Resümee der absoluten Vergänglichkeit alles Geschaffenen.[36] Die sich aus allgemein weisheitlichen Sentenzen und Bildern zur Sterblichkeit speisende Collage zeigt deutlich, dass Ben Sira die sich vom alten Mesopotamien bis zum antiken Griechenland nachweisbare Vorstellung von der Freudlosigkeit des Daseins in der Unterwelt und der generellen Todverfallenheit teilt.[37] Angesichts der Endgültigkeit des Todes ist es die Aufgabe des Menschen, dieses Leben in Verantwortung gegenüber dem Nächsten (אח) und gegenüber Gott (אלהים) zu genießen. Dabei liegt der Schwerpunkt von V.19 auf der Hinfälligkeit jeglichen menschlichen Werks. Der menschlichen Hoffnung, aus eigener Kraft etwas schaffen zu können, das den eigenen Tod überdauert, wird eine Absage erteilt. Ben Siras universale Formulierung „alle seine Taten" (כל מעשיו) schließt dabei zeitgenössische monumentale Bauwerke und Mausoleen, die scheinbar für die Ewigkeit errichtet sind, ebenso ein wie die Etablierung politischer Macht oder die Produktion von Schriften, die in großen Bibliotheken wie in Alexandria gesammelt werden.

Der griechische Text entspricht prinzipiell der Tendenz von H[A]. Allerdings fehlt in G eine Entsprechung zur Aufforderung, das Gute und Schöne in diesem Leben in Achtung vor Gott zu tun.[38] Die Korrelation der Verantwortung gegenüber dem Nächsten und Gott ist durch die objektlose Formulierung des Imperativs „gib" (δός) weniger deutlich als in H[A]. Der Schwerpunkt der Abschlusssentenz liegt auf der Vergänglichkeit des Menschen selbst, nicht seines Werks; letzteres wird gegenüber H[A] ausdrücklich

---

36. Cf. Koh 2,24–26; 3,12; 5,17–19; 7,14; 8,15; 9,7–10.

37. Cf. Sir 17,27–28; 41,1–4; Hi 10,20–22; 14,7–12; Koh 9,4–5; Theognis, *Elegien* 973–978; Aischylos, *Perser* 840–842; Gilgamesch Meissner-Millard Tafel III,1–10, übersetzt von Karl Hecker (*TUAT* 3:665–66); Harfnerlied im Grab des Königs Antef, übersetzt von Jan Assmann (*TUAT* 2:905–6); siehe dazu auch Otto Kaiser, „Carpe diem und Memento mori in Dichtung und Denken der Alten, bei Kohelet und Ben Sira", in *Zwischen Athen und Jerusalem*, 247–50.

38. Die Passage in H[A] und in Syr wird daher häufig als ein von Koh 9,10 beeinflusster sekundärer Einschub angesehen (Skehan und Di Lella, *The Wisdom of Ben Sira*, 258; siehe auch Kaiser, *Weisheit*, 36).

als ein „vermoderndes" (σηπόμενον) qualifiziert,[39] so dass zumindest theoretisch auch die Möglichkeit besteht, ein beständiges Werk zu schaffen. Damit deutet sich eine ethische Differenzierung des Todesgeschicks an. In der lateinischen Version erscheint dieser Gedanke ausdrücklich.

So bringt L mittels des dreifachen Gebrauchs der Wurzel *ius-** auf den Punkt, dass es bei der Gestaltung des sozialen und religiösen Lebens um Gerechtigkeit (*iustitia*) geht. Sie spitzt die Aussagen zur allgemeinen Vergänglichkeit ethisch und eschatologisch („vor deinem Abgang … am Ende") zu (cf. Sir 14,13 [L]). Letzteres wird durch die gegenüber allen anderen Versionen hinausgehende Antithese unterstrichen, dass „jedes auserlesene Werk" (*opus electum*) gerechtfertigt wird und es dem, der es getan hat, Ehre (*honor*) einbringt. Der Zusatz kann sich innerweltlich auf postmortalen Ruhm beziehen,[40] ist aber offen für einen Bezug zu einem Totengericht, wie es sich auch an anderen Stellen des lateinischen Sirach zeigt (cf. Sir [L] 10,28; 15,8; 20,28 u.v.a.).[41] In jedem Fall beschließt L den dritten Buchteil nicht negativ mit der Aussicht auf den Tod als absoluter Grenze, sondern positiv mit der Verheißung einer den Tod überdauernden Ehrung durch Gott (cf. Sap 19,22[20]). Neben den vergänglichen Menschen tritt der von Gott gerichtete und geehrte.

Die syrische Version setzt nochmals eigene Akzente. Zwar bietet auch sie in Sir 14,15–19 eine Beschreibung der allgemeinen Vergänglichkeit (V.18). Sie enthält aber keine Aussage zur absoluten Freudlosigkeit in der Unterwelt und betont vielmehr, dass alle menschlichen Werke vor Gott offenbar sind. Damit teilt S den von L ausdrücklich eingespielten

---

39. σηπόμενον dürfte attributiv als Partizip Aktiv zu übersetzen sein (so auch Johannes Marböck, *Jesus Sirach 1–23. Übersetzt und ausgelegt*, HThK.AT [Freiburg: Herder, 2010], 181; Benjamin G. Wright, „Sirach", in *A New English Translation of the Septuagint*, hrsg. von Albert Pietersma und Benjamin G. Wright [New York: Oxford University Press, 2007], 730; Rey, „L'espérance", 272–73—anders Eve-Marie Becker, „Sophia Sirach", in *Septuaginta Deutsch. Das griechische Alte Testament in deutscher Übersetzung*, 2. Auflage, hrsg. von Wolfgang Kraus und Martin Karrer [Stuttgart: Deutsche Bibelgesellschaft, 2010], 1109 [Partizip Passiv: „verfault"] und *Die Bibel. Einheitsübersetzung der Heiligen Schrift. Gesamtausgabe, vollständig durchgesehene und überarbeitete Ausgabe*, hrsg. von der Deutschen Bischofskonferenz u.a. [Stuttgart: Katholische Bibelanstalt, 2016], 794 [prädikativ: „modert und …"]).

40. Cf. Sir 37,26; 39,10–11 (G); 41,11–13; 44,13–15; Prov 10,7; Hi 18,17.

41. Siehe dazu Kearns, *The Expanded Text*, 82–88; 141–42; Legrand, „La version latine", 231–32; Rey, „L'espérance", 274–75; siehe weiterhin Sap 3,11; 1 Hen 97,5–6; T. Ab. 13; 2 Hen 63,4.

Gedanken des göttlichen Gerichts,[42] differenziert dieses aber nicht aus, sondern formuliert universal (cf. Röm 14,10; 2 Kor 5,10). Der Schwerpunkt verlagert sich von der Anthropologie auf die Theologie, vom Bild des vergehenden und gerichteten Menschen hin zum richtenden Gott, vor dem nichts verborgen ist (cf. Sir 42,18–20). Komprimiert zeigt sich hier der für das gesamte Sirachbuch in allen seinen Versionen charakteristische enge Zusammenhang von Theologie und Anthropologie.

5. Von der *imago dei* zur *imitatio dei* (Sir 18,13–14)

Sir 18,13–14 beschließt *den* Abschnitt des Sirachbuches, in dem am grundsätzlichsten über das Wesen des Menschen und seine Stellung in der Welt und vor Gott nachgedacht wird (Sir 16,24–18,14). Die Passage ist ab Sir 16,27 nur in der griechischen, lateinischen und syrischen Version erhalten, so dass sich eine Nachzeichnung des mutmaßlich ältesten Argumentationsgangs an G orientieren muss. Unter Rückgriff auf die biblische Urgeschichte, zumal auf Gen 1–3 und Gen 9, auf einzelne Psalmen (u.a. Ps 8 und 144) und das Hiobbuch, auf die Sinaiperikope und auf Deuterojesaja, aber auch auf stoische Vorstellungen wird der Mensch als ein von Gott geschaffenes, mit Vernunft begabtes, gleichwohl von Gott durch die Sünde und die Vergänglichkeit kategorial unterschiedenes Wesen beschrieben, das mittels der als „Gesetz des Lebens" (Sir 17,11; 45,5[6]) bezeichneten Tora Zugang zu einer heilvollen Gottesnähe hat.[43] Vom „Gott des Alls" (Sir 36[33],1 cf. 18,1) zur Gottesebenbildlichkeit geschaffen, die sich in der Herrschaft über die Tiere und in der Anlage zu ethischer, intellektueller und religiöser Erkenntnis niederschlägt, findet der Mensch sein Lebensziel in der Erziehung durch und der Entsprechung zu Gott.

---

42. Smend, *Weisheit*, 136, Wido Th. van Peursen, *Language and Interpretation in the Syriac Text of Ben Sira. A Comparative Linguistic and Literary Study*, Monographs of the Peshitta Institute Leiden 16 (Leiden: Brill, 2007), 35–36. Demgegenüber bestreitet Kearns, *The Expanded Text*, 225–226, eine eschatologische Dimension von Sir 14,19 (S) und versteht den Stichos im Sinn der allgemeinen Kenntnis Gottes (cf. Sir 16,17–23; 17,15–20; 23,18–20; Prov 15,11; 24,12).

43. Siehe dazu Markus Witte, „,Das Gesetz des Lebens'. Eine Auslegung von Sir 17,11", in *Texte und Kontexte*, 109–21.

G	L	S
[13] Die Barmherzigkeit eines Menschen gilt seinem Nächsten, aber die Barmherzigkeit des Herrn gilt allem Fleisch. Er weist zurecht und erzieht und lehrt und wendet zurück wie ein Hirte seine Herde.	(12) Das Mitleid eines Menschen kreist um seinen Nächsten, aber die Barmherzigkeit Gottes ergeht über alles Fleisch, (13) der, der Barmherzigkeit hat und lehrt, erzieht wie ein Hirte seine Herde.	[13] Die Barmherzigkeit des Menschen bezieht sich auf den Verwandten seines Fleischs, aber die Barmherzigkeit Gottes bezieht sich auf alle seine Diener. Er macht sie weise und unterweist sie und lehrt sie und führt sie wie ein guter Hirte, der seine Herde hütet.
[14] Derer, die (seine) Erziehung annehmen, erbarmt er sich, und derer, die zu seinen Urteilen eilen.	(14) Es möge sich erbarmen, der die Lehre zum Mitleid annimmt, und die in/bei seinen Urteilen eilen.	[14] Glücklich sind die, die auf seine Barmherzigkeit warten und die seine Urteile annehmen.

Ein besonderes Kennzeichen der Theologie des Sirachbuches ist, dass es in der Fluchtlinie der aus Ex 34,6–7 bekannten Gnadenformel die Barmherzigkeit Gottes besonders betont und—soweit angesichts der Überlieferungslage erkennbar—erstmals im Bereich der israelitisch-jüdischen Literatur Gott ausdrücklich als *den* Barmherzigen (רחום, ὁ ἐλεήμων) bezeichnet (Sir 50,19).[44] Charakteristisch für das Sirachbuch ist weiterhin, dass die Barmherzigkeit als Kriterium zur Unterscheidung von Gott und Mensch verstanden wird. Wie Ewigkeit und Endlichkeit, Heiligkeit und Sündhaftigkeit Gott und Mensch unterscheiden, so bilden universale und partikulare Barmherzigkeit eine wesentliche Differenz zwischen Gott und Mensch. Der Mensch erscheint dadurch erstens auf Barmherzigkeit angewiesen, zweitens zur Barmherzigkeit aufgerufen und drittens hinsichtlich der Barmherzigkeit zwar defizitär, aber entwicklungsfähig. Der göttliche Vierklang in V.13c–d (ἐλέγχων καὶ παιδεύων καὶ διδάσκων καὶ ἐπιστρέφων) markiert die grundsätzliche Bildbarkeit des Menschen (cf. Ps 94,12; Hi 5,17; PsSal 3,4). Er unterstreicht die Vorstellung, dass der Mensch stets im Werden ist. Die in der Schöpfung verliehene *imago dei* verwirklicht

---

44. Zu den Vorläufern dieser Gottesbezeichnung gehören die Verwendung von רחום in prädikativer Stellung (Ps 78,38; 103,8) und die auf Gott bezogene partizipiale Wendung מרחם (Jes 49,15; 54,10; Ps 116,5; cf. Sir 15,20 [H^A]), cf. Markus Witte, „Barmherzigkeit und Zorn Gottes im Buch Jesus Sirach", in *Texte und Kontexte*, 83–105.

sich in der *imitatio dei*. Am Ende der an die Erfüllung der Gebote der Tora, als deren Kern gemäß Sir 17,14 (G) der Dekalog angesehen werden kann, gebundenen und selbst erfahrenen göttlichen Barmherzigkeit soll das Üben menschlicher Barmherzigkeit stehen. Sir 18,13–14 (G) erweist sich hier, wie schon Sir 4,10 (G), als Wegbereiter der Mahnung des lukanischen Jesus: *Werdet/seid barmherzig (οἰκτίρμονες), wie auch euer Vater barmherzig (οἰκτίρμων) ist* (Lk 6,36).[45]

Während G göttliche und menschliche Barmherzigkeit (ἔλεος) strikt parallel betrachtet, unterscheidet L (nach der Mehrzahl der Handschriften) hier zwischen menschlichem Mitleid (*miseratio*) und göttlicher Barmherzigkeit (*misericordia*). L betont dadurch den Unterschied zwischen Mensch und Gott. Weitergehend hebt L die Barmherzigkeit Gottes besonders hervor.[46] Sie verkürzt den Vergleich[47] und unterstreicht die Vorstellung von der Bildbarkeit des Menschen, indem sie diesen in der Rolle eines Schülers sieht, der die Lehre (*doctrina*) seines Meisters annimmt. Ist sich G abschließend der Barmherzigkeit Gottes über die Gesetzestreuen gewiss, so gipfelt L (nach den wichtigsten Textzeugen) offenbar in dem Wunsch bzw. der Erwartung, dass der von Gott belehrte Mensch sich nun seinerseits erbarmen möge.[48]

Gegenüber den universalen Barmherzigkeitsaussagen von G und L in V.13 lässt S die göttliche Barmherzigkeit auf die Frommen (ʿbdwhy) beschränkt sein. Dies entspricht zwar der auch von G und L artikulier-

---

45. Siehe oben S. 8.

46. Die Lesart *misericordiam habet* könnte auf eine Verwechslung von ἐλέγχων und ἐλέων/ἐλῶν zurückgehen (so Norbert Peters, *Das Buch Jesus Sirach oder Ecclesiasticus*, EHAT 25 [Münster: Aschendorff, 1913], 150) oder auf die Lesart ἐλεήμων (Smend, *Weisheit*, 165), allerdings finden sich keine lateinischen Varianten, und keine griechische Handschrift bietet ἐλέων/ἐλῶν oder ἐλεήμων.

47. Peters, *Das Buch Jesus Sirach*, 150, nimmt den Ausfall eines *reducit* als Äquivalent zu ἐπιστρέφων an, was aber keinen Anhalt in der textlichen Überlieferung hat.

48. In diesem Sinn versteht auch *Vulgata Deutsch* den Text (Andreas Beriger, Widu-Wolfgang Ehlers, Michael Fieger, Hrsg., *Hieronymus Biblia Sacra Vulgata*, III, [Berlin: de Gruyter 2018], 1095. Für die Diskussion des lateinischen Textes danke ich herzlich Frau Kollegin Barbara Feichtinger und Frau Dd. Sophie-Christin Holland). Folgt man hingegen den Varianten *excipientis* oder *excipientibus*, entspricht L dem griechischen Text. Sperrig bleibt in jedem Fall 14b. Wollte man den Wechsel des Subjekts (Gott – Mensch) vermeiden, könnte man auch überlegen, *misereatur* als „echtes" Passiv zu verstehen, allerdings wird *misereor* im lateinischen Sirach durchgehend als Deponens gebraucht.

ten Tendenz von V.14, nivelliert aber den Gedanken, dass sich Gott und Mensch gerade hinsichtlich der Bezugsgrößen und Bezugsdimension der Barmherzigkeit unterscheiden. So bietet S insgesamt eine stärker auf die Frommen ausgerichtete Sentenz, die mittels der Seligpreisung derer, die auf Gottes Barmherzigkeit warten (*sk'*) und Gottes Gericht annehmen, eine eschatologische Note bekommt. Am Ende der ausführlichen Antwort auf die Frage, was der Mensch sei, die G, L und S bieten, steht damit noch einmal die Kennzeichnung des Menschen als eines *hoffenden Wesens*. Schließlich bildet die so nur von S gebotene Qualifikation des Hirten als eines *guten* Hirten (*r'y' ṭb'*) eine Brücke zum johanneischen Christus, der sein Leben für seine Schafe gibt (Joh 10,11.14).[49] Die Erlösungsbedürftigkeit des Menschen wird damit ebenso festgestellt wie die Möglichkeit und Wirklichkeit der Erlösung.

6. Der Wert der Gottesfurcht und des Toragehorsams (Sir 23,27)

Auch der Abschluss des ersten großen Buchteils (Sir 1,1–23,27) ist bisher nur in G, L und S erhalten, so dass wie im Fall von 18,13–14 der griechische Text den Ausgangspunkt bildet.[50]

G	L	S
[27] Und es werden erkennen die, die zurückgelassen sind, dass nichts besser ist als die Furcht des Herrn und nichts süßer ist als das Achten auf die Gebote des Herrn.	[(37)] Und es werden erkennen die, die zurückgelassen sind, dass nichts besser ist als die Furcht des Herrn und nichts süßer als das Achten auf die Gebote des Herrn.	[27] Und alle Bewohner der Welt werden erkennen, und alle, die auf der Erde übrig sind, werden verstehen, dass nichts besser ist als die Furcht Gottes und nichts angenehmer als seine Gebote zu halten.
G-II		
[28] Großen Ruhm bedeutet es, Gott zu folgen,	[(38)] Und großen Ruhm bedeutet es, dem Herrn zu	

---

49. Siehe dazu auch Segal, ספר בן־סירא, 110, sowie die Diskussion über den „Zusatz"*ṭb'* bei van Peursen, *Language and Interpretation*, 117, 120, 139, 193, 425–426, und bei Robert J. Owens, „Christian Features in the Peshitta Text of Ben Sira: the Question of Dependency on the Syriac New Testament", in *The Texts and Versions of the Book of Ben Sira. Transmission and Interpretation*, hrsg. von Jean-Sébastien Rey und Jan Joosten, JSJSup 150 (Leiden: Brill, 2011), 184–85.

50. Bisher fehlen hebräische Äquivalente zu Sir 23,12–25,6.

aber Länge der Tage, dass	folgen,
du von ihm aufgenommen	denn Länge der Tage
wirst.	erhält[51] man von ihm.

Die Sentenz beschließt die Beschreibung einer Ehebrecherin und die Folgen ihrer als Verstoß gegen die Tora und die Treue ihres Mannes verstandenen Tat. Der konkrete Fall dient als Ausgangspunkt zu einem generellen Lobpreis der Gottesfurcht und der Beachtung der Gesetze (cf. Sir 1,1–21). Implizit ergeht der Appell, Gott zu fürchten und die Tora zu halten. Dass der erste Buchteil vor dem großen Selbstlob der kosmischen Weisheit (Sir 24) gerade mit Ausführungen zur Sexualethik endet, zeigt die hohe Bedeutung, die das Sirachbuch der ehelichen Gemeinschaft von Mann und Frau als dem Zentrum der Familie beimisst. In Kontinuität zur israelitischen Tradition kommt für Sirach der Ehe zwischen Mann und Frau eine wesentliche ökonomische und religiöse Sicherungsfunktion zu. Dass der Mensch in geschlechtlicher Differenzierung geschaffen ist (cf. Gen 1,27; 2,22–24), steht für Sirach im Schatten der Tora ebenso fest wie die Dominanz des Mannes und die rechtliche und gesellschaftliche Ungleichbehandlung von Mann und Frau.

Der erweiterte griechische Text (G-II) und L weisen eine zusätzliche Motivation zur Gottesfurcht auf. In beiden Fällen, deutlicher noch in G-II, wird der Bewahrung der Gebote grundsätzlich eine den Tod überdauernde Bedeutung zugeschrieben. So berührt sich die Formulierung von G-II eng mit dem Ausblick auf die postmortale Aufnahme des Frommen in die Herrlichkeit Gottes in Ps 72,24 (LXX).[52] Wie schon in der lateinischen Version von Sir 6,16–17 und 14,19(21) erscheint der Tod hier nicht mehr als absolute Grenze des Menschen.

Demgegenüber bleibt S bei einem auf dieses Leben bezogenen Lob der Gottesfurcht und der Gebotsbewahrung, bietet aber gleichsam eine über G hinausreichende Universalisierung. Aus einem Lernbeispiel für die Nachkommen der Ehebrecherin bzw. für die, die sie überleben, ist in S die prophetische Erwartung einer universalen Gotteserkenntnis und Gottesfurcht geworden (cf. Ez 29,6; 32,15; Hab 2,14).[53]

---

51. Zu dieser Übersetzung von *adsumetur* siehe Peters, *Das Buch Jesus Sirach*, 193.

52. So auch Segal, ספר בן־סירא, 144; Skehan und Di Lella, *The Wisdom of Ben Sira*, 326. Zu L (und dem möglichen Bezug auf Ps 49,16) siehe Kearns, *The Expanded Text*, 167–68, 292.

53. Aufgrund seiner poetischen Geschlossenheit (zwei Bikola) wird gelegentlich

7. Leben im Schatten der Weisheit (Sir 33[36],7–15)

Der Lobpreis der Gottesfurcht und des Toragehorsams in Sir 23,27 beendet nicht nur den ersten großen Buchteil. Er leitet auch zum zweiten Hauptabschnitt über, der mit dem Selbstlob der kosmischen Weisheit, die sich am Jerusalemer Tempel niederlässt und in der Tora Gestalt annimmt, eröffnet wird (Sir 24,1) und der mit einem Schöpfungshymnus endet, der selbst in einem Bekenntnis zur eingeschränkten Erkenntnis des Menschen und zur Gabe der Weisheit an die Frommen mündet (Sir 43,33). Einzelne Unterabschnitte dieses zweiten großen Buchteils schließen jeweils mit zentralen anthropologischen Ausführungen. Unter diesen ragt aufgrund seines Umfangs und seiner Mischung aus genuin israelitisch-jüdischen Traditionen mit stoischen Konzeptionen der Abschnitt Sir 33(36),7–15 hervor, in dem Ben Sira die Erfahrungen von Gut und Böse auf eine duale, kontrastive Einrichtung des Kosmos zurückführt. Otto Kaiser hat ausführlich dargelegt, wie Ben Sira bei seiner Gegenüberstellung von Gut und Böse, Leben und Tod, hell und dunkel auf das stoische Konzept vom „dualen Kontrast aller Dinge" zurückgreift und so die Frage der Gerechtigkeit Gottes mit der Vorstellung von der Freiheit Gottes und der notwendigen paarweisen, antithetischen Anordnung alles Geschaffenen beantwortet.[54]

Ich beschränke mich daher auf die Benennung von grundsätzlichen Gemeinsamkeiten und charakteristischen Unterschiede der Versionen. Diese bieten alle die im Alten Orient und in der klassischen Antike weit verbreitete Metapher von der Erschaffung des Menschen aus Ton,[55] mit-

---

vermutet, dass S der mutmaßlichen hebräischen Vorlage näher stünde als G, wobei dann umstritten ist, ob sich die rekonstruierte Wendung יושבי ארץ auf die Bewohner des Landes (so Peters, *Das Buch Jesus Sirach*, 190) oder auf die Bewohner der ganzen Erde bezieht (so Skehan und Di Lella, *The Wisdom of Ben Sira*, 320; Marböck, *Jesus Sirach 1–23*, 271). Zur Frage, ob die universale Perspektive von S in 23,27 eine spezifisch christliche Tendenz aufweise, siehe van Peursen, *Language and Interpretation*, 89.

54. Kaiser, „Die stoische Oikeiosis-Lehre", 62; Kaiser, „Göttliche Weisheit und menschliche Freiheit", 55–58; Beentjes, „Theodicy", 272 und ausführlich Ursel Wicke-Reuter, *Göttliche Providenz und menschliche Verantwortung bei Ben Sira und in der Frühen Stoa*, BZAW 298 (Berlin: de Gruyter, 2000), 224–73.

55. Cf. Gen 2,7; Hi 10,9; 33,6; Ps 103,14. Aus der Fülle der vorderorientalischen und ägyptischen Belege siehe Atramchasis I,200–230, übersetzt von Wolfram von Soden (*TUAT* 3:612–45); Gilgamesch I,ii,34, übersetzt von Karl Hecker (*TUAT* 3:671–744); Enki und Ninmach 31–32; 58–59, übersetzt von Willem H. P. Römer (*TUAT* 3:386–401); Kosmologie des kalû-Priesters 25, übersetzt von Karl Hecker

tels derer sowohl die Vergänglichkeit und Zerbrechlichkeit menschlichen
Wesens als auch dessen Beziehung zu der ihn in Freiheit erschaffenden
Gottheit ausgedrückt wird (33[36],10):

H^E	G	L	S
[Und jeder Mensch ist ein Gefä]ß aus Ton, und aus Staub wurde אדם geschaffen.	Und alle Menschen sind vom Erdboden, und aus der Erde wurde Adam erschaffen	(10b) Und alle Menschen sind vom Erdboden und aus der Erde, aus der Adam erschaffen wurde.	Und alle Menschen wurden also aus Ton erschaffen, und aus Staub wurde Adam erschaffen

Während der von H^E in V.10b gebotene Text sich sowohl auf die Erschaf-
fung des Menschen als auch auf die Adams beziehen lässt, verstehen G,
L und S das zweite Kolon eindeutig im Sinn des Eigennamens und der
Anspielung auf Gen 2–3. Dafür, dass letzteres wohl auch für H^E anzunehmen ist,[56] spricht die hohe Bedeutung, die Adam im Sirachbuch hat (cf.
Sir 40,1; 49,16). Die auf die Erschaffung folgende Ausdifferenzierung der
Menschheit, die Sirach in Anlehnung an die biblische Urgeschichte ganz
knapp referiert (V.11), führt H^E auf die Weisheit selbst zurück,[57] während
G, L und S explizit Gott als Subjekt und die göttliche Weisheit als Mittel
der Unterscheidung verstehen. Die nur in H^E und S gebotene Notiz, dass
die Menschen zu Bewohnern der Erde eingesetzt wurden (V.11), spielt
deutlicher als G und L neben Gen 1 noch Gen 10–11 ein, während sich
die Aussage über die Unterscheidung der Wege des Menschen sowohl in
lokaler als auch in ethisch-religiöser Hinsicht als Generalisierung von Gen

(*TUAT* 3:604–5); ludlul bēl nēmeqi IV,110, übersetzt von Wolfram von Soden (*TUAT*
3:110–25); Babylonische Theodizee 277, übersetzt von Wolfram von Soden (*TUAT*
3:143–57); Lehre des Amenemope XXIV,13–14, übersetzt von Irene Shirun-Grumach
(*TUAT* 3:222–50); Mythos von der Geburt des Gottkönigs II,3, übersetzt von Heike
Sternberg-el Hotabi (*TUAT* 3:991–1005); Chnum-Hymnus aus Esna, übersetzt von
Jan Assmann (*TUAT* 2:909–10). Aber auch in griechischen und römischen Mythen
begegnet das Motiv, wenn Prometheus die Menschen aus Lehm und Wasser erschafft
(Apollodor, *Bibliothek* I,45; Properz, *Elegien* IV,5).

56. Cf. Peters, *Jesus Sirach*, 271; Charles Mopsik, *La Sagesse de ben Sira: Traduction
de l'hébreu, introduction et annotation* (Lagrasse: Verdier, 2003), 197; Kaiser, *Weisheit*,
77. Dagegen Skehan und Di Lella, *The Wisdom of Ben Sira*, 394; Sauer, *Jesus Sirach*, 232;
Morla, *Los manuscritos hebreos*, 393, 484; Zapff, *Jesus Sirach 25–51*, 213: „Mensch".

57. Cf. Sauer, *Jesus Sirach*, 232; Mopsik, *La Sagesse*, 198; Morla, *Los manuscritos
hebreos*, 393, 484; Wicke-Reuter, *Göttliche Providenz*, 244.

12–13 verstehen lässt. In anthropologischer Hinsicht ist entscheidend, dass die Differenzierung der Lebensräume und Lebenswege des Menschen als von Gott bestimmt betrachtet werden. Ein Widerspruch zu der von Ben Sira in 15,11–17 in Anlehnung an Dtn 30,15–20[58] formulierten Entscheidungsfreiheit des Menschen muss darin nicht gesehen werden: Innerhalb des von Gott gesetzten Raums hat der Mensch Freiheit. Auch die folgenden Ausführungen zur unterschiedlichen Verteilung von Segen und Fluch, Erhöhung und Erniedrigung, Gottesnähe und Gottesferne, die allgemein formuliert sind (V.12), hinter denen aber die Erzählungen über die Erzväter sowie über Mose, Aaron und ihre Gegner (Korach, Datan und Abiram) aufleuchten,[59] lassen dem Menschen die Möglichkeit zur Entscheidung in den von Gott gesetzten Grenzen. Gleichwohl besteht zwischen der Betonung der menschlichen Freiheit in Sir 15 und der göttlichen Freiheit in Sir 33 eine Spannung, mit der die Versionen in unterschiedlicher Weise umgehen (V.13).

H[E]	G	L	S
13 … Töpfer zu halten/ergreifen gemäß (seinem) Wohlgefallen … sein Sch[öpfer], sich vor [ihm] hinzustellen, hat er zugeteilt.	13 wie Ton des Töpfers in seiner Hand, ihn zu formen gemäß seinem Wohlgefallen, so sind die Menschen in der Hand dessen, der sie schuf, ihnen zu vergelten gemäß seinem Urteil.	13 wie Ton des Töpfers in seinen eigenen Händen, jenen zu formen und anzuordnen, (14) alle seine Wege gemäß seiner Anordnung, so ist der Mensch in der Hand jenes, der ihn gemacht hat, er wird ihm vergelten gemäß seinem Urteil.	13 wie Ton, der geformt ist in der Hand des Töpfers, (14) so ist der Mensch in der Hand seines Schöpfers, um ihn in den Bereich[60] all seiner Werke zu stellen.

---

58. Cf. Dtn 11,26–28; Jer 21,8.

59. Sir 33,12; cf. Gen 12–13; Ex 3–6; Num 16–17. In Sir 33,12d zeigt sich eine kleinere Differenz zwischen den Versionen, wenn H[E] von der Vertreibung „von ihren Tätigkeiten" (מעבדיהם) bzw. G und L von der Vertreibung aus ihrer „besonderen Stellung" (ἀπὸ στάσεως αὐτῶν, a separatione ipsorum) sprechen, womit auf die Abstellung zum Priesterdienst Bezug genommen wird, und in S von der Vertreibung aus „ihren Wohnungen" (mn mdyryhwn) die Rede ist, was auf eine Exilierung hinweist.

60. Zu dieser Wiedergabe der Präposition b siehe Victor Ryssel, „Die Sprüche

Der nur fragmentarisch erhaltene und hinsichtlich der Übersetzung des zweiten Kolons umstrittene hebräische Text,[61] lässt zumindest die Vorstellung erkennen, dass Gott den Menschen als sein Gegenüber geschaffen hat (cf. Jes 64,7; Jer 18,6). In die Geschöpflichkeit ist der Gottesbezug integriert. Ob mit der Formulierung להתיצב der generelle Stand des Menschen vor Gott gemeint ist oder speziell ein gottesdienstliches, anbetendes Stehen (cf. 1QHª XI,22), muss offenbleiben. Jedenfalls liegt es in der Freiheit des Menschen, *wie* er seinen grundsätzlichen Stand vor Gott lebt.[62]

G und L betonen demgegenüber stärker das Handeln Gottes, der dem Menschen nicht nur als Schöpfer, sondern auch als Richter begegnet. L konstatiert, wie auch zahlreiche griechische Handschriften,[63] darüber hinaus als zweites Kolon (als Dublette?), dass Gott alle Wege des Menschen anordnet (*disponere*). Der Gedanke der Determination wird damit (in Entsprechung zu V.11) verstärkt.

Hingegen unterstreicht S den Charakter des Menschen als Teil der göttlichen Schöpfung. Die Ambivalenz menschlicher Existenz, die sich zwischen geschöpflicher Hinfälligkeit und Gott geschenkter Leistungsfähigkeit bewegt, wird damit im Schatten von Gen 1–2 auf knappstem Raum ausgedrückt. Sollte in der Formulierung *bkl ʿbdwhy* eine Anspielung auf

---

Jesus' des Sohnes Sirachs", in *APAT* 1:396; Smend, *Weisheit*, 299, Wicke-Reuter, *Göttliche Providenz*, 229; Zapff, *Jesus Sirach 25–51*, 214.

61. Ich verstehe להתיצב reflexiv, lese חֵלֶק und deute מפניו im Sinn von לפניו (cf. Gen 31,35; Lev 19,32), cf. Sauer, *Jesus Sirach*, 232. Demgegenüber liest Wicke-Reuter, *Göttliche Providenz*, 229, חֶלְק („daß von ihm das Geschick festgesetzt wird"), ähnlich Zapff, *Jesus Sirach 25–51*, 214; Morla, *Los manuscritos hebreos*, 395, 485. Mopsik, *La Sagesse*, 198, vokalisiert חָלָק („glatt") und paraphrasiert: „apparaît devant lui comme une pierre lisse". Kaum plausibel ist der Vorschlag von Tadeusz Penar, חֹלֵק zu punktieren und dies als göttliches Epitheton im Sinn von „der Schöpfer" zu verstehen, das angeblich auch in Jer 10,16; Ps 119,57 und Thr 3,24 belegt sei (*Northwest Semitic Philology and the Hebrew Fragments of Ben Sira*, BibOr 28 [Rom: Pontificio Istituto Biblico, 1975], 55–56). Gleichwohl schließt sich Pancratius C. Beentjes, „Theodicy in Wisdom of Ben Sira", in *Happy the One who Meditates*, 270, Penar an.

62. Anders Wicke-Reuter, *Göttliche Providenz*, 259: „So wie der Töpfer den Ton nach seinem Willen formt, so bestimmt Gott, indem er den Menschen schafft, zugleich sein Leben, indem er ihm sein ,Teil' festsetzt".

63. Zur Diskussion des texkritischen Befundes in G siehe ausführlich Eve-Marie Becker, Heinz-Josef Fabry und Michael Reitemeyer, „Sophia Sirach", in *Septuaginta Deutsch. Erläuterungen und Kommentare zum griechischen Alten Testament*, II, hrsg. von Martin Karrer und Wolfgang Kraus [Stuttgart: Deutsche Bibelgesellschaft, 2011], 2217–18.

das Motiv des *dominium terrae* aus Gen 1,26 (cf. Ps 8,7) vorliegen, würde der Schwerpunkt auf der Funktion der Erschaffung des Menschen liegen.[64]

Hinsichtlich der paradigmatischen Auflistung polarer Phänomene in V.14(15) weisen die Versionen erneut kleine Differenzen auf. Während alle Versionen die Größen Gut und Böse sowie Leben und Tod auflisten, verweisen nur H^E und S zusätzlich auf Licht und Finsternis und unterstreichen im Anschluss an Gen 1 die kosmische Dimension göttlichen Handelns. Menschliche Existenz ist damit explizit in die von Gott bestimmten Abläufe der Natur eingebettet. Hingegen bieten nur H^E, G und L eine ausdrückliche ethische Differenzierung des Menschen in Gut und Böse, wobei G und L spezifischer religiös gefärbt sind und zwischen dem Frommen (εὐσεβής, *vir iustus*) und dem Sünder (ἁμαρτωλός, *peccator*) unterscheiden. Die Viergliedrigkeit von H^E mit der Aufzählung von Gut und Böse, Leben und Tod, einem guten und einem bösen Menschen sowie Licht und Finsternis dürfte ursprünglich sein.[65] Ein besonderer Akzent von S besteht darin, die Polarität nicht nur zu konstatieren, sondern ausdrücklich auf das Geschaffensein (*'tbry*) durch Gott zurückzuführen.[66]

Die die Perikope in V.15 beschließende summarische Feststellung, dass alle Werke Gottes paarweise und antithetisch zueinander geschaffen sind, ist in den Versionen identisch. Allerdings steht dem an den Leser des hebräischen, griechischen und lateinischen Buches gerichteten Imperativ, selbst jedes Werk zu betrachten und so zur Erkenntnis der dualen Anlage der Schöpfung zu kommen, in S die Feststellung gegenüber, Gott habe die paarweise Struktur alles Geschaffenen aufgezeigt (*hwy*). So werden in H^E, G und L die Vorstellung von der grundsätzlichen menschlichen Erkenntnis- und Reflexionsfähigkeit des Menschen sowie die Pragmatik des Sirachbuches als eines auf die Bildung des Menschen zielenden Werks deutlicher als in S.

---

64. In diesem Sinn übersetzen Calduch-Benages et al., *Wisdom of the Scribe*, 200 („in order to place him over all his works") und Morla, *Los manuscritos hebreos*, 395, allerdings würde man dann eher die Präposition 'al erwarten.

65. So auch Sauer, *Jesus Sirach*, 232–34, und Kaiser, *Weisheit*, 77, während Peters, *Das Buch Jesus Sirach*, 271, und Skehan und Di Lella, *The Wisdom of Ben Sira*, 396 und 401, G (und L) folgen (cf. Wicke-Reuter, *Göttliche Providenz*, 396).

66. Cf. van Peursen, Language and Interpretation, 47.

8. Auf dem Weg zur Überwindung des Todes (Sir 39,11)

Ben Siras Anleitungen zur Gottesfurcht, zum Erwerb von Weisheit und zur Beachtung der Tora gipfeln in einem Lobpreis des Schriftgelehrten (סופר / γραμματεύς, Sir 38,24–39,11). In der Tradition des vor allem aus ägyptischen Lehren[67] bekannten Lobs des Schreibers erscheint der jüdische Weise, der sich mit den Schriften der Väter beschäftigt, mittels Inspiration den Geheimnissen Gottes nachgeht, sich im Gebet an Gott wendet und im täglichen Leben der Tora folgt, als *der ideale Mensch*. Die abschließende Eulogie in Sir 39,11 ist vollständig nur in G, L und S erhalten.[68] In allen drei Fällen scheint der überlieferte Text des Schlussverses gestört zu sein. Bleibt man bei dem von den Versionen repräsentierten Text, ergibt sich folgendes Bild:

G	L	S
[11] Wenn er (der schriftgelehrte Weise) standhaft bleibt[69], wird er einen Namen hinterlassen mehr als tausend andere. Und wenn er zur Ruhe kommt, nimmt er (der Name) ihm noch zu.	[(15)] Wenn er standhaft gewesen sein wird, wird er tausend Namen hinterlassen, und wenn er zur Ruhe gekommen sein wird, wird er/es ihm nützen.	[11] Wenn er (etwas) wünscht, wird er von tausend gepriesen[70], und wenn er schweigt, von einem kleinen Volk (?)

---

67. Siehe z.B. die auf der Rückseite des Papyrus Chester Beatty IV (50–145) gesammelten Lobeshymnen auf den Schreiber (Hellmut Brunner, *Die Weisheitsbücher der Ägypter. Lehren für das Leben*, 2., verbesserte Auflage [Düsseldorf: Artemis & Winkler, 1988], 218–30) und dazu Johannes Marböck, „Sir 38,24–39,11: Der Schriftgelehrte Weise", in *Gottes Weisheit unter uns. Zur Theologie des Buches Sirach*, hrsg. von Irmtraud Fischer, HBS 6 (Freiburg: Herder, 1995), 29–51.

68. H[B] bietet nur Sir 38,24–27.

69. So nach *LEH* s.v. ἐμμένω (cf. Wright, „Sirach", 751; Michael Reitemeyer, „Sophia Sirach" in *Septuaginta Deutsch. Das griechische Alte Testament in deutscher Übersetzung*, 2. Auflage, hrsg. von Wolfgang Kraus und Martin Karrer [Stuttgart: Deutsche Bibelgesellschaft, 2010], 1144)—oder: „lange lebt" (Takamitsu Muraoka, *A Greek-English Lexicon of the Septuagint* [Louvain: Peeters, 2009], 226; *Einheitsübersetzung*, 818; Peters, *Das Buch Jesus Sirach*, 323; Skehan und Di Lella, *The Wisdom of Ben Sira*, 447; Sauer, *Jesus Sirach*, 269; Kaiser, *Weisheit*, 90; Burkard M. Zapff, *Jesus Sirach 25–51*, NEchtB 39 [Würzburg: Echter, 2010], 267).

70. Die Lesart *nštbḥ* wird gelegentlich auf ein mutmaßlich ursprüngliches יאשר

In G scheint der Vers die Vorstellung zu spiegeln, dass der Ruf, den sich ein Mensch erworben hat, den Tod überdauert.[71] Das positive Gedenken ist gemäß traditioneller israelitischer Vorstellung die einzige Form einer postmortalen Existenz. Burkard M. Zapff spricht in diesem Zusammenhang treffend von dem Lebensweg des Weisen als einem „Sonderweg zur Bewältigung des allgemeinen Todesgeschicks".[72] Im „Lob der Väter" (Sir 44–49.50) wird diese Vorstellung an einzelnen Figuren der Geschichte Israels entfaltet.[73] Der Weise, der schon in diesem Leben besondere Achtung genoss, wird damit beispielsweise den hellenistischen Herrschern gegenübergestellt, deren Namen auch noch Jahrzehnte oder gar Jahrhunderte nach ihrem Tod bekannt sind. Entscheidend für einen solchen postmortalen Ruhm, der sogar noch wächst, sind weder politische oder militärische Leistungen noch besondere kulturelle oder bauliche Maßnahmen—alles menschliche Werk ist, wie in Sir 14,19 schon notiert, vergänglich—, sondern das Leben in und mit der Tora, das sich in Schriftstudium, einem entsprechenden Ethos und im Gebet niederschlägt. Dieser Weg ist prinzipiell jedem (Mann) offen—vorausgesetzt, er hat dazu die ökonomischen Mittel, denn „nur, wer wenig Arbeit hat, kann weise werden" (Sir 38,24). Weite und Begrenztheit der sirazidischen Anthropologie zeigen sich an dieser Stelle besonders.

L scheint dem überlieferten, aber häufig geänderten griechischen Text[74] grundsätzlich zu entsprechen, wobei die Formulierung „er/es wird jenem nützen" (*proderit illi*) offen lässt, ob der verstorbene Weise aufgrund seines außergewöhnlichen, den göttlichen Geboten voll entsprechenden Lebens ein besonderes jenseitiges Geschick hat, welches das Fortleben des Namens, und sei es in der Vielgestaltigkeit von Namen, wie sie eigent-

---

zurückgeführt (Segal, ספר בן־סירא, 260; siehe auch Sauer, *Jesus Sirach*, 269; Zapff, *Jesus Sirach 25–51*, 267).

71. Cf. Sir 37,26; 41,11–13; 44,13–15; Prov 10,7; Hi 18,17.

72. Zapff, *Jesus Sirach 25–51*, 267.

73. Sir 44,14; 45,1; 46,11; 49,1.

74. Seit Smend, *Weisheit*, 356, wird anstelle von ἐμποιεῖ (so die Mehrzahl der Handschriften) frei ἐκποιεῖ konjiziert (cf. Rahlfs, *Septuaginta*; Vattioni, *Ecclesiastico*; Ziegler, *Sapientia*); zu handschriftlich belegten Varianten siehe Ziegler, *Sapientia*. Auch Reitemeyer, *Sophia Sirach*, 1144, liest ἐκποιεῖ und versteht dies im Sinn von „vollenden" (cf. Becker, Fabry, Reitemeyer, „Sophia Sirach", 2232), wobei dann an die Vorstellung gedacht zu sein scheint, dass sich in einem guten Tod, das heißt in einem Sterben zur rechten Zeit („alt und lebenssatt") das gesegnete Leben des Weisen vollendet (cf. Gen 25,8; 35,29; 1 Chr 29,28; Hi 42,17).

lich nur Göttern oder vergöttlichten Herrschern zukommt, übertrifft. In diesem Sinn böte L eine Parallele zu Sir 14,21 (L): Weisheit, Gottesfurcht und Gesetzestreue zahlen sich auch im Jenseits aus, in dem der ideale Mensch durch Gott seine Vollendung findet. Dementsprechend wäre der lateinischen Version von Sir 39,11(15) dann Mt 16,26 zur Seite zu stellen:

Denn was nützt es [prodest] einem Menschen, wenn er die ganze Welt gewinnt, aber an seiner Seele einen Schaden erleidet? Oder was wird ein Mensch als Tausch für seine Seele geben?

Demgegenüber bleibt S eindeutig bei einem rein immanenten Verständnis, wobei das zweite Kolon unklar ist.

9. Gotteslob und Erkenntnisgrenzen (Sir 43,32–33)

Der gesamte achte Unterabschnitt des Buches (Sir 39,12–43,33) kreist um das Thema Schöpfung und die Stellung des Menschen in ihr. Entsprechend der Zeichnung des idealen Menschen, der sich im Gebet an Gott wendet (Sir 39,6), bietet Ben Sira am Ende dieser Ausführungen, die zugleich den zweiten Hauptteil des Buches beschließen, einen ausführlichen Hymnus auf Gottes Schöpfungswerke (Sir 42,15–43,33). Der Hymnus hat zahlreiche Parallelen in den Psalmen (cf. besonders Ps 104; 147–148) und in der ersten Gottesrede des Hiobbuches (Hi 38–39). Ähnlich wie Hiob am Ende der Gottesreden (Hi 42,2) bekennt sich das betende Ich von Sir 42,15–43,33 abschließend zur umfassenden Macht des Schöpfers und zu den Grenzen menschlicher Erkenntnis (Sir 43,32–33 cf. Hi 26,14).

G	L
[32] Viele verborgene Dinge sind (noch) größer als das, denn (nur) wenige haben wir gesehen von seinen Werken.	[36] Viele verborgene Dinge sind (noch) größer als das, denn (nur) wenige haben wir gesehen von seinen Werken.
[33] Denn alles hat der Herr gemacht, und den Frommen hat er Weisheit gegeben.	[37] Alles aber hat der Herr gemacht, und denen, die fromm handeln, hat er Weisheit gegeben

In H^B sind von V.32–33 nur noch sehr wenige Wörter lesbar, wobei hier entsprechend der Eröffnung des Hymnus in Sir 42,15 der Beter in der 1. Person Singular spricht (ראיתי). Dies dürfte ursprünglich sein (cf. Sir 39,12). L entspricht dem griechischen Text. S weist in Sir 43,11–43,33 eine Lücke auf, so dass der Hymnus dort mit der Feststellung der astralen Ordnung durch Gott endet (Sir 43,10, cf. Gen 1,14–19; Hi 38,31–33; Ps 104,19). Anthropologisch ist entscheidend, dass der Mensch grundsätzlich, wenn auch begrenzt, auf Erkenntnis hin angelegt ist. Diese zielt auf eine Verortung seiner selbst in einer von Gott planvoll geschaffenen Welt und auf das Gotteslob. Im Gegensatz zu den Gottesreden im Hiobbuch ist in Sir 42,15–43,33—trotz eines vergleichbaren kosmisch-meteorologischen Schwerpunkts—der Mensch *ausdrücklich* in die hymnische Beschreibung einbezogen (Sir 42,18; 43,11.24.27–33). Die Weisheit, mit der der Hymnus auf die Eröffnung des zweiten Buchteils in Sir 24 rekurriert, ist hingegen eine Gabe, die nur den Frommen geschenkt wird (Sir 43,33). Weisheit ist demnach noch mehr als die Wahrnehmung der Wunder der Schöpfung. Universales und partikulares Denken, das das Sirachbuch durchgehend prägt, zeigt sich auch hier. Dabei klingt die nur in G und L erhaltene Frage, wer Gott gesehen habe, wer ihn adäquat beschreiben und lobpreisen könne (Sir 43,31), wie eine Kritik an Hiobs Schlussbekenntnis, nun habe *sein Auge* Gott gesehen (Hi 42,5; cf. 1QS XI,3.6). Auch wenn das Sirachbuch dem Weisen die Möglichkeit zur Ergründung besonderer Geheimnisse zugesteht (Sir 39,7), scheint es eine unmittelbare Gottesschau wie die Hiobs auszuschließen. So lässt Sirach auch Mose nur die Stimme Gottes hören und sich dem Wolkendunkel Gottes nur nähern (Sir 45,5; cf. 1QS XI,3.6). Sirachs Theologie und Anthropologie entspricht hier eher dem Gottes- und Menschenbild der dem Hiobbuch später zugewachsenen Elihureden (Hi 37,23–24, cf. Hi 28,28):

> 23 Schaddaj, ihn finden wir nicht.
> Gewaltig ist er an Kraft und Recht[75],
> und die Fülle der Gerechtigkeit beugt er nicht.
> 24 Deshalb fürchten ihn die Männer,
> nicht jeder, der weisen Herzens ist, vermag (das) zu sehen.

10. Der wahre Mensch (Sir 50,22–24)

Das Stichwort der „Frommen", denen Gott seine Weisheit gibt (Sir 43,33), leitet zugleich zum letzten großen Buchteil und zum „Lob der Väter" (Kap. 44–49.50) über. In dieser aus Elementen israelitisch-jüdischer Geschichtspsalmen und paganer hellenistischer Enkomien gemischten Galerie ausgewählter Figuren der Geschichte Israels entfaltet das

---

75. ומשפט gehört gegen die masoretische Segmentierung zu 23aβ.

Sirachbuch wahre Frömmigkeit, um dann mit einem Lobpreis auf den Hohenpriester Simeon zu schließen (Sir 50,1–24). Dieser erscheint in seiner an Adam erinnernden Herrlichkeit (Sir 50,20 cf. 49,16) und in seinem den Kosmos repräsentierenden Ornat (Sir 50,6) als *der wahre Mensch*.

H^B	G	L	S
[22] Jetzt segnet doch Jahwe, den Gott Israels, der wunderbar an der Erde handelt, der den Menschen groß zieht von Mutterleib an und an ihm handelt gemäß seinem Wohlgefallen (cf. 33,11).	[22] Und jetzt segnet den Gott des Alls/ von allem, der große Dinge tut in allem, der unsere Tage erhöht von Mutterleib an und an uns handelt gemäß seiner Barmherzigkeit.	[(24)] Und jetzt bittet den Herrn von allem, der große Dinge getan hat auf der ganzen Erde, der unsere Tage vom Leib unserer Mutter an vermehrt hat und der an uns gemäß seiner Barmherzigkeit gehandelt hat.	[22] Und das Volk des Landes pries Gott, der Wunder im Land getan hat/tut, der die Menschen aus dem Leib ihrer Mutter erschaffen hat/erschafft und der sie geleitet hat/leitet nach seinem Willen,
[23] Er gebe euch Weisheit des Herzens, und er[76] sei im/als Frieden unter euch.	[23] Er gebe uns Freude des Herzens und dass Frieden werde in unseren Tagen in Israel gemäß den Tagen der Ewigkeit.	[(25)] Er gebe uns Freude des Herzens und dass Frieden werde in unseren Tagen in Israel während ewiger Tage,	[23] um ihnen Weisheit des Herzens zu geben, und es wird Frieden unter ihnen sein,
[24] Fest stehe mit Simeon seine Treue, und er erhalte ihm den Bund des Pinhas, dass er nicht gebrochen werde, ihm und seinen Nachkommen gemäß den Tagen des Himmels.	[24] Es sei in Treue mit uns seine Barmherzigkeit, und in unseren Tagen soll er uns erlösen.	[(26)] dass Israel glaube, dass die Barmherzigkeit Gottes mit uns sei, damit er euch[77] in seinen Tagen befreie.	[24] und mit Simeon wird Treue gehalten und mit seinen Nachkommen gemäß den Tagen des Himmels.

---

76. Das heißt: Gott selbst (cf. Mopsik, *La Sagesse*, 320; Skehan und Di Lella, *The Wisdom of Ben Sira*, 554; Sauer, *Jesus Sirach*, 338; Zapff, *Jesus Sirach 25–51*, 384). Peters, *Jesus Sirach*, 433, und Morla, *Los manuscritos hebreos*, 345, streichen die Präposition ב und verstehen שלום als Subjekt (cf. G, L, S).

77. Var.: *nos* („uns").

Die Schlussverse des Enkomiums auf den Hohenpriester bieten eine Zusammenfassung der Menschenbilder des hebräischen Sirachbuches. Der von Gott *gesegnete Mensch* (Sir 50,20) soll zugleich *der Gott segnende, das heißt lobpreisende Mensch* sein (V.22). Der von Gott geschaffene und von diesem in Freiheit geleitete Mensch (cf. Sir 33,7–15) findet seine Erfüllung in der Begabung mit der göttlichen Weisheit und in der Frieden stiftenden Gemeinschaft mit Gott (V.23).[78] Als Mittler des Segens, der Weisheit und des Gottesfriedens fungiert der in der Sukzession Aarons stehende (Sir 45,6–22), für die Dauer der Zeit (כימי שמים)[79] eingesetzte Hohepriester. Auf Israel bezogene Geschichts- und Bundestheologie ist hier mit einer Schöpfungstheologie verbunden.

Liegt der Schwerpunkt von H[B] auf der Beziehung dieses Gottes zu Israel,[80] der grundsätzliche Aussagen zum Menschen untergeordnet sind, so zeigt sich in G ein universaler Zug. In G fehlt vor allem die Bitte für den Hohenpriester, was textgeschichtliche Gründe haben kann,[81] aber auch zeitgeschichtlich bedingt sein kann, insofern zur Zeit des griechischen Übersetzers der „Bund mit Pinhas" (Sir 45,23–25 H[B]; 50,24 cf. Num 25,13) tatsächlich zerbrochen war und die zadokidische Dynastie Simeons nicht mehr als Jerusalemer Hohepriester amtierte (cf. 2 Makk 4,26.34). Die Tendenz von G ist eindeutig. Neben der universalen Perspektive (Sir 36[33],1; 43,27) kennzeichnen den griechischen Text die starke Applikation des Gebets auf die Beter selbst, die Konzentration auf Gottes Barmherzigkeit (ἔλεος), der Wunsch um Freude (εὐφροσύνη) anstelle um Weisheit und der abschließende Erlösungswunsch. Deutlicher als in H[B] wird das grundsätzliche Angewiesensein des Menschen auf die Barmherzigkeit Gottes und die unmittelbare Erlösung durch Gott herausgestellt.

L entspricht weitgehend G, setzt aber eigene Akzente, insofern aus dem Lobpreis Gottes ein Gebet *zu* Gott wird und Israel als handelnde Größe in

---

78. V.22c–d und 23 dürften generell zu verstehen sein (cf. Skehan und Di Lella, *The Wisdom of Ben Sira*, 554; Sauer, *Jesus Sirach*, 340), nicht exklusiv im Blick auf Simeon bzw. dessen Söhne (so aber tendenziell Zapff, *Jesus Sirach 25–51*, 384, und ausdrücklich Jeremy Corley, *Sirach*, The New Collegeville Bible Commentary 21 [Collegeville: Liturgical Press, 2013], 143–144, mit Hinweis auf Sir 45,25–26).

79. Sir 50,24 cf. Sir 45,15; Dtn 11,21; Ps 89,30; Bar 1,11; PsSal 14,4; *KAI5* 266:3.

80. Cf. Sir 24,23 (die kosmische Weisheit schlägt sich in der Tora Israels nieder), 44,1–49,16 (in der Geschichte Israels finden sich die beispielhaft frommen und weisen Menschen), 50,1–24 (der Kult Israels repräsentiert den wahren Kult).

81. Die Lesung μεθ' ἡμῶν könnte auf einer Verlesung von μετὰ Σιμων beruhen (so Ryssel, „Die Sprüche Jesus'", 470).

das Gebet einbezogen wird. Auch wenn sich die zusätzliche Erwähnung Israels in V.24(26) textgeschichtlich auf die Lesart עַם / עָם („Volk") anstelle von עִם („mit") zurückführen lässt, ist offen, ob der Übersetzer Israel als ein Gegenüber zu den von sich in der 1. Person Plural sprechenden Betern oder als eine die Beter einschließende Größe versteht. In jedem Fall betont L, dass der Zeitpunkt des Befreiens (*liberet*)[82] allein in Gottes Händen liegt.

Auch S unterstreicht die Aktivität Gottes. Dabei bietet S anstelle eines an die Leser des Buches gerichteten Gebetsaufrufs eine Beschreibung des Gotteslobs und anstelle der Bitte um Weisheit oder Freude des Herzens die Gewissheit, dass Gott den Menschen mit der Weisheit begabt. So steht am Ende des Väterlobs des syrischen Sirachs noch einmal der von Gott geschaffene, geführte und mit Weisheit ausgestattete Mensch (cf. Sir 17,7 [S]: *Mit Weisheit und Verstand füllte er ihre Herzen. Gut und Böse zeigte er ihnen*).

11. Das wahre Leben (Sir 50,28–29)

H^B	G	L	S
28 Glücklich ist der Mann, der über diese Dinge nachsinnt, und der, der sie auf sein Herz legt, wird weise werden.	28 Glücklich ist, wer bei diesen Dingen verweilen wird, und, nachdem er sie auf sein Herz gelegt hat, wird er weise gemacht werden.	(30) Glücklich, wer in diesen Gütern verweilt, wer jene in sein Herz legt, wird immer weise sein.	28 Glücklich ist der Mann, der über diese Dinge nachdenkt und sie lernt und durch sie weise wird und sie tut.
29 Denn die Furcht Jahwes ist Leben.	29 Denn wenn er sie tut, wird er zu allem Kraft haben, weil die Furcht des Herrn seine Spur ist.	(31) Denn wenn er dies getan haben wird, wird er zu allem fähig sein, weil das Licht Gottes seine Spur ist.	Die Höhe der Furcht des Herrn ist über alles erhöht. Beachte sie genau, mein Sohn, und lass sie nicht dahingehen.
	G-II Und den Frommen hat er Weisheit gegeben. Gelobt sei der Herr in Ewigkeit. Es geschehe, es geschehe.		

---

82. So nach dem Obertext im *Liber Hiesu Filii Sirach* und bei Vattioni, *Ecclesiastico*. Weber und Gryson, *Biblia Sacra*, bevorzugen die Variante *sanet* („er heile").

Bezeichenderweise enden die weisheitlichen und auf die Erziehung des jüdischen Mannes zielenden Sprüche Ben Siras mit einem an Ps 1,1–2 erinnernden Makarismus (cf. 4Q525 frag. 2,ii + 3,1.6). Weisheitliche Bildung und Toragehorsam (cf. Dtn 6,6; 11,18) werden abschließend nochmals eng zusammen gesehen, unter dem Begriff der Gottesfurcht vereint und als Quelle des Lebens selbst angesehen (cf. Prov 14,27; 19,23). Die Gottesfurcht erscheint wie in Sir 6,37 (H^A) und 40,26–27 (H^B) als wahres Lebensmittel des Menschen, der für Ben Sira grundsätzlich bildbar und erkenntnisfähig, frei und bis zum bzw. in den Tod im Werden ist. Pointiert lautet das Schlusswort des hebräischen Sirach (vor dem dreigliedrigen Anhang in Kap. 51) „Leben" (חיים), was gemäß der eingangs beschriebenen weisheitlichen Tradition dem fundamentalen Interesse des gesamten Buches an einem gelingenden Leben des Menschen entspricht (cf. Sir 6,15[16]; 15,17; 17,11; 45,5).[83]

Auch G betont den engen Zusammenhang von Erziehung zur Weisheit, erfolgreicher Bewältigung des Lebens und Gottesfurcht, lässt aber weniger deutlich den Bezug zu Ps 1 und zur Beachtung der Tora erkennen. Hingegen wird in einem gegenüber H^B zusätzlichen, aus poetologischen Gründen wohl als ursprünglich anzusehenden vierten Kolon (V.29a) die aktive Umsetzung des Gelernten unterstrichen. Denken und Handeln bilden demnach eine Einheit. Durch die passivische Formulierung von V.28b wird die Rolle Gottes als dem eigentlichen Lehrer des Menschen betont. Die Gottesfurcht (φόβος κυρίου) erscheint schließlich weniger als ein Mittel denn als ein Kennzeichen (ἴχνος)[84] des Lebens des Frommen. G-II hebt diese zwei Gedanken mittels der Wiederholung von Sir 43,33b hervor. Dass es eigentlich Gott ist, der am Menschen zu dessen Heil handelt, betont dann auch Paulus, wenn er in einer Art christologischer Transformation von Sir 50,29 (G) bekennt: *Ich habe zu allem Kraft (ἰσχύω) durch den, der mich stark macht, Christus* (Phil 4,13). Dass Sir 50,28–29 schon früh in der christlichen Überlieferung christologisch verstanden werden konnte, zeigt der *Codex Venetus*, der in V.29 von φόβος χριστοῦ spricht (cf. Eph 5,21).

Die lateinische Version setzt gegenüber H^B und G nochmals eigene Akzente, indem sie erstens die weisheitlichen und pädagogischen Gegenstände des Nachdenkens ausdrücklich als gut (*bona*) qualifiziert, zweitens

---

83. Cf. Prov 3,18; 4,22; 8,35; 14,27; 19,23.

84. Bei der Lesart λύχνος („Leuchte") handelt es sich um eine freie Konjektur (cf. Ziegler, *Sapientia*, 470).

dem, der sie befolgt, fortwährendes Weisesein zusagt (*sapiens erit semper*) und drittens die umfassende Bevollmächtigung nicht auf die Furcht, sondern, wie die Mehrzahl der griechischen Handschriften, die φῶς κυρίου bieten, auf das „Licht Gottes" (*lux dei*) zurückführt. So steht am Ende des lateinischen Sirach der im Licht Gottes wandelnde Mensch. Damit kann ein Leben im Gehorsam gegenüber dem Wort Gottes gemeint sein (cf. Ps [Vg] 118,105; Prov 6,23; Jes 2,5) wie auch ein von Gott selbst geleitetes Leben (cf. Ps [Vg] 118,33), das sich im Kontext der christlichen Bibel dann auf ein von Christus als dem Licht Gottes (cf. Joh 12,46) geführtes Leben bezieht.

Noch deutlicher als G und L hebt S den Zusammenhang von Meditation der im Sirachbuch niedergelegten Weisheit, Lernen, weise Werden und Handeln, mithin den Weg vom Intellekt zum Ethos hervor, um dann mit einem Lobpreis der Gottesfurcht und einer formelhaften, direkten Ermahnung des Schülers Sirachs und des Lesers seines Buches zu schließen (cf. Sir [S] 6,27; 25,11–12; 40,26).

12. Ausblick: Der betende und segnende Mensch (Sir 51,1–30)

In allen seinen Versionen stellt das Sirachbuch den Menschen als ein von Gott geschaffenes Wesen dar, das auch in seiner Endlichkeit auf Gott bezogen, zur Erkenntnis Gottes befähigt und zu einem an den Geboten der Tora orientierten Leben aufgerufen ist. Komprimiert zeigt sich die prozesshafte, theologische Anthropologie des Sirachbuches nochmals am Ende in den drei Anhängen in Kap. 51, wenn dort der für sich und in der Gemeinschaft *betende* sowie *der Weisheit suchende* und Gott *segnende Mensch* dargestellt werden (Sir 51,1–12; 51,12a–o; 51,13–30). Die von Bernd Janowski für die alttestamentliche Anthropologie herausgearbeitete Vorstellung, wonach sich in der Situation vor Gott, mithin in Gebet und Segen, Menschwerdung ereigne, gilt in besonderer Weise für das Sirachbuch (cf. Sir 51,1–12; 23,1.4 [G]).[85] Dabei weist das Sirachbuch insgesamt eine doppelachsige Anthropologie auf, insofern es eine allgemeine und eine spezielle, auf Israel bezogene Anthropologie vertritt. Zwischen beiden Achsen entwickelt sich der Mensch, dessen allgemeines Ideal der Weise und dessen Verkörperung wahren Menschseins der Hohepriester ist. Der *ideale* Mensch ist von der

---

85. Cf. Janowski, „Mensch", 1057, und zur Bedeutung des Gebets im Sirachbuch Werner Urbanz, *Gebet im Sirachbuch. Zur Terminologie von Klage und Lob in der griechischen Texttradition*, HBS 60 (Freiburg: Herder, 2009).

Furcht Gottes geprägt, meditiert die heiligen Schriften Israels, wendet sich im Gebet an Gott und begegnet seinem Mitmenschen mit Barmherzigkeit und Wahrhaftigkeit. Mittels des *wahren* Menschen, dem Jerusalemer Hohenpriester, erfährt er Sühne und Segen seitens *des* Gottes, der sowohl der Gott des Alls als auch der Gott Israels ist.

Die Vielgestaltigkeit des Menschenbildes des Sirachbuches zeigt sich vor allem vor dem Hintergrund seiner unterschiedlichen hebräischen, griechischen, lateinischen und syrischen Überlieferungsgestalten, die jeweils eigene Akzente setzen, über je eigene intertextuelle Bezüge und je eigene Rezeptionsgeschichten verfügen. Ausweislich der hier exemplarisch behandelten anthropologischen Texte zeigt sich in G tendenziell eine Verstärkung der in H angelegten Vorstellung, dass die Gottesebenbildlichkeit des Menschen in der Nachahmung Gottes Gestalt gewinnt. S ist in einzelnen ethischen Mahnungen grundsätzlicher und betont die Erlösungsbedürftigkeit des Menschen als eines von Hoffnung gekennzeichneten Wesens stärker als die anderen Versionen. L blickt am deutlichsten über dieses Leben und den Tod hinaus, deutet eine ethische Differenzierung des Todesgeschicks und den Gedanken eines Totengerichts an und weist im Kontext der aus Altem und Neuem Testament bestehenden Bibel das höchste Maß einer auf das Handeln Gottes in Jesus Christus hin transparenten Lesbarkeit des Sirachbuches auf.

G = image = imitation gán shape

Anthropologie bei Ben Sira im Zusammenspiel von לב, נפש und יצר

Franz Böhmisch

ABSTRACT: In Ben Sira's anthropology, נפש and לב form the center of dynamics and the center of a person's orientation. Each of them must be realized in its entirety (holistically). According to Ben Sira, it is a fundamental evil if they are split. This corresponds to his view of the theology of creation as a theory that implies the unity of contrasting entities in the world. At the same time, Ben Sira introduces the typically theological term יצר. The analysis of this term within the Hebrew version of Ben Sira (Sir 15:14 in MS A and once in the medieval paraphrase of the book) in addition to the loanword ܝܨܪܐ in the Syriac translation (Sir 17:31; 21:11; 27:5–6) leads to a clear understanding of the term. It refers to the vital human conditions of disposition, personality, characteristic traits and nature. The creator (yoṣer) molds (yaṣar) the disposition of the human being (yeṣer). According to Ben Sira, man remains constantly turning back to his creator: "the day will turn to night, if there is no sun" (Sir 17:31). The term yeṣer is never split within the book of Ben Sira.

1. Begriffsnetz der Anthropologie bei Ben Sira

Ben Sira verbindet mit der traditionellen Nefesch-Leb-Basar-Ruach-Anthropologie innovativ den Begriff יצר. Was will er damit spezifisch ausdrücken? Der psychologische Kern der Anthropologie bei Ben Sira ist mit Oda Wischmeyer[1] als psychologischer Rationalismus anzusprechen, weshalb geklärt werden muss, wie die irrationalen Strömungen der נפש, die Ben Sira feststellt und diskutiert, eingebunden sind. Das Denken in Polaritäten in der Schöpfungslehre bei Ben Sira ist damit zu konfrontieren,

---

1. Oda Wischmeyer, *Die Kultur des Buches Jesus Sirach*, BZNW 77 (Berlin: de Gruyter, 1995), 201–47.

wenn der Mensch eingespannt ist zwischen Erhabenheit als Gottes Ebenbild und seiner Kreatürlichkeit in Staub und Asche. Wie wirkt sich diese
Grundspannung anthropologisch und psychologisch aus? Ist bei Ben Sira
die *jeṣær*-Anthropologie abzuheben von den anderen anthropologischen
Ansätzen oder ergänzen sich die Begriffe? Sind die anthropologisch-psy-
chologischen Ansätze bei Ben Sira konsistent oder widersprechen sie sich?
Dabei steht auch die schon öfter diskutierte Frage im Raum, ob Ben Sira
schon in Richtung der rabbinischen Scheidung von *jeṣær haṭṭob* und *jeṣær
hara'* denkt[2] oder ein Verständnis von *jeṣær* als Neigung (inclination) entwickelt hat.

Die Anthropologie bei Ben Sira könnte man mit Carol A Newsom einordnen in ein universales Koordinatensystem anthropologischer Ansätze[3]
oder zunächst einmal bescheidener das Begriffsnetz im Buch des Ben Sira
rekonstruieren, wie es hier versucht ist. Wenn man aus einer Schrift ein
Netz der leitenden Begriffe und ihr Zusammenspiel nachzeichnet, zeigen
sich das anthropologische Konzept, oder falls ein Werk nicht konsistent
oder absichtlich mehrdimensional arbeitete, die kontextuell verschiedenen anthropologischen Konzepte.

Zur Lösung des Problems, dass für diese Fragen entscheidende Passagen des Sirachbuches bis heute hebräisch teilweise nicht vorliegen,
in denen יצר nach Ausweis der Übersetzungen Verwendung gefunden
haben könnte, wird hier stark auf die syrische Übersetzung des Buches
(SirSyr) zurückgegriffen, in der das Lehnwort ܝܨܪܐ *jaṣro* in Sir 15,14;
17,31 und Sir 21,11 verwendet wird und zudem an diesen Stellen die
Metaphorik zur Erklärung des יצר durch Ben Sira sprachlich besonders
gut erkennbar ist. So bietet sich beim Fehlen von hebräischen Textzeugen zu יצר die syrische Version als Ausgangspunkt der Analyse an, ohne
hebräische Rekonstruktionsversuche (z.B. von Moshe Segal oder Rudolf
Smend) zugrunde zu legen.

Aus dem Netz der Begriffe ergibt sich hoffentlich eine Klarstellung des
Verständnisses der jeweiligen Begriffe bei diesem Autor Ben Sira. Dazu
gehören auch spezifische Verbundbegriffe wie תאות נפש oder לב פחז.

---

2. So Johann Cook, „The Origin of the Tradition of the יצר הטוב and יצר הרע", *JSJ*
38 (Leiden: Brill, 2007), 80–91; dagegen aber die umfangreichen Untersuchungen von
Ishay Rosen-Zvi und Miryam T. Brand (siehe unten).

3. Vgl. Carol A. Newsom, „Models of the Moral Self: Hebrew Bible and Second
Temple Judaism", *JBL* 131 (2012): 5–25.

Zusätzlich ist zu beachten, dass in einigen Abschnitten, in denen Ben Sira sehr grundsätzlich gegen etwas opponiert, er Positionsgrenzen setzt, sozusagen rote Linien, die gegenüber einer falschen These eine Abgrenzung definieren. Wenn Ben Sira z.B. in Sir 15,11–16,14 den freien Willen des Menschen verteidigt, dann geschieht das in Auseinandersetzung mit Thesen von Gegnern, die diese Willensfreiheit und Entscheidungsfähigkeit anzweifeln. Ben Sira setzt hier eine klare Kante für die Willensfreiheit und eine rote Linie gegen einen grundlegenden Zweifel. Durch solche Abgrenzungen entsteht bei Ben Sira ein Rahmen, innerhalb dessen Ben Sira Anthropologie denkt. Anthropologie bei Ben Sira ist der Raum zwischen den roten Linien, die er zieht. Die einzelne rote Linie in einem Textabschnitt ist noch nicht seine ganze Anthropologie.

Ben Sira sagt jedoch in solchen Abschnitten wenig über die komplizierten innerpsychischen Vorgänge, die den Menschen in kritischen Situationen schließlich zur freien Entscheidung führen, zu der er befähigt ist, wenn er von seinem Wesen weiß und dementsprechend weise nachdenkt und handelt. Sein Verständnis dieser innerpsychischen Voraussetzungen des freien Willens und des Handelns erläutert er jedoch an anderen Stellen und führt diese psychologischen Vorgänge dort aus, z.B. in den Abschnitten über die Träume in Sir 34 und Sir 40 oder auch im Gebet in Sir 22,27–23,6 oder in den Abschnitten über das Reden und Schweigen.

Psychology

2. Zu den Grundlagen der Anthropologie des Ben Sira

Eine Mitte seiner Psychologie und Anthropologie beschreibt Ben Sira in poetisch-metaphorischer Sprache, wenn er über die integrale Einheit des Menschen im לב als Orientierungszentrum für die נפש handelt.

Oda Wischmeyer hat die psychologischen Ansätze bei Ben Sira unter der treffenden Überschrift „Seelenleitung" analysiert.[4] Ben Sira ist der klassisch alttestamentlichen Anthropologie verpflichtet, die die Motivationen, Affekte und Strebungen des Menschen in der נפש bündelt.[5]

---

4. Wischmeyer, *Kultur*, 201–47.

5. Vgl. ausführlicher Franz Böhmisch, „Spiegelungen der Seele und Gesichter: Traumkritik im Sirachbuch", in *Geistes-Gegenwart: Vom Lesen, Denken und Sagen des Glaubens: Festschrift für Peter Hofer, Franz Hubmann und Hanjo Sauer*, hrsg. Franz Gruber, Linzer philosophisch-theologische Beiträge 17 (Frankfurt a.M.: Lang, 2009), 19–30.

Mit der נפש, „jenem inneren Kräfteensemble, das den Menschen ausmacht", ist bei Ben Sira die Kreatürlichkeit des Menschen in seiner Orientierungslosigkeit ausgedrückt, welcher der לב mit der Orientierung an Weisheit und Gottesfurcht eine Richtung geben soll. Daraus resultiert eine „Kultur des Herzens"[6] mit dem Herz als dem Verstandeszentrum, das sich an der Weisheit orientieren muss und damit die destruktiven Tendenzen der נפש eindämmen und die kreativen Tendenzen der נפש entfalten muss.

Wiederholt schärft Ben Sira in der Tradition der Weisheitsliteratur ein, dass die irrationalen Strebungen des Menschen durch die Ausrichtung an Weisheit, Tora und Gottesfurcht gesteuert werden müssen.

„Sirach steht in dieser Diskussion ganz eindeutig und betont auf der Seite des Rationalen. Medizinische Einsichten in die somatische Bedingtheit schlechter und schwerer Träume rücken Sirach zudem inhaltlich in die Nähe des hippokratischen Traktats Über die Diät" und sind ein Zeugnis für sein ärztliches Interesse. Daß Sirach unter den Träumen gerade die Angst- und Verfolgungsträume erwähnt, gehört zu seinem psychologisch-ärztlichen Realismus."[7]

Am Beispiel der Träume hat Ben Sira sein Konzept ausgearbeitet: Wenn das Herz sich in Träumen den Spiegelungen der eigenen Seele hingibt, dann verliert es die Orientierung. Ben Sira hat eine sehr kritische Position gegenüber der Introspektion in die eigene Psyche. Objektive äußere Intervention durch Gesetz und Weisheit müssen das Herz leiten, damit es nicht fehlgeht.

Sir 34,1–8

1 Nichtiges sucht die Hoffnung auf Lüge, / und Träume erfreuen die Narren.

2 Wie einer, der nach Schatten greift und dem Wind nachjagt, / so ist einer, der auf Träume vertraut.

3 Dieser ist wie jener: Spiegel und Traum, / gegenüber dem Gesicht das Abbild des Gesichts.

4 Wie kann Reines von Unreinem kommen? / Wie kann Wahres von der Lüge kommen?

5 Wahrsagung, Zeichendeuterei und Träume sind nichts, / was du erhoffst, macht das Herz sich vor.

---

6. Wischmeyer, *Kultur*, 213.
7. Wischmeyer, *Kultur*, 222.

6 ~~Wenn sie~~ nicht vom Höchsten gesandt sind zur Warnung, / gib ihnen dein Herz nicht hin.

7 Viele verloren den Weg durch Träume und scheiterten auf ihrem Lebenswandel.[8]

8 Ohne Lüge erfüllt sich das Gesetz / und Weisheit wird in einem ehrlichen Mund vollendet.

Wenn das Herz auf einen Traum vertraut, dann fällt es zurück in die Orientierungslosigkeit der נפש und spiegelt sich selbst, macht sich also selber etwas vor (außer in den Fällen, in denen der Traum von Gott als Warntraum geschickt ist).

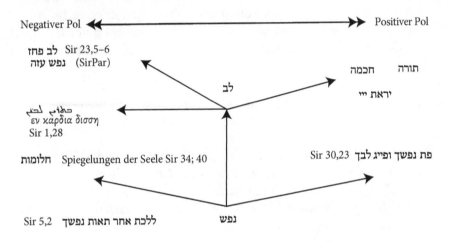

Abb. 1: Das Energiezentrum נפש und das Orientierungszentrum לב

Abbildung 1 zeigt den Versuch einer Visualisierung des psychologischen Konzepts von נפש und לב bei Ben Sira. Das Energiezentrum des Menschen נפש treibt den Menschen ungerichtet voran, doch das Orientierungszentrum לב muss die negativen und positiven Strebungen des Menschen in die richtigen Bahnen lenken. Die chaotische Selbstbespiege-

---

8. Zur Übersetzung von Sir 34,7 mit Hilfe des hebräischen Textes aus SirSyr und der gereimten Sirachparaphrase in T-S NS 108.43:רבים תעו דרך בחלומות ויכשלו בהליכתם, vgl. Franz Böhmisch, Die Vorlage der syrischen Sirachübersetzung und die gereimte hebräische Paraphrase zu Ben Sira aus der Ben-Ezra-Geniza, in *Texts and Contexts of the Book of Sirach / Texte und Kontexte des Sirachbuches*, hrsg. Gerhard Karner, Frank Ueberschaer und Burkard M. Zapff, SCS 66 (Atlanta: SBL Press, 2017), 232.

lung der Seele in Träumen (חלומות), das Nachgehen nach den Begierden der Seele (Sir 5,2 תאות נפשך) etc. treiben den Menschen auf den negativen Pol zu, das Ausrichten der inneren Kräfte und Strebungen auf die Gottesfurcht יראת יי und die Orientierung an Tora תורה und Weisheit חכמה führen zum positiven Pol. Bereits in Sir 1,28–30 macht Ben Sira klar, dass die ungespaltene Einheit des Menschen grundlegend ist für ein gelingendes Leben: Man soll sich Gott in Gottesfurcht und nicht mit einem zwiespältigen Herz nähern.

Diese Bedeutung der integralen Einheit des Menschen für das Verstehen der anthropologischen und psychologischen Begrifflichkeit bei Ben Sira, die sowohl hier beim לב als auch später beim יצר wichtig wird, zeigt sich generell im Umgang mit Polaritäten bei Ben Sira. Er versucht, Polaritäten in einer Einheit zusammenzubinden, was man bei ihm ein „Gesetz von der Einheit der Polaritäten" nennen könnte, und konsequenterweise ist ihm innerpsychisch jede Aufspaltung ein Gräuel.

3. Polare Strukturen in der Anthropologie Kohelets als Kontrast zu Ben Sira

Ben Sira arbeitet etwas anders, als es vor ihm Kohelet tat, mit Hilfe polarer Strukturen das anthropologische Profil des Menschen heraus:[9]

Bei Kohelet wird eine traditionelle Weisheit (Pol A) mit einer eigenen Beobachtung konfrontiert (Pol B) und nun nicht einfach die Gültigkeit der Schlussfolgerung gegenüber der traditionellen Weisheit behauptet, sondern beides als „Windhauch" relativiert.[10] Selbst diese neuentdeckte „Kohelet-Weisheit", die aufgrund eigener Beobachtung kritisch zur tradierten Weisheit steht, hinterfragt Koh wiederum in Hinblick auf andere Beobachtungen und kommt zu der Entscheidung, dass auch diese abgeleitete Weisheit wiederum „Windhauch" sei (vgl. Koh 2,11–17).

---

9. Vgl. die ausführlichere Ausarbeitung dieser biblischen Ansätze in Auseinandersetzung mit Hermann Hesse in Franz Böhmisch, *Weisheitliche Krisenbewältigung bei Hermann Hesse und in der alttestamentlichen Weisheitsliteratur*, PzB 10 (Klosterneuburg: Österreichisches Katholisches Bibelwerk, 2001), 95–103.

10. Vgl. J. A. Loader, *Polar Structures in the Book of Qohelet*, BZAW 152 (Berlin: de Gruyter, 1979).

Possession

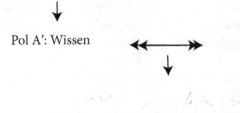

Pol A: Besitz   ←→   Pol B: kein Vorteil

No benefit

הבל Windhauch

=> Wissen: Relativierung des Besitzes

Pol A′: Wissen   ←→   Pol B′: Gleiches Geschick von Wissendem und Unwissendem

הבל Windhauch

=> Pol A″: … usw.

=> Glück als Anteil Gottes für den Menschen

Abb. 2: Relativierungsketten bei Kohelet (nach J. A. Loader, Polar structures)

Mit Hilfe solcher Polaritäten baut Kohelet Relativierungsketten zu Positionen traditioneller Weisheit auf. Doch er endet nicht im Nihilismus. Er relativiert und überwindet auch seinen krisenhaften Lebensüberdruss aufgrund der Beobachtung von Glück im Leben des Menschen. Da für Kohelet Gott zwar ferne ist, dessen Letztverantwortlichkeit für die Schöpfung aber trotz aller Relativierungen nicht zur Disposition steht, ergibt sich als letzte Polarität die zwischen dem „Windhauch" (hebräisch הבל *hæbæl*), der allen Phänomenen zu eigen ist, und dem Glück, das als Geschenk Gottes im Leben des Menschen auch beobachtet werden kann.

> But this polar relation differs from all the others in that *joy is not merely an antithesis of hebel but a consequence* thereof.[11]

Dieses Glück zu ergreifen ist für Kohelet der Anteil am Leben, den Gott schenkt:

---

11. Loader, *Polar Structures*, 111.

Koh 3, 12–13: Ich hatte erkannt: Es gibt kein in allem Tun gründendes
Glück, es sei denn, ein jeder freut sich, und so verschafft er sich Glück,
während er noch lebt, wobei zugleich immer, wenn ein Mensch isst und
trinkt und durch seinen ganzen Besitz das Glück kennenlernt, das ein
Geschenk Gottes ist.

Bei Kohelet sind also die Grundbegriffe הבל *hæbæl* (Windhauch) und טוב
ṭôb (Glück) dominant, die jedoch bei Ben Sira keine Rolle spielen. Wenn
man davon ausgeht, dass Ben Sira Kohelet kennt, ist es bezeichnend, wie
er seine Anthropologie anders aufbaut.

[handwritten: Polarity in BS / tries to unify behind it . in Creation]

4. Die Einheit der Polarität bei Ben Sira

Ben Sira, der anscheinend grundsätzlich traditionellere Positionen als
Kohelet vertritt, geht in der Frage polarer Strukturen einen Schritt weiter als
dieser und versucht hinter der Polarität eine höhere Einheit der Schöpfung
zu entdecken. Dabei kommt er zu einem im Kontext alttestamentlicher
Theologie ungewöhnlichen und originären Weg der Krisenbewältigung,
dem Grundgesetz von der gottgewollten Entsprechung der Polaritäten in
der Schöpfung:

Sir 33,13–15 (nach HE)[12]

> [13] Wie Ton in der Hand des Töpfers,
>   um ihn zu formen nach Belieben,
>   so ist der Mensch in der Hand seines Schöpfers,
>   so dass sich einstellt von ihm her der Anteil.
> [14] Gegenüber dem Bösen ist das Gute,
>   und gegenüber dem Leben der Tod,
>   gegenüber dem Guten ist der Frevler
>   und gegenüber dem Licht die Finsternis.
> [15] Schau hin auf jegliches Werk Gottes:
>   Alle sind sie paarweise, eins gegenüber dem andern.

Dieses Gesetz der Einheit der Bipolarität in der Schöpfung ist bei Ben Sira
kein Dualismus und formuliert auch keinen Determinismus, wie auch das
Töpfergleichnis in Jer 18,6, worauf diese Passage aufbaut, die „Freiheit der

---

12. Vgl. Wicke-Reuter, *Providenz* (Anm. 39), 224–73.

missratenen Gefäße" beinhaltet.[13] Mit diesem Grundgesetz kann er die Krise der weisheitlichen Deutung der Welt in der Theodizee, wie sie bei Job und Koh aufbricht, verarbeiten und eine neue Synthese anbahnen.

Dieser Dominanz der Einheit der Polaritäten in der Schöpfung bei Ben Sira korrespondiert in seiner Psychologie und Anthropologie die Betonung der Einheit, während die innere Spaltung des Menschen (vgl. 1,18 zwiespältiges Herz) Ausgangspunkt von Fehlhaltungen ist:

5. יצר-Belege bei Ben Sira

In diesem Zusammenhang müssen wir nun überprüfen, ob der יצר im Sirachbuch und wie er mit den anderen anthropologischen Begriffen in Beziehung steht und ob es eine bei Ben Sira moderne *jeṣær*-Anthropologie gibt, die über die anderen Konzepte hinausgeht.[14] Belege für יצר in Sirach finden sich hebräisch oder syrisch in Sir 15,14 (MS A); 17,31 (SirSyr); 21,11 (SirSyr); 23,2 (Sirachparaphrase mit SirSyr) und 27,6 (MS A).

Sir 15,14

אלהים *מראש ברא אדם) וישיתהו ביד חותפו(ויתנהו ביד יצרו

Gott schuf von Anfang an den Menschen (und versetzte ihn in die Hand seines Häschers) undgab ihn in die Hand seines Naturells.

ܐܠܗܐ ܗܘ ܡܢ ܒܪܝܫܝܬ ܒܪܐ ܗܘ ܠܐܢܫܐ. ܘܐܫܠܡܗ ܒܐܝܕܐ ܕܝܨܪܗ.

SirSyr 15,14 belegt die Übersetzung von יצר mit ܝܨܪܐ. Der hebräische Text aus MS A (mit der Randkorrektur Bm *מראש statt מבראשית) enthält zu Sir 15,14, wie in der Literatur oftmals bestätigt wird,[15] eine eingeschobene Ergänzung „und er brachte ihn in die Hand seines Häschers", die den יצר

---

13. Vgl. Wicke-Reuter, *Providenz* (Anm. 39), 257; Jan Liesen, *Full of Praise: An Exegetical Study of Sir 39:12–35*, JSJSup 64 (Leiden: Brill, 2000), 260–61.

14. Analyse zu den *jeṣær*-Konzepten und zum *jeṣær* bei Ben Sira bieten Ishay Rosen-Zvi, *Demonic Desires: „Yetzer Hara" and the Problem of Evil in Late Antiquity* (Philadelphia: University of Pennsylvania Press, 2011), und Miryam T. Brand, *Evil Within and Without: The Source of Sin and Its Nature as Portrayed in Second Temple Literature*, JAJSup 9 (Göttingen: Vandenhoek & Ruprecht, 2013).

15. Vgl. Roland E. Murphy, *Yēṣer in the Qumran Literature*, Biblica 39 (Leuven: Peeters, 1958), 335; Johannes Marböck, *Jesus Sirach 1–23*, HThKAT (Freiburg: Herder,

mittelalterlich in den Text hineininterpretiert in Richtung einer negativen
dämonischen Kraft, wie sie später in der rabbinischen Literatur auftritt.
Dieser Einschub findet sich aber in den alten Übersetzungen nicht und
ist mit Miryam Brand u.a. als interpretierender mittelalterlicher Einschub
im hebräischen Fragment zu erklären. Ursel Wicke-Reuter übersetzt יצר
in der Tradition eines voluntaristischen Ansatzes mit „Wille" und hebt auf
die Entscheidungsgewalt des Menschen ab.[16] Wenn man versucht, יצר an
den verschiedenen Stellen im Sirachbuch möglichst einheitlich zu übersetzen, kommt man jedoch mit „Wesensart", „Charakter" oder „Naturell"
weiter; „Naturell" drückt im heutigen Deutsch das Geschaffensein aus, die
Identität des Einzelnen und bindet das Willenszentrum ein und trifft, wie
die folgenden Ausführungen zeigen sollen, wohl eher das, was יצר und
ܐܝܨ meint.

Englisch steht für diese Bedeutung zumeist „character" wie im hebräischen Begriffslexikon von Clines.[17]

In Sir 15,14 ist also mit Hilfe der Übersetzungen der mittelalterliche
Einschub herauszunehmen und dann zu übersetzen:

> Gott schuf von Anfang an den Menschen [] und gab ihn in die Gewalt
> seines Naturells.

Der Mensch ist sich selber überantwortet, seiner Freiheit, seinem Willen,
aber auch seinem angeborenen Naturell. Durch den Einschub in MS A
„und er brachte ihn in die Hand seines Häschers" erhält der Satz in rab-
binischer Interpretation einen ganz anderen Sinn, der über die Sicht Ben
Siras hinausgeht. In den Lexika ist diese Fortentwicklung in MS A weg
vom hebräischen Text von Ben Sira nicht ohne weiteres ersichtlich. Dieses
Problem muss daher in Texteditionen kommentiert werden, sonst könnte
auch in einer Sirachsynopse für Nutzer, die sich der Fortentwicklung auch
der hebräischen Version in mittelalterliche hebräischer Tradition nicht
bewusst sind, ein Missverständnis entstehen.

Sir 15,14 verbindet den יצר = das Naturell des Menschen mit der
Erschaffung durch Gott, ohne das Verständnis detailliert auszuführen.

2010), 199, und ausführlich Brand, *Evil Within and Without*, 99, „The Medieval Gloss
in Sir 15:14".

16. Ursel Wicke-Reuter, *Göttliche Providenz und menschliche Verantwortung bei
Ben Sira und in der Frühen Stoa*, BZAW 298 (Berlin: de Gruyter, 2000), 115–22.

17. David J. A. Clines, „יצר", *DCH* 4 (Sheffield: Sheffield Phoenix, 1998), 270–71.

Sir 17,6

ܡܕܡ ܟܝܢ̈ܐ ܦܘܡܐ ܘܠܫܢܐ ܘܥܝܢ̈ܐ ܘܐܕܢ̈ܐ܂ ܘܠܒܐ ܠܡܣܬܟܠܘ ܦܠܓ ܠܗܘܢ܀

Und er schuf ihnen [Mund und] Zunge und Augen und Ohren
und ein Herz zum Verstehen teilte er ihnen zu.

διαβούλιον καὶ γλῶσσαν καὶ ὀφθαλμούς, ὦτα καὶ καρδίαν ἔδωκεν διανοεῖσθαι
αὐτοῖς.

Entscheidungsfähigkeit und Zunge und Augen, Ohren und Herz gab er
Ihnen zum Überlegen.

Miryam Brand rekonstruiert mit Moshe Segal u.a. in diesem Vers, der
hebräisch nicht erhalten ist, aus dem griechischen διαβούλιον ein Beleg des
Nomens יצר.[18] Dagegen ist mit vielen Exegeten[19] und aktuell Marko Marttila[20] einzuwenden, dass alle Bicola in Sir 17,1–6 jeweils ein Verb im Teil
a und ein Verb in Teil b enthalten und so auch die syrische Übersetzung
in 17,6 das Verb ܦܠܓ statt διαβούλιον, woraus der Schluss gezogen wird,
dass dahinter יצר bzw. ויצר anzunehmen ist, das in der griechischen Übersetzung als Nomen gedeutet wurde, in der syrischen Übersetzung (wohl
stimmig) als Verbum. Auffällig ist das Vorkommen von „creavit" in Sir
17,5 und 17,6 in der Vetus Latina.[21]

Bei Ben Sira ist also das nomen agentis „Jôṣer" יוצר (vgl. Sir 27,5;
33,13), das Verb „jaṣar" יצר als Vorgang der Erschaffung und Begabung
des Menschen mit Sinnes- und Verständnisorganen durch Gott (Sir 17,6
uö.) und das nomen qualitatis „jeṣær" יצר (Sir 15,14; 17,31; 21,11; 23,2;
27,6) in Gebrauch.

Sir 17,31

Ausgangspunkt ist der syrische Text, der das Lehnwort ܝܨܪܐ enthält und
für seine Vorlage יצר voraussetzt:

---

18. Vgl. Brand, *Evil Within and Without*, 102.

19. Vgl. Marböck, *Jesus Sirach 1–23*, 210.

20. Marko Marttila, *Foreign Nations in the Wisdom of Ben Sira: A Jewish Sage
between Opposition and Assimilation*, DCLS 13 (Berlin: de Gruyter, 2012), 49.

21. Vgl. Francesco Vattioni, *Ecclesiastico: testo ebraico con apparato critico e versioni greca, latina e siriaca*, (Napoli: Istituto Orientale di Napoli, 1968), 84.

Sir. 17,31–32[22]

ܡܐ ܕܥܒܪ ܫܡܫܐ ܡܢ ܐܝܡܡܐ. ܐܦ ܗܘ ܗܘܐ ܠܗ ܚܫܘܟܐ
ܗܟܢܐ ܗܘ ܒܪܢܫܐ ܕܠܐ ܟܒܫ ܝܨܪܗ. ܡܛܠ ܕܒܣܪܐ ܗܘ ܘܕܡܐ.
ܚܝܠܘܬܐ ܕܫܡܝܐ ܕܐܢ ܐܠܗܐ. ܐܦ ܠܒܢܝ ܐܢܫܐ ܕܗܢܘܢ ܥܦܪܐ ܘܩܛܡܐ.

31 Wenn die Sonne verschwindet vom Tag: dann wird sogar dieser Finsternis. So ist der Mensch, der nicht presst sein Naturell יצר, weil er von Fleisch ist und von Blut. Die Heere des Himmels richtet Gott und auch alle Menschen, die Staub und Asche sind.

Diese poetische Ausarbeitung des *jeṣær* ist erhellend: So wie der Tag nur Tag ist, solange die Sonne scheint, und in einer Sonnenfinsternis zur Finsternis wird, so ist der Mensch, der sein Naturell nicht in Richtung Sonne (Gott) ausrichtet, nur Fleisch und Blut, nur Staub und Asche.

Der griechische Text weicht in 17,31–32 davon sehr stark ab und erscheint mir nicht schlüssig und durch den griechischen Übersetzer verunklart (Übersetzung nach Marböck):[23]

Was ist heller als die Sonne? Auch die lässt nach,
und Böses planen Fleisch und Blut.
Er selbst beobachtet die Macht der Himmelshöhe,
und die Menschen sind alle Staub und Asche.

Gegen den griechischen Text spricht, dass in Sir 17,25–27 mit dem Thema der Umkehr und der (Finsternis der) Unterwelt in allen Versionen der Text, den SirSyr 17,30–31 bietet, gut vorbereitet und in der Interpolation in SirGII 17,26b

er selbst wird dich führen aus der Finsternis zum Licht [der Gesundheit]

die Metaphorik aus SirSyr 17,30–31 bereits vorweggenommen wird und den Ergänzern thematisch evtl. vorgelegen hat.

In SirSyr 17,30–31 zeigt sich ein Verständnis von יצר im Sinne von Naturell als geschaffener und bedürftiger Wesensnatur des Menschen.

---

22. Syrischer Text nach 7h1 und der Edition Paul Anton de Lagarde, *Libri veteris testamenti apocryphi syriace*, (Leipzig: Brockhaus, 1861), 17, während in 7a1 Umstellungen von Sonne und Tag festzustellen sind.

23. Vgl. Marböck, *Jesus Sirach 1–23*, 219.

Hier kann ܪܨܝܢ nicht mit „Wille" übersetzt werden, weil der *jeṣær* ja Objekt des willentlichen Tuns ist. Das Konzept des Ausrichtens des *jeṣær* auf Gott in SirSyr 17,30–31 ist grundlegend für die theologische Anthropologie des Ben Sira, weil es Freiheit der Entscheidung, Ganzheitlichkeit der Persönlichkeit und zugleich Bipolarität der menschlichen Möglichkeiten (Ebenbildlichkeit Gottes und Staub und Asche) zusammendenkt.

Sir 21,11

Sir 21,11a ܚܢܰܟ ܡܳܪ ܐܰܠܳܗܐ ܠܟ ܐܰܠܳܗܐ ܕܢܰܓܕܠ ܨܶܒܝܳܢ ܐܶܠܝ ܪܶ̈ܚܡܰܬܐ ܢܰܚ̈ܠܐ

Wer das Gesetz einhält, zwingt sein Naturell, und wer Gott fürchtet, dem wird nichts mangeln.

Das b-Kolon gilt in SirSyr als verunstaltet und wohl im Griechischen besser bewahrt:

Ὁ φυλάσσων νόμον κατακρατεῖ τοῦ ἐννοήματος αὐτοῦ, καὶ συντέλεια τοῦ φόβου Κυρίου σοφία.

Wer das Gesetz einhält, ist Herr seines Denkens, und Vollendung der Furcht des Herrn ist Weisheit.

Dieser Beleg mit ܪܨܝܢ, der leider hebräisch nicht erhalten ist, zeigt ebenfalls deutlich, dass die Übersetzung von יצר bei Ben Sira mit „Wille" verengt wäre. Es geht gerade darum, den יצר willentlich einzuhegen, zu zwingen, zu pressen. Der יצר ist auch hier Objekt des willentlichen Tuns. Zusätzlich trägt dieser kurze Vers die Orientierung an der Tora bei, die nach Ben Sira Voraussetzung ist, um das Naturell an Gott auszurichten.

Sir 23,2

In der von Joseph Marcus aufgefundenen und von Ezra Fleischer edierten Sirachparaphrase (SirPar) aus der Geniza[24] findet sich auch eine Strophe über Sir 22,27–23,6, die die Vorlage יצר in Sir 23,2 belegt. Das Vorliegen von יצר an dieser Stelle hatte bereits Smend postuliert.[25] Hier hat SirSyr

---

24. Vgl. Böhmisch, *Vorlage*, 199–237.
25. Rudolf Smend, *Die Weisheit des Jesus Sirach erklärt* (Berlin: Reimer, 1906), 192.

Franz Böhmisch

zwar nicht mit ܚܪܝ übersetzt, sondern mit ܚܘܫܒܐ, das ebenso in SirSyr
27,5 als syrische Übersetzung von יצר dient (hebräisch dort belegt durch
MS A—siehe unten). Die Grundannahme dieses Aufsatzes, dass syrisches
ܚܪܝ in der Vorlage יצר voraussetzt, bedeutet umgekehrt also nicht, dass
jedes belegte Vorkommen von יצר im hebräischen Sirach im Syrischen mit
ܚܪܝ übersetzt ist.

In der SirPar zu Sir 22–23 ist bzgl. eines Rückschlusses zur Bedeutung
des Begriffs יצר bei Ben Sira Vorsicht geboten, da die SirPar mehrfach in
Richtung eines dämonischen יצר הרע mittelalterlicher jüdischer Tradition
ausgestaltet ist. Es ist daher von den Sirachübersetzungen auszugehen und
aus der SirPar sind einzelne Phrasen und Termini als Vorlage zu erweisen.
Das funktioniert bei Sir 23,2 sehr gut: Bereits Moshe Segal,[26] Menachem
Kister[27] und Ishay Rosen-Zvi[28] arbeiten mit begründeten Rekonstruktionen des Verses Sir 23,2 aus der hebräischen SirPar, wobei mir diejenige
von Segal nach der syrischen Vorlage mit dem hebräischen Wortschatz aus
der gereimten Sirachparaphrase am stichhaltigsten erscheint:[29]

ܡܢ ܕܝܢ ܢܩܘܡ ܥܠ ܬܪܥܝܬܝ، ܢܓܕܐ. ܘܥܠ ܠܒܝ ܡܪܕܘܬܐ ܕܚܟܡܬܐ

τίς ἐπιστήσει ἐπὶ τοῦ διανοήματός μου μάστιγας καὶ ἐπὶ τῆς καρδίας μου
παιδείαν σοφίας

(Menahem Kister) *מי יתן על יצרי שוט   ועל לבי שבט מוסר*

(Moshe Segal)*מי יקים על יצרי שוט   ועל לבי שבט מוסר*

---

26. Moshe Ş. Segal, ספר בן־סירא השלם (Jerusalem: Bialik, [3]1972), S. קלו.
27. Menahem Kister, "יצר לב האדם", הגוף והטיהור מן הרע: מטבעות תפילה ותפיסות
עולם בספרות בית שני ובקומראן וזיקתם לספרות חז"ל ולתפילות מאוחרות / "'The Imagination of Man's Heart': Body and Purification from Evil: Prayer Formulas and Concepts
in Second Temple Literature and Their Relationship to Later Rabbinic Literature",
Meghillot 8 (2010): 265.
28. Rosen-Zvi, *Demonic Desires*, 163, Anm. 7.
29. Moshe Segal hat in seiner Vorliebe für G I auch in Sir 22–23 zumeist eine
Rekonstruktion eines hebräischen Textes aus der griechischen Übersetzung und der
gereimten Sirachparaphrase hergestellt, die die Vorlage von G I hätte sein können,
selber wohl wissend, dass der hebräische Text der Sirachparaphrase strukturell und im
Wortbestand eher mit der syrischen Version dieses Kapitels zusammengeht.

Die Parallelismus-Stellung von יצר mit לב in Sir 23,2 verdeutlicht, dass יצר auf dem לב aufbaut. Während es in der ersten Strophe des Gebets (Sir 22,27–23,1) in allen Versionen Gr I, Gr II, VL und SirSyr um Reden und Schweigen geht, um das falsche Verhalten von Zunge und Sprache und die Eindämmung einer gefährlichen Wirkung einer Äußerung auf die Umwelt, geht es in der zweiten Strophe (Sir 23,2–6), die formal mit (1) Wer-Frage, (2) Zweck, (3) Gebetsanrede אל אבי ואדון חיי und (4) Gebetsbitte gleich aufgebaut ist, um die zugrundeliegende innere Haltung, die nach außen wirkt. Für beides wird bei Ben Sira mit innovativer Gebetssprache der eindämmende Beistand Gottes erbeten, da Gott der Einzige ist, der diese Hilfestellung für den יצר des Geschöpfes leisten kann. Es geht also in Sir 23,2 nicht nur um den Verstand oder den Willen, sondern um die ganze Persönlichkeit, eben um יצר: das Naturell. Sir 23,5–6 nach SirSyr und SirPar

גבה עינים אל תתנני ולב פחז הרחק ממני
נפש עזה אל תמשל בי ...

ܚܣܟ ܘܙܗܪܐ ܠܐ ܬܬܠ ܠܝ. ܘܠܒܐ ܦܫܝܛܐ ܐܪܝܡ ܡܢܝ.
ܘܦܫܝܛܐ ܕܟܣܝܐ ܠܐ ܢܛܥܝܢܝ. ܘܢܦܫܐ ܣܢܝܐܬܐ ܠܐ ܬܐܚܠܛ ܒܝ.

5   Hochmütige Augen gib mir nicht
     und ein lüsternes Herz halte fern von mir.
6   Und die Verdorbenheit des Fleisches soll mich nicht verleiten
     und eine freche Seele mich nicht beherrschen.

Für ܘܦܫܝܛܐ ܕܟܣܝܐ ܠܐ ܢܛܥܝܢܝ „und die Verdorbenheit des Fleisches soll mich nicht verleiten" findet sich eine Zeile weiter unten in der SirPar פחזי יצר אל יחפיזוני „die Verdorbenheiten des jeṣær sollen mich nicht verleiten". Die griechischen Übersetzungen und VL belegen hier κοιλίας bzw. ventris, was entweder freie Übersetzung von בשר oder wörtliche Übersetzung von בטן, jedenfalls nicht Übersetzung von יצר ist. Segal und Kister rekonstruieren daher פַּחַז בשר am Anfang von Sir 23,6, wobei jedoch Kister mit Recht ein dickes Fragezeichen danebensetzt.[30] Die SirPar trägt hier ein negatives Vorverständnis von יצר und das Wort selbst in das Piyyut-Gedicht ein. Nach Ausweis der Übersetzungen stand in Sir 23,6 nicht יצר im hebräischen Sirachtext.

---

30. Vgl. Kister „יצר לב האדם" / ‚The Imagination of Man's Heart', 265.

Die Ausdrücke לב פחז, גבה עינים und נפש עזה sind durch SirPar für Sir 23,5–6 verifiziert und bezeichnen einen יצר, der sich nicht richtig orientiert. Dann ergreifen diese ungeordneten Kräfte der נפש in der Sicht von Ben Sira Besitz vom Menschen: die Gier, das verdorbene Herz und die hochmütige Seele. Gott kann in dieser Situation der Bedürftigkeit des Geschöpfs jedoch noch rettend eingreifen und wird daher im Gebet um Bewahrung angefleht.

Dieses Gebet in Sir 22,27–23,6 wird in Sir 18,30–31 thematisch vorbereitet: Wenn die נפש nicht gesteuert wird, kann sie sogar zum inneren Feind werden (vgl. Sir 18,30–31).[31]

Der Begriff יצר im Gebet in Sir 22,27–23,6 (23,2) funktioniert als ein integrierender Begriff, der das Ensemble der psychischen und physischen Konstitution des Menschen meint und dabei die Bedürftigkeit des Geschöpfs hervorhebt, seine Kreatürlichkeit, seine Geschöpflichkeit.[32] Menahem Kister hat die in diesem Gebet verwendeten Bilder als „dämonologisch" benannt. Ishai Rosen-Zvi folgt ihm darin: „As Kister meticulously shows, Sirach uses demonological imagery".[33] Doch es ist fraglich, ob dieses Vokabular als „dämonologisch" zu bezeichnen ist. Ben Sira entwirft seine Psychologie in poetischer Einkleidung. Er beschreibt dabei innere Kräfte, nicht jedoch Kräfte, die von außen „dämonologisch" in den Menschen hineinwirken. Vielmehr sind es destruktive innere psychische Tendenzen, die dann mit Hilfe dieses „apotropäischen Gebetes תפילה אפוטרופאית"[34] (M. Kister) abgewehrt werden sollen, im Unterschied z.B. zum Gebet des Levi, das Kister vergleichend heranzieht, in dem externe Kräfte wie der frevlerische Geist oder ein Satan abgewehrt werden.[35]

Der psychologische Realismus des Ben Sira besteht gerade darin, die psychologischen Vorgänge nicht wie in solchen Schriften wie dem Test-Lev mit externen dämonologischen Instanzen aufzuladen und mit „Satan" oder „Dämonen" in Verbindung zu bringen, sondern die innere psychische Zerrüttung mit ähnlichen Begriffen anzusprechen und in einem Gebet abzuwehren. Menahem Kister schließt:

---

31. Vgl. Marböck, *Jesus Sirach 1–23*, 233.
32. Mit der Übersetzung „Geschöpflichkeit?" für יצר experimentiert Marböck, *Jesus Sirach 1–23*, 199, zu Sir 15,14.
33. Rosen-Zvi, *Demonic Desires*, 170, note Anm. 79.
34. Vgl. Kister, „יצר לב האדם" / ,*The Imagination of Man's Heart*', 264.
35. Vgl. Kister, „יצר לב האדם" / ,*The Imagination of Man's Heart*', 265.

בפסקה זו בבן סירא דומה מאוד להתייחסות אל היצר (או היצר הרע) בספרות
חז"ל

„In diesem Abschnitt bei Ben Sira besteht eine große Ähnlichkeit zur Behandlung des יצר (oder des יצר הרע) im Schrifttum der jüdischen Weisen". (Übersetzung: Franz Böhmisch)

Im Blick auf die Diskussion in der Judaistik zwischen einem Modell, das auch im rabbinischen Schrifttum nur einen יצר annimmt (Ishay Rosen-Zvi[36]), und dem Modell mit zwei יצרים, ist hier zunächst für Ben Sira festzuhalten: Der יצר bei Ben Sira ist nirgends etwas, das von außen an den Menschen herantritt, sondern ein Ensemble innerpsychischer Kräfte. Der יצר bei Ben Sira wirkt von innen nach außen.

Sir 27,5–6

Dieser kleine, aber wichtige Abschnitt aus zwei Versen ist hebräisch nur erhalten, weil er in MS A weit weg vom originalen Standort in Kapitel 6 zwischen die Verse 22 und 26 eingefügt wurde, da Sir 27 ansonsten hebräisch in den Sirachhandschriften nicht erhalten ist:[37]

כלי יוצר לבער כבשן, וכמהו איש על חשבונו
על עבדת עץ יהי פרי, כן חשבון על יצר אחד

5 Das Gefäß des Töpfers ist gemäß dem Brennen des Ofens:
   und wie dieses ein Mann über seinem Gedanken.
6 Über die Baumpflege wird die Frucht (künden):
   so der (geäußerte) Gedanke über das Naturell des Einzelnen.

In SirSyr ist nur Vers 6 belegt:

ܐܝܟ ܘܦܐܪܗܐ ܕܐܝܠܢܐ ܗܒ ܦܐܪܐ ܗܟܢܐ ܕܚܘܫܒܐ ܕܐܢܫܐ ܥܠ ܬܪܥܝܬܗܘܢ
ܘܟܢ ܐܝܟܢ.

Wie die Pflege eines Baumes Früchte hervorbringt, so ihre (geäußerten) Gedanken über die Einstellungen der Menschen.

---

36. Vgl. Ishay Rosen-Zvi, „Two Rabbinic Inclinations? Rethinking a Scholarly Dogma", *JSJ* 39 (2008): 513–39.
37. Vgl. Brand, *Evil Within and Without*, 101–2.

Im Lexikon von Clines wird hier יצר treffend mit engl. „character" über-setzt.[38] Ich verwende „Wesensart, Wesensnatur" oder eben „Naturell" im Deutschen: das, was einen Menschen ausmacht.

Man könnte diese poetische Beschreibung des יצר bei Ben Sira folgen-dermaßen umschreiben:

Die Qualität eines Tongefäßes zeigt, wie optimal die Hitze im Brenn-ofen war, und genauso steht es auch mit den Gedankenäußerungen eines Menschen. Und so wie die Frucht zeigt, wie der fruchttragende Baum gepflegt wurde und „vom Stamm her" dasteht, so zeigt der geäußerte Gedanke eines Menschen die Entwicklung (=Pflege) seines Charakters / Naturells.

Es handelt sich bei Ben Sira m.E. um eine einheitliche יצר-Vorstellung ohne dämonologische Vorstellung im Hintergrund. Im Gegenteil: Der יצר/ der Charakter, das Naturell kann sich veredeln oder verwildern, wie man bei Fruchtbäumen sagen würde.

Ishay Rosen-Zvi resümiert in seinem umfangreichen Werk über die Entwicklung des יצר letztendlich seine Einsicht in „the basic neutral cha-racter of *yetzer* in Sirach.... I accept Cohen Stuart's conclusion that we should not read the later rabbinic meaning of the *yetzer* into Sirach".[39] Die Diskussion der יצר-Texte Sir 17,30–31 und des Gebetes in Sir 22,27–23,6 hat darüberhinaus gezeigt, dass der יצר-Begriff bei Ben Sira eine tiefe Abhängigkeit des Geschöpfes vom Schöpfer beinhaltet.

6. Folgerungen

Für die Anthropologie bei Ben Sira kann man zusammenfassen

1. dass der Mensch in seinem Herzen (לב) sich an Weisheit, Tora und Gottesfurcht orientieren muss, um der Orientierungslosigkeit der נפש eine Richtung zu geben. Hier zeigt sich Ben Siras psychologischer Rati-onalismus (Oda Wischmeyer). Die Gefahr liegt in einem gespaltenen Herzen (Sir 1,28). Diesen Gedanken hat der Jakobusbrief aufgenommen und warnt davor, ein ανήρ δίψυχος zu sein (Jak 1,8), ein Mensch mit zwei Seelen bzw. im Sirachbuch mit zwei Herzen bzw. zwiespältigem Herzen in Sir 1,27–28.

right orientation

---

38. Clines, „יצר", DCH 6 (1998): 270–71.

39. Rosen-Zvi, *Demonic Desires*, 163, Anm. 10. Die Argumente von Cook, *The Origin of the Tradition*, 80–91, greifen daher zu kurz.

Unity in polaty

2. Die Einheit der Gegensätze in der Welt und der Polaritäten korrespondiert mit der Einheit des menschlichen לב.   , Introspection + giving

3. Der Mensch ist gehalten, sich nicht selbst zu spiegeln (z.B. in to
Träumen, die sich die נפש selbst vormachen kann) und nicht der Selbst- self
täuschung der eigenen נפש in der Introspektion zu erliegen, sondern als bad
Hörer des Wortes Ausschau nach göttlicher Weisung zu halten. Kommt
ungesteuert die Begierde der נפש durch (תאות נפש „Gier der Seele" Sir req'g
5,2; ܢܦܫܐ ܪܓܬܐ. „Verlangen deiner Seele" und ܨܒܝܢ ܕܢܦܫܟ „Wille deiner
Seele" in SirSyr 18,30), so kehrt sich das eigene Innere gegen den Menschen contrl
selbst wie ein innerer Feind (SirSyr 18,30). Der יצר des Einzelnen spiegelt
sich im Außen, im geäußerten Gedanken, in der Rede (Sir 27,5–6), wie
sich die Pflege eines Baumes an seinen Früchten zeigt. יצר ist als integra-
tiver theologischer Begriff bei Ben Sira verwendet, um die Kreatürlichkeit
/ Geschöpflichkeit des Menschen zum Ausdruck zu bringen. Dieser theologische Begriff drückt zugleich (Vgl. das Gebet Sir 22,27–23,6 und die
Lichtmetaphorik in Sir 17,31) stärker die Bedürftigkeit und Abhängigkeit
des menschlichen Geschöpfes von seinem Schöpfer aus als לב und נפש.

4. Der Jozer (יוצר „Töpfer, Bildner") gestaltet den Menschen und gibt
ihm den Jezer (יצר „das Gebilde, sein Naturell, seine Wesensart, seine
Geschöpflichkeit"). Der Mensch ist in der Hand des Schöpfers (Sir 33,13),
der wie ein Töpfer (יוצר) dem Menschen einen Anteil (חלק) mitgegeben
hat, den der Mensch nun entfalten muss. Der Mensch ist zugleich sich
selbst und seinem Naturell aufgegeben, das er steuern muss (Sir 15,14).
Die Tora gibt die Richtung an, um den יצר zu steuern (Sir 21,11). Die יצר-
Theologie bei Ben Sira bindet das Naturell des Menschen permanent an
Gott zurück und begründet, warum der Mensch ohne Orientierung an
Gott in die Finsternis der Existenz in Staub und Asche (17,32) zurückfal-
len kann. Mit Hilfe der Toraweisheit jedoch entfaltet sich in der Sicht Ben
Siras die Gottesebenbildlichkeit (17,1–10) des Menschen.

Variants and Facets of Anger in Sirach

Werner Urbanz

ZUSAMMENFASSUNG: Der Zorn gilt als eine der stärksten menschlichen Emotionen und verweist in biblischen Texten immer wieder auf die Relation von Anthropologie und Theologie. Der Beitrag bietet nach einem kurzen Überblick zum Zorn im Alten Testament einen Streifzug durch die antike (primär) griechische Philosophie und Literatur als kultureller „Matrix" der Sirachtexte. Ausgehend von einer Übersicht zur im ganzen Sirachbuch verwendeten Terminologie des Begriffsfeldes Zorn werden exemplarisch Texte (Sir 1,21–22, 3,16; 4,2f.; 5,4; 16,11; 27,30–28,8; 36,8.11; 45,15–16) und deren Aspekte untersucht. Hierbei zeigen sich in Sirach interessante Parallelen zur aristotelischen Mesotes-Lehre: Es geht in der weisheitlichen Ethik um einen Balance der Affekte. Menschlicher Zorn soll durch Einsicht in größere Zusammenhänge und Weisheit kontrolliert werden. Der strafende Zorn wird letztlich Gott alleine überlassen.

Anger (one's own or others') is an issue in every person's life. So it is not surprising that in Sirach, as a book teaching wisdom and practical skills for life, this topic is included. It is a topic that can be found again and again at the intersection of anthropology and theology, because the subject matter is treated both with divine and human protagonists, not only in Sirach but in the context of the whole Old Testament.[1]

This short essay attempts to trace a few aspects and facets that characterize this topic in Sirach and within the intellectual and cultural context of its time. Therefore the focus lies in particular on statements from contemporary philosophy or its later developments. This happens, of course, in an act of gleaning after the vintage (Sir 33:16). Núria Calduch-Benages

---

1. Bruce Edward Baloian, *Anger in the Old Testament*, AUSTR 99 (New York: Lang, 1992); Deena E. Grant, *Divine Anger in the Hebrew Bible*, CBQMS 54 (Washington, DC: Catholic Biblical Association of America, 2014).

offered a detailed explanation of the aspects of human wrath in the text
passage of Sir 27:30–28:7 and beyond.[2] Markus Witte has expanded on
the theological facets of mercy and wrath of God.[3] Oda Wischmeyer has
pointed out important aspects of the overall background of emotions,
under the term of affect theory, which has been an integral part of Greek
philosophy and ethics with regard to the guidance of the soul as one of the
main tasks of the philosopher and the wise since Aristotle's *De Anima*.[4]

In a first step, this essay gives a very brief overview of the terminology of anger in biblical texts (§1). This first examination is followed by
some statements about the understanding and handling of the matter in
(primarily) Greek literature and philosophy as the cultural matrix of the
Sirach texts (§2). This will provide a heuristic framework for a brief look
at the terminology and selected text passages in Sirach itself (§3). A few
observations complete the study (§4).[5]

1. Anger and the Old Testament—in Highly Simplified Terms

Anger is one of humanity's strongest emotions; but the word describes
a wide range of feelings from being upset to the affective loss of action
control. Anger has anthropological, theological, social, and political
dimensions, which, like the consequences of anger, are already discussed
in biblical and extrabiblical literature.[6] The strong emotional impulse of
anger cannot easily be distinguished terminologically or objectively from

---

2. Núria Calduch-Benages, "Es mejor perdonar que guardar rencor: Estudio de
Sir 27,30–28,7," *Greg* 81 (2000): 419–39.

3. Markus Witte, "'Barmherzigkeit und Zorn Gottes' im Alten Testament am
Beispiel des Buchs Jesus Sirach," in *Divine Wrath and Divine Mercy in the World of
Antiquity*, ed. Reinhard G. Kratz and Hermann Spieckermann, FAT 2/33 (Tübingen: Mohr Siebeck, 2008), 176–202 (= "Barmherzigkeit und Zorn Gottes im Buch
Jesus Sirach," in *Texte und Kontexte des Sirachbuchs: Gesammelte Studien zu Ben Sira
und zur frühjüdischen Weisheit*, ed. Markus Witte, FAT 98 [Tübingen: Mohr Siebeck,
2015], 83–105).

4. Oda Wischmeyer, *Die Kultur des Buches Jesus Sirach*, BZNW 77 (Berlin: de
Gruyter, 1995), 207–8.

5. The focus of this article lies on the Hebrew and Greek text traditions. The special features in Syriac and Latin are not incorporated; cf. for Syriac, e.g., 17:25 and
18:11.

6. Christian Frevel, "Zorn," *HGANT*, 474.

the emotions of wrath and other related terms in Bible translations.[7] The same words are translated differently in different contexts.[8] Different concepts can be used in the same way both for the wrath of humans and for the wrath of God. However, the Old Testament speaks of the wrath of God far more frequently than of the wrath of humans.[9]

In general, the perception of emotions never seems neutral. Emotions are always perceived as something good or bad (see Prov 15:1; 27:4). Due to the power of emotions, there are many instructions for their proper handling, especially in wisdom literature. It often emphasizes the ideal of balance, in particular the mastery of negative emotions, and gives warnings of the destructive effects emotions may have (Prov 14:30). Often, the close connection between emotion and communication is explicitly addressed. For example, negative feelings such as displeasure, anger, or hatred are considered to be the cause of strife (e.g., Prov 10:12; 15:1, 18).[10]

2. The Cultural Matrix of Anger in Antiquity

Anger is one of the most violent affects/emotions in Greco-Roman philosophy.[11] Τὰ κάκιστα τῶν παθῶν, οἷόν ἐστιν ἡ ὀργή ("the worst of his emotions, such as anger," Plutarch, *De cap.* 8 [90c]). This negative evaluation of

---

7. Stephen H. Travis, "Wrath of God (NT)," *ABD* 6:998.

8. In addition to the classic terminology overviews in the theological dictionaries (*TDOT* and *TDNT*), see John Goldingay, "Anger," *NIBD* 1:156 and Deena Grant, "Wrath," *NIBD* 5:932. See also the classification of Ellen J. van Wolde, "Sentiments as Culturally Constructed Emotions: Anger and Love in the Hebrew Bible," *BibInt* 16 (2008): 7–14.

9. Baloian (*Anger*, 189) names 518 instances for divine and 196 for human wrath; Stefan Wälchli, "Zorn (AT)," *WiBiLex*, https://www.bibelwissenschaft.de/stichwort/35502/, 1.

10. Susanne Gillmayr-Bucher, "Emotion und Kommunikation," in *Biblische Anthropologie: Neue Einsichten aus dem Alten Testament*, ed. Christian Frevel, QD 237 (Freiburg im Breisgau: Herder, 2010), 286–87.

11. For the following consult in detail Petra von Gemünden, "Umgang mit Zorn und Aggression in der Antike und der Bergpredigt," in *Affekt und Glaube: Studien zur Historischen Psychologie des Frühjudentums und Urchristentums*, ed. Petra von Gemünden, NTOA 73 (Göttingen: Vandenhoeck & Ruprecht, 2009), 163–89; von Gemünden, "Emotions and Literary Genres in the Testaments of the Twelve Patriarchs and the New Testament: A Contribution to Form History and Historical Psychology," *BibInt* 24 (2016): 514–35; Susanne Luther, *Sprachethik im Neuen Testament*, WUNT 2/394 (Tübingen: Mohr Siebeck, 2015), 67–81.

anger is, however, not uncontested in antiquity. In the context of extensive treatises, ancient philosophy deals with the subject of anger. The focus is especially on the nature of the affect, the way it can be controlled, and the critical evaluation of human contact with anger.[12] Overall, however, there is no uniform picture.

For Plato, anger is attributed either to a person's irritable nature or lack of education (παιδεία), for right parenting can provide the ability to control anger. In the ideal state, the right education (*Resp.* 440a–441a) takes place as part of the child rearing by the guards. Laws should make people feel fear and shame and thus motivate them to refrain from and prevent angry interactions with their neighbors.[13]

Aristotle defines anger "as an impulse, accompanied by pain, to a conspicuous revenge for a conspicuous slight directed without justification towards what concerns oneself or towards what concerns one's friends" (Aristotle, *Rhet.* 2.2 [1378a]).[14] In doing so, he takes into account the affective, evaluative, and volitional aspects of anger and places it in relationships in which one can rightly expect to be respected by others.[15] None of these human behaviors is innate, but must be acquired through "habituation" and must be formed by education, practice, and correct actions. Aristotle does not interpret anger as negative but constructs a relation between the affect, which always appears to be reactive, and its purposeful use; for if something excites the wrath of a person, their inner disposition determines the subsequent action. Any attitude can be realized in three ways, two faulty, marked by excess and inadequacy, and one right: the middle (μεσότης).[16] This is referred to as Aristotle's "doctrine of the mean," which is applicable to all attitudes and actions except for those of which there can be no shortage, because they are bad in themselves. The list of examples for intrinsically bad attitudes given by Aristotle includes spite, shamelessness, and envy but not anger: "With regard to anger also there is an excess, a deficiency, and a mean. Although they can scarcely be said to have names,

---

12. Luther, *Sprachethik*, 67.

13. Luther, *Sprachethik*, 68–69.

14. English text from W. Rhys Roberts at https://tinyurl.com/SBL0474a.

15. Douglas Cairns, "Der iliadische Zorn und die transkulturelle Emotionsforschung," in *Handbuch Literatur und Emotionen*, ed. Martin von Koppenfels and Cornelia Zumbusch, Handbücher zur kulturwissenschaftlichen Philologie 4 (Berlin: de Gruyter, 2016), 184.

16. See also Aristotle, *Eth. nic.* 1106b.

yet since we call the intermediate person good-tempered let us call the mean good temper; of the persons at the extremes let the one who exceeds be called irascible, and his vice irascibility, and the man who falls short an inirascible sort of person, and the deficiency inirascibility" (*Eth. nic.* 1108a).[17]

On the other hand, the Stoics do see anger as intrinsically bad. While Aristotle argues that reason can guide anger and direct it toward the good, anger and reason are in absolute contradiction for the Stoics. Consequently, the problem cannot be solved by finding the right balance, but only by the complete elimination of anger. The polemic against Aristotle and his school led to problematic simplifications. Thus the Stoic Seneca can speak of Aristotle in an undifferentiated manner as a *defensor irae*—as a defender of wrath—as if he had approved of any kind of anger.[18]

Hellenistic-Jewish philosophy largely takes up the Stoic theory of emotions. Thus Philo of Alexandria counts wrath among the emotions that a person should try to overcome and advocates the Stoic ideal of ἀπάθεια ("insensibility to suffering," Philo, *Spec.* 2.100–102; 3.131.140; *Prov.* 1.56.66). By connecting Stoic and Old Testament traditions, he considers God as ἀπαθή. His concept of *homoiosis theou* implies the transfer of this ethical norm to humanity.[19]

In different studies of the topic, philosophy is always in the foreground. As a further foundation of antiquity, however, Homer's writings are worth a further glance. Anger (μῆνιν) stands at the beginning of Western literature (the *Iliad*).[20] In contrast to the later classical Greek, in which ὀργή and θυμός are the main terms for anger, Homeric Greek has a multitude of terms that are usually translated as forms or aspects of anger.[21] While in Classical Greek, θυμός is simply the regular and prosaic word for anger, in

---

17. Luther, *Sprachethik*, 70. Translation from Ross at https://tinyurl.com/SBL0474b.

18. Gemünden, "Umgang mit Zorn," 166. However, Seneca's line of argument is definitely interesting for the biblical context. Anger leads to hatred, which is why a person should overcome it by cultivating an appropriate inner disposition, an inner greatness. The drastic examples chosen by Seneca are designed to lead his readers to adopt this attitude. Instead of letting one's anger out, he recommends interpersonal correction, applied with discretion. See Luther, *Sprachethik*, 71–72.

19. Luther, *Sprachethik*, 75.

20. Peter Schenk, "Darstellung und Funktion des Zorns der Götter in antiker Epik," in Kratz and Spieckermann, *Divine Wrath and Divine Mercy*, 153.

21. Cairns, "Iliadische Zorn," 187.

Homeric Greek, there are a number of terms that can be used in the context of anger but may also include other forms of emotional arousal or the expression of emotion. In the Homeric conception, θυμός is a whole series of interrelated motives and impulses.[22]

3. Facets of Anger in the Texts of Sirach

Sirach is standing between the Jewish traditions and the forms of Hellenistic παιδεία. Also in terms of language, the study of the book and its different text versions leads us into this intermediate world. While many studies on anger in the Old Testament understandably analyze primarily the Hebrew text of the Tanak, in Sirach we must look at both the Hebrew and the Greek text traditions.[23] The following table tries to give an overview of the terms that were used in the Hebrew and Greek versions.[24]

	ὀργή	θυμός	μῆνις κτλ	אף	others
1:21	ὀργήν GII			x	x
1:22		θυμός		x	x
		θυμοῦ			
3:16	παροργίζων				ומכעיס A
					וזועם C
4:2	παροργίσῃς			—	—
4:3	παρωργισμένην			—	—
5:4		(μακρόθυμος)		(ארך) אפים A	
5:6	ὀργή			ואף A+C	
		θυμός			רוגזו A+C

---

22. Douglas Cairns, "Ψυχή, Θυμός, and Metaphor in Homer and Plato," *Études platoniciennes* 11 (2015): 32, http://etudesplatoniciennes.revues.org/566.

23. See also Angela Thomas, *Anatomical Idiom and Emotional Expression: A Comparison of the Hebrew Bible and the Septuagint*, HBM 52 (Sheffield: Sheffield Phoenix, 2014), for anger esp. 161–89.

24. The terms are listed in order of their appearance in the text. The occurrences of the terms are clustered. In G, nominal and verbal variants of ὀργή and θυμός are quoted separately; in H, only אף and its derivatives. For H, the manuscripts are listed and also if there are no fragments (x). If there are no relevant equivalents, the sign "—" is used. For the texts, the standard editions (Beentjes, Ziegler) were used.

5:7	ὀργή				זעמו A+C
7:16	ὀργή				(עכרון) A
8:16		θυμώδους			אף (בעל) A
10:6			μηνιάσῃς		תשלֵים רע A
10:18	ὀργὴ θυμοῦ	<=			ועזות אף A
16:6	ὀργή				חֵמֶ(ה) A חמה B)
16:11	ὀργή				ואף A
	ὀργήν				רגזו A
18:24		θυμοῦ		x	x
19:21	παροργίζει GII			x	x
20:2		θυμοῦσθαι		x	x
23:16	ὀργήν			x	x
25:15		θυμὸς ὑπὲρ θυμόν		x	x
25:22	ὀργή				— C
26:8	ὀργή			x	x
26:28		θυμός		x	x
27:30	ὀργή		Μῆνις	x	x
28:3	ὀργήν			x	x
28:5			μῆνιν	x	x
28:7			μηνίσῃς	x	x
28:8		θυμώδης		x	x
28:10	ὀργήν	θυμός		x	x
28:19		θυμῷ		x	x
30:22			(μακροημέρευσις)	האריך אפו B	
30:23	—	—	—		וקצפון B
					בקצפון B
30:24		θυμός		וֹאׅף B	
31:29			ἐρεθισμῷ		בתחרה B
			ἀντιπτώματι		וכעס B
31:30		θυμόν		—	— B

32:19	—	—	—	B תתקצף
36:8	θυμόν		אף B	
	ὀργήν			חמה B
36:11	ὀργῇ πυρός		—	— B
39:23	ὀργήν			זעמו B
39:28		θυμῷ		ובאפם ? M
		θυμόν		
40:5		θυμός	—	—²⁵
			μηνίαμα	תהרה B
41:21	—	—	—	אפי B²⁶
43:2	—	—	—	חמה B
44:17	καιρῷ ὀργῆς		—	— B, M
45:18		θυμῷ καὶ ὀργῇ	בעזוז אפם B	
45:19			ויתאנף B	
		θυμῷ ὀργῆς	בחרון אפו B	
46:7	—	—	—	חרון B
47:20	ὀργήν		אף B	
48:10	ὀργήν πρὸ θυμοῦ		אף B	

Starting with the Greek version, there is a strong focus on a few terms, mostly in nominal use. ὀργή (twenty times) and θυμός (sixteen times) are used most often. Derivatives of μῆνις can be found only a few times (five times).[27] Greek ὀργή and θυμός seem to represent interchangeably the

_____

25. In MS B אך "only" is often changed into אף in translation, because of G and Syriac; Georg Sauer, *Jesus Sirach/Ben Sira*, ATD.A 1 (Göttingen: Vandenhoeck & Ruprecht, 2000), 275 n. 195.

26. אפי of MS B is often quoted as a reading error (MS M פני); Sauer, *Jesus Sirach*, 285; Víctor Morla, *Los manuscritos hebreos de Ben Sira: Traducción y notas*, ABE 59 (Estella: Verbo Divino, 2012), 256–57. Maybe the different readings are not mutually exclusive, because פני can also be associated with anger: Thomas, *Anatomical Idiom*, 179.

27. Maybe the verb προσοχθίζω (not directly relevant in this article) can be added: 6:25; 25:2; 38:4; 50:25.

larger variety of Hebrew expressions of anger.[28] Noticeable is the really small spectrum of terms.[29] In Hebrew, only אף is widely used (fourteen times), much less others like forms of זעם (five times) and חמה (three times), but there are many more different terms in use than in Greek.[30] From a terminology point of view, Sirach fits in both textual traditions in the broader context of LXX and Greek literature in general.

A few text examples below are intended to show first interpretation lines and at the same time open up a semantic range.

Sirach 1:21–22

[[21] The fear of the Lord repels sins,]
[and when it endures, it will turn away all wrath (ὀργήν).]
[22] Unjust anger [θυμός] can never be justified,
for the weight of his anger [θυμοῦ] is his downfall.[31]

In verse 21 we find a contrasting statement as the conclusion of an instruction on the fear of the Lord and wisdom (Sir 1:11–21).[32] This addition in GII is building on the first concretization of fear of the Lord, which results in "danger prevention." The wrath (ὀργή) of God stands for fair

---

28. Travis, "Wrath of God (NT)," 996 also points out that the tendency in Classical Greek is to represent the inner emotions of anger with θυμός, while ὀργή "stands for its outward expression."

29. Generally, the range of words used in the LXX is smaller than in Classical Greek (cf. χόλος "gall, bitter anger" and κότος: Oscar Grether and Johannes Fichtner, "ὀργή," TDNT 5:409–12). Katja Maria Vogt, "Anger, Present Injustice and Future Revenge in Seneca's De Ira," in Seeing Seneca Whole: Perspectives on Philosophy, Poetry and Politics, ed. Katharina Volk and Gareth D. Williams, CSCT 28 (Leiden: Brill, 2006), 62. This tendency is also present in Sirach.

30. Comparing the broader range of terms in Hebrew Ben Sira with the Greek Sirach seems to be almost a bit like comparing Homeric and Classical Greek; Cairns, "Iliadische Zorn," 187.

31. The English translations for Greek are taken from NETS and for Hebrew from the Ben Sira English translation by Benjamin H. Parker and Martin G. Abegg Jr. in Accordance (OakTree Software, Inc. 2008).

32. Also Sir 24:22; Prov 1:22–33; 8:32–36; Johannes Marböck, Jesus Sirach 1–23, HThKAT (Freiburg im Breisgau: Herder, 2010), 56, 59. Verse 21 can also be seen as the beginning of a new section: Josef Schreiner, Jesus Sirach 1–24, NEchtB 38 (Würzburg: Echter, 2002), 20.

judgment, which should be motivating for one's own actions.[33] The theme
forms a hinge to the next part, where the unjust anger (θυμός) of humanity
is addressed.[34] Although there is an old discussion of whether the anger
in verse 22 is divine or human,[35] verse 23, in contrast to verse 22, directs
the view to the patient person. In any case, both God and humanity are
connected in this subject area. Fear of the Lord gives a fundamental orientation and connects the human action to God's actions, in the present and
with eschatological overtones.[36]

Sirach 3:16

> [16 (A)] The presumptuous man despises his father
> and he who curses his mother arouses the anger [ומכעיס] of his Creator.
> [16 (C)] The one who forsakes his father is like a blasphemer
> and he who curses [וזוע] God shall drag off his mother.
> [16] Like a blasphemer is the one who neglects a father,
> and cursed by the Lord is the one who angers [παροργίζων] his mother.

The first concretization of the foundations of fear of the Lord and wisdom
takes place in an early commentary on the commandment to honor one's
parents of the Decalogue (Sir 3:1–16). In this we see the same interweav-
ing of human anger and God's anger that shows up in 1:21–22. Here also
we have a contrasting statement with motivating character at the end
of an instruction. It is very interesting that all textual witnesses (MS A,
MS C, G) highlight different aspects in the interpretation of the case.
There seems to be a particular proximity of MS A to G, because the LXX
uses παροργίζω for כאס.[37] Which version really offers a weakening rendi-

33. So also the addition in diverse MSS in 2:11 μακρόθυμος καὶ πολυέλεος; Rudolf
Smend, *Die Weisheit des Jesus Sirach* (Berlin: Reimer, 1906), 21.

34. See Maurice Gilbert, "L'addition de Siracide 1,21: Une énigme," in *Palabra,
prodigio, poesía: In memoriam P. Luis Alonso Schökel*, ed. Vicente Collado Bertomeu,
AnBib 151 (Rome: Biblical Institute Press, 2003), 320–22.

35. Norbert Peters, *Das Buch Jesus Sirach oder Ecclesiasticus*, EHAT 25 (Münster:
Aschendorff, 1913), 16 (divine); and Smend, *Weisheit des Jesus Sirach*, 15 (human).

36. See also in the same line the eschatological additions in Syriac in 1:22–27;
Núria Calduch-Benages, Joan Ferrer and Jan Liesen, eds., *La sabiduría del escribe:
Edición diplomática de la versión siriaca del libro de Ben Sira según el Códice Ambro-
siano, con traducción española e inglesia*, Biblioteca Midrásica 26 (Estella: Verbo
Divino, 2003), 50–51.

37. Morla, *Manuscritos hebreos de Ben Sira*, 29.

tion of the facts is not so easy to determine.[38] All in turn emphasize the connection between human and divine experience of anger and anger response.[39]

Sirach 4:2-3

> [2] A hungry soul do not grieve,
> and do not anger [παροργίσῃς] a man in his difficulty.
> [3] An angry [παρωργισμένην] heart do not trouble,
> and do not delay giving to one in need.

In 4:2-3 the keyword παροργίζω from 3:16 is applied again. The topic is now extended beyond the family circle and connected with another social aspect in a warning against bad behavior toward the poor (Sir 4:1-10). The text places a strong emphasis on the human-psychic side of misbehavior and the importance of almsgiving. In verse 3 of MS A, a lacuna before מעי (belly, internal organs) is often supplemented with תחמיר, which matches the "boiling pot" as a metaphor for anger.[40] Verse 6 takes up the theme of the curse and refers to the context of creation (cf. Sir 3:16).[41]

---

38. G "softens" H: Smend, *Weisheit des Jesus Sirach*, 27; Christian Wagner, *Die Septuaginta-Hapaxlegomena im Buch Jesus Sirach: Untersuchungen zur Wortwahl und Wortbildung unter besonderer Berücksichtigung des textkritischen und übersetzungstechnischen Aspekts*, BZAW 282 (Berlin: de Gruyter, 1999), 249; vice versa: Marböck, *Jesus Sirach 1-23*, 72.

39. This is especially interesting in comparison with Aristotle's reciprocal definition of anger: "a conspicuous revenge for a conspicuous slight directed without justification toward what concerns oneself or toward what concerns one's friends" (Aristotle, *Rhet.* 2.2, 1378a); Cairns, "Iliadische Zorn," 184. Here, the parents seem to be in a very close relationship with God, so that any affront to them is really an affront to God, which will provoke God's reaction.

40. For the supplement, see Patrick William Skehan and Alexander Di Lella, *The Wisdom of Ben Sira: A New Translation with Notes*, AB 39 (New York: Doubleday, 1987), 166; Morla, *Manuscritos hebreos de Ben Sira*, 35-36. For a detailed analysis see Bradley C. Gregory, *Like an Everlasting Signet Ring: Generosity in the Book of Sirach*, DCLS 2 (Berlin: de Gruyter, 2010), 298-99. For the metaphor for anger, see Andreas Wagner, "Emotionen in alttestamentlicher und verwandter Literatur: Grundüberlegungen am Beispiel des Zorns," in *Emotions from Ben Sira to Paul*, ed. Renate Egger-Wenzel and Jeremy Corley, DCL.Y 2011 (Berlin: de Gruyter, 2012), 44-45.

41. Gregory, *Like an Everlasting Signet Ring*, 261.

Sirach 5:4 (5:6–7) and 16:11

> 4 (A) Do not say, "I have sinned, but who will do anything to me?"
> for God is slow to anger [ארך אפים].
> Do not say, "The LORD is compassionate. All my iniquity will be blotted
> out."
> 4 Do not say, "I sinned, and what has happened to me?"
> For the Lord is long-suffering [μακρόθυμος].

The context speaks of measured trust in wealth and at the same time of God's forbearance. One should not overestimate oneself, because this puts one in danger of underestimating, indeed of belittling, the actions of God.[42] The warning of God's long-suffering wait for anger is justified by the creed of Israel (e.g., Exod 34:6; Num 14:18; Neh 9:17; Ps 86:15; 103:8; 145:8 Joel 2:13; Jonah 4:2), which includes the passionate intervention of God.[43] This facet is even more obvious in Hebrew and Greek, when אף and θυμός are included in the linguistic formulation of "long-suffering." The continuation (5:6) shows this clearly: mercy/compassion and anger are both passionate expressions of God's will to justice. But the fury (רגז) is upon the sinners. Therefore, it is necessary to repent in time (5:7) before his rage (זעם/ὀργή) will break forth (יצא/ἐξέρχομαι). Here Sirach has a strong prophetic feature, which understands love and anger (as a moment of justice) on the whole as an expression of the will of God to have a tangible relationship with humanity.[44]

Sirach 16:11 is standing in the same line. As a completion of a historical-theological reflection, the text summarizes the dual aspect of judgment (wrath) and reward (mercy) of God in the service of his righteousness. It is only in this dialectic that one can speak of God's relation to the world and humanity.[45]

---

42. Hermann Spieckermann, *Lebenskunst und Gotteslob in Israel: Anregungen aus Psalter und Weisheit für die Theologie*, FAT 91 (Tübingen: Mohr Siebeck, 2014), 126.

43. Marböck, *Jesus Sirach 1–23*, 101.

44. Friedhelm Hartenstein, "Die Theologie der Gefühle Jhwhs," in *Theologie der Gefühle*, ed. Roderich Barth and Christopher Zarnow (Berlin: de Gruyter, 2015), 229 speaks of a tangible relationship with God ("erfahrbare Gottesbeziehung") against the background of the prophetic divine hermeneutics, which sees continuity in God's actions over time. Both God's love and his anger, resulting in the punishment of Israel and Judah, mean that God will never stop caring for his people.

45. Witte, "Barmherzigkeit und Zorn Gottes," 183–86, 201.

Sirach 27:30; 28:3, 5, 7–8

³⁰ Ire and anger [μῆνις καὶ ὀργή], these also are abominations,
and a sinful man will have possession of them.
³ A person harbors wrath [ὀργήν] against a person—
and will he seek healing from the Lord?
⁵ His being flesh maintains ire [μῆνιν]—
who will make atonement for his sins?
⁷ Remember commandments, and do not be irate [μηνίσῃς] with your fellow,
and remember the covenant of the Most High, and overlook a mistake.
⁸ Refrain from strife, and you will reduce sins,
for a hot-tempered [θυμώδης] person will kindle strife.

The section Sir 27:30–28:12 (only in G) contains multiple aspects of anger between the two poles of resentment and forgiveness on the part of God and of the people in the context of quarrel.[46] The first two lexemes [μῆνις καὶ ὀργή] characterize the further course of the text very clearly. Striking is the strong emphasis on the otherwise rarely used μῆνις at the top position and in the frequency (27:30; 28:5, 7).[47] The question that arises, of course, is whether this constitutes an antithesis to the wrath of Achilles sung at the beginning of the Iliad. In any case, such attitudes are not praised. The warning against vengeance is very strong, because if a person is doing so, God will also operate in this way. Therefore, as the solution of offense, Sirach recommends forgiveness, especially the seeking for forgiveness. And this solution and basic attitude will also shape the relationship between God and humanity, especially in the context of prayer as an expression of the search for this relationship.[48] This concept of humanity does not negate such emotions, but it motivates to a "let go" attitude (no grudge).

---

46. For a detailed treatment, see Calduch-Benages, "Es mejor perdonar que guardar rencor."

47. The word ὀργή in 27:30; 28:3, 10; θυμός only in the second half (28:8, 10). See Benjamin G. Wright, "Sirach 10:1–18: Some Observations on the Work of the Translator," in *Texts and Contexts of the Book of Sirach/Texte und Kontexte des Sirachbuches*, ed. Gerhard Karner, Frank Ueberschaer, and Burkhard M. Zapff, SCS 66 (Atlanta: SBL Press, 2017), 174.

48. Werner Urbanz, *Gebet im Sirachbuch: Zur Terminologie von Klage und Lob in der griechischen Texttradition*, HBS 60 (Freiburg im Breisgau: Herder, 2009), 82–84.

This most carefully designed and theologically significant text is in fact a productive commentary on the section Lev 19:17–18, (34): as no to grudges in the Greek self-image and as a positive contribution to the image of humanity.[49] The neighbor is not only the other, but the same; the person who forgives acts, according to Sirach, as the merciful, forgiving God.

Sirach 36:8, 11

8 (B) Stir up your anger [העיר אף] and pour out your wrath [ושפוך חמה]
8 Raise up anger [ἔγειρον θυμόν], and pour out wrath [ἔκχεον ὀργήν];
11 In wrath of fire [ἐν ὀργῇ πυρός] let him who survives be consumed,
and may those who harm your people find destruction.

In the prayer for salvation (Sir 36:1–22), the different genre also reveals a different style with a strong emotional tone and powerful vocabulary.[50] The fluid metaphors used are reminiscent of the theme of the outpouring of wrath in prophecy (Isa 42:25; Jer 10:25). There is also the theme of the "enemy," which in the course of the book in Sir 50:25 finds a special conclusion.[51] In Sir 36 we have a very strong apocalyptical and eschatological emphasis, much more than in other parts of the book. May God act for his people and consequently, make himself known among the peoples (36:5, 22).

Sirach 45:18–19

18 (B) And strangers burned with anger [ויחרו] against him [[ ]]
and were envious of him in the wilderness.
The men who followed Dathan and Abiram [[ ]]
and those who gathered around Korah in their vigorous anger [בעזוז אפם].
18 Strangers conspired against him,
and they envied him in the wilderness,

---

49. Hans-Winfried Jüngling, "Der Nächste als der Andere und der Gleiche," in *Evangelium und Kultur: Begegnungen und Brüche; Festschrift für Michael Sievernich, SJ,* ed. Mariano Delgado and Hans Waldenfels, Studien zur Religions- und Kulturgeschichte 12 (Fribourg: Academic Press; Stuttgart: Kohlhammer, 2010), 237–55.

50. Maria Carmela Palmisano, *"Salvaci, Dio dell'universo!" Studio dell'eucologia di Sir 36H,1–17,* AnBib 163 (Rome: Biblical Institute Press, 2006), 206–13.

51. Marko Marttila, *Foreign Nations in the Wisdom of Ben Sira: A Jewish Sage between Opposition and Assimilation,* DCLS 13 (Berlin: de Gruyter, 2012).

the men with Dathan and Abiron
and the gathering of Kore in wrath and anger [ἐν θυμῷ καὶ ὀργῇ].
19 (B) And the LORD saw it and was provoked to wrath (ויתאנף) [[ ]]
and brought them to their end by the fury of his anger [בחרון אפו].
And he provided a sign for them [[ ]]
and he consumed them with his burning fire.
19 The Lord saw and was not well pleased,
and they were destroyed by wrath of anger [θυμῷ ὀργῆς];
he performed wonders among them,
to consume them in the fire of his flame.

The theme of anger is clearly present in the historical retrospect Hymn of
the Fathers (Sir 44–50). We find it in the context of Noah (44:17), Joshua
(46:7), Solomon (47:20), and Elijah (48:10) and in our example with Moses
and Aaron (45:18–19). The strong terminology describing the revolt of
Korah (Num 16) against Aaron (in Sirach, Moses plays no role) suggests
that the divine order in the context of the cult is a delicate matter, in the
past and also in the present.[52] Again, God reacts to human, aggressive
actions with strong emotion to restore the (just) order.

affect reveals wisdom [handwritten]   *What about Philo* [handwritten]

4. A Little Review

The strong emotional impulse of anger does not correspond to the wisdom
ideal of moderation of feelings, especially not to the ataraxia of Hellenistic popular philosophy, which is why human anger is seen negatively
throughout late wisdom.[53] The character of a person is determined by
their manner of dealing with the affect: the patient person is praised as the
true sage, while the irascible is condemned as a fool. The ideal of wisdom
lies in the balance of the affects, that is, in learning an appropriate way of
dealing with the affects. Here we find many parallels to Aristotle: the relational character of anger and the control of the affect in balance (*mesotes*).
Nonetheless, a person has to suppress their anger (cf. Seneca).

Anger and resentment are characteristic of the sinner and are contrary
to the fear of the Lord (Sir 1:21). In Old Testament-Jewish wisdom, anger
is associated with folly and godlessness. Unjust human anger is an affront
to God for Jesus Sirach, because punitive anger is reserved for God (fear of

---

52. Burkard M. Zapff, *Jesus Sirach 25–51*, NEchtB 39 (Würzburg: Echter, 2010), 332.

53. For this review, see again Frevel, "Zorn," 475; Luther, *Sprachethik*, 78; and
Gemünden, "Umgang mit Zorn," 172–86.

God). Nevertheless, there is also just anger (Sir 26:28), which is why God's wrath is fundamentally different in history and in the final judgment (Sir 5:6–8; 18:24; 36:8).

What can humans do? They can forgive (28:2). Furious wrath destroys the person, it is not right (Sir 10:18), while the fear of God averts anger (Sir 1:11–12). So we find two motives that help to handle anger: (1) one's own sinfulness, which makes a person ask for divine forgiveness and in the end makes it impossible for them to hold on to anger and resentment against one's fellow human (28:3–5) and (2) the knowledge of human transience (28:6).

The sage has learned to control his anger, leaving punitive wrath to God alone. It is not the elimination, but the control of the affect through insight and wisdom, that is at the center of the ethical instructions.

BS doesn't just repeat HB.
Focus on pedagogical
Another diff genres Israel's mercy story

"A Human Being Has Pity on His Neighbor, the Lord on Every Living Being" (Sir 18:13ab): Mercy in the Book of Ben Sira

Nuria Calduch-Benages

ZUSAMMENFASSUNG: Barmherzigkeit ist ein wichtiges Thema in der Lehre Ben Siras, und zwar sowohl im zwischenmenschlichen Bereich als auch im Zusammenhang mit Gott. Die folgende Untersuchung erhebt keinen Anspruch auf Vollständigkeit, sondern konzentriert sich auf die Barmherzigkeit als eine Eigenschaft Gottes und auf ihr Verhältnis zur Furcht des Herrn, zur Gerechtigkeit, zur Vergebung, zur Erlösung, zur menschlichen Schwachheit und zum Gebet. Ben Siras Darstellung der Barmherzigkeit Gottes ist, was ihre Form und ihren Inhalt anbetrifft, weder eine bloße Wiederholung überkommener Texte, noch ist sie einheitlich oder eintönig. Verschiedene literarische Gattungen, unterschiedliche thematische Assoziationen und unterschiedliche Zusammenhänge veranschaulichen, wie sich der Weise das barmherzige Angesicht Gottes vorstellte und wie er diese Vorstellung seinen Jüngern vermittelte.

Both in its human and divine dimensions, mercy is a major theme in Ben Sira's teaching. Our study, far from being exhaustive, intends to examine mercy as a divine attribute and in relation with the fear of the Lord, justice, forgiveness, salvation, human frailty, and prayer. After a brief *status quaestionis* and some remarks on the vocabulary, we will deal with this topic in two sections: first, we will examine human mercy and, then, focus our attention on mercy as an attribute of God. Finally, we will end with some concluding reflections.

For a Spanish version of this essay, see Nuria Calduch-Benages, "'El ser humano se compadece de su prójimo; el Señor de todo viviente' (Si 18,13ab): La misericordia en el Sirácida," *EstBib* 75 (2017): 103–25.

1. A Brief *Status Quaestionis*

God's mercy for human beings is a recurring, "almost obsessive," as Victor Morla Asensio says, subject in the book of Ben Sira.[1] It is therefore surprising that we do not yet have a complete study on it, like those published on other important topics of the book, such as the fear of God, wisdom, the law, theodicy, friendship, or women. The studies that have been published up to now—mostly articles—are limited to particular passages or very specific aspects, as we shall see below.

In my doctoral thesis, published in 1997, I focused on Sir 2:1–18, studying in detail the role of divine mercy in verses 7, 9, 11, and 18 of this passage, which culminates in the exaltation of the divine attribute par excellence.[2] The disciple who chooses to follow the Lord knows right from the outset that he can count on his infinite and unconditional mercy.

Five years later, in 2002, the volume *Ben Sira's God* was published. It gathers the lectures given at the International Ben Sira Conference held in Durham, Ushaw College in 2001.[3] Three of the articles in that book touch on our subject. The first, in the printed order, is a very brief essay by Jeremy Corley, in which the author compares the New Testament conception of God as merciful Father with the portrait of God that emerges in the book of Ben Sira.[4] Second, Pancratius C. Beentjes presents a detailed terminological study of רחם (*piel*), רחום, and רחמים, as well as of the corresponding Greek, Syriac, and Latin terms, in order to illustrate the methodological problem that the scholar faces when dealing with an incomplete Hebrew text and its different versions.[5] Finally, Maurice Gilbert concentrates on the analysis of a long section of the book, Sir 15:11–18:14, the only passage that deals explicitly with God, sin, and mercy. He proposes to describe

---

1. Víctor Morla Asensio, *Eclesiástico: Texto y Comentario*, Mensaje del Antiguo Testamento 20 (Estella: Verbo Divino, 1992), 34; Morla Asensio, *Libros sapienciales y otros escritos*, IEB 5 (Estella: Verbo Divino, 1994), 234. Unless otherwise noted, all translations, ancient and modern, are by the author.

2. Nuria Calduch-Benages, *En el crisol de la prueba. Estudio exegético de Sir 2,18*, ABE 32 (Estella: Verbo Divino, 1997).

3. Renate Egger-Wenzel, ed., *Ben Sira's God: Proceedings of the International Ben Sira Conference Durham, Ushaw College 2001*, BZAW 321 (Berlin: de Gruyter, 2002).

4. Jeremy Corley, "God as Merciful Father in Ben Sira and the New Testament," in Egger-Wenzel, *Ben Sira's God*, 33–38.

5. Pancratius C. Beentjes, "God's Mercy: 'Racham' (pi.), 'Rachum', and 'Rachamim' in the Book of Ben Sira," in Egger-Wenzel, *Ben Sira's God*, 101–17.

step-by-step the argumentative process used by the sage, who begins by exonerating God from all responsibility for the sin of humans. Human beings are free and responsible for their actions. Not one action goes unnoticed by the Lord, who repays them all, whether good or bad, with justice. The Lord is a righteous God who does not leave the sinner unpunished. That is why Ben Sira invites others to conversion and sings a hymn to the merciful God, in which his greatness contrasts with human frailty: the greater is human frailty, the greater is God's mercy.[6]

In 2006, Johannes Marböck published a short article on Sir 17:30–18:14, the hymn that concludes the section we have just discussed, Sir 15:11–18:14.[7] The author's main objective is theological: he wants to illustrate the close tie between God's mercy and people's conversion. To do this, he first deals with conversion and the return to God and then with divine mercy as an opportunity and objective of conversion. Two years later, in 2008, Otto Kaiser briefly dealt with the aforementioned hymn (according to him, Sir 18:1–14) in an article intended to elucidate some anthropological aspects of Sir 16:24–18:14.[8] That same year, Markus Witte published a study—the most complete to date—on God's mercy and wrath in the Old Testament, taking as an example the book of Ben Sira, which he considers a "compendium of biblical theology."[9] Witte analyzes the most significant texts (Sir 2:11; 5:6; 16:11; 18:11; 36:7; 50:19), focusing his attention on several formal aspects, facets of the content, and pragmatic features.

---

6. Maurice Gilbert, "God, Sin and Mercy: Sirach 15:11–18:14," in Egger-Wenzel, *Ben Sira's God*, 118–35.

7. Johannes Marböck, "Einladung ins Erbarmen Gottes: Sir 17,30–18,14 als ein Beitrag zur Rede von Gott im Sirachbuch," in *"Gott bin ich, kein Mann": Beiträge zur Hermeneutik der biblischen Gottesrede; Festschrift für Helen Schüngel-Straumann zum 65. Geburtstag*, ed. Ilona Riedel-Spangenberger and Erich Zenger (Paderborn: Schöningh, 2006), 196–205.

8. Otto Kaiser, "'Was ist der Mensch und was ist sein Wert?' Beobachtungen zur Anthropologie des Jesus Sirach nach Jesus Sirach 16,24–18,14," in *Was ist der Mensch, dass du seiner gedenkst? (Psalm 8,5): Aspekte einer theologischen Anthropologie; Festschrift für Bernd Janowski zum 65. Geburtstag*, ed. Michaela Bauks, Kathrin Liess, and Peter Riede (Neukirchen-Vluyn: Neukirchener Verlag, 2008), 215–25.

9. "Kompendium biblischer Theologie"; Markus Witte, "'Barmherzigkeit und Zorn Gottes' im Alten Testament am Beispiel des Buchs Sirach," in *Divine Wrath and Divine Mercy in the World of Antiquity*, ed. Reinhard G. Kratz and Hermann Spieckermann, WUNT 2/33 (Tübingen: Mohr Siebeck, 2008), 177.

2. Some Remarks on the Terminology

In the book of Ben Sira, the following terms express the concept of mercy, compassion, or pity: in Greek ἔλεος ("mercy"), ἐλεέω ("to show mercy"), ἐλεήμων ("merciful"), οἰκτείρω ("to feel compassion, pity"), οἰκτιρμός ("compassion, mercy, pity"), and οἰκτίρμων ("merciful"). The main Hebrew equivalents are: רחום ("compassionate"), רחמים (lit., "entrails"; fig., "compassion, pity, commiseration"), רחם ("to love, to pity, to feel compassion"), and חסד ("compassion, kindness, piety, loyalty, fidelity"). It is noteworthy that, in the LXX, ἔλεος most often translates the noun חסד (172x) and only rarely רחמים (6x). This, however, is not the case in Ben Sira, where, given the fragmentary state of the Hebrew text and leaving aside the litany after 51:12, the ratio is more even: ἔλεος translates חסד (13x) and רחמים (8x).

The use of חסד is concentrated, apart from 7:33, in the second part of the book (Sir 24–51), while רחמים appears, except for 51:8a, only in the first (Sir 1–23). As for the use of the above-mentioned terms, there are examples of fluctuation between חסד and רחמים (cf. 51:3, 8), as well as between ἔλεος and οἰκτιρμός, which translate them without distinction (cf. 5:6a, c). The same occurs with the verbs ἐλεέω and οἰκτείρω (cf. 33[36]:17, 18).[10]

The situation is even more complicated if one takes into account the Syriac version, where the root רחם and its derivatives translate a variety of Hebrew verbs and nouns.[11]

3. The Human Being's Mercy

In the book of Ben Sira, mercy as a religious human virtue is attested in several texts and in various contexts. For example, in Sir 18:13ab and 28:4 human mercy appears in relation to divine mercy.

In 18:13ab (which we have quoted in the title of this paper), the relation is explicit; it is formulated by means of an antithetical parallelism that emphasizes the universal dimension of divine mercy in contrast to the much limited human dimension: "The mercy [ἔλεος] of the human being reaches his neighbor; the Lord's is upon all living [ἐπὶ πᾶσαν σάρκα]" (Sir 18:13ab).

---

10. Calduch-Benages, *En el crisol*, 107–9, 283–84 (appendix 2).
11. Beentjes, "God's Mercy," 102.

Conversely, in 28:4 the relationship is implicit and expressed by a rhetorical question: "If a person does have no mercy [οὐκ ἔχει ἔλεος] on another, how dare he implore [God is inferred] for his own sins?" (Sir 28:4).[12] This question reveals the lack of inner coherence of the person who asks God to do for them what they have not done for their neighbor: they want God to grant them forgiveness while they do not forgive their brother. Demanding salvation, mercy, and forgiveness from God while denying all these things to one's neighbor denotes not only incoherence (i.e., lack of judgment, of wisdom) but also a lack of any religious sense. Even worse, these demands, devoid of all human and religious logic, really challenge the Lord. These ideas are echoed in rabbinic thought. We find a good example in the Talmud: "He who is merciful to others, mercy is shown to him by Heaven, while he who is not merciful to others, mercy is not shown to him by Heaven" (b. Shabb. 151b).

Chapter 29 is an instruction on matters relating to money (loans, bonds, economic autonomy).[13] It begins with a verse in which mercy, charity, and the observance of the law go hand in hand: "The one who practices mercy [ὁ ποιῶν ἔλεος] lends to his neighbor, and the one who comes to his aid keeps the commandments" (Sir 29:1). The parallelism is perfectly synonymous: practicing mercy corresponds to helping one's neighbor and making a loan (i.e., to the needy) to accomplishing the law. It is clear, then, that for Ben Sira lending to one's neighbor when they are in need is an act of piety and obedience to the precepts of the law. That is how the righteous person behaves, and the Lord will reward them for it (Pss 37:26; 112:5; Prov 19:17).

In Israel's history there are many examples of famous people renowned for their compassion or piety. They are known as the "men of piety" (אנשי חסד, Sir 44:1) who, having received goodness or mercy from God, exercise them toward others.[14] Among them are three memorable figures:

---

12. See also Nuria Calduch-Benages, "Es mejor perdonar que guardar rencor: Estudio de Sir 27,30–28,7," *Greg* 81 (2000): 432–33.

13. Maurice Gilbert, "Prêt, aumône et caution," in *Der Einzelne und seine Gemeinschaft bei Ben Sira*, ed. Renate Egger-Wenzel and Ingrid Krammer, BZAW 270 (Berlin: de Gruyter, 1998), 179–89; Bradley C. Gregory, *Like an Everlasting Signet Ring: Generosity in the Book of Sirach*, DCLS 2 (Berlin: de Gruyter, 2010), 133–63.

14. The Greek version translates "illustrious men" (ἄνδρας ἐνδόξους). According to Alonso Schökel that indicates "a choice in the mind of the author: benefactors." (Luis Alonso Schökel, *Proverbios y Eclesiástico*, Los Libros Sagrados 8.1 [Madrid: Cristiandad, 1968], 305–6).

Moses, "a merciful man" (ἄνδρα ἐλέους), who gained the favor of all (Sir 44:23–45:5; cf. Exod 2:5–10; 16–22; 11:3);[15] Joshua, who in Moses's time "accomplished an act of piety/showed faithfulness" (עשה חסד/ἐποίησεν ἔλεος) (Sir 46:7; cf. Num 14:6–10); and Josiah, who in violent times "did good/was compassionate" (עשה חסד) (Sir 49:3; cf. 2 Kings 22:17).[16]

Also worthy of consideration is Sir 12:13–14, a peculiar text containing a negative view of human mercy: "Who feels pity [יוחן/ἐλεήσει] for the snake charmer who has been bitten or for someone who approaches ferocious beasts?" (v. 13). This rhetorical question serves to illustrate the following statement: "Likewise, no one commiserates with someone who associates himself with an arrogant person and defiles himself with their crimes" (v. 14).[17] In other words, the person who goes along with the arrogant deserves no more pity than a snake charmer who has been bitten or someone who does not keep away from wild beasts. Here, Ben Sira is perfectly in line with the classical conception of mercy found in Aristotle ("Pity is aroused by a person's unmerited misfortune," Poet. 12.1453a4) or in Andronicus ("Pity is distress for the wicked, for the undeserved suffering of others," Pass. 2 [SVF 3.414]).[18]

4. Mercy as a Divine Attribute

The texts on mercy as a divine attribute—certainly one of Ben Sira's favorite subjects—are much more numerous in comparison with those mentioned in the previous section. This emphasis on divine mercy is closely related to Israel's election, an issue that Greg S. Goering dealt with in his doctoral dissertation.[19] The awareness of being the chosen people and the Lord's unlimited mercy are not literary inventions or illusions of the author but true faith experiences, rooted in an event that is emblematic for Israel: the

---

15. The Hebrew manuscript (MS B) presents a text with lacuna.

16. The Greek version translates "in a time of impious men he restored piety [κατίσχυσεν τὴν εὐσέβειαν]."

17. With Patrick W. Skehan and Alexander A. Di Lella, The Wisdom of Ben Sira: A New Translation with Notes, Introduction, and Commentary, AB 39 (New York: Doubleday, 1987), 244; and Víctor Morla Asensio, Los manuscritos hebreos de Ben Sira: Traducción y notas, ABE 59 (Estella: Verbo Divino, 2012), 115, we correct MS A (the arrogant woman). The Greek version translates "the sinful man."

18. Quoted in Calduch-Benages, En el crisol, 109 n. 39.

19. Greg S. Goering, Wisdom's Root Revealed: Ben Sira and the Election of Israel, JSJSup 139 (Leiden: Brill, 2009).

liberation from slavery in Egypt (Exod 14). This divine initiative indelibly marked the relationship between the Lord and his people. From that moment on, mercy becomes the most outstanding divine attribute. Let us now see how Ben Sira presents it.

4.1. Mercy and Fear of the Lord

In the book of Ben Sira, ἔλεος appears for the first time in relation with the fear of the Lord, that is, the inner disposition of the pious Israelite that consists, according to Louis Derousseaux, in "faithfully adhering to Yahweh as the God of the covenant."[20] The text in question is Sir 2:7–9. It is delimited by the inclusion found in 7a (τὸ ἔλεος αὐτοῦ) and 9b (ἔλεος), and the initial triple anaphora (οἱ φοβούμενοι κύριον) in 7a, 8a, and 9a.[21] Since we do not have the Hebrew text, we offer a translation of the Greek version in Joseph Ziegler's edition.[22]

> 7a You who fear the Lord, wait for his mercy,
> 7b and do not deviate, in order to avoid falling.
> 8a You who fear the Lord, trust in Him;
> 8b you will not be deprived of your salary.
> 9a You who fear the Lord, hope for good things,
> 9b everlasting joy and mercy.

The earnestness and urgency of this exhortation suggest interpreting divine mercy as a beneficent action, that is, concrete and effective help from the Lord for his fidelity in times of tribulation.[23] The teacher's resolute tone does away with any possible doubt about divine intervention. Indeed, the strength of this teaching lies in the deep conviction of the one

---

20. Louis Derousseaux, *La crainte de Dieu dans l'Ancient Testament: Royauté, Alliance, Sagesse dans les royaumes d'Israël et de Juda*, LD 63 (Paris: Cerf, 1970), 221.

21. In this context, Alonso Schökel remarks, the verb "fear" indicates "the general attitude of devotion and fidelity to God" (*Proverbios y Eclesiástico*, 150).

22. Joseph Ziegler, ed., *Sapientia Iesu Filii Sirach*, 2nd ed., SVTG 12.2 (Göttingen: Vandenhoeck & Ruprecht, 1980). See also Alfred Rahlfs, ed., *Septuaginta: Id est Vetus Testamentum graece iuxta LXX interpretes*, 9th ed. (Stuttgart: Deutsche Bibelgesellschaft, 1982).

23. Note the allusions to an incipient conflict in the rest of the chapter (vv. 1, 2, 4, 5, 11, 12–14, 18). See Nuria Calduch-Benages, *Un gioiello di sapienza: Leggendo Siracide 2*, Cammini nello Spirito 45 (Milan: Paoline, 2001), 159–60.

who proclaims it and in its historical foundation, which is mentioned in the subsequent verses (Sir 2:10–11). Hence, the Lord's help is not a fallacy but a reality proven by Israel's history and witnessed to by its representatives, including Ben Sira himself (cf. Sir 51:1–12).

Those who fear the Lord are called to put their trust in him and to hope in his mercy. At first glance, this invitation seems to be out of place, because the vocative "you who fear the Lord" supposes that these disciples have already reached a certain degree of spiritual perfection; that is, they have put their trust in the Lord. That impression, however, is inaccurate. The sage's exhortation reveals the gradualness of divine instruction, which requires the disciple's constant collaboration. Without his continuous effort, the goal cannot be reached. Thus, "those who fear the Lord" are still on the way. Yet, despite the difficulties, they can truly hope to receive "good things, everlasting joy and mercy" since—according to the vision of the sage—the reward for their fidelity is given to them in this life. It is noteworthy that the Syriac version translates "salvation" (ܦܘܪܩܢܐ/purqana') instead of mercy, and the long version of the Greek text (GII) adds: "for his reward is an eternal gift, together with joy" (Sir 2:9c), an explanatory gloss that emphasizes the eschatological character of the divine reward.[24]

4.2. Mercy, Forgiveness, and Salvation

We continue with chapter 2, specifically verses 10–11. Here Ben Sira appeals to the authority of the past generations to reinforce his argument. His reference to tradition begins with an invitation (10a), continues with a series of rhetorical questions (10bcd), and ends with a conclusive sentence (11ab) that serves to justify the preceding questions. Let us begin by reading the text:

10a Consider the past generations and see:
10b Who trusted the Lord and was disappointed?

---

24. Calduch-Benages, *En el crisol*, 104. Di Lella considers Sir 2:9c a Christian addition, see Alexander A. Di Lella, "Fear of the Lord and Belief and Hope in the Lord amid Trials: Sirach 2,1–18," in *Wisdom, You Are My Sister: Studies in Honor of Roland E. Murphy, O. Carm., on the Occasion of His Eightieth Birthday*, ed. Michael L. Barré, CBQMS 29 (Washington DC: Catholic University of America Press, 1997), 191. For a detailed study of the addition, see Severino Bussino, *The Greek Additions in the Book of Ben Sira*, AnBib 203 (Rome: Gregorian & Biblical Press, 2013), 72–76.

10c Who persevered in fear of him and was forsaken?
10d Who called upon him and was disregarded?
11a For the Lord is compassionate and merciful;[25]
11b he forgives sins and saves in time of tribulation.

We are especially interested in the last verse, that is, the conclusion of the passage. Introduced by the causal conjunction ὅτι ("because") verse 11 consists of two clauses: a statement about the Lord (he is compassionate and merciful) and an explanation of his behavior (he forgives sins and saves in time of tribulation). We will look at them separately.

The two attributes of the Lord (οἰκτίρμων καὶ ἐλεήμων) correspond in the Hebrew to רחום וחנון, a combination frequently found in the Hebrew Bible. Undoubtedly the most remarkable of its eleven occurrences is found in Exod 34:6. There, these two adjectives are part of the so-called *Gnadenformel* or formula of mercy:[26] "The Lord is compassionate and merciful, slow to anger and rich in grace and truth." The biblical authors quote this self-revelation of the Lord in many different ways: with slight variations (Joel 2:13; Jon 4:2; Pss 86:15; 103:8; 145:8; Neh 9:17); partially and with free adaptations (e.g., Exod 20:5, 22, 26; Deut 4:31; Isa 48:9; Pss 78:38; 111:4; Neh 9:31; 2 Chr 30:9), or even summarized to the maximum in the expression "rich in mercy" (Eph 2:4).[27]

Ben Sira 2:11 belongs to the second category of texts. Ben Sira omits "slow to anger and rich in grace and truth" in order to give greater emphasis to "compassionate and merciful," two adjectives that belong to the sphere of love. In this way, mercy, or loving compassion, becomes the most important aspect of the Lord's self-presentation. His mercy then reappears in 2:18, the concluding verse of the passage: "Let us fall into the hands of the Lord and not into hands of humans, for his mercy equals his greatness." Taking his inspiration from 2 Sam 24:14, here the sage Ben Sira combines two essential elements of his instruction: the disciple's trust and the Lord's mercy. Both synthesize, in an endearing way, the relationship between the

---

25. Some Greek manuscripts add: μακροθυμος και πολυελεος (see Ziegler's edition).

26. This term was coined by Hermann Spieckermann in his study "Barmherzig ist der Herr...," *ZAW* 102 (1990), 1–18.

27. According to the rabbinic interpretation, Exod 34:6–7 contains "the three attributes of divine mercy" that were revealed to Moses when he asked God to forgive the people of Israel after the episode of the golden calf, see b. Rosh Hash. 17b.

Lord and the human being. The latter abandons himself into the hands of the Lord, and the Lord shows him his infinite mercy. Not without reason, Norbert Peters describes Sir 2:18 as "a highpoint of individual piety in the Old Testament."[28]

Let us now consider the second part of verse 11. In the second colon, divine mercy is expressed by forgiveness and salvation: the Lord "pardons sins [ἀφίεσιν ἁμαρτίας] and saves in time of affliction [σῴζει ἐν καιρῷ θλίψεως]." According to one possible, although hypothetical, reconstruction of the Hebrew text, the first clause consists of two key terms in Old Testament theology: the verb סלח ("to forgive, remit, excuse") and the noun עון ("iniquity, offense, fault"). These words often appear together in petitions addressed to the Lord by those praying for forgiveness (Exod 4:9; Num 14:19; Ps 25:11) and in promises of forgiveness made by the Lord to his people (Jer 31:34; 33:8; 36:3). Psalm 103 deserves special mention because of the parallelism established in verse 3a between the Lord's forgiveness and his healing power: "He is the one who forgives all your offenses, who heals all your diseases."

The Lord who forgives sins also saves in times of affliction or tribulation. In the Old Testament the concept of salvation is expressed predominantly by the verb ישע, which the LXX renders, in most cases (including Sir 2:11b), with σῴζω and its derivatives. Now, let us ask ourselves: What exactly is salvation? What does it mean to be saved? Our text does not answer these questions. In our view, there are two concurrent reasons for this: a theological one and a didactic one. According to Ben Sira, the disciple's aim is not to discover what salvation is but to be able to recognize its divine origin. The sage's message is clear and unambiguous, and there can be no confusion about it: salvation comes from the Lord. By way of conclusion, we could say that the Lord's forgiveness and salvation are fruits of his infinite mercy.[29]

4.3. Mercy and Justice

As we have just seen, the description of the Lord offered in Sir 2:11 highlights his mercy and its fruits. Yet, it clearly leaves aside another important

---

28. "Ein(en) Höhepunkt individueller Frömmigkeit im A.T."; Norbert Peters, *Das Buch Jesus Sirach oder Ecclesiasticus*, EHAT 25 (Münster in Westf.: Aschendorff, 1913), 27, quoted in Witte, "Barmherzigkeit und Zorn Gottes," 183 n. 23.

29. For this entire section, cf. Calduch-Benages, *En el crisol*, 142–47.

quality of his being—his anger (Exod 24:7). Although at first glance, mercy and anger seem incompatible, they are in fact closely related. The relationship between the two, as José Luis Barriocanal Gómez rightly points out, is asymmetrical: "While Yahweh's wrath is a passing state or quality, his merciful love is everlasting."[30]

There are two texts in the book of Ben Sira that complete the description given in Sir 2:11, namely, Sir 5:6 and 16:11–14. There, the Lord manifests himself in a persistent polarity. If, in 2:11, we have contemplated the Lord lavishing his mercy on those who fear him, in 5:6 and 16:11–14 we will see him compassionate and merciful, irritated and angry, forgiving and discharging his wrath on the wicked.

Let us begin with the first passage. Sirach 5:6 is part of an instruction dedicated to preventing the negative consequences that come from excessive self-confidence (Sir 5:1–8).[31] According to Witte, it is "a small theodicy," in which the human being's sin, the Lord's forgiveness and his relentless anger come into play.[32]

In this case, we have a Hebrew text in MSS A (complete text) and C (fragmentary text), which almost entirely coincides with the Greek version. The most striking difference is that the Hebrew text uses two distinct roots to refer to sin (חטה, v. 4a and עון, vv. 4d, 5b, 6b), whereas the Greek version always uses the same root (ἁμαρτάνω, v. 4a; ἁμαρτία, 5b, 6b; ἁμαρτωλός, 6d). To make it easier to understand Sir 5:6, we are going to read it in its immediate context.

1a Do not trust your wealth,
1b or say: "The power is in my hand."
1c Do not trust your strength
1d to go after what you want.
2a Do not let yourself be carried away [lit., do not go after] by your heart and your eyes

---

30. José Luis Barriocanal Gómez, *La imagen de un Dios violento*, Espíritu-Norte (Burgos: Monte Carmelo, 2010), 163.

31. On the Hebrew text of this passage, see Pancratius C. Beentjes, "Ben Sira 5,1–8: A Literary and Rhetorical Analysis," in *The Literary Analysis of Hebrew Texts: Papers Read at a Symposium Held at the Juda Palache Institute, University of Amsterdam (5 February 1990)*, ed. Emile G. L. Schrijver, Niek A. van Uchelen, and Irene E. Zwiep, Publications of the Juda Palache Institute 7 (Amsterdam: Juda Palache Institute, 1992), 45–59.

32. "Eine kleine Theodizee"; Witte, "Barmherzigkeit und Zorn Gottes," 186.

²ᵇ to follow your bad desires.³³

³ᵃ Do not say: "Who can have power over me?"

³ᵇ because the Lord will hold you accountable [lit., catches up with what is fleeing].

⁴ᵃ Do not say, "I have sinned, and what has happened to me?³⁴ Nothing!"³⁵

⁴ᵇ because God is slow to anger.

⁴ᶜ Do not say, "The Lord is merciful

⁴ᵈ and erases all my faults."³⁶

⁵ᵃ Do not trust in forgiveness,

⁵ᵇ and go on heaping up fault upon fault,

⁶ᵃ saying: "His mercy is great;

⁶ᵇ he will forgive my many sins."

⁶ᶜ For, mercy and wrath are with him,

⁶ and his wrath is upon the wicked.

⁷ᵃ Do not postpone turning to him,

⁷ᵇ nor delay from one day to the next,

⁷ᶜ because his anger explodes suddenly,

⁷ᵈ and on the day of vengeance you shall perish.

⁸ᵃ Do not put your trust in deceitful riches,

⁸ᵇ for on the day of wrath they will be of no use.³⁷

By using the literary form "do not say (saying)" (vv. 1b, 3a, 4a, 4c, 6a), Ben Sira denounces self-sufficiency, arrogance, the defiant attitude, and bold presumption that take for granted that the Lord will forgive all one's sins. The insolent words of the hypothetical sinner are opposed to the motivations advanced by the sage with the aim of defending, at all costs, God's justice (theodicy). In his discourse, the sage presents a God torn between mercy and anger (רחמים ואף/ἔλεος γὰρ καὶ ὀργή, 6c). Thus, the patient and merciful God who forgives sins is at the same time the God who directs his anger upon sinners. Luis Alonso Schökel comments: "His personal reaction to sin is both compassion and anger. If compassion seems always to persevere, anger can suddenly explode: it is justified but unforeseeable for the human being."³⁸ The fact that Ben Sira spared no effort in describing

---

33. Verse 2 seems to be a duplicate of 1cd. Cf. Skehan and Di Lella, *Wisdom of Ben Sira*, 180.

34. MS C mistakenly reads ומה יהיה לו ("and what was this for him?").

35. Only in MS A (מאומה).

36. Sir 5:4cd is only found in MS A.

37. Sir 5:8 is missing in MS C.

38. Alonso Schökel, *Proverbios y Eclesiástico*, 169.

divine wrath is demonstrated by the use of five different terms—some of which are synonyms—in this single passage: אף ("wrath, anger, irritation," 4b, 6d), רגז ("fury, tremor," 6d), זעם ("anger, indignation," 7c), נקם ("vengeance, retaliation, revenge," 7d), and עברה ("anger, wrath, fury," 8b). This word range evokes the image of God as a stern judge who, when the time of judgment comes, does not leave the sinner unpunished. For Witte, "the reference to God's wrath functions as a counterpart that is necessary from a theological viewpoint to confess his mercy."[39]

The sage condemns not only the form of presumption related to material goods, as one might think when looking only at the beginning (v. 1) and the end (v. 8) of the passage. There are also those who boast of their own strength, abilities, resources, and power. These, along with wealth, are the false assurances that deceive a person, nourish their self-esteem, and make them feel excessively satisfied with themselves, to the point of daring to defy God and presuming of his infinite compassion.[40]

From all this emerges the urgency of conversion (v. 7), for the day of wrath (יום עברה), the day of vengeance (יום נקם), will come unexpectedly, and its outcome will be devastating. In light of the prophetic tradition, we interpret this day as the day of divine judgment, the day when the apparent security of human beings will vanish in the presence of the Lord. In the concluding verse, we seem to hear the voice of the author of the book of Proverbs: "On the day of wrath, riches are of no use, but righteousness saves from death" (Prov 11:4; cf. 10:2).

Let us conclude this section with Sir 16:11–14, a text that is part of a theological reflection on Israel's history (Sir 16:1–16) that includes the topic of divine retribution. God appears, giving the good and the bad their due reward. We will follow the text of MS A:

11a[41] And even if one had only been stiff-necked,
11b it would have been a miracle for him to go unpunished,
11c for mercy and wrath are with him:

---

39. "Der Verweis auf Gottes Zorn (Sir 5,4.6) dient als theologisch notwendiges Gegenüber zum Bekenntnis zu Gottes Barmherzigkeit" (Witte, "Barmherzigkeit und Zorn Gottes," 184).

40. According to Alonso Schökel, this form of presumption is "more refined and dangerous" than the preceding ones (*Proverbios y Eclesiástico*, 160).

41. Before v. 11, GII introduces this addition: "punishing, showing pity [ἐλεῶν], striking, healing, the Lord persevered in mercy [ἐν οἰκτιρμῷ] and correction" (v. 10cd). See Bussino, *Greek Additions*, 169–76.

11d he absolves and forgives,
11e but he also wreaks his wrath (upon the wicked).
12a As great as his mercy is his punishment,
12b and he judges each person according to his works.
13a He does not let the wicked man escape with his prey/loot,
13b nor does he fail to fulfill the desires of the righteous.
14a He who accomplishes good [lit., righteousness] will have his reward,
14b and each person will receive according to his works.[42]

The expression "stiff-necked" (מקשה ערף/σκληροτράχηλος/cervicatus) sends us back to Exod 32:9; 33:3, 5; 34:9, where it is used in reference to the people of Israel. Using the same expression as in Sir 5:6c ("for mercy and wrath are with him"), this time in a much more extended sense, the sage presents us with a God who is very merciful and, at the same time, very severe, giving to each person what they deserve. The last two verses explain in what God's impartial judgment consists: punishment for the sinner and recompense for the righteous/charitable person.

4.4. Mercy and Human Frailty

Another important aspect of divine mercy is its relation with the creation of the human being. The text that best illustrates this subject is Sir 18:8–14. The passage is part of a hymn to the compassionate God (Sir 18:1–14), which in turn functions as the conclusion of a long section about creation and divine providence (Sir 16:24–18:14).[43] Since we do not have the Hebrew text, we will follow the Greek version:

8a What is the human being? Of what use is he?
8b What is his good and what is his evil?
9a The days of the human being are numbered, a hundred years is a lot;
9b and the most unpredictable (day) of all is that of death.[44]

---

42. Verses 15–16, also in GII and Syr, are a later expansion of the text. See Alonso Schökel, *Proverbios y Eclesiástico*, 198; Skehan and Di Lella, *Wisdom of Ben Sira*, 270; Beentjes, "God's Mercy," 110.

43. On this, see Gian Luigi Prato, *Il problema della teodicea in Ben Sira: Composizione dei contrari e richiamo alle origini*, AnBib 65 (Rome: Pontifical Biblical Institute, 1975), 262–99; Ursel Wicke-Reuter, *Göttliche Providenz und menschliche Verantwortung bei Ben Sira und in der Frühen Stoa*, BZAW 298 (Berlin: de Gruyter, 2000), 143–87.

44. An addition of GII that is missing in Syr and La.

10a Like a drop of seawater and a grain of sand
10b are those few years[45] compared to a day of eternity.
11a Therefore, the Lord is patient with them [i.e., the human beings],
11b and pours his mercy out over them.
12a He sees and knows that their end is miserable,
12b hence he multiplies his forgiveness.
13a A human being's compassion (reaches) their neighbor,
13b that of the Lord, every living being.
13c He rebukes, corrects, teaches,
13d and leads his flock like a shepherd.
14a He has pity on those who accept instruction,
14b and on those who eagerly seek his decrees.

Echoing Ps 8:5 (cf. Job 17:7; Ps 144:3), Ben Sira asks about the essence, utility, and nature of human beings, not to demonstrate their superiority over creation as the psalmist did but to emphasize once again how frail and fleeting they are (cf. Sir 17:1). The sage insists on the fragile and transitory character of human nature to justify the need for divine mercy (ἔλεος, 11b, 13a, b; ἐλεάω, 14a). In fact, verse 11 begins with διὰ τοῦτο ("for that"), which links it to the previous verses. Knowing the human beings' miserable destiny, God generously offers them patience (μακροθυμέω), mercy (ἔλεος), and forgiveness (ἐξιλασμόν). Thus, human weakness, in fact, increases divine mercy, which, unlike that of the human being, is universal and unlimited. This sublime idea is taken up by the author of the book of Wisdom in his digression on God's moderation: "You have pity on all, for you can do all things; you close your eyes to the sins of human beings so that they may repent. You love all beings and you do not hate anything that you have created; if you had hated anything, you would not have made it" (Wis 11:23–24).

Nevertheless, God's mercy is not blind mercy that ignores human responsibility. Rather, it has a pedagogical aim. God uses it to educate human beings in the pursuit of wisdom (ἐλέγχω, παιδεύω, διδάσκω). Education and correction, patience and mercy go hand in hand (cf. Sir 16:10cGII; Wis 12:19–22). As Alonso Schökel puts it: "God's compassion is not good-natured indifference that lets everything pass, but it has the personal character of one who seeks to correct and redirect the one whom he

45. The Lucianic recension and MS 743 read "a thousand years" (cf. Ps 90:4) and MS 795 "one hundred," whereas Syr offers an eschatological interpretation of the text: "A thousand years of this world are not like a day in the world of the righteous."

forgives; and that is why he demands human collaboration, the acceptance of correction, and the effort to obey the law."[46]

4.5. Mercy and Prayer

Ben Sira is particularly interested in prayer. In fact, prayer is a part of his daily life (Sir 39:5–6). In his book, he speaks about prayer more than twenty times, much more often than his predecessors and the author of the book of Wisdom. In addition to a great deal of practical advice on prayer, the sage offers concrete examples of prayers, both individual (Sir 22:27–23:6; 51:1–12) and collective (Sir 36:1–17). In other words, Ben Sira combines speaking about God with speaking to God. It should be noted that mercy also appears in the prayers, and most remarkably in relation with what could be called the "national spirit," that is, the consciousness of being the chosen people and, hence, worthy of being treated by God differently than others.

Ben Sira 35:14–26 is a beautiful text about the mercy of God for society's most vulnerable: the poor and the oppressed, orphans and widows. Curiously, in the last few verses, Ben Sira casually passes from the individual level to the collective one, until an unexpected change takes place in his discourse. Giving free rein to his patriotism, he implores God to exterminate the nations and do justice to his people and comfort them with salvation (MS B)/with his mercy (G) (Sir 35:25). "This 'descent into the political arena,'" comments Morla Asensio, "serves as a preparation to Ben Sira's prayer for the liberation of Israel that comes next."[47] Literally speaking, the mention of mercy in 35:25–26 functions as a link to the cry in 36:1 "Save us (H)/Have mercy on us, Lord (G), God of the universe" with which he begins prayer for his people (Sir 36H:1–17).[48] The bold and passionate tone, as well as the tension perceived in the text, suggests situating this prayer at the time of the Seleucid government in Palestine. Maria Carmela Palmisano, who studied this prayer in depth in her doctoral thesis, dares to be even more precise. In her opinion, the historical background reflected in the eucology is the failed attempt of Heliodorus (an officer of

---

46. Alonso Schökel, *Proverbios y Eclesiástico*, 206.

47. Morla Asensio, *Eclesiástico*, 175.

48. Sir 31G:1–22 according to Ziegler's numbering. The phrase, situated within the great transposition of Sir 33:16–36:13a after 30:24–25, figures in all the Greek manuscripts.

Seleucus IV) to loot the treasure of the temple of Jerusalem shortly before
175 BCE (cf. 2 Macc 3:1–40; Dan 11:20).[49]

Because of our subject, we are especially interested in the third stanza
of this prayer (Sir 36H:11–14). Here is the translation of the Hebrew text
of MS B:

11a Gather all the tribes of Jacob
11b and let them inherit as in the days of old.
12a Have compassion[50] on the people called by your name,
12b of Israel, whom you named firstborn.
13a Have pity[51] on your holy city,
13b on Jerusalem, the place of your dwelling.
14a Fill Zion with your majesty,
14b and your temple with your glory.

The national consciousness that we mentioned above emerges here with all
its force. It is highlighted by the concentration of several proper names (one
per verse), all of which are emblematic for an Israelite. Its arrangement in
the stanza follows a centripetal movement, that is, starting from the periph-
ery it moves toward the center (Jacob, Israel, Jerusalem, Zion, the temple).
This is diametrically opposed to what happens in Sir 24:10–12, where we
contemplate Wisdom establishing herself first in the holy tent, then in Zion,
in Jerusalem and, finally, in the people (centrifugal movement).

If, in the second stanza (Sir 36:6–10), Ben Sira vehemently asks the
Lord to release his wrath against the foreign nations, here he invokes
divine mercy on his people and on Jerusalem. For this, he uses the *piel*
imperative of the root רחם ("to have compassion"), a verbal form that is
not attested in the Hebrew Bible. It is surprising that the sage uses it to
address God directly, since this use of רחם is not found elsewhere in the
book. As Beentjes has observed, the almost immediate repetition (vv. 12a,
13a) of the imperative and the abundant use of the possessive (by means of

---

49. Maria Carmela Palmisano, 'Salvaci, Dio dell'universo': Studio dell'eucologia di
Sir 36H,1–17, AnBib 163 (Rome: Biblical Institute Press, 2006), 305–14.

50. In G: ἐλέησον, the same verbal form as in v. 1. H does not have this correspondence.

51. While H repeats the same verb from v. 12 (רחם, *piel* impv.), G replaces ἐλέησον
with οἰκτίρησον.

the suffix of second person singular -kā) are rhetorical means that the sage uses to rouse the Lord's mercy.[52]

To support his plea, Ben Sira refers, on the one hand, to the people's origins, which go back to the exodus out of Egypt, and, on the other hand, to God's divine fatherhood. The image of the "firstborn" (בכור) echoes the text of Exod 4:22 ("And you shall say to Pharaoh, thus says the Lord: 'Israel is my son, my firstborn'") and some prophetic oracles such as Hos 11:1 ("When Israel was a child, I loved him; from Egypt I called my son") and Jer 31:9 ("All will come crying, and I will guide them among consolations; I will lead them to torrents of water, on a flat road without stumbling blocks. I will be a father for Israel, Ephraim will be my firstborn").

From the time of its birth and throughout its history, especially during exile, Israel has enjoyed the unconditional love of the Lord who, despite unceasing betrayals and reparations, has never abandoned it. The arguments of the sage are certainly convincing, indeed to such an extent that God will see himself obliged to intervene. At least that is what the sage hopes. How could he stop doing so? If God does not come to help his people (his son) who are suffering injustice, he would be behaving like a bad father and would be dishonoring his fidelity and holiness. Ben Sira is confident that his plea will be heard. Therefore, drawing on the experience of the past, he implores the Lord's merciful love, so that his people, stifled by foreign oppression, can be reborn and reestablish the covenant relationship with its God.

We conclude with two other texts of prayer in which the faithful appeal for divine mercy. The first text is Sir 50:24, the last verse of an invitation to praise the Lord (Sir 50:22–24). In the Hebrew manuscript (MS B), it is directly related to the high priest Simon and functions as the conclusion to his eulogy: "Let his faithfulness [חסד] remain with Simon, and may the alliance with Phinehas be fulfilled in him; may he not take it away from him or his descendants as long as heaven lasts." Yet, in the Greek version, the text is transformed into a general intercession for all Israel, because at the translator's time the corruption of the high priesthood was a hard fact, and, consequently, the alliance that Ben Sira speaks about had already been broken. It was, therefore, better not to mention that dark page of history. Here is the Greek version: "May his mercy [ἔλεος] remain faithfully with us and deliver us in our days."

---

52. Beentjes, "God's Mercy," 111.

The second text, placed at the end of the book, is part of a psalm of thanksgiving (Sir 51:1–12), which according to Antonio José Guerra Martínez, "sums up everything the author understands by prayer."[53] We are referring to Sir 51:8. It is the only verse in the book that contains the word pair "mercy/goodness" (חסד/רחמים), which is quite frequent in biblical poetry.[54] We propose the translation of the Hebrew text according to MS B:

> I remembered (then) the Lord's mercy[55]
> and his goodness [lit., his benefits],[56] which has always existed (is eternal),
> that frees those who take refuge in him
> and rescues them from all evil.[57]

The person praying—probably Ben Sira himself—gives thanks to God for having delivered him from many perils, and especially from the slander of adversaries who wanted his death. In his prayer, the sage recalls the extreme situation in which he found himself and how he called on the Lord like a son his father (cf. Sir 51:1, 10), with blind trust in his help. The paternal image of God, on the one hand, and his extraordinary power in face of the enemies, on the other, are reminiscent of the prayer for Israel in Sir 36:1–17. Just as the Lord saved Ben Sira from mortal danger, so he will save Israel from its enemies. As a father cares for his son, so the Lord responds to the call of the afflicted, for his mercy is great (Sir 51:3).

5. Conclusion

"Asking oneself about the relationship between the divine attributes of mercy and justice is like descending to the level of the fundamental com-

---

53. Antonio José Guerra Martínez, *El poder de la oración: Estudio de Sir 51,1–12*, ABE 50 (Estella: Verbo Divino, 2010), 13.

54. E.g., Isa 63:7; Pss 25:6; 40:12; 51:3; 69:17; 103:4; Lam 3:22. See Beentjes, "God's Mercy," 113; and Guerra Martínez, *El poder de la oración*, 169–70.

55. G adds a vocative at the end of 8a (χύριε) and, unlike H, uses the direct style: the entire verse is formulated in the second person singular.

56. G: "of your works" (τῆς εὐεργεσίας σου). See Guerra Martínez, *El poder de la oración*, 160.

57. G: "from the hand of the wicked" (Ziegler's edition), "from the hand of the enemies" (Rahlfs's edition), "from the hand of the nations" (Cod. B and Vulg.). See Guerra Martínez, *El poder de la oración*, 162–64.

ponents of the divine figure as it is presented in the Bible; it implies, so to speak, getting to the divine core, where two constitutive forces interact, God's justice and his merciful *ḥesed*." This statement was recently made by Jean-Pierre Sonnet in an article on divine justice and mercy in the narrative texts of the Pentateuch.[58]

I do not know if our study has brought us any closer to that divine core that, despite our efforts to shorten distances, remains submerged in the mystery of what is incomprehensible and unreachable for humans. Our investigation, limited to the book of Bem Sira, has focused basically on a single attribute, that of mercy, and on its relationship with the fear of the Lord, justice, forgiveness, salvation, human frailty, and prayer.

At first sight, it seems that Ben Sira says nothing new about divine mercy, nothing different from what his ancestors already said. However, this impression is not correct, because it fails to take into account the way in which the sage reads, quotes, and interprets Scripture. While always remaining faithful to his people's history and tradition, Ben Sira does not hesitate to adapt the ancient texts so that they concord with his doctrine and the objectives of his teaching.

Let us review our texts. In Sir 2:7–9, mercy appears in relation to the fear of the Lord, one of the theological foundations of the book and an essential condition for attaining wisdom. Divine mercy is the answer to/ reward for the faithful and trusting attitude of those who fear the Lord, that is, of the disciples who, despite life's vicissitudes (Hellenistic influence), remain strongly attached to the faith of their fathers. In Sir 2:10–11, the sage evokes the example of the ancestors to underpin his teaching, and he ratifies it with the formula of mercy in Exod 34:6, adapting it to the new context. Finally, in Sir 2:18, he demonstrates, through a rereading of 2 Sam 24:14, that the Lord's mercy surpasses his justice.

Sirach 5:6 and 16:11–14, situated within a context of divine justice and retribution, clearly show the two opposing, but not incompatible, faces of divine love: mercy and anger. Both texts present God as a judge

---

58. "S'interroger à propos de la relation des attributs divins de miséricorde et de justice, c'est, de manière analogue, descendre au niveau des constituants les plus fondamentaux du personnage divin tel qu'il est mis en scène dans la Bible; c'est, pour ainsi dire, accéder au noyau divin, où interagissent deux puissances constitutives, la justice et la *ḥesed* miséricordieuse de Dieu." Jean-Pierre Sonnet, "Justice et miséricorde: Les attributs de Dieu dans la dynamique narrative du Pentateuque," *NRT* 138 (2016): 3–4.

who punishes with justice and forgives with mercy, which can be interpreted as "a demonstration of his surprising freedom."[59]

In Sir 18:1–14, the contrast between God's greatness and the human condition finds a path to conciliation through divine mercy. God, the creator and eternal author of inaccessible wonders, takes pity on the human beings. He feels compassion for their frailty, that is, for their transience and the limitations of their condition. His universal and unlimited mercy is a pedagogical instrument that, together with timely correction, leads the disciple along the right path.

In the texts of prayer, the link between mercy and the national conscience stands out, as also do the destruction of the enemy and divine paternity. Israel, conscious of being the chosen people, asks the Lord to take pity on his firstborn son and let his hand fall upon the foreign nations (Sir 36:1–17). In Sir 50:22–24H, the request refers to the high priest Simon and his descendants, that is, the person praying pleads for the continuity of the Aaronite priesthood. Finally, in Sir 51:8, the personal testimony of Ben Sira, who has experienced the Lord's mercy in his own flesh, puts the finishing touch on our itinerary.

From the formal point of view, it should be noted that the texts presented here belong to different literary genres: instruction (Sir 2:1–18), negative series (Sir 5:1–8), theological reflection (Sir 16:1–16), hymn (Sir 18:1–14), collective supplication (Sir 36:1–17), doxology (Sir 50:22–24), and individual thanksgiving (Sir 51:1–12). This variety of literary genres is a feature of Ben Sira's book that fits its sapiential character perfectly. Because of this, the sage's teaching on divine mercy acquires a greater capacity of persuasion while opening up a broader interpretive horizon.

In conclusion, Ben Sira offers us a presentation of divine mercy that, both in form and content, is neither a repetition of ancient texts nor is it homogeneous or monochrome. Various literary genres, thematic associations, and different contexts contribute to illustrate the understanding that the wise Ben Sira had of the Lord's merciful character and how the sage transmitted it to his disciples.

---

59. Sonnet, "Justice et miséricorde," 4.

Anthropologische Konzepte der biblischen Urgeschichte bei Jesus Sirach

Burkard M. Zapff

ABSTRACT: This essay deals with the way in which the book of Ben Sira makes reference to the biblical *Urgeschichte*. For this study, not only textual allusions to Gen 1–3 in the Hebrew text fragments are examined but also those in the Greek and Syriac versions of Ben Sira. The essay raises the question of how the texts were perceived and came to form the anthropological conception of Ben Sira and whether the different language versions display different emphases in this respect. It can be seen that Ben Sira uses the text of Gen 1–3 in various ways, for example, with regard to the nature of man or the question of the responsibility of the (first) woman for the common fate of death. At the same time, he integrates the text into his own anthropology and theology. In so doing, he is not always guided by the original meaning of the text, even though he remains fundamentally faithful to central biblical anthropological statements. Moreover, the interpretation process of these texts is continued in the Greek and Syriac versions, where the authors acted not only as translators of a Hebrew *Vorlage* but also at the same time as interpreters. Thus, in the comparison of the reception of Gen 3:6, 19 in the three language versions of Sir 25:24, one can say that it is only in the Syriac version that a clear statement regarding woman's responsibility for the common fate of death can be found; the Hebrew and Greek versions, in contrast, can be understood to mean that the (first) woman serves merely as a paradigm showing how sin leads to death. The conclusion, then, is that an interpretation of Ben Sira would ideally start from a comparison of these three language versions and that each of them would have to be assessed separately.

1. Hinführung zur Fragestellung

Wer sich die Frage nach dem Verständnis des Menschen in seinem Gegenüber zu Gott in der Hebräischen Bibel stellt, der ist zwar nicht nur, aber doch in besonderer Weise auf die beiden Schöpfungserzählungen am Beginn des Buches Genesis verwiesen.[1] Bekanntlich findet sich in der priesterschriftlichen Schöpfungserzählung eine Schilderung der Weltschöpfung, in deren Zusammenhang auch das Wesen des Menschen als zweigeschlechtlich bestimmt wird und sein Verhältnis zu seiner belebten Umwelt, sowie nicht zuletzt zum Schöpfergott Elohim beschrieben wird, der ihn in analogiefreier Weise in die Existenz gerufen hat.[2] In der zweiten, nichtpriesterlichen Schöpfungsgeschichte engt sich der Fokus auf den Menschen ein. Aus einer Weltschöpfungserzählung wird eine Erzählung der Erschaffung des Menschen. So gerät der Mensch insbesondere als stoffliches Wesen (so Gen 2,7a) in seiner unbedingten Abhängigkeit von JHWH-Elohim—veranschaulicht durch das direkte Einblasen des Lebensatems in die Nase des Menschen—sowie seine Natur als Beziehungswesen in den Blick (vgl. Gen 2,18 und die anschließende narrative Entfaltung in Gen 2,19–24). Die folgende Paradiesesgeschichte trägt ätiologische Züge, insofern sie Erklärungen für die z.T. harten Lebensumstände des Menschen, seine Eigenart als moralisches Wesen und seinen nicht mehr unmittelbaren und vertrauten Umgang mit dem Schöpfergott bietet (Gen 3,16–19.22–24). Für die ersten drei Kapitel des AT eine passende Bezeichnung zu finden, ist bekanntlich schwierig. So spricht man im Hinblick auf die zweite Schöpfungserzählung gerne von „Anthropogonie", eine Erzählung also, die mit der Entstehungsgeschichte des Menschen zugleich zentrale Wesenszüge des Menschen aufzuweisen sucht.[3] Erstaunlicher-

---

1. Neuere Literatur zu Gen 1–3: Lothar Ruppert, *Genesis. Ein kritischer und theologischer Kommentar. 1. Teilband: Gen 1,1–11,26*, FzB 70 (Würzburg: Echter, 2003²); Othmar Keel und Silvia Schroer, *Schöpfung. Biblische Theologien im Kontext altorientalischer Religionen*, (Göttingen: Vandenhoeck & Ruprecht, 2008/2002); Walter Bührer, *Am Anfang…: Untersuchungen zur Textgenese und zur relativ-chronologischen Einordnung von Gen 1–3*, FRLANT 256 (Göttingen: Vandenhoeck & Ruprecht, 2014).

2. Das Verhältnis zu Elohim bedenkt die „Gottesebenbildlichkeit" des Menschen in V.26a und V.27a, insbesondere durch die Kombination von בצלמנו „nach unserem Bild" und כדמותנו „uns ähnlich"; das Verhältnis zur belebten Umwelt klärt V.26b; die grundlegende Zweigeschlechtlichkeit und damit die Gleichursprünglichkeit der Geschlechter als Verwirklichung des Menschseins wird in V.27b festgehalten: ausführlich Odil Hannes Steck, *Der Schöpfungsbericht der Priesterschrift. Studien zur literarkritischen und überlieferungsgeschichtlichen Problematik von Gen 1,1–2,4a*, FRLANT 115 (Göttingen: Vandenhoeck & Ruprecht, 1981).

3. So z.B. Reinhard G. Kratz, *Die Komposition der erzählenden Bücher des Alten Testaments*, UTB 2157 (Göttingen: Vandenhoeck & Ruprecht, 2000), 256.

weise werden nun beide Schöpfungserzählungen in der Hebräischen Bibel kaum rezipiert.[4] Sie bilden im Gesamt der Hebräischen Bibel beinahe so etwas wie eine Insel, die zwar für die christlich-jüdische Anthropologie bis zum heutigen Tag von erheblicher Bedeutung ist, in der Hebräischen Bibel selbst jedoch nicht die Rolle spielt, wie man es eigentlich erwarten würde.

Anders ist dies in der Literatur, die man gemeinhin der Zeit zwischen den Testamenten zuweist und zu der auch das Buch Jesus Sirach gehört. Hier finden sich eine ganze Reihe von Bezügen nicht nur zur biblischen Urgeschichte als Ganze—zu denken ist etwa an das Lob der Väter, wo bedeutende Gestalten der Urgeschichte aufgezählt werden (vgl. Sir 44,16.17–18; 49,16)—sondern auch zu jenen drei ersten Kapitel der Genesis. Um daher etwas über das Verständnis des Menschen bei Jesus Sirach in Erfahrung zu bringen, liegt es nicht zuletzt nahe, nach der Art der Rezeption dieser Texte im Sirachbuch zu fragen.

Folgende Vorgehensweise scheint hier sinnvoll. Zunächst sollen die Textstellen genannt werden, an denen Sirach direkt Bezug auf die ersten drei Kapitel der Genesis und darüber hinaus auf die biblische Urgeschichte nimmt, insofern sie in irgendeiner Form Relevanz für seine Sicht des Menschen haben. Dass dabei eine Auswahl getroffen werden muss, die auf bestimmte zentrale Thematiken fokussiert ist, dürfte selbstverständlich sein.

Angesichts der schwierigen Textsituation sollen dabei, soweit dies notwendig erscheint, wesentliche Unterschiede zwischen den hebräischen Fassungen, den griechischen Fassungen und der syrischen Fassung benannt werden. Bei letzterer ist ja bekanntlich die Textüberlieferung wesentlich unproblematischer und einheitlicher. Dass dies zugleich ein Ertrag einer sich derzeit in Arbeit befindlichen Erstellung einer diplomatischen Sirachsynopse[5] ist, sei nur am Rande erwähnt. Sporadisch soll dabei auch die lateinische Fassung des Sirach Berücksichtigung finden, die auf

---

4. Eine der wenigen Ausnahmen bildet Ps 8, wo insbesondere das Verhältnis des Menschen zu seiner belebten Umwelt in ähnlicher Weise reflektiert wird wie in Gen 1,26b und 28b und auch das Verhältnis des Menschen zu JHWH näher bestimmt wird (vgl. V 6); zur Rezeption von Gen 1–3 in der Literatur des Antiken Judentums vor der Zerstörung des Jerusalemer Tempels, vgl. den Überblick bei Christfried Böttrich, Beate Ego und Friedmann Eißler, *Adam und Eva in Judentum, Christentum und Islam* (Göttingen: Vandenhoeck & Ruprecht, 2011), 29–43.

5. Nähere Informationen zur Durchführung des Projektes finden sich unter www.sirach-synopse.uni-saarland.de.

der Basis wichtiger Handschriften der vetus latina ebenfalls in der Sirachsynopse dokumentiert wird.

Schließlich soll danach gefragt werden, wie und in welcher Weise
Sirach auf den hebräischen Text Bezug nimmt, was er zitiert, was er
unterschlägt und was er verändert, um daraus nicht nur die Art der
Rezeption seiner Vorlage, sondern auch das ihn offensichtlich leitende
Verständnis von Menschsein im Gegenüber zu Gott und zum Mitmen-
schen zu erschließen.

Responsibility [handwritten annotation]

2. Sir 15,14–17—Zur Verantwortung des Menschen

Die erste einschlägige Stelle findet sich in Sir 15,14–17.[6] Der hebräische
Text wird hier durch die Manuskripte A und B bezeugt.[7] Die Verse sind
eingebunden in ein Kapitel, in dem es um die Herkunft von Sünde und
Schuld geht. Der Abschnitt beginnt in V.11 mit der Ablehnung einer
These, wie sie bei Sirach öfter erscheint: „Sag nicht: von Gott kommt
mein Frevel", אל תאמר מאל פשעי; die griechische Fassung ist hier sogar
noch konkreter, wenn sie übersetzt: „Sage nicht: wegen des Herrn bin ich
abgefallen" μὴ εἴπῃς ὅτι διὰ κύριον ἀπέστην.[8] Die syrische Fassung per-
sonalisiert hier sogar noch die Aussage, wenn es dort heißt: „von Gott
her[9] tat ich Unrecht"[10] ܡܢ ܐܠܗܐ ܥܘܠܐ ܣܥܪܬ. Damit aber macht sie Gott

---

6. Eine ausführliche Kommentierung findet sich bei Alexander A. Di Lella,
„Free Will in the Wisdom of Ben Sira 15:11–20. An Exegetical and Theological
Study", in *Ben Sira's God*, ed. Renate Egger-Wenzel, BZAW 321 (Berlin: de Gruyter,
2002), 282–301.

7. Die Textdarstellung orientiert sich an Pancratius C. Beentjes, *The Book of Ben
Sira in Hebrew: A Text Edition of All Extant Hebrew Manuscripts and a Synopsis of
All Parallel Hebrew Ben Sira Texts*, VTSup 68, (Atlanta: Society of Biblical Literature,
2006); Rekonstruktionen des hebräischen Textes orientieren sich an Francesco Vattioni, *Ecclesiastico. Testo ebraico con apparato critico e versioni greca, latina e siriaca*,
Pubblicazioni del Seminario di Semitistica 1 (Neapel: Istituto Orientale di Napoli,
1968) bzw. Moshe Zevi Segal, ספר בן־סירא השלם (Jerusalem: Bialik Foundation,
1953/1997⁴).

8. Merkwürdigerweise spricht die lateinische Fassung in V 11 von einer „Abwe-
senheit", offensichtlich der Weisheit: „per Deum abest".

9. Rudolph Smend, *Die Weisheit des Jesus Sirach* (Berlin: Reimer, 1906), 141: „von
Seiten Gottes".

10. Auffällig ist hier, dass S sich an den verbalen Ausdruck von G anschließt, vgl.
Smend, Weisheit, ebenda; dies könnte auf eine gemeinsame hebräische Vorlage oder
ein direktes Abhängigkeitsverhältnis hinweisen.

Creatureliness

zu dem, der den Menschen sündigen lässt. Hier setzt Sirach bei seinen Adressaten offenbar eine Sicht voraus, die Sünde als etwas, das mit der Geschöpflichkeit des Menschen verbunden ist, versteht. Tatsächlich findet sich eine solche Auffassung in den Reden der Freunde des Ijob, insbesondere der Rede des Elifas, wo es in Ijob 4,17 heißt: „Ist wohl ein Mensch vor Gott gerecht, ein Mann vor seinem Schöpfer rein?"[11] Ausgehend von dieser Aussage, könnte man also durchaus zur These kommen, die Sündhaftigkeit des Menschen wurzle in seiner Kreatürlichkeit, der Mensch sei demnach für sein Tun nicht voll verantwortlich. Dieser These tritt Sirach nun mit einigen grundsätzlichen Aussagen bezüglich des Verhältnisses Gottes zur Sünde entgegen, die vor allem durch das die Vv.11–13 rahmende Leitwort „hassen" bestimmt sind. Entsprechend V.11b tut JHWH nicht, „was er hasst" und nach V.13a „hasst" Gott das „Böse und jeglichen Gräuel". Ausgehend von dieser These, wonach Gott nicht tun kann, was er hasst, folglich die Sünde des Menschen nicht ihren Ursprung in Gott hat, machen nun die Vv.14–17 einige grundsätzliche Aussagen hinsichtlich des Wesens des Menschen und seines Verhältnisses zu Gutem und Bösem. Dabei findet sich eine Reihe von schriftgelehrten Rückbezügen, insbesondere auf Gen 1 und 2. Zunächst jedoch ein Blick auf die hier in Form von Manuskript A und B überlieferten hebräischen Versionen, auf die griechische Fassung und schließlich die syrische Übersetzung, mit ihren je eigenen Schwerpunktsetzungen.

So fällt auf, dass beide hebräischen Versionen eine doppelte Bestimmung des Menschen kennen: Entsprechend V.14b wurde der Mensch von Gott zum einen „in die Hand seines Räubers" übergeben (ביד חותפו), zum anderen „in die Hand seines Trachtens" ביד יצרו. Die syrische Version hingegen bietet einen verkürzten Satz, insofern sie „Räuber" nicht übersetzt und nur von der „Hand ihrer—nämlich der Menschen—Neigung" spricht, ܒܐܝܕ ܝܨܪܗܘܢ. In ähnlicher Weise verkürzt hier auch G und gibt יצרו mit διαβουλίου αὐτοῦ „seines Ratschlusses" wieder. V.15 lautet in der hebräischen Fassung von MS A „Wenn es dir gefällt, wirst du das Gebot halten, und Klugheit ist es, seinen Willen zu tun. Wenn du an ihn glaubst, wirst

11. Vgl. Markus Witte, *Vom Leiden zur Lehre. Der dritte Redegang (Hiob 21–27) und die Redaktionsgeschichte des Hiobbuchs*, BZAW 230 (Berlin: de Gruyter, 1994). Er weist Hi 4,17 einer von ihm als „Niedrigkeitsredaktion" beschriebenen Bearbeitung des Hiobbuches zu, die mit anderen Texten des Sirachbuches in Kontakt steht, z.B. Sir 17,30–32 LXX, vgl. 194–98.

auch du leben".[12] Auch in V.15 bietet die syrische Übersetzung gegenüber der hebräischen und griechischen Version eine kürzere Fassung, wenn sie das „Tun des Willens Gottes" bzw. „Treue zu halten" (so G) in V.15b unübersetzt lässt. Diese Veränderung mag der Neigung der syrischen Fassung geschuldet sein, möglichst einen Parallelismus membrorum beider Satzteile herzustellen.[13] Demgegenüber fällt in G V.15d „wirst auch du leben" ersatzlos aus.

V.17 lautet in der hebräischen Fassung von MS A: „Vor dem Menschen sind Leben und Tod; was ihm gefällt, wird ihm gegeben werden"[14]. Hier fällt auf, dass die syrische Version wiederum auf die Herstellung einer parallelen Struktur bedacht ist, wenn sie übersetzt: „Denn es wurde den Menschen Leben und Tod gegeben, damit sie das Leben wählen und den Tod liegen lassen".[15] So wird das Wortpaar „Leben" und „Tod" aus V.17a in V.17b wieder aufgegriffen. Außerdem wird als Ziel der Gabe von Leben und Tod eine bewusste Wahl des Lebens und der Verwerfung des Todes angegeben, so dass es also darum geht, das erhaltene Geschenk anzunehmen.

Welche Aussagen werden hier nun unter Rückgriff auf die Urgeschichte gemacht? 1. Auf den ersten Schöpfungsbericht weist gleich der Beginn von V.14 zurück, wo aus Gen 1,1 zwei Stichworte aufgegriffen werden: אלהים מבראשית, wörtl. „Gott von im Anfang".[16] Gleichzeitig weisen

---

12. אם תחפץ תשמר מצוה ותבונה לעשות רצונו אם תאמין בו גם אתה תחיה; MS B liest anstelle von תבונה „Klugheit" אמונה „Treue".

13. So lautet die syrische Fassung: „Und wenn du willst, wirst du seine Gebote halten, und wenn du an ihn glaubst, wirst auch du leben"; im zweiten Teil liegt aller Wahrscheinlichkeit nach ein Anklang an Hab 2,4 vor: ܒܗܝܡܢܘܬܗ ܢܚܐ „durch seinen Glauben wird er leben", so bereits Norbert Peters, *Das Buch Jesus Sirach oder Ecclesiasticus*, EHAT 25 (Münster: Aschendorff, 1913), 131.

14. וכל שיחפץ אשר יחפץ ינתן לו; MS B liest anstelle von יחפץ ein לפני אדם חיים ומוות אשר יחפץ ינתן לו „und alles, was ihm gefällt".

15. Bereits Smend, *Sirach*, 143, meint hinsichtlich V 17bα eine Reminiszenz auf Dtn 30,15.19, insbesondere PeshDtn 30,19 (ܘܓܒܝ / ܚܝܐ) feststellen zu können; dagegen jedoch Willem Th. van Peursen, *Language and Interpretation in the Syriac Text of Ben Sira. A Comparative Linquistic and Literary Study*, MPIL 16 (Leiden: Brill, 2007), 107–8.

16. So MS A; Smend, *Sirach*, 142, weist darauf hin, dass es sich in MS A um eine aramäische Verbindung handelt; vgl. S; entsprechend Jes 46,10 müsste es eigentlich heißen: מראשית „von Anfang an"; zur Diskussion über die Ursprünglichkeit von מבראשית vgl. James K. Aitken, „Divine Will and Providence", in *Ben Sira's God*, ed. Renate Egger-Wenzel, BZAW 321 (Berlin: de Gruyter, 2002), 289. Er meint, dass eine

ברא und אדם auf Gen 1,26 hin, wobei MS A den fehlenden Artikel über der Zeile einfügt.

Merkwürdig ist dabei die Formulierung „von Anfang an", angesichts dessen, dass Gen 1,1 mit בראשית „im" oder „als" Anfang einsetzt.[17] Tatsächlich gibt hier MS B den Text mit הוא מראש „er hat von Beginn an (erschaffen)" wieder, ähnlich wie auch G mit αὐτὸς ἐξ ἀρχῆς „von Anfang an" übersetzt.[18] In jedem Fall soll mit dem Partitivpartikel מן offensichtlich der Ausgangspunkt einer Bewegung, in diesem Fall einer zeitlichen Spanne im Sinne von „seit", zum Ausdruck gebracht werden. Dann aber meint „von im Anfang" (MS A) oder „von Anfang an" (MS B), dass Gott nicht nur am Anfang die Erschaffung des Menschen bewirkt hat, sondern offensichtlich von Anfang an an der Erschaffung eines jeden Menschen beteiligt war, sich also hier so etwas wie eine creatio continua des Menschen abzeichnet. Daraus wiederum ergibt sich, dass das, was für den ersten Menschen auch für jeden seiner Nachkommen in gleicher Weise gilt.[19] Es geht hier also nicht um einen Urstand, der durch die Schuld des Menschen verloren wurde, sondern um eine Wirklichkeit, die von Anfang an für jeden Menschen Gültigkeit besitzt, der von Gott erschaffen wird. Unter diesem Vorzeichen wäre sogar zu überlegen, ob man das ברא nicht vielleicht als aktives Partizip vokalisieren sollte: „schafft Gott".

Davon ausgehend beschreibt nun der Folgesatz V.14b die mit der Erschaffung des Menschen verbundene, grundsätzliche Wirklichkeit. Entscheidend sind dabei die beiden suffigierten Nomen חותפו und יצרו.

---

nachträgliche Verstärkung der Bezugnahme auf Gen 1,1 durch die Einfügung jener Formel wahrscheinlicher sei als deren nachträgliche Tilgung in MS B.

17. Zur syntaktischen Problematik von בְּרֵאשִׁית, vgl. die Zusammenstellung von Michaela Bauks, *Die Welt am Anfang. Zum Verhältnis von Vorwelt und Weltentstehung in Gen 1 und in der altorientalischen Literatur*, WMANT 74 (Neukirchen-Vlyun: Neukirchener Verlag, 1997), 65–85.

18. Die Ersetzung des הוא in MS B durch אלהים in MS A (vgl. dazu V mit „Deus"), deutet darauf hin, dass es sich tatsächlich bei מבראשית um eine nachträgliche Harmonisierung mit Gen 1,1 handeln könnte; bezüglich הוא vgl. van Peursen, *Language*, 401.

19. Maurice Gilbert, „God, Sin and Mercy: Sirach 15:11–18:14", in: *Ben Sira's God*, ed. Renate Egger-Wenzel, BZAW 321 (Berlin: de Gruyter, 2002), 118–35, drückt diesen Sachverhalt folgendermaßen aus: "Now, from the moment of his origin, man was 'given' over to the power of his *yésèr*" vgl. auch Ursel Wicke-Reuter, *Göttliche Providenz und menschliche Verantwortung bei Ben Sira und in der frühen Stoa*, BZAW 298 (Berlin: de Gruyter, 2000) 116: „Die Befähigung des Menschen, verantwortlich zu handeln, entspringt folglich dem göttlichen Willen und ist Teil der Schöpfungsordnung".

Das erste der beiden bedeutet so viel wie „Wegreißer" oder „Räuber".
Die genaue Deutung ist schwierig, zumal sich die Wurzel nur noch an
zwei Stellen in der Hebräischen Bibel findet.[20] In jedem Fall drückt sich
darin eine Gefährdung des Menschen aus, die, setzt man die Verbform
in Entsprechung zum folgenden יצרו, offensichtlich aus dem Inneren
des Menschen kommt, sich also auf geistiger Ebene bewegt. Es könnte
sich dabei auf die Neigung beziehen, sich selbst des Gutes des Lebens zu
berauben, möglicherweise in Anspielung auf den Griff nach der verbo-
tenen Frucht im Paradiesgarten (vgl. Gen 3,6). Die Tatsache, dass diese
Wendung in der syrischen, griechischen und lateinischen Version unübersetzt bleibt, wird in der Forschung in der Weise gedeutet, dass es sich hier
um eine spätere Ergänzung handelt.[21] Diese Ergänzung könnte mit der
Intention verbunden sein, das hinsichtlich seiner Konnotation zunächst
ambivalente יצר stärker negativ zu bestimmen. Womöglich aber wurde
diese vermeintliche Glossierung ob der Schwierigkeit ihres Verständnisses
oder der damit verbundenen negativen Einschätzung des Menschen von
G und S schlicht nicht rezipiert.[22] Klarer ist dies bei der folgenden Wendung „in die Hand seines Trachtens" ביד יצרו. Zwar wird in der neueren
Forschung immer wieder herausgestellt, dass יצר hier im neutralen Sinn
zu verstehen und nicht wie in der späteren rabbinischen Literatur[23] bereits
negativ geprägt sei,[24] doch wird dabei nicht berücksichtigt, dass damit ja

---

20. In Ijob 9,12 ist die Wurzel als Verbform und in Spr 23,28 als Abstractum
belegt; dort gibt sie T mit dem aramäischen טרף wieder, was ebenfalls „wegreißen,
rauben" bedeutet; im Syr. hat die Wurzel ܬܒܪ die Bedeutung „zerbrechen".

21. Vgl. z.B. Wicke-Reuter, Göttliche Providenz, 112, Anm. 29.

22. Patrick W. Skehan und Alexander A. Di Lella, The Wisdom of Sira. A New
Translation with Notes, AB 39 (New York: Doubleday, 1987), 269, weist auf die Ähnlichkeit mit dem syrischen Text von Sir 4,19b hin (ܚܕ ܒܝܕ). Dort sei die Formulierung durchaus sinnvoll, was man jedoch hier nicht sagen könne. Der Sinn der
Verwendung der Formulierung in V.14 könnte allerdings darin bestehen, die negative Konnotation von יצר vor dem Hintergrund von Gen 6,5 zu verstärken. Hingegen
scheint G mit ἐν χειρὶ διαβουλίου αὐτοῦ durchweg etwas Positives i.S. von Überlegung
und freiem Willen verstanden zu haben, vgl. Johannes Marböck, Jesus Sirach 1–23,
HThKAT (Freiburg: Herder, 2010), 201.

23. So z.B. im Targum Pseudo-Jonathan, der—im Unterschied zum Targum Neo-
fiti etwa—das verhärtete Herz des Pharao regelmäßig mit יצר übersetzt und dieses
Nomen dabei grundsätzlich negativ konnotiert verwendet. Die Datierung des Targum
ist allerdings umstritten. Sie reicht vom 1. bis 4. Jhd. n. Chr.

24. So ausführlich Wicke-Reuter, Göttliche Providenz, 117–119; Marböck, Jesus
Sirach, 201.

auch ein Begriff aus dem Vorspann der Sintfluterzählungen in Gen 6,5 aufgegriffen wird,[25] wo JHWH ausdrücklich feststellt, dass alles „Trachten" des menschlichen Herzens immer nur böse sei: וכל־יצר מחשבת לבו רק רע כל־היום, eine Aussage, die in Gen 8,21 nochmals wiederholt wird. Zumindest wird vor diesem Hintergrund יצר—bereits von der hebräischen Bibel her (!)—auch eine potentiell negative Konnotation beigefügt, die den Menschen vor eine besondere Herausforderung stellt, ohne dass deshalb die negativen Seiten dieses Trachtens JHWH als Schöpfergott angelastet werden oder den Menschen determinieren. Tatsächlich wird im Folgesatz, trotz dieser Vorprägung, die grundsätzliche Freiheit des Menschen zur Gebotserfüllung und damit in V.15c die Möglichkeit, das Leben zu erreichen, betont,[26] wobei es dabei natürlich um ein gelungenes Leben geht. Die Auslieferung des Menschen an sein eigenes Trachten ist vielmehr eine schöpfungsmäßige Realität, vor deren Bewältigung der Einzelne steht, ohne dass deren negative Seiten deshalb JHWH angelastet würden.

3. Sir 17,1–9—Das Wesen des Menschen

Das zweite Beispiel findet sich in Sir 17,1–9. Der Abschnitt ist eingebunden in einen Vorspann in Sir 16,26–30, der ebenfalls auf den priesterschriftlichen Schöpfungsbericht Bezug nimmt, allerdings in sehr allgemeiner Weise. In erster Linie dient der Vorspann der Klärung des Weltverständnisses des Sirach. Folgende Aspekte sind dabei entscheidend: 1. Wiederum erscheint entsprechend der Variante von MS B in Sir 15,14 die Formulierung מראש „von Anfang an" zusammen mit der speziell in der priesterschriftlichen Schöpfungsgeschichte verwendeten Wurzel ברא „erschaffen", wenn Sirach in 16,26 schreibt (MS A): „als Gott seine Werke von Anfang an schuf" כברא אל מעשיו מראש. Auch hier klingt in der Partitivpartikel (מן) der Gedanke der *creatio continua* an, wonach die Erschaffung keine abgeschlossene Tat Gottes ist, sondern sich bis in die Gegenwart hinein fortsetzt. 2. Die Erschaffung geht entsprechend der

exhort to prayer

---

25. Darauf weist neuerdings Paul E. Dion, *God and the Evil Men according to Ben Sira 15:11–18:14*, ScEs 59/2–3 (2007): 143–52, 147 hin.

26. Vgl. Timo Veijola, „Law and Wisdom. The Deuteronomistic Heritage in Ben Sira's Teaching of the Law", in *Leben nach der Weisung. Exegetische und historische Studien zum Alten Testament*, ed. Walter Dietrich, FRLANT 224 (Göttingen: Vandenhoeck & Ruprecht, 2008), 154.

syrischen Fassung mit der Zuteilung von Gesetzen, syr. ܬܘܩܦܝܗܘܢ einher,[27]
bzw. entsprechend G mit der Unterscheidung von Anteilen, griech. μερίδας
bzw. partes, so der Lateiner, die den einzelnen Werken zugewiesen werden.
3. Die Werke erfüllen den ihnen zugewiesenen Zweck ohne zu ermatten
(V.27b). 4. Die Werke treten nicht in Konkurrenz zueinander—der Syrer
spricht hier sogar davon, dass sie einander nicht hassen, syr. ܣܢܐ ܠܐ. ܚܕ
ܡܢ—und übertreten nicht das Wort Gottes—syr. ܠܐ / ܥܒܪܝܢ ܦܬܓܡܗ /
griech. οὐκ ἀπειθήσουσιν τοῦ ῥήματος αὐτοῦ (V.28). Es ist leicht ersichtlich,
dass sich in diesem Vorspann stoisches Denken spiegelt, was sich z.B. in
dem Gedanken der Gesetzmäßigkeit der Weltwirklichkeit und damit ihrer
Harmonie niederschlägt.[28] Natürlich geht Sirach dabei entsprechend der
alttestamentlichen Schöpfungsvorstellung von einem Schöpfergott aus,
der seiner Schöpfung gegenübersteht und nicht in ihr aufgeht, so dass die
Weltwirklichkeit entsprechend der Stoa selbst göttlichen Charakters wäre.

Vv.29/30 schließlich bilden den Übergang[29] zu den Ausführungen
zum Menschen, wiederum unter Bezug auf den ersten Schöpfungsbericht, allerdings mit veränderter Reihenfolge: Erst blickt Gott die Erde an,
hier spiegelt sich wohl Gen 1,31 wieder, dann erfüllte er sie mit seinen
Gütern, wobei der Syrer hier vom „Segnen mit seinen Gütern" spricht,
gedacht ist wohl an die Nahrungszuteilung entsprechend Gen 1,29–30
und schließlich bedeckt Gott—der Syrer spricht hier von „erfüllt"—das
Angesicht der Erde mit Lebewesen, womit auf Gen 1,20–25 Bezug genommen wird. Die veränderte Reihenfolge zwischen Nahrungszuweisung und
anschließender Erschaffung der Tierwelt geht wohl auf den Gedanken
der göttlichen Providenz zurück, womit Sirach sich wiederum stoischem
Denken nähert. Der Vorspann endet in V.30b entsprechend G (MS A ist
hier nicht mehr erhalten) mit dem Hinweis der Rückkehr der Lebewesen zur Erde: καὶ εἰς αὐτὴν ἡ ἀποστροφὴ αὐτῶν. Damit aber wird die das
Strafwort in Gen 3,19 beschließende Aussage JHWH-Elohims an Adam

---

27. Zur möglichen Rekonstruktion der hebräischen Version in MS A aufgrund
des erhaltenen spiegelverkehrten Abdruckes der MS AVI verso Z.1–4 vgl. Gerhard
Karner, „Ben Sira Ms A Fol. I Recto and Fol. VI Verso (T-S 12.863) Revisited", *RdQ* 27
(2015): 177–203 (Vgl. dazu: Eric D. Reymond, „New Hebrew Text on Ben Sira Chapter 1 in Ms A (T-S 12.863)", *RdQ* 27 (2015): 83–98.

28. Vgl. Wicke-Reuter, *Göttliche Providenz*, 273.

29. Marböck, *Jesus Sirach*, 213; Gilbert, God, 215: „Possibly 16:29–30 is a
necessary transition between the cosmos and man, because these verses already refer
to the earth, with vegetation and animals, before referring to man on the earth".

(כי־עפר אתה ואל־עפר תשוב) zu einer allgemeinen, schöpfungsmäßig festgelegten Selbstverständlichkeit: Wer auf der Erde ist, kehrt zur Erde zurück.[30] Interessant ist, dass die syrische Fassung in V.30bβ nur recht unbestimmt davon spricht, dass Gott alle ihrer—wohl der Lebewesen—Werke inmitten der Erde gesammelt hat: ܘܡܢܗ ܠܓܘܗ ܕܐܪܥܐ ܟܢܫ ܐܢܘܢ.

An diesen Vorspann knüpft nun Sir 17,1–9 mit seinen Ausführungen über den Menschen an, insofern G in V.1 mit ἀπέστρεψεν αὐτόν „er wird ihn zurückkehren lassen" und εἰς αὐτήν „zu ihr" zwei wichtige Stichworte aus Sir 16,30 (εἰς αὐτήν; ἀποστροφή) aufgreift. Dabei verbindet Sirach die in Gen 2,7 beschriebene Erschaffung des Menschen, nun allerdings unter Verwendung des Verbs „erschaffen" ἔκτισεν, das wohl die hebräische Wurzel ברא wiedergibt (vgl. S: ܒܪܝܗ), mit der das Strafwort an Adam beschließenden Aussage Gen 3,19, welche in Sir 16,30 für alle Lebewesen gemacht wurde und überträgt sie nun auf den Menschen. Der Erschaffung des Menschen[31] aus Erdreich entspricht seine Rückkehr zur Erde.[32] Im Unterschied zu Gen 3,18 allerdings wird auch diese Rückkehr zur Erde analog zur Erschaffung des Menschen direkt von Gott bewirkt.[33] Anfang und Ende des Menschen verdanken sich damit einem direkten Handeln Gottes. Dieser Vorstellung entspricht auch der nächste Vers, wonach dem Menschen von Gott eine bestimmte Zahl an Tagen zugewiesen ist. D.h. das Leben des Menschen ist nicht nur hinsichtlich seiner Existenz,

---

30. Vgl. Otto Kaiser, „‚Was ist der Mensch und was ist sein Wert?'. Beobachtungen zur Anthropologie des Jesus Sirach nach Jesus Sirach 16,24–18,14", in *Was ist der Mensch, dass du seiner gedenkst? Aspekte einer theologischen Anthropologie. FS Bernd Janowski zum 65. Geburtstag*, ed. Michaela Bauks (Neukirchen-Vluyn: Neukirchener Verlag, 2008), 220: „Das Erstaunliche an diesen Versen ist, daß Ben Sira hier weder die Sterblichkeit des Menschen noch seine Unterscheidungsfähigkeit zwischen Gut und Böse auf den Sündenfall des Urmenschen zurückführt, sondern den Menschen nicht anders als alle übrigen Lebewesen auf Erden von Anfang an als sterblich erschaffen (V.1) und von Anfang an mit einem sittlichen Unterscheidungsvermögen ausgestattet betrachtet (V.7)".

31. Im Unterschied zu G gebraucht S „Adam" als Eigenname, während G hier von ἄνθρωπος spricht.

32. Vgl. Wicke-Reuter, *Göttliche Providenz*, 156: „Indem in 17,1b Jahwe das Subjekt von ἀποστρέφειν ist und nicht wie in Gen 3,19 der Mensch selbst, ist die ‚Rückkehr' des Menschen zur Erde in den Schöpfungsakt hineingenommen".

33. Vgl. Gilbert, *God*, S.125, der dies folgendermaßen beschreibt: „The Lord is the chief actor. He creates (16:26a; 17,1a) the universe and man…. But when he creates, God gives to each series of his work a function; moreover, the scope of this function is to assure order in creation".

sondern auch seines zeitlichen Umfangs vollständig von Gott bestimmt. Hier nähert sich Sirach stoischem Weltordnungsdenken an, wonach sich das menschliche Leben nach bestimmten Vorgaben der Weltordnung vollzieht, die eben auch die Dauer menschlichen Lebens betrifft. Die Vollmacht, die entsprechend V.2b Gott dem Menschen über alles gegeben hat, ist als Umsetzung der Aussage in Gen 1,28 zu verstehen: ורדו בדגת הים ובעוף השמים ובכל־חיה הרמשת על־הארץ. Dabei spricht die syrische Version ausdrücklich davon, dass Gott den Menschen „über alles herrschen ließ" ܫܠܜ, womit jegliche menschliche Herrschaft von Gott ermöglicht ist und damit wiederum die Souveränität Gottes herausgestellt wird. V.3 interpretiert die Gottesebenbildlichkeit, von der Gen 1,27 spricht. Wiederum fällt auf, dass die Reihenfolge der Bezugnahme auf die biblische Vorlage vertauscht ist. An erster Stelle steht die Herrschaft, die in V.3 mit der Gottesebenbildlichkeit des Menschen in einen Bezugszusammenhang gebracht wird:[34] „Sich selbst entsprechend bekleidete er sie mit Stärke und nach seinem Bild machte er sie". καθ᾽ ἑαυτὸν ἐνέδυσεν αὐτοὺς ἰσχὺν καὶ κατ᾽ εἰκόνα αὐτοῦ ἐποίησεν αὐτούς. Die griechische Fassung nimmt dabei mit κατ᾽ εἰκόνα αὐτοῦ „nach seinem Abbild" den entsprechenden Fachterminus aus Gen 1,26 LXX auf. Gottesebenbildlichkeit besteht hier in der Stärke[35] des Menschen. Was darunter zu verstehen ist, expliziert der folgende V.4. Interessant ist, dass die syrische Fassung in keiner Weise von Gottesebenbildlichkeit spricht. S greift vielmehr allem Anschein nach auf die Bekleidungsszene vor der Vertreibung aus dem Paradies in Gen 3,21 zurück und deutet diese metaphorisch. So ist hier davon die Rede, dass Gott den Menschen „in seiner Weisheit mit Stärke bekleidete" und „sie mit Furcht bedeckte"—möglich wäre auch „ihnen die Furcht bedeckte"— ܗܒܬܕܬܗ ܐܠܒ ܐܢܘܢ ܒܚܝܠܝܢܗ ܘܕܚܠܬܐ ܐܢܘܢ ܐܣܚ ܒܣܪܐ. In V.4 treffen sich nun alle Versionen wieder: Die Gottesebenbildlichkeit in Gestalt seiner Stärke zeigt sich in der Furcht allen Fleisches vor dem Menschen. Wie

---

34. Georg Sauer, *Jesus Sirach/Ben Sira*, ATD.A 1, (Göttingen: Vandenhoeck & Ruprecht, 2000), 141: „Für Ben Sira besteht offensichtlich die Gottebenbildlichkeit in der Möglichkeit, so wie Gott Macht über die Schöpfung auszuüben", so bereits Josef Schreiner, *Jesus Sirach 1–24*, NEchtB AT 38 (Würzburg: Echter, 2002), 94: „Der Mensch als Abbild soll die Präsenz Gottes, des eigentlichen Herrn, darstellen und Verantwortung für die geschaffenen Wesen übernehmen. Dazu gab er Macht, der seinen ähnlich und von ihm abgeleitet, dem Menschen übertragen wie in einer Investitur".

35. V, die hier eine Versumstellung vornimmt (V.3b wird zu 17,1 und V.3a zu 17,2), spricht davon, dass er „ihn sich selbst entsprechend mit Tugend bekleidete": „et secundum se vestivit illum virtutem".

leicht zu erkennen ist, nimmt Sirach hier auf den noachitischen Segen in Gen 9,2 Bezug, ohne dabei zwischen vorsintflutlicher und nachsintflutlicher Zeit zu unterscheiden. Die Furcht der Tierwelt vor dem Menschen ist damit bereits eine schöpfungsmäßige Kategorie und nicht der nachsintflutlichen Zeit zuzuschreiben, durch die eine Gebrochenheit in die Schöpfung gekommen ist, wie dies der Duktus in der hebräischen Bibel nahelegt. Ohne Bezug auf die biblischen Schöpfungserzählungen[36] schildert V.6 die Ausstattung des Menschen mit Sinnesorganen. Dabei rahmen in der griechischen Fassung die Organe der Ratio, „Überlegung" und „Herz", die Organe „Zunge", „Augen" und „Ohren"[37], während in der syrischen Fassung, die hier eine Versvertauschung vornimmt, ein besonderer Nachdruck auf dem Herzen liegt. So spricht V.6(S) in Entsprechung zu V.7(G) davon, dass Gott den Menschen und zwar sein Herz (nur in S) mit Weisheit und Verstand, erfüllt habe. V.7(S) entsprechend V.6(G) mündet ausgehend von Mund und Zunge, Augen und Ohren in das Herz ein, das dem Verständnis dient. Durch die Versvertauschung in S und die nochmalige Erwähnung des Herzens in V.7(S) wird damit dem Herzen als entscheidendem Organ des Menschen ein Vorrang eingeräumt, welches dann auch der Erkenntnis der im folgenden V.8 in S genannten Machttaten Gottes dient. V.7b (in S V.6b) schließlich nimmt allem Anschein nach auf Gen 2,17 und 3,5 Bezug, wenn es nun um Gut und Böse geht, was dem Menschen zur Kenntnis gebracht wird: „Gutes und Böses zeigte er ihnen" ἀγαθὰ καὶ κακὰ ὑπέδειξεν αὐτοῖς. Während in Gen 3,5 der Drang des Menschen, Gut und Böse zu erkennen, zur Übertretung des Verbotes, vom Baum der Erkenntnis zu essen, führt, ist es hier nun eigenartigerweise Gott selbst, der dem Menschen Gut und Böse „zeigt"—so die griechische Fassung—bzw. „lehrt" ܐܠܦ—so die syrische Fassung. Von einem Verbot oder gar einer Versuchung des Menschen, durch diese Fähigkeit, Gut und Böse zu erkennen und wie Gott werden zu wollen, ist in keiner Weise die Rede.[38] Erkenntnis ist vielmehr eine Gabe Gottes und die Unterscheidung

---

36. Vgl. Otto Kaiser, „Göttliche Weisheit und menschliche Freiheit bei Ben Sira", in *Auf den Spuren der schriftgelehrten Weisen, FS Johannes Marböck* ed. Imtraud Fischer et al., BZAW 331 (Berlin: de Gruyter, 2013), 295.

37. Marböck, *Jesus Sirach*, 214: „Für Sir 17,6 ist ein Bezug auf die auch in Test Naft II,5-8 begegnende Rede von fünf Sinnen im Haupt des Menschen wahrscheinlich"; Schreiner, *Jesus Sirach*, 94, hält den Vers für einen Nachtrag, der „griechische Philosophie ein(trägt)" und „aus der Lehre der Stoa" schöpft.

38. Marböck, *Jesus Sirach*, 214.

von Gut und Böse geht direkt auf die Unterweisung seitens Gottes zurück.[39] Tatsächlich erscheint das Paar „Gut und Böse" noch einmal in Sir 11,11, wo es seinen Ursprung direkt in Gott hat, wenn es dort heißt: „Gut und Böse sind von Gott". Beide zu erkennen, hat also etwas mit Erkenntnis der Schöpfungswerke Gottes und damit der Größe des Schöpfers selbst zu tun.[40] Die Erkenntnisfähigkeit des Menschen ist damit bei Sirach keine Folge unerlaubter Grenzüberschreitung, sondern entspricht Gottes Willen. Auf diese Weise wird eine schwierige Aussage der biblischen Paradiesesgeschichte in traditionelle alttestamentliche Weisheit eingeordnet: Gott selbst ist der eigentliche Weisheitslehrer des Menschen und er selbst hat die Organe der Erkenntnis, allen voran das Herz, geschaffen.

In V.8 wird ein weiterer Grund deutlich, weshalb die syrische Fassung eine Versumstellung vorgenommen hat. Demnach dienen die Erkenntnisorgane des Menschen, allen voran das Herz, dazu, die Wunder der Werke Gottes zu sehen und zu verstehen. So schließt die syrische Version mit einem Finalsatz an V.7. an: „um ihnen die Wunder seiner Werke zu zeigen" ܠܡܚܘܝܘ ܐܢܘܢ ܠܬܕܡܪܬܐ ܕܥܒܕܘܗܝ.

Demgegenüber bringt die griechische Fassung[41] einen neuen Aspekt ins Spiel, nämlich die „Furcht" vor Gott, einen zentralen Begriff der Theologie des Sirach. Mit ἔθηκεν τὸν φόβον αὐτοῦ ἐπι „er legte die Furcht vor ihm auf (ihre Herzen)" greift Sir 17,8 eine Formulierung aus V.4 auf.[42] Was in Bezug auf das Verhältnis zwischen allem Fleisch und dem Menschen gilt, gilt nun auch für das Verhältnis zwischen Gott und dem Menschen. Wie das grundlegende Verhältnis der Tierwelt zum Menschen durch

---

39. Kaiser, „Göttliche Weisheit", 296.

40. Wicke-Reuter, *Göttliche Providenz*, 159: „Man kann geradezu, cum grano salis, von einer natürlichen Gotteserkenntnis sprechen, die das Auge des Herzens den Menschen eröffnet. Freilich ist damit nicht die Erkenntnis des göttlichen *Wesens*, sondern allein seiner Größe gemeint".

41. Mit Ziegler; dagegen Rahlfs: ἔθηκεν τὸν ὀφθαλμὸν αὐτοῦ ἐπὶ τὰς καρδίας αὐτῶν „Und er richtete sein Auge auf ihre Herzen"; Gilbert, *God*, 216, bevorzugt diese Lesart, insofern damit Gott, nachdem er dem Menschen gezeigt hat, was Gut und Böse ist, nun ihre Wahl beobachtet. Demnach setze V.8a V.7b logisch fort. Allerdings macht dann der Anschluss von V.8b Schwierigkeiten, selbst wenn man den Infinitiv partizipial auffassen will. Während die Furcht Gottes durchaus die Wahrnehmung der Größe seiner Werke erschließt, ergibt sich daraus, dass Gott sein Auge auf die Herzen der Menschen richtet, nicht, dass er ihnen die Größe seiner Werke zeigt.

42. Marböck, *Jesus Sirach*, 215: „die Variante der Furcht würde hierarchisch die Parallele zu 4a betonen".

die Furcht bestimmt ist, die entsprechend Sir 16,26 sozusagen zu einem Grundgesetz der Schöpfungswirklichkeit gehört, so ist die Grundhaltung menschlicher Existenz gegenüber Gott demnach ebenfalls die „Furcht", die damit zur adäquaten Haltung des Menschen gegenüber Gott wird. D.h. die Gottesebenbildlichkeit des Menschen, von der in V.3 die Rede war, wird insofern konkretisiert, als das Verhältnis der Tierwelt zum Menschen in derselben Weise beschrieben wird, wie das des Menschen zu Gott. Für die Tierwelt ist damit der Mensch gottähnlich.[43] Gegenüber Gott befähigt die Haltung der Gottesfurcht den Menschen entsprechend der griechischen Version, die Größe der Werke Gottes wahrzunehmen. Diese Bestimmung des Menschen mündet schließlich in den Lobpreis Gottes ein, „als höchste Erfüllung der gottgeschenkten Ausstattung des Menschen".[44] D.h. Menschsein wird hier eingeordnet zwischen Tierwelt und Gott und jeweils relational durch den Begriff „Furcht" näher bestimmt.

4. Die Frau und die Sünde

Ein weiterer Bezug auf die biblische Urgeschichte liegt in Sir 25,24 vor, einem Vers, der nicht zuletzt rezeptionsgeschichtlich von erheblicher Bedeutung ist.[45] Er findet sich im Rahmen der Beschreibung der bösen Frau in Sir 25,13–26. Dort heißt es zunächst in der hebräischen Version von MS C: „von einer Frau ist/war der Anfang der Sünde und wegen ihr verscheiden wir zusammen", יחד / מאשה תחלת עון ובגללה גוענו, was sprachlich und syntaktisch weitgehend der griechischen Fassung entspricht: ἀπὸ γυναικὸς ἀρχὴ ἁμαρτίας καὶ δι' αὐτὴν ἀποθνήσκομεν πάντες. Der Syrer liest hier: „Von einer Frau begannen die Sünden und wegen ihr sterben wir alle", ܡܢ ܐܢܬܬܐ ܫܪܝ ܚܛܗ̈ܐ ܘܡܛܠܬܗ ܚܢܢ ܟܠܢ ܡܝܬܝܢ. Der Unterschied zwischen den zwei bzw. drei Versionen liegt schlicht darin, dass in der hebräischen und griechischen Fassung das „wegen ihr" sich sowohl auf

---

43. Gilbert, *God*, 216, spricht hier mit Recht von einer Art „hierarchical order: animals fear or revere man, and man fears or reveres the Lord".

44. Marböck, ebenda.

45. So etwa in 1Tim 2,13–14: „Denn zuerst wurde Adam erschaffen, danach Eva. Und nicht Adam wurde verführt, sondern die Frau ließ sich verführen und übertrat das Gebot"; vgl. dazu Böttrich, Ego, und Eißler, *Adam und Eva*, 79–137; zur Wirkungs- und Rezeptionsgeschichte von Gen 1-3 in biblischer Zeit, vgl. Helen Schüngel-Straumann, „,Von einer Frau nahm die Sünde ihren Anfang, ihretwegen müssen wir alle sterben' Sir 25,24. Zur Wirkungs- und Rezeptionsgeschichte der ersten drei Kapitel der Genesis in biblischer Zeit", *BiKi* 53 (1998): 11–20.

den „Anfang der Sünde" עון תחלת /ἀρχή ἁμαρτίας bzw. die „Sünde" עון /
ἁμαρτία wie auf die „Frau" אשה /γυνή beziehen kann. Dabei ist die zuerst
genannte syntaktische Beziehung jeweils die wahrscheinlichere, da „wegen
ihr" direkt auf die femininen Nomina „Anfang" bzw. „Sünde" folgen. Beim
Syrer ist diese Uneindeutigkeit beseitigt, insofern sich wegen der plurali-
schen Form „Sünden" ܚܛܗܐ und der verbalen Auflösung des hebräischen
„Anfang" תחלת in „begannen" ܐܬܫܪܝ das „und wegen ihr" ܘܡܛܠܬܗ nur auf
die Frau beziehen kann. D.h. in der hebräischen und griechischen Fassung
kann der Vers zunächst so verstanden werden, dass durch eine Frau, die
gesündigt hat, der Tod in die Welt gekommen ist und demzufolge wir alle
sterben müssen.[46] Es würde sich hier also der Gedanke einer Ursprungssünde, die zum Tod aller führt, abzeichnen, welche der ersten Frau
angelastet wird.[47] Diese Interpretation vertritt ausdrücklich die syrische
Übersetzung, die, wie oftmals angenommen wird, unter christlichem Einfluss verfasst wurde.[48] Das Problem dieser Interpretation besteht jedoch
darin, dass Sirach—unterstellt man ihm ein widerspruchsfreies Denken—
sich hier widersprechen würde.[49] So wurde in den oben behandelten Texten

Contradicts [handwritten annotation]
other places [handwritten annotation]

---

46. So die übliche Deutung, vgl. Sauer, *Jesus Sirach*, 192: „So kommt Ben Sira zu
der einseitigen Feststellung, es läge an dem Verhalten der Frau, daß die Sünde in die
Welt gekommen sei". So auch noch Burkard M. Zapff, *Jesus Sirach 25–51*, NEchtB 39
(Würzburg: Echter, 2010), 148.

47. Ein früherer Versuch, die hebräischen und griechischen Versionen auf andere
Weise zu verstehen, als dass angeblich Eva für den allgemeinen Tod verantwortlich
sei, findet sich bei Jack Levison, „Is Eve to blame? A Contextual Analysis of Sirach
25:24", *CBQ* 47 (1985): 617–23. Er meint, dass es sich bei der in Sir 25,24 genannten
Frau nicht um Eva, sondern entsprechend des Kontextes um die böse Frau handle.
Bei ihr sei der Beginn der Sünde. Dann aber wäre eben zu erwarten, dass hier nicht
absolut „von der Frau" gesprochen würde, sondern eben, wie Levinson ergänzen will,
„von der bösen Frau".

48. Vgl. Nuria Calduch-Benages, Joan Ferrer und Jan Liesen, *La sabiduría del
escriba: Edición diplomática de la versión siriaca del libro de Ben Sira según el Códice
Ambrosiano, con traducción española e inglesa / Wisdom of the Scribe: Diplomatic Edition of the Syriac Version of the Book of Ben Sira according to Codex Ambrosianus, with
Translations in Spanish and English*, Biblioteca Midrásica 26 (Estella: Verbo Divino,
2003), 39–40.

49. So Wicke-Reuter, *Göttliche Providenz*, S.156, unter Verweis auf ein Zitat von
John J.Collins, *Jewish Wisdom in the Hellenistic Age*, OTL (Louisville: Westminster
John Knox, 1997), 59: „Sirach 25:24 ascribes the original sin to Eve,… but this explanation of the origin of sin and death is anomalous and unsupported by anything else
in Ben Sira".

deutlich, dass der Tod von Anfang an zum menschlichen Leben gehört, und nicht auf eine wie auch immer geartete Ursprungssünde zurückgeht (vgl. vor allem Sir 17,1). Die Alternative zu dieser Sicht besteht in einer Deutung des Verses wie ihn die hebräische und griechische Fassung ebenfalls zulässt, wonach es hier grundsätzlich um die Folge jeder Sünde geht, unter der jedermann zu leiden hat. Dieses zeigt sich eben paradigmatisch in der Sünde der ersten Frau. Dann geht es hier nicht darum, dass der Tod, den jeder Mensch erleiden muss, eine Folge der Sünde der ersten Frau ist, sondern darum, dass Sünde grundsätzlich den Tod nach sich zieht. Dies ist dann aber nicht im absoluten Sinn zu verstehen, wonach es vorher keinen Tod gegeben hätte, sondern wohl im Sinne eines verfrühten Todes. Mit einer Frau begann sozusagen dieses Unheilsgeschehen und deshalb ist der Umgang mit der bösen Frau—letztere Charakterisierung ist wohl auch im moralischen Sinn zu verstehen—verhängnisvoll. In diese Richtung weist auch V.20, wo es um die Gefahr geht, auf eine schöne Frau hereinzufallen, eine Mahnung, die sich auch in der traditionellen Weisheit findet, z.B. Spr 7,5–27. So verstanden fügt sich die Aussage in die Reihe der anderen Aussagen über die böse Frau recht stimmig ein, geht es doch jeweils um eine Lebensminderung. Tatsächlich verlängert sich umgekehrt nach Sir 26,1 die Zahl der Tage eines Mannes, der sich einer guten Frau rühmen darf, ohne dass hier natürlich an eine unbegrenzte Verlängerung des Lebens gedacht ist. Die nicht mit einem Namen benannte erste Frau wird demnach hier zum Paradigma dafür, wie durch Sünde der Tod zu einem Menschen kommt und sein Leben verkürzt.

5. Der Sohn als Abbild seines Vaters

In einer weiteren, nicht sofort erkennbaren Weise wird auch in Sir 30,4 auf die biblische Urgeschichte Bezug genommen. Dort geht es um die Bedeutung, die ein Sohn für seinen Vater hat. Die hebräische Fassung ist nicht erhalten, deshalb bildet hier die griechische Fassung die Grundlage der Ausführungen. Dort heißt es über den wohlerzogenen Sohn: „Und stirbt sein Vater, ist es, als ob er nicht gestorben ist, denn einen ihm ähnlichen hat er nach sich hinterlassen", ἐτελεύτησεν αὐτοῦ ὁ πατὴρ καὶ ὡς οὐκ ἀπέθανεν ὅμοιον γὰρ αὐτῷ κατέλιπεν μετ' αὐτόν. Im Hintergrund dieser Vorstellung scheint Gen 5,3 zu stehen,[50] wo von Adam erzählt wird, dass

---

50. Zapff, *Jesus Sirach*, 187; möglicherweise stehen im Hintergrund auch ägyp-

er einen Sohn, ihm ähnlich, nach seinem Abbild zeugte. Allerdings besteht
dabei keine sprachliche Übereinstimmung zwischen der G-Fassung von
Gen 5,3 und Sir 30,4. Anders ist dies hingegen in Gen 1,26, wo G das
hebräische כדמותנו „uns ähnlich" mit καθ᾽ ὁμοίωσιν übersetzt. Während
nun in Gen 5,3 Grund der Ähnlichkeit des Sohnes mit dem Vater das Zeugungsgeschehen ist, so wird entsprechend dem Kontext von Sir 30,4 die
Ähnlichkeit durch ein vorgängiges Erziehungsgeschehen bewirkt. Dieses
Erziehungsgeschehen wiederum gewährleistet ein Weiterleben des Vaters
im Sohn über den individuellen Tod hinaus, so dass für ihn angesichts
des Todes für Trauer kein Anlass besteht. Vorausgesetzt wird hier also die
Formung eines Sohnes durch Erziehung, die eine Überwindung der Todesgrenze erlaubt, wofür das Faktum der Nachkommenschaft allein keinerlei
Gewähr bietet (vgl. auch Sir 41,8–12). Auch hier wiederum bleibt Sirach
seinem Ansatz treu, wonach der Tod das natürliche Ende des Menschen
ist, zeigt aber unter Rückgriff auf die biblische Urgeschichte bei gleichzeitiger Verknüpfung mit einem Erziehungsideal einen Weg auf, um den Tod
nicht fürchten zu müssen. Vielmehr wird Erziehung zu einem geistigen
Zeugungsgeschehen, welches die traditionelle Vorstellung eines Fortle-
bens, etwa des eigenen Namens in den Söhnen, bei weitem übertrifft.[51]

6. Des Menschen Schicksal

Ein weiterer Rückgriff auf die biblische Urgeschichte findet sich in Sir
33,10–15.[52] Hier geht es um das Schicksal des Menschen, welches ihm von
Gott zuteil wird.

---

tische Einflüsse, die der in Ägypten wirkende griechische Übersetzer kreativ verar-
beitet hat. Darauf verweist etwa Joachim Kügler, „Der Sohn als Abbild des Vaters.
Kulturgeschichtliche Notizen zu Sir 30,4–6", BN 107/108 (2001): 82: So erscheint der
Sohn dort „im Kontext der *Kamutef* Konstellation … als Wiederverkörperung des
Vaters, aber nicht nur seines Vaters, sondern genauer eines überindividuellen genea-
logischen Prinzips, das beiden gemeinsam ist und das vor dem Sohn in seinem Vater
verkörpert war".

51. Wicke-Reuter, *Göttliche Providenz*, 124, verweist in diesem Zusammenhang
auf Sir 16,1–4. Dort wird die im AT anzutreffende Hochschätzung des Kinderreich-
tums als Garantie, über den Tod hinaus Dauer zu haben, problematisiert. Dies gilt nur,
„sofern die Kinder selbst in Gottesfurcht und ohne Frevel ihren Weg gehen (V.1 f.)".

52. Eine ausführliche Interpretation der Verse insbesondere hinsichtlich der
Frage nach der hier anscheinend zu findenden Prädestinationslehre findet sich bei
Wicke-Reuter, *Göttliche Providenz*, 224–73.

Der Abschnitt gehört zu einem größeren Ganzen, in dem es um die Unterscheidung innerhalb gleicher Größen geht. So ist in V.7, der in MS E nur fragmentarisch erhalten ist, entsprechend G (und S) von verschiedenen Tagen die Rede, wiewohl alles Licht der Tage eines Jahres von der Sonne kommt: „Was (unterscheidet) einen Tag vom anderen, denn alles Licht eines Jahres (kommt) von der Sonne?"[53] Damit wird offensichtlich auf Gen 1,5 Bezug genommen, wo nach der Scheidung von Licht und Finsternis die Tagzählung beginnt und damit die Abhängigkeit aller sieben Tage in ihrer Unterschiedlichkeit vom Licht deutlich wird. Entsprechend V.8 wird die Unterscheidung der Tage dabei als Werk JHWHs gesehen, wobei es unter ihnen Versammlungstage gibt: ויש מהם מועד[ים]. Durch diesen Begriff wiederum greift Sirach ein Stichwort auf, das sich auch in der Beschreibung des vierten Schöpfungstages in Gen 1,14 findet, wo die Lichter am Himmelsgewölbe u.a. zur Bestimmung von Festzeiten, eben מועדים dienen. Im V.9 spricht Sirach davon, dass Gott „von ihnen einen segnete und heiligte" מהם] ב[רך והקדשו und nimmt damit allem Anschein nach auf die Segnung des siebten Tages in Gen 2,3 Bezug[54]. Dort ist bekanntlich davon die Rede, dass Gott den siebten Tag „segnete" ויברך und „heiligte" ויקדש. Ausgehend von dieser Unterscheidung von Tagen unterschiedlichen Charakters, die zwar alle vom Licht der einen Sonne bestimmt sind, nimmt nun Sirach in Vv.10–15 auch den Menschen und sein Geschick in den Blick. V.10 entspricht dabei V.7, insofern nun auch beim Menschen die allen Menschen eigene Gemeinsamkeit herausgestellt wird. Wiederum nimmt Sirach dabei Bezug auf die Schöpfungserzählungen und zwar auf Gen 2,7. Dabei entspricht vor allem V.10b vom Wortbestand her Gen 2,7a, ist allerdings passivisch formuliert. Dies ist wohl im Sinne eines *passivum divinum* zu verstehen: „und aus Staub ist der Mensch/Adam gebildet": ומן עפר נוצר אדם. Dieser Aussage wird im Vordersatz in Form eines *parallelismus membrorum* eine, zumindest auf den ersten Blick synonyme Aussage vorangestellt, die daraus eine für jeden Menschen in gleicher Weise geltende Aussage macht: „jedermann ist aus Lehmgeschirr": [וכל איש מכ[לי חמר. Notwendig war dieser Vorspann offensichtlich nicht nur aus formalen Gründen, sondern auch deshalb, weil in V.10b „Adam" als individuelle Persönlichkeit verstanden wird, so dass die in der Schöpfungsgeschichte auf Adam bezogene Aussage hier verallgemeinert wird. Noch deutlicher

---

53. מה יו[ם] יום כי כלו אור שונה [מ]על שמש] rekonstruiert nach G: διὰ τί ἡμέρα ἡμέρας ὑπερέχει καὶ πᾶν φῶς ἡμέρας ἐνιαυτοῦ ἀφ᾽ ἡλίου.

54. Wicke-Reuter, *Göttliche Providenz*, 236.

wird dies in der griechischen[55] und syrischen Fassung[56], wo von ἄνθρωποι πάντες bzw. ܒܪܢܫܐ ܟܠܗܘܢ ܒܪ „alle Menschen" gesprochen wird, so dass das, was für Adam gilt, eben auch für alle Menschen Geltung hat. Betont wird also hier, ähnlich wie bei den Tagen in V.7, die grundsätzliche Gleichheit aller Menschen qua Materie, von denen entsprechend Sir 17,1 gilt, dass sie zur Erde zurückkehren. Dass dabei in der hebräischen Fassung, soweit erkennbar, von „Lehmgeschirr" gesprochen wird, ein Begriff, der in Gen 2,7 nicht erscheint, hat noch einen weiteren Grund, auf den weiter unten zurückzukommen ist.

Der hebräische Text von V.11 ist vor allem im zweiten Teil des Verses nicht eindeutig. V.11a spricht davon, dass die Weisheit JHWHs die Menschen voneinander getrennt habe: חכמת יְי' תבדילם und V.11b, dass JHWH sie zu Bewohnern der Erde gemacht und ihre Wege geändert habe: וישם [...]ושנ [...]הא דרי אותם; dabei ist „ihre Wege" דרכיהם nur durch eine Marginalie bezeugt, die allerdings durch G bestätigt wird. Gedacht ist hier entsprechend der Völkertafel in Gen 10 wohl an die Ausbreitung der Menschheit in verschiedene Völker der Erde, die auf dem Erdboden wohnen.[57] In dieser Weise hat wohl auch die syrische Fassung den Vers verstanden, macht allerdings bereits in V.11a JHWH selbst zum Subjekt des Satzes und lässt gleichzeitig jene etwas unverständliche Formulierung vom „Verändern ihrer Wege" entfallen. Umgekehrt verfährt hier G. Sie spricht überhaupt nicht davon, dass Gott die Menschen zu Bewohnern der Erde gemacht hat, und bezieht allem Anschein nach die Unterscheidung der Menschen auf ihre Wege und damit ihre Schicksale:[58] „In der Fülle des Verstandes hat der Herr sie getrennt, und er hat ihre Wege verändert", ἐν πλήθει ἐπιστήμης κύριος διεχώρισεν αὐτοὺς καὶ ἠλλοίωσεν τὰς ὁδοὺς αὐτῶν. Das heißt, innerhalb der Versionen lägen hier unterschiedliche Deutungen vor. Wie der Vers nun auch immer zu verstehen ist, ob im Hinblick auf eine Unterscheidung der Menschen hinsichtlich ihres Wohnortes und

---

55. καὶ ἄνθρωποι πάντες ἀπὸ ἐδάφους καὶ ἐκ γῆς ἐκτίσθη Αδαμ „und alle Menschen sind aus Lehm und aus Erde wurde Adam erschaffen".

56. ܘܐܦ ܒܪ ܐܢܫܐ ܟܠܗܘܢ ܡܢ ܛܝܢܐ ܐܬܒܪܝܘ. ܘܡܢ ܥܦܪܐ ܐܬܒܪܝ ܐܕܡ. „Und alle Menschen sind aus Lehm gemacht und aus Staub wurde Adam erschaffen".

57. Gelegentlich wird ein Bezug auf Gen 11,1–9 vermutet, jedoch klingt hier nichts von der dortigen negativen Akzentuierung einer Zerstreuung der frühen Menschheit an; vgl. Wicke-Reuter, *Göttliche Providenz*, 245–46.

58. Wicke-Reuter, *Göttliche Providenz*, 245, interpretiert דרכיהם als unterschiedliche Wege, „die die Rechtschaffenen und Frommen einerseits und die Frevler und Gottlosen andererseits einschlagen".

völkischen Charakters, so S, oder ihres Geschicks, so wohl G, in jedem Fall entspricht V.11 der Aussage in V.8, wonach es unter den grundsätzlich gleichen Menschen Unterschiede gibt, die durch die Weisheit JHWHs bzw. JHWH bestimmt sind.

In V 12a lässt sich die fragmentarische hebräische Fassung mittels der weithin gleichlautenden griechischen und syrischen Fassung etwa folgendermaßen rekonstruieren: „Von ihnen segnete und erhöhte er welche und von ihnen heiligte er welche und ließ sie ihm nahen"[59]. Der Vers greift dabei zwei Stichworte auf, die bereits in V.9 verwendet wurden, nämlich „segnen", und „heiligen". Durch das doppelte „von ihnen" מהם (entsprechend ܡܢܗܘܢ in S) sind offensichtlich zwei Gruppen von Menschen im Blick. Bei „segnen" und „erhöhen" והרים entsprechend ἀνύψωσεν / רגתא ist nicht zuletzt aufgrund des sprachlichen Anklangs harim wohl an Abraham und seine Nachkommen zu denken.[60] Damit aber dürfte hier die Berufung Abrahams in Gen 12,3 im Blick sein.[61] Die zweite Gruppe bezieht sich durch das Stichwort „heiligen" und „nahen lassen" aller Wahrscheinlichkeit nach auf das aaronidische Priestertum, wird doch letztere Formulierung mit dem Subjekt Gott ausschließlich in diesem Kontext verwendet (vgl. Ex 29,8; Num 16,5.9).[62] Im Unterschied zu V.9, wo ja nicht von einer Verfluchung der Tage gesprochen wird, ist in V.12bα nun ausdrücklich von einer Verfluchung von Menschen und deren Erniedrigung die Rede. Die zum Teil rekonstruierte hebräische Version lässt sich folgendermaßen übersetzen: „Von ihnen verfluchte und erniedrigte er welche und stürzte sie um von ihrem Tun".[63] Ist V.12aα vor dem Hintergrund der Segnung und Erhebung Abrahams zu lesen und zu verstehen, könnte dies

---

59. [מהם ברך והרי]ם מה [ו]מהם הקדיש וא[ליו הקריבם] rekonstruiert nach G: ἐξ αὐτῶν εὐλόγησεν καὶ ἀνύψωσεν καὶ ἐξ αὐτῶν ἡγίασεν καὶ πρὸς αὐτὸν ἤγγισεν.

60. Gelegentlich wird die Segnung und Verfluchung im Rahmen der Fluch- und Segensverheißung über Kanaan und Sem in Gen 9,25ff. interpretiert, so dass sich V.12a auf Israel und V.12b auf die Völker Kanaans beziehen würde. Belege bei Wicke-Reuter, *Göttliche Providenz*, 247, Anm. 107. Allerdings ist von einer Segnung in Gen 9,24ff. nur im Hinblick auf Gott („Gesegnet sei JHWH, der Gott Sems"), nicht aber auf Sem die Rede. Anders verhält es sich hingegen in Gen 12,3, wo tatsächlich von zwei Menschengruppen gesprochen wird, von denen die eine gesegnet, die andere aber verflucht wird.

61. So bereits Di Lella, *Wisdom*, 400; Zapff, *Jesus Sirach*, 214.

62. So bereits Wicke-Reuter, *Göttliche Providenz*, 248.

63. [מהם קלל ו]השפילם ודחפם ממעבד]יה[ם] rekonstruiert nach G: ἀπ' αὐτῶν κατηράσατο καὶ ἐταπείνωσεν καὶ ἀνέστρεψεν αὐτοὺς ἀπὸ στάσεως αὐτῶν.

auch für V.12bα gelten. So verwendet Sirach hier wohl die (rekonstruierte) Wurzel קלל „verfluchen", die mit dem Subjekt JHWH in Gen 12,3
das erste Mal erscheint, während die Rede vom Erniedrigen wohl eher der
Entsprechung zur Erhöhung in V.12aα und nicht einem bestimmten biblischen Bezugszusammenhang geschuldet ist.[64] Es handelt sich dann um all
diejenigen, die Abraham verwünschen. V.12bβ macht bezüglich der Interpretation einige Probleme. Setzt man ihn in Parallele zu V.12aβ, so geht es
hier offensichtlich um eine Entfernung aus dem Amt. Womöglich stehen
im Hintergrund konkrete zeitgeschichtliche Entwicklungen, insbesondere hinsichtlich des Kampfes um das Hohepriesteramt. Auffällig ist, dass
hier die syrische Fassung deutlich abweicht, wenn sie davon spricht, dass
JHWH sie „aus ihren Wohnungen entwurzelt" ܘܐܢܐ ܡܢ ܩܝܐ ܐܩܪ ܐܢܘܢ
und dabei mit der Wurzel ܩܝܐ inhaltlich auf V.11 zurückverweist, wo von
den Bewohnern der Erde die Rede ist. Hier könnte nun tatsächlich auf die
Vertreibung der Kanaaniter zugunsten Israels Bezug genommen werden.

Die Segnung und Heiligung bestimmter Tage wird hier also auf die
Auswahl bestimmter Menschen bzw. Menschengruppen—sei es das Got-
tesvolk als Ganzes, sei es das Priestertum in Israel—bezogen und damit
Heilsgeschichte in Bezug zur Schöpfungsgeschichte gesetzt. Während es
keine verfluchten Tage gibt, gibt es unter der Menschheit solche, die unter
dem Fluch und der Erniedrigung Gottes stehen, ohne dass dafür konkrete
Gründe genannt werden.[65]

V.13 stellt einen Rückbezug zu V.10 her, wo davon die Rede ist, dass
jeder Mensch aus Lehmgeschirr ist. Hier wird nun der weitere Sinn dieser
Ergänzung deutlich. Der Mensch ist nicht nur aus Lehm geschaffen, sondern auch hinsichtlich seines Seins und seiner Existenz „wie Lehm in der
Hand des Formers, gehalten nach dem Gefallen"[66]. Es ist natürlich leicht
zu erkennen, dass Sirach hier eine im AT mehrfach verwendete Metaphorik aufgreift (vgl. Jes 29,16; 45,9 und 64,7). Besonders enge Verbindungen

---

64. Wicke-Reuter, *Göttliche Providenz*, 249, meint, dass V.12bβ als Gegenpart zu
V.12aβ zu deuten „und als eine Anspielung auf die Verstoßung einer anderen Gruppe
aus dem Priesteramt zu verstehen" sei. Im Hintergrund könnte dann auch Num 16
stehen, vgl. Zapff, ebenda.

65. Die damit implizierte Aussage zielt in jedem Fall auf die Souveränität Gottes
gegenüber dem menschlichen Geschick in gleichzeitiger Ablehnung des Wirkens
einer wankelmütigen Schicksalsmacht (Tyche) im hellenistischen Umfeld, vgl. Zapff,
Jesus Sirach, 213–14.

66. ‏[כחומר ביד ה]יוצר לאחוז כרצון‎ rekonstruiert nach G: ὡς πηλὸς κεραμέως ἐν
χειρὶ αὐτοῦ.

bestehen zum Töpfergleichnis in Jer 18,4.6. Hier finden sich etwa die Formulierung כחמר ביד היוצר „wie Lehm in der Hand des Formers" und auch
die Vorstellung, dass der Töpfer jeweils nach seinem Gefallen handelt,[67]
vgl. V.4. Nun allerdings wird diese Vorstellung, die sich bei Jeremia kollektiv auf Israel bezieht, auf den einzelnen Menschen übertragen, von dem es
bereits in V.10 heißt, dass er ein Lehmgefäß ist. Zu welchem Zweck nun
dieses Bild auf den Menschen übertragen wird, davon spricht der Nach-
satz in V.13bβ. Die hebräische Version ist hier nur schwer verständlich:
„um vor ihn gestellt zu werden als Anteil" להתיצב מפני[ו] חלק. Vermutlich
geht es dabei um die Zuteilung des persönlichen Geschicks, wie aus der
griechischen Version erkennbar wird, die hier mit: „um ihnen (den Menschen) entsprechend seiner (nämlich Gottes) Entscheidung zu erstatten"
ἀποδοῦναι αὐτοῖς κατὰ τὴν κρίσιν αὐτοῦ. Dies wiederum würde sich in den
gesamten Sinnduktus einfügen, wo V.12 vom unterschiedlichen Geschick
der Menschen spricht, das durch Gott bedingt ist. Dass die hebräische
Vorlage schwierig zu verstehen ist, bestätigt indirekt auch die syrische
Version, die hier übersetzt: „um ihn zu" oder „über all seine(n) Werken zu
stellen", ܠܗܡܚܬܐ ܟܗܠ ܟܗܪܬܗܡ. Entweder geht es hier um den Herrscher-
auftrag des Menschen oder aber es setzt sich das Bild vom Töpfer fort, der
seine fertigen Gefäße zu seinen übrigen Gefäßen stellt, so eben auch Gott
den Menschen.

In jedem Fall wird hier Gott nicht nur zum Urheber der materiellen
Existenz des Menschen, sondern auch zum Former seines Geschicks. Die
EÜ paraphrasiert dies mit der Aussage: „von ihm (also von Gott) erhält
er (also der Mensch) sein Geschick". Es deutet sich damit so etwas wie
eine Prädestination des Menschen an, insofern das Bild von der Formung
des Menschen aus dem Staub des Ackerbodens in Gen 2,7 mit dem Töpfergleichnis in Jeremia verbunden wird und sich nun nicht mehr allein
auf die materielle Konsistenz des Menschen bezieht, sondern auch auf
sein Geschick.[68] Vv.14–15 schließlich verbinden das in V.12 beschriebene, gegensätzliche Geschick des Menschen mit einer grundsätzlichen

---

67. Wicke-Reuter, *Göttliche Providenz*, 257, zieht daraus die Schlussfolgerung,
dass es hier nicht nur um die Tatsache gehe, dass Gott das menschliche Geschick
in deterministischer Weise bestimme, sondern auch die Souveränität besitze, dieses
ändern zu können: Gottes Ratschlüsse sind nicht unabänderlich.

68. Vgl. Wicke-Reuter, *Göttliche Providenz*, 259: „So wie der Töpfer den Ton nach
seinem Willen formt, so bestimmt Gott, indem er den Menschen schafft, zugleich sein
Leben, indem er ihm sein ‚Teil' festsetzt".

Aussage über die Schöpfungsordnung, ein Gedanke, der sich im Sirachbuch an verschiedener Stelle findet (vgl. Sir 42,21–25). Demnach besteht
die Schöpfungsordnung aus Gegensätzlichkeiten, die jeweils paarweise
einander gegenüberstehen, womit, wie immer wieder beobachtet wurde,
Sirach einen Gedanken Chrysipps aufgreift.[69] Auch das unterschiedliche
Geschick des Menschen entspricht der insgesamt von Sirach als harmo-
nisch dargestellten Schöpfungsordnung. Nicht nur der Mensch ist damit
Teil der Schöpfungsordnung, sondern auch sein Geschick. Die sich daraus
ergebende Konsequenz besteht darin, sich in diese Unterschiedlichkeit
zu fügen. Wicke-Reuter fasst dies folgendermaßen zusammen: „Was
bei der Erfahrung der Wechselfälle des menschlichen Lebens zunächst
widersprüchlich erschien, wird nun im Aufblick zur Schönheit der gottge-
schaffenen Natur als sinnvoll begründet. Bei genauem Hinsehen erschließt
sich die hinter dem Phänomen liegende Ordnung".[70]

Zusammenfassend lässt sich sagen, dass Sirach die biblische Vorgabe
zwar kennt und benutzt, aber nichtsdestoweniger sie seiner Sicht des
Menschen ein- und unterordnet. Dabei wird insbesondere die Souveränität Gottes herausgestellt, der sich der einzelne Mensch zu unterwerfen
hat. Dennoch besteht für den Menschen die Möglichkeit, sich gegenüber
dieser Vorgabe zu verhalten, so dass der Mensch im Rahmen der Schöpfungsordnung also nicht gänzlich unfrei ist. Die Erkenntnisfähigkeit des
Menschen wird als Gabe und Aufgabe Gottes ausdrücklich hervorgehoben
und geschätzt. Trotz unverkennbarer Einflüsse stoischen Denkens, bleibt
damit Sirach hinsichtlich seines Menschenbildes zumindest zentralen
biblischen Vorgaben treu. Man kann ihn demnach als wirklichen Schriftgelehrten bezeichnen, der angesichts zeitgenössischer Herausforderungen
auf der Basis der biblischen Überlieferungen eine Sicht des Menschen entwickelt, die sich zwischen Determination und absoluter Freiheit bewegt
und damit vielleicht auch für aktuelle Fragestellungen einiges an Potential
bereit hält.

---

69. Chrysipp: „Denn da das Gute dem Bösen konträr entgegengesetzt ist, müssen
notwendig beide sich einander gegenüberstehen, und als etwas zusammenbestehen,
was sich sozusagen gegeneinander anstemmt und sich dadurch wechselseitig stützt
und bedingt", Gell. VII 1,2.6, zitiert nach Otto Kaiser, *Des Menschen Glück und Gottes
Gerechtigkeit. Studien zur spätbiblischen Weisheit und Hermeneutik*, BZAW 392
(Berlin: de Gruyter, 2008), 133.

70. Wicke-Reuter, *Göttliche Providenz*, 267.

The Explicit Precepts Referred to by Ben Sira

Maurice Gilbert, SJ

ZUSAMMENFASSUNG: Elf Texte im Sirachbuch beziehen sich explizit auf Gebote der Tora. Für jede dieser Stellen werden im Folgenden die hebräischen Texte mit den antiken griechischen, lateinischen und syrischen Versionen konfrontiert. Es gibt zwei Verweise auf den Dekalog (Sir 3,6 und 23,23), zwei auf Lev 19 (Sir 19,17 und 28,6–7), zwei auf Gen 2,17 oder 3,19 (Sir 14,11.12.17 und 41,3–4), zwei beziehen sich auf Priestertum und Kult (Sir 7,31 und 35 [32],1–7), einer auf bedürftige Personen (Sir 29:1–2a.9.11) und zwei auf biblische Charaktere (Sir 45:7 und 46:13–14). All diese Texte sind über das gesamte Sirachbuch verstreut, und die meisten erheben die Forderung, die Menschenwürde zu wahren.

In 1970, Gerhard von Rad wrote in his famous book *Weisheit in Israel* these two statements:

No, the Torah is not a subject of particular interest to Sirach. He knows about it, it has a part to play, but basically for Sirach it is of relevance only in so far as it is to be understood on the basis of, or as it is otherwise connected with, the great complex of wisdom teachings.

All this should not, of course, be taken to mean that the Torah plays only a negligible part in Sirach's thought. It is simply a question of determining the theological point at which it exercises its specific function. One is immediately struck by the way in which it always appears in remarkably formal terms, as an entity *sui generis*, as "the Torah," "the commandments." Nowhere does Sirach deal with it in any greater detail, but he does consider it necessary to refer to it.[1]

---

1. I quote the English translation: Gerhard von Rad, *Wisdom in Israel*, trans. James D. Martin (London: SCM, 1972), 247, 244.

These statements could be discussed, of course, especially in dialogue with many studies on the relation between torah and wisdom that have appeared since von Rad's book.[2] But this is not the only question to pursue. It seems to me that there are several texts of Ben Sira where the connection between his teaching and explicit precepts of the torah has something to say about his social and moral understanding of life.[3]

---

2. See Maurice Gilbert, "L'éloge de la Sagesse (Siracide 24)," *RTL* 5 (1976): 345–48; Johannes Marböck, "Gesetz und Weisheit: Zum Verständnis des Gesetzes bei Jesus ben Sira," *BZ* 20 (1976): 1–21; Eckhard J. Schnabel, *Law and Wisdom from Ben Sira to Paul: A Tradition Historical Enquiry into the Relation of Law, Wisdom, and Ethics,* WUNT 2/16 (Tübingen: Mohr, 1985); José Ramón Busto Saiz, "Sabiduría y Torá en Jesús ben Sira," *EstBib* 52 (1994): 229–39; Joseph Blenkinsopp, *Wisdom and Law in the Old Testament: The Ordering of Life in Israel and Early Judaism,* rev. ed. (Oxford: Oxford University Press, 1995), 140–45; Georg Sauer, "Weisheit und Tora in qumranischer Zeit," in *Weisheit ausserhalb der kanonischen Weisheitsschriften,* ed. Bernd Janowski, Veröffentlichungen der Wissenschaftlichen Gesellschaft für Theologie 10 (Gütersloh: Kaiser, 1996), 107–27; Gian Luigi Prato, "Sapienza e Torah in ben Sira: Meccanismi comparativi culturali e conseguenze ideologico-religiose," *RStB* 10 (1998): 129–51; Shannon Burkes, "Wisdom and Law: Choosing Life in Ben Sira and Baruch," *JSJ* 30 (1999): 253–76; Marcello Milani, "Rilettura sapienziale della Legge nel recupero dell'"identità nazionale' di Israele," *RStB* 15 (2003): 109–31; Tiziano Lorenzin, "Sapienza e legge: L'autoelogio della sapienza (Sir 24)," *PaVi* 48 (2003): 23–30; Timo Veijola, "Law and Wisdom: The Deuteronomistic Heritage in Ben Sira's Teaching of the Law," in *Ancient Israel, Judaism, and Christianity in Contemporary Perspective: Essays in Memory of Karl-Johan Illman,* ed. Jacob Neussner et al., Studies in Judaism (Lanham, MD: University Press of America, 2006), 429–48; Friedrich V. Reiterer, "Das Verhältnis der חכמה zur תורה im Buch Ben Sira: Kriterien zur gegenseitigen Bestimmung," in *Studies in the Book of Ben Sira: Papers of the Third International Conference on the Deuterocanonical Books, Shime'on Centre, Pápa, Hungary, 18–20 May, 2006,* ed. Géza G. Xeravitz and Jozsef Zsengellér, JSJSup 127 (Leiden: Brill, 2008), 97–133; Angelo Passaro, "Torah e Sapienza: Ben Sira ovvero della metamorfosi del sapiente," *RStB* 22 (2008): 103–11; Benjamin G. Wright, "Torah and Sapiential Pedagogy in the Book of Ben Sira," in *Wisdom and Torah: The Reception of 'Torah' in the Wisdom Literature of the Second Temple Period,* ed. Bernd Schipper and D. Andrew Teeter, JSJSup 163 (Leiden: Brill, 2013), 157–86; Pancratius C. Beentjes, "The Book of Ben Sira: Some New Perspectives at the Dawn of the Twenty-First Century," in *"With All Your Soul Fear The Lord" (Sir 7:27): Collected Essays on the Book of Ben Sira II,* ed. Pancratius C. Beentjes, CBET 87 (Leuven: Peeters, 2017), 13–18.

3. I simply call to mind that תורה appears twelve times in the Hebrew fragments of Ben Sira, מצוה nine times, and חק twenty-two times. In the Greek version of his grandson, νόμος appears twenty-four times and ἐντολή/ἐντολαί eighteen times. In the Greek additions, νόμος appears only once and ἐντολαί twice. On חק, see Marko

As far as I can see, only Eckhard J. Schnabel analyzed some of these texts under the title "The Function of the Law."[4] He mentioned, for instance, Sir 19:17; 23:23; 28:6–7; 29:9, 11; 35:1–7 as "Norms of Moral and Social Behavior" (46–49); Sir 7:31; 35:6–7 under the subtitle "Rule for Cult and Jurisdiction" (51–52); and Sir 45:1–5 with the subtitle "Foundation for Teaching" (52–55). I will come back to these texts, including also a few others: Sir 3:6; 14:11–12, 17; 29:1–2a; 41:3–4; 45:7; 46:13–14.[5]

Here all Ben Sira's texts in which a reference to an explicit precept of the torah appears will be presented and analyzed in groups sharing some similarities. Since the transmission of these texts is sometimes complicated, four versions, three in English, will be proposed, using recent translations.[6]

1. Two References to the Decalogue

3:6

Hebrew: [lacking, except] who honors his mother.
Greek: He who glorifies his father will prolong his days, and he who listens to the Lord will give rest to his mother.

Martilla, "'Statute' or 'Covenant'? Remarks on the Rendering of the Word חק in the Greek Ben Sira," in *Scripture in Transition: Essays on the Septuagint, Hebrew Bible, and the Dead Sea Scrolls in Honor of Raija Sollamo*, ed. Anssi Voitila and Jutta Jokiranta, JSJSup 126 (Leiden: Brill, 2008), 73–87.

4. Schnabel, *Law and Wisdom*, 46–55.

5. In my *status quaestionis*, Maurice Gilbert, "Siracide," *DBSup* 12 (1996): 1389–437, esp. col. 1429, I mentioned a few of these texts, namely, Sir 3:1–16; 7:31; 23:23; 28:7; 29:9; 35:6–7.

6. Hebrew: Patrick W. Skehan and Alexander A. Di Lella, *The Wisdom of Ben Sira: A New Translation with Notes*, AB 39 (New York: Doubleday, 1987). Greek: Benjamin G. Wright, "Wisdom of Iesous Son of Sirach," in *A New English Translation of the Septuagint and the Other Greek Translations Traditionally Included under That Title*, ed. Albert Pietersma and Benjamin G. Wright (Oxford: Oxford University Press, 2007), 715–62. Vulgate: Francesco Vattioni, ed., *Ecclesiastico: Testo ebraico con apparato critico e versioni greca, latina e siriaca*, Pubblicazioni del Seminario di Semitistica 1 (Naples: Istituto Orientale di Napoli, 1968); the text of the Vulgate edited there was prepared by Jean Gribomont and Guy Dominique Sixdenier; see pp. liii–liv. Syriac: Nuria Calduch-Benages, Joan Ferrer, and Jan Liesen, eds., *La Sabiduría del escriba/ Wisdom of the Scribe: Edición diplomática de la Peshitta del libro de Ben Sira según el Códice Ambrosiano con la traducción española e inglesa/Diplomatic Edition of the Peshitta of the Book of Ben Sira according to Codex Ambrosianus with Translations in Spanish and English*, Biblioteca Midrásica 26, 2nd ed. (Estella: Verbo Divino, 2015).

Latin: qui honorat patrem suum vita vivet longiore et qui obaudit patrem[7] refrigerabit matri.

Syriac: He who honors his father, his days will be numerous, and he who honors his mother obtains good rewards from God.

After two introductory chapters, on wisdom and fear of the Lord and on conditions to be a true disciple (Sir 1–2), Sir 3:1–16 comments on the fourth commandment of the Decalogue (Exod 20:12; Deut 5:16).[8] The main problem of 3:1–16 is that the Hebrew text (MS A) begins with the two last words of 3:6b and that 3:7 is lacking in Hebrew.[9] According to the Greek version, 3:1–16 is clearly a teaching addressed to the disciples. After two introductory verses, 3:3–7 presents the same structure "He who." Only from 3:8, a disciple (singular) is addressed (3:8, 10, 12–15). Therefore the context of 3:6 shows a normative teaching that has to be received by the disciple.

Now, the transmission of 3:6 is full of variations. Only the Greek version refers to the precept of the Decalogue, as mentioned above. Even if Andrzej Kondracki prefers the Syriac version, the Greek one is sure, at least for ὁ εἰσακούων κυρίου. In 3:6a, ὁ δοξάζων is not the verb of Exod 20:12 and Deut 5:16, where the verb is τιμάω, but this verb comes in 3:3, 5a, 7a, 8a, whereas ὁ δοξάζων appears in 3:4. This is just a stylistic variation.

The key point of 3:1–16, expressed from verse 12, is the respect and care of parents when they become old. Therefore the Decalogue precept is used in a context of sympathy toward old parents: צדקה/ἐλεημοσύνη (3:14a), which means charity toward people who have lost their strength.

---

7. MS H: qui obaudit domino (Munich eighth–ninth century, corrected on the Gr during the fourth or the fifth century).

8. See Reinhold Bohlen, *Die Ehrung der Eltern bei Ben Sira: Studien zur Motivation und Interpretation eines familienethischen Grundwertes in frühhellenistischer Zeit,* TThSt51 (Trier: Paulinus Verlag, 1991); Andrzej Kondracki, "La צדקה che espia i peccati: Studio esegetico di Sir 3,1–4,10" (PhD diss., Pontifical Biblical Institute, 1996), 3–45 [textual criticism: 15–18 for Sir 3:6]; Jeremy Corley, "Respect and Care for Parents in Sirach 3:1–16," in *Family and Kinship in the Deuterocanonical and Cognate Literature,* ed. Angelo Passaro, DCL.Y 2012/2013 (Berlin: de Gruyter, 2013), 139–72. Theophil Middendorp, *Die Stellung Jesu ben Siras zwischen Judentum und Hellenismus* (Leiden: Brill, 1973), 59, speaks of Ben Sira's neglect of the Decalogue apart from the command to honor parents.

9. Sir 3:7a comes from Gr II.

23:23

Hebrew: [lacking]
Greek: Now, first, she disobeyed the Law of the Most High, and second, she committed a wrong against her husband and third, she committed adultery by an illicit act and presented children by another man.
Latin: Primo enim in lege Altissimi incredibilis fuit et secundo virum suum dereliquit. Tertio in adulterio fornicata est et ex alio viro filios statuit sibi
Syriac: First, she has been unfaithful to the Law of God and second, to the husband of her youth and third, in (committing) {the fornication of}[10] adultery: by a stranger she has raised a child.

Sirach 3:6 was at the beginning of Ben Sira's teaching; 23:23 perhaps concludes the first redaction of his book. Both texts concern family problems, here an adulteress. Again the Hebrew text is lacking, but, contrary to 3:6, the ancient versions have the same interpretation. In 23:23a, the reference is again to a precept of the Decalogue (Exod 20:14; Deut 5:18) applied to a woman.

Sirach 23:23 is inserted in a large pericope starting in 22:27. This verse opens a prayer of the master asking the Lord to control his tongue and his sexuality (22:27–23:6). Then Ben Sira proposes his teaching on these two matters: first, on ways of speaking to be avoided and here he addresses himself to the disciples (23:7–15); second, on sexual sins committed by men (23:16–21) and finally by women (23:22–27), in both cases without any address to the disciple.[11]

It seems that, according to 23:22–23, the woman acted without the knowledge of her husband, and her adultery was fruitful: she gave birth to a child (23:22) or even to children (23:23d). It is not clear if the husband was impotent: she gave him an heir (23:22b).

That woman will be prosecuted by the assembly, and this supposes that she was caught in the act, like the adulteress of John 8:2–11. Note that,

---

10. "{}words in the manuscript omitted for the sake of the translation" (Calduch-Benages, Ferrer, and Liesen, *Sabiduría del escriba*, 62).

11. On Sir 23:22–27, see Ibolya Balla, *Ben Sira on Family, Gender, and Sexuality*, DCLS 8 (Berlin: de Gruyter, 2011), 130–37. Nuria Calduch-Benages, "Ben Sira 23:27: A Pivotal Verse," in *Wisdom for Life: Essays Offered to Honor Prof. Maurice Gilbert, SJ on the Occasion of His Eightieth Birthday*, ed. Nuria Calduch-Benages, BZAW 445 (Berlin: de Gruyter, 2014), 186–200.

as in John 8, the adulterer is not apprehended, and this is not according to the torah (Lev 20:10; Deut 22:22). But here the emphasis of Ben Sira is on the woman.

Lastly, she "committed a wrong." In the LXX of the Pentateuch, the verb πλημμελέω always translates a word of the root אשם, which indicates an offense, a trespass, a fault, guilt. In the Hebrew fragments of Ben Sira, אשם appears in 9:13c, and the root מעל, "perfidy, perfidiousness, treachery," in 10:7b; 38:10a. In short, the behavior of that adulterous wife was unjust.

2. Two References to Leviticus 19

19:17[12]

> **Hebrew:** [lacking]
> **Greek:** Question your fellow before threatening, and give a place to the Law of the Most High.
> **Latin:** [17] Corripe proximum antequam commineris [18] et da locum timori Altissimi
> **Syriac:** Reprove an evildoer who deals falsely with many and do not believe him in whatever he says.[13]

This verse comes at the end of a teaching that begins in 19:13. Ben Sira speaks to a disciple who heard about a friend or a fellow accused of having committed a wrong: do not believe it too quickly, but go and speak to him in order to clarify the point. Verse 17 concludes with an explicit reference to Lev 19:16–18:

> [16] You shall not go around as a slanderer among your people, and you shall not profit by the blood of your neighbor: I am the LORD. [17] You shall not hate in your heart anyone of your kin; you shall reprove your neighbor or you will incur guilt yourself. [18] You shall not take vengeance or bear a grudge against any of your people.... (NRSV)

Here again the Hebrew text is lacking. The Latin version, instead of "the law of the Most High," has *timori Altissimi*. As Joseph Ziegler observed,

---

12. On Sir 19,13–17, see James L. Kugel, "On Hidden Hatred and Open Reproach: Early Exegesis of Leviticus 19:17," *HTR* 80 (1987): 43–61; Jeremy Corley, *Ben Sira's Teaching on Friendship*, BJS 316 (Providence: Brown Judaic Studies, 2002), 155–73.

13. This is not in fact a translation of Sir 19:17, but another reading of Sir 19:15.

the same change appears in Sir 28:7 (Vulg. 8) and 37:12 (Vulg. 15).[14] The Syriac version does not truly translate 19:17.

In the expanded Greek version (Gr II), there is an addition: γινόμενος ἄμηνις, "do not be angry" or more literally: "becoming without resentment," which is an allusion to Lev 19:18: ולא־תטר/καὶ οὐ μηνιεῖς: these two verbs, Hebrew and Greek, mean "to keep resentment or grudge." This Lucianic Greek addition anticipated Sir 28:7a; and it is worthy to note that the end of Lev 19:18 has the first mention of the precept of loving your neighbor as yourself.

28:6–7[15]

> Hebrew: [lacking]
> Greek: [6] Remember the end of things, and cease to be at enmity remember[16] corruption and death, and cleave to the commandments. [7] Remember commandments, and do not be irate with your fellow, and remember[17] the covenant of the Most High, and overlook a mistake.
> Latin: [6] memento novissimorum et desine inimicari [7] Tabitudo enim et mors imminet in mandatis [8] ‹Memorare› timorem Dei et non irascaris ‹proximo› [9] Memorare testamenti Altissimi et despice ignorantiam proximi
> Syriac: [6] Remember death and set aside enmity and (remember) Sheol and perdition and refrain from sinning. [7] Remember the commandment and do not hate your companion before God and give to him what is lacking to him.

Here again the Hebrew text is lacking. In the Greek version of 28:7a, "commandments" is in the plural, but the singular appears in some textual traditions and in Syriac, as Ziegler mentioned. The Latin version *timorem Dei*, as explained above, could also be in favor of the singular. In 28:7b, the Greek version has διαθήκην ὑψίστου. If we agree with Marko Martilla, the Hebrew text should have been written חק עליון.[18]

---

14. Joseph Ziegler, ed., *Sapientia Iesu Filii Sirach*, SVTG 12.2 (Göttingen: Vandenhoeck & Ruprecht, 1965), 213.

15. On this text, see Nuria Calduch-Benages, "Es mejor perdonar que guardar rencor: Estudio de Sir 27,30–28,8," *Greg* 81 (2000): 419–39.

16. Lacking in Greek.

17. Lacking in Greek.

18. Martilla, "'Statute' or 'Covenant'?"

27:30–28:7 is an invitation given to the disciple not to keep resentment toward a neighbor but to forgive him. This teaching is unparalleled in the Old Testament, though Lev 19:17 advises avoiding sin by offering reproof toward an erring neighbor, and more similarly, Ps 37:8 commands refraining from anger and forsaking wrath. Every Christian will remember the same teaching of Jesus (Matt 6:12, 14–15; 18:35; Eph 4:32; Col 3:13), and indeed the Syriac of 28:7d seems to echo Matt 5:42; Luke 6:30 (cf. Deut 15:8).

Grudge or rancor is the main theme: the word or the verb appear in 27:30a at the beginning of the verse, then in 28:5a, and finally in 28:7a. Instead of resentment, Ben Sira considers that compassion (ἔλεος) is the right behavior (28:4a).

3. Two references to Genesis 2:17 (3:19)

14:11, 12, 17[19]

> **Hebrew:** [11] My son, use freely whatever you have, and enjoy it as best you can. [12] Remember that death does not tarry, nor have you been told the grave's appointed time. [17] All flesh grows old like a garment; the age-old law is: all must die.
>
> **Greek:** [11] Child, even as you have, treat yourself well, and bring offerings to the Lord worthily. [12] Remember that death will not tarry, and the covenant of Hades has not been shown to you. [17] All flesh becomes like a garment, for the covenant of old is, "By death you shall die!"
>
> **Latin:** [11] Fili si habes benefac tecum et Deo *bonas*[20] oblationes *offer* [12] *Memor esto* quoniam mors non tardat et testamentum inferorum quia demonstratum est tibi testamentum enim huius mundi morte morietur [18] omnis caro sicut faenum veterascit
>
> **Syriac:** [11] If you have (something), my son, attend yourself and if you have (something), do well to yourself. [12] Remember that up till now you did not see death and the decree of Sheol was not visible for you. [17] Because all human beings fail with age and the generations of the world die away.

---

19. On Sir 14:11–19, see Maurice Gilbert, "Qohelet et Ben Sira," in *Qohelet in the Context of Wisdom*, ed. Antoon Schoors, BETL 136 (Leuven: Peeters, 1998), 171–78.

20. See Vattioni, *Ecclesiastico*, liv: "les éléments probablement corrompus ont été imprimés en italiques."

14:11–19 is addressed to the disciple. After a description of an envious miser (14:3–10), Ben Sira invites his disciple to enjoy life with his possessions and to be generous to friends. The argument of the master, who did not have any perspective of an afterlife, is that death is inevitable and, therefore, better to be happy in the meantime.

Manuscript A has the Hebrew text, and, for the three verses 14:11, 12, 17, there is no textual problem. Note that in 14:12b, the English translation "the grave's appointed time" covers in Hebrew וחוק לשאול. Note again the Hebrew text of 14:17b וחוק עולם גוע יגוע. The expression גוע יגוע is translated into Greek as θανάτῳ ἀποθανῇ. The Hebrew formula of 14:17b never appears elsewhere in the Old Testament. It is possible that Ben Sira refers to Gen 2:17, where the double verb is מות. His grandson used the Greek way of translating Gen 2:17 in the LXX.

The Greek version, followed by the Latin one, has in 14:11b a reading that seems out of context; in any case, the Syriac version is in agreement with the Hebrew text. Again in 14:12b, 17b Greek and Latin, διαθήκη/testamentum translate חוק, like in Sir 28:7b, as already mentioned above.[21]

In 14:12, 17, Ben Sira reminds his disciple of the universal law of human death, probably referring to Gen 2:17. Genesis 3:19 is behind it, but not textually alluded to. The reason is not clear why Ben Sira does not employ the vocabulary of Gen 2–3 here, but perhaps it is simply for poetic variation.

41:3–4[22]

Hebrew: [3] Fear not death, the decree for you; remember it embraces those before you and after.[23] [4] From God this is the decree for all flesh; why then should you reject the Law of the Most High?
Greek: [3] Do not be wary of death's judgment; remember those before you and the last ones. [4] This is the judgment of the Lord for all flesh—and why should you reject the good pleasure of the Most High?

---

21. No connection with Isa 28:15, 18; the Hebrew and Greek are different.

22. On Sir 41:1–13, see Gian Luigi Prato, *Il problema della teodicea in Ben Sira: Composizione dei contrari e richiamo alle origini*, AnBib 65 (Rome: Biblical Institute Press, 1975), 332–63; Andrzej Piwowar, *La vergogna come criterio della fama perpetua: Studio esegetico-teologico di Sir 40,1–42,14* (Katowice: Emmanuel, 2006), 163–242.

23. On that theme, see L. J. Prockter, "'His Yesterday and Yours Today' (Sir 38:22): Reflection on Ben Sira's View of Death," *JSem* 2 (1990): 44–56 (Stoic influence).

seems a stretch

Latin: [5] Noli metuere iudicium mortis memento quae ante te fuerunt et quae superventura sunt tibi [6] Hoc iudicium a Domini omni carne et quid superveniet in beneplacita Altissimi

Syriac: [3] Do not be afraid of death, because this is your lot; remember that the ones before and the ones after are near you, [4] because this is the end of all human beings for God.

The Hebrew text is correctly reflected in Greek and Latin. The Syriac version does not translate 41:4b. In the Hebrew text of 41:3a, for the translation "the decree for you," one read חוקיך MS Masada, or חקך MS B. In 41:4a, MS B gives חלק, which means "portion, lot," but MS Masada reads קץ, "the end," accepted by Charles Mopsik, who sees a reference to Gen 6:13; with Gian Luigi Prato, the reading of MS B is acceptable, even if 41:4a in Syriac has "the end," like MS Masada.[24]

In Hebrew 41:3a, the expression "the decree for you," means in English something like "when your time comes." There could be an allusion to Gen 6:3 in 41:4a, when the Lord decided that human life would not go beyond 120 years. In 41:4b (cf. Jer 6:19), instead of the Hebrew text "the law [תורה] of the Most High," the Greek version, followed by the Latin one, read רצון, which never appears elsewhere for תורה and for words like commandments in the Hebrew fragments; perhaps, even if it is strange, the manuscript of the grandson was damaged, and he read תרצה, Tirsa, and translated that word as in LXX of Cant 6:4 by εὐδοκία.[25]

In this chapter (Sir 41) the mention of death intends to emphasize the importance of leaving a good reputation after death, as it is explicitly written in 41:12–13: do not fear death, but try to leave after you a good name, which will remain forever. Only this should remain, according to this master who did not have any perspective of an afterlife; and the right track to leave a good name is through mercy and alms (40:17, 24: צדקה/ἐλεημοσύνη/misericordia), fear of the Lord (40:26–27), and showing wisdom (41:14–15), always, except 40:24, at the end of a paragraph.

---

24. Charles Mopsik, *La Sagesse de ben Sira: Traduction de l'hébreu, introduction et annotations*, Les Dix Paroles (Lagrasse: Verdier, 2004), 242.

25. In Sir 32 (35):14b, he translated with εὐδοκία the Hebrew word מענה "answer."

4. Two References to Priesthood and Cult

7:31

> **Hebrew:** Honor God and respect the priest; give him his portion as you have been commanded.
> **Greek:** Fear the Lord, and honor a priest, and give him his portion, as it has been commanded of you.
> **Latin:** [33] Honora Deum ex tota anima tua et honorifica sacerdotes ... [34] Da illi partem sicut mandatum est tibi.
> **Syriac:** Praise him and honor his priests also and give them their due according to what you were commanded.

In 7:29–31, Ben Sira invites his disciple to honor the priest and to give him his portion, as prescribed by the torah. In 7:31cd, he mentions some of these requirements, but the Hebrew text is problematic.[26] At the beginning the Greek version mentions the first fruits (cf. Deut 18:4; 26:1–11), then sacrifice for reparation (cf. Lev 5:6), offering of shoulders (cf. Deut 18:3), sacrifice of sanctification (?), and either sacred donations or contributions to the sanctuary (cf. Exod 36:6; Lev 22:12) or for priests (Neh 13:5). The Latin version is still more confused and the Syriac one has reduced the text: "the bread of offerings and the first-fruit of your hands."[27] In any case, in these offerings, there are portions reserved to the priests.

The reason is that priests do not have any other means of subsistence, except the people's offerings (see 45:20–22): they depend on the generosity of the people, exactly as old parents (7:27–28;[28] cf. Tob 4:4) and as the poor, the afflicted, and the sick (7:32–36). In fact, for Ben Sira, traditional priesthood is the only hope for the future of God's people (cf. the Hebrew text of 45:26; 50:22–24).

---

26. See the translations of Skehan and Di Lella, *Wisdom of Ben Sira*, 204; Mopsik, *Sagesse de ben Sira*, 113; Bradley C. Gregory, *Like an Everlasting Signet Ring: Generosity in the Book of Sirach*, DCLS 2 (Berlin: de Gruyter, 2010), 225–26 and for text criticism 304–6.
27. See Calduch-Benages, Ferrer and Liesen, *Sabiduría del escriba*, 106.
28. Sir 7:27–28 are lacking in Hebrew because of a homoioarcton.

35 (32 LXX):1–7[29]

> **Hebrew:** [lacking]
> **Greek:** [1] He who keeps the Law multiplies offerings. [2] One who makes a sacrifice for deliverance is one who pays heed to the [commandments]. [3] One who repays kindness is one who offers the finest flour, [4] and he who does an act of charity is one who makes a sacrifice of praise. [5] A good pleasure to the Lord it is to withdraw from wickedness, and it is atonement to withdraw from injustice [6] Do not be seen empty in the presence of the Lord, [7] for all these things are for the sake of a commandment.
> **Latin:** [1] Qui conservat legem multiplicat orationem [2] sacrificium salutare adtendere mandatis … [6] Non apparebis ante conspectum Dei vacuus [7] Haec enim omnia propter mandatum ‹Domini›[30] fiunt
> **Syriac:** [1] If you have done what is written in the law, you have increased worship. [2] and he who observes the commandment, his spirit is happy. [3] He who brings an offering, piles up good rewards [4] He who give alms observes the law. [5] (To do) the will of God is to turn aside from all evil and restrain your strength, lest you do what He hates. [6] Do not appear before Him empty-handed. [7] Because everyone, who does what is fair, observes the commandment.

These verses go together when one considers the inclusion between 35:1–2 and 35:7. In the Greek version as well as in the Latin one, "all these things" (35:7) means everything mentioned in 35:1–6. In 35:6, the reference is to Exod 23:15; 34:20; Deut 16:16. The two central distichs, 35:3–5, point to the message of Ben Sira, in agreement with Isa 1:10–17: not an opposition between legal sacrifices and correct behavior, because both are complementary and also requested by the torah.

In this context, ἐλεημοσύνη, "act of charity" in this translation of 35:4, refers to Deut 15:11, where the commandment is explicit. Therefore, no liturgical act is accepted by the Lord if there is not at the same time justice and alms to the poor.

For the Greek and the Latin versions, the commandment not to go before the Lord in his temple empty-handed is addressed to the disciple. In the Syriac version, 35:1, 5b–6 are also addressed to him. It would not

---

29. See Gregory, *Like an Everlasting Signet Ring*, 237–40 and for text criticism 326–27. Renato De Zan, *Il culto che Dio gradisce: Studio del "Trattato sulle offerte" di Sir^Gr 34,21–35,20*, AnBib 190 (Rome: Gregorian & Biblical Press, 2011), 311–73.

30. See Vattioni, *Ecclesiastico*, liv: "Les éléments qui représentent probablement une interpolation ont été mis entre crochets."

be wrong to say that the precept about alms to the poor in 35:4 is also addressed to him, as it was in 29:9, 11 (see the discussion below).

About priesthood and cult, the conclusion is that Ben Sira still has poverty in mind.

5. Commandments to Help the Needy Person

29:1–2a, 9, 11[31]

Hebrew: [lacking]

Greek: [1] He who does mercy will lend to his fellow, and he who prevails with his hand keeps the commandments. [2] Lend to your fellow in his time of need. ... [9] On account of the commandment, assist a needy person, and according to his need do not turn him away empty. ... [11] Dispose your treasure according to the commandments of the Most High, and it will profit you more than gold.

Latin: [1] Qui facit misericordiam foenerat proximum et qui praevalet manu mandata servat [2] Foenera proximum tibi in necessitate illius. ... [12] Propter mandatum adsume pauperem et propter inopiam eius ne dimittas illum vacuum. ... [14] Pone thesaurum tuum in praeceptis Altissimi et proderit tibi magis quam aurum.

Syriac: [1] He who lends to his companion is piling up good rewards and he who takes (him) by the hand observes the commandment. [2] Lend to your companion in the time of his need. ... [8] But with a poor person, be patient with him [9] And give him time so as to keep the commandment, and if there is a loss, do not take (it) to {your} heart. ... [11] Gather for yourself a treasure with justice and with love and it will be better for you than all that you have.

Sirach 29:1–20 forms a unit: 29:1–7 is about loans, 29:8–13 about alms, and 29:14–20 about guarantee or bail. Earlier in his book, Ben Sira was more than prudent concerning loans and bails: he advises against both in 8:12–13.

Sirach 29:1–2a concerns the commandments of the torah about lending (ἐντολάς/mandata; cf. Exod 22:24; Lev 25:35–38; Deut 15:8; 23:20): given to a member of the people (πλησίον: 29:1a, 2a), any loan, according to the torah,

31. See Maurice Gilbert, "Prêt, aumône et caution (Sir 29,1–20)," in *Der Einzelne und seine Gemeinschaft bei Ben Sira*, ed. Renate Egger-Wenzel and Ingrid Krammer, BZAW 270 (Berlin: de Gruyter, 1998), 179–89; Gregory, *Like an Everlasting Signet*, 128–220.

has to be interest-free. Here Ben Sira's position is more positive than in 8:12, but before him Pss 37:26; 112:5 consider that the one who has mercy and lends is a just person. In 29:2a, this precept of the torah is clearly addressed to the disciple. 29:2b–7 concern the borrower. The Syriac version understood 29:8–9 as bound with the former verses about restitution of a loan.

As for lending, 29:14–20 about guarantee is more positive than 8:13 and the ancient wisdom tradition in Prov 6:1–5; 17:18; 22:26–27. But in Sir 29:14–20, there is no mention of any commandment.

It is evident that for Ben Sira, giving alms to a needy person is preferable to lending and being a guarantor. Twice, in 29:9, 11, the Greek version, followed by the Latin one, refers to the commandment in Deut 15:11, implicitly referred to in Sir 35 (32 LXX):4, as explained above. Unlike loan and guarantee, alms are given without any hope of return, except in the heart of the poor (29:13): the Latin version adds in its verse 29:15: "Conclude elemosynam in corde pauperis et haec pro te exorabit ab omni malo." Now, in Greek the concept of alms (ἐλεημοσύνη) is connected with mercy, in Hebrew with justice (צדקה), and in Christianity with charity. Several times, wisdom literature commends alms to the poor (Job 31:19–20; Prov 19:17; 28:27; Tob 4:7–11, 16; 12:8–9). For Ben Sira in 3:30, like in Tob 12:9, giving alms purifies from sins.[32]

Giving alms is not only to be done according to the commandment of the Lord, but also according to the need of the beggar (29:9 Greek); and this one is also a brother, as says 29:10a—the Latin version correctly translated: "Perde pecuniam pro frate et amico" (Vulg. 29:13). For his part, the Syriac translator of 29:11 put "with justice and with love" instead of "the commandments of the Most High": justice and love are the primordial design of the divine precepts.

6. Two Characters of Biblical History

45:7[33]

Hebrew: He made his office perpetual when he endowed him with its dignity.

---

32. According to Kondracki, "La צדקה che espia i peccati," 73 n. 87, here צדקה/
ἐλεημοσύνη means "beneficence."

33. See Friedrich V. Reiterer, "Aaron's Polyvalent Role according to Ben Sira," in *Rewriting Biblical History: Essays on Chronicles and Ben Sira in Honor of Pancratius C.*

Greek: He established him as an everlasting covenant and gave him a priesthood of the people;
Latin: [8] Statuit ei testamentum aeternum et dedit illi sacerdotium gentis et beatificavit illum in gloria
Syriac: And He constituted him for a strengthening of the people and He bestowed him {from} his honor and his praise.

In the *Laus Patrum* (Sir 44–49), only twice do divine decisions concern famous characters: Aaron in 45:5 and Samuel in 46:13–14. About Aaron, the Lord "made his office perpetual": in Hebrew וישימהו לחק עולם. This expression comes from Exod 29:9: לחקת עולם. There is no literal equivalent in LXX. In Num 25:13, the Hebrew text gives: ברית כהנת עולם, and in LXX: διαθήκη ἱερτείας αἰωνία, a literal translation. In the Greek version, as well as in the Latin one, even if there is some similarity with the Greek version of Num 25:13, the translator, according to his habit, translated חק with διαθήκη.[34]

The perpetual office given by the Lord to Aaron was also to pass on to his descendants, but at the beginning, it was attributed to a single person, Aaron, even if he was not directly addressed. Finally, 45:21–22 must be called to mind: Aaron and his descendants have no property and depend on the generosity of the people, as it was already stated apropos of 7:31.

46:13–14

Hebrew: [13] Friend of his people and favored by his Maker[35] pledged in a vow from his mother's womb, As one consecrated to the LORD[36] in the prophetic office was Samuel, the judge who offered sacrifice. At God's word he established the kingdom and anointed princes to rule the people. [14] By LORD's precept, he ordered the assembly[37] and he made the rounds of the settlements of Jacob.

Beentjes, ed. Jeremy Corley and Harm van Grol, DCLS 7 (Berlin: de Gruyter, 2011), 33–34.

34. See Martilla, "'Statute' or 'Covenant'?"

35. I take this line of the Hebrew from the translator's note. Skehan translated it from the Greek.

36. Literally: "*nazir* of the LORD," as well as in Syriac; cf. 1 Sam 1:11 and an addition present in 4QSam[a] 1:22.

37. The translators note that "lines 13e–18 in MS B are damaged." I translate 14a from the edition of Vattioni.

Greek: [12] Having received glory of human beings, [13] beloved by his Lord was Samouel;[38] a prophet of the Lord, he established a kingdom and anointed rulers over his people. [14] By the law of the Lord he judged a gathering, and the Lord watched over Jacob.

Latin: [16] Dilectus a Domino suo Samuhel propheta Domini renovavit imperium et unxit principes in gente sua [17] In lege Domini iudicavit congregationem et vidit Dominus Iacob.

Syriac: [13] And beloved by his Creator who was asked for from the womb of his mother a Nazirean by prophecy, Samuel, judge and priest, by whose word the kingdom was established and he anointed rulers and kings for the people. [14] By his law he ordered the assembly according to what the Lord of Jacob had ordered, and also.

With Samuel, we are no longer in the Pentateuch, but if torah should mean, as in Sir 24:23, the complete revelation of God to his people, we could insert Sir 46:13–14 in our analysis. "At God's [word][39] he established the kingdom": 1 Sam 8:9, 22 recall the word of the Lord to Samuel, giving him the order to establish a king. Samuel anointed Saul (1 Sam 10:1) and, later, David (1 Sam 16). "By [the law of the Lord he judg]ed a gathering":[40] the activity of Samuel as judge is mentioned in 1 Sam 7:6, 15–17, but not "by the law of the Lord."[41] In fact Samuel was fully at the service of the Lord and of his people. Indicating to the community the right way (1 Sam 12:23), he never took advantage of his position, as he himself acknowledged, and there was no contestation from the people (1 Sam 12:1–5). He was truly a free man.

7. Conclusion

This list of eleven texts, explicitly mentioning the Lord's precepts in Ben Sira, was never previously put together, as far as I can see. Seven points

---

38. Note of the translator: "Perhaps *among the sons of humankind, having received glory of human beings. Beloved by his Lord was Samouel*" (Wright, "Wisdom of Iesous son of Sirach," 757). But this one is properly the common text of the manuscripts!

39. The Hebrew word דבר is lacking in MS B. In the Greek and Latin versions, "At God's word" was not translated.

40. The Hebrew letters in brackets are lacking in MS B. They are translated from the three versions.

41. On Sir 46:14a, see Andrzej Demitrów, *Quattro oranti nell'Elogio dei Padri (Sir 44–49): Studio dei testi e della tradizione*, Opolska Biblioteka Teologiczna 124 (Opole: University of Opole, Faculty of Theology, 2011), 124 (textual criticism) and 173–75 (commentary).

seem to summarize the enquiry. (1) Except in Sir 14:17; 41:3–4; 46:14a, references to divine precepts in earlier scriptural passages are easy to detect. (2) When Ben Sira refers to a precept, his teaching is individualized: he speaks to somebody or about somebody. (3) In a few cases, that person is either generalized (23:23: the adulteress) or personalized as a character of the past (45:7: Aaron; 46:13–14: Samuel). (4) All the other cases, even in 3:6 and 35:4 on account of the context, are addressed to one disciple: "you" singular. (5) Poverty or misery are often evident from the text itself (29:1–2a, 9, 11; 35:4) or from the context (3:6; 7:31; 45:7). (6) Anxiety before death (14:12, 17; 41:3–4) or injustice (19:17; 23:23; 28:6–7) is also the context in which Ben Sira refers to a divine precept. Even 46:14 refers implicitly to the sins of the people. (7) All these texts are to be found throughout the book of Ben Sira, and most references to the torah call for the protection of human dignity.

*wordstudy
why did No theory*

Anthropomorphic Language in the
Descriptions of God in Ben Sira

Ibolya Balla

ZUSAMMENFASSUNG: Der Gebrauch von Metaphern und Analogien ist durchweg ein bedeutendes Merkmal des Sirachbuches. Das trifft insbesondere auf die Textstellen zu, in denen Handlungen und Emotionen Gottes oder seine Beziehung zur Schöpfung und zum erschaffenen Individuum dargestellt werden. Ihm, als dem Herrn über die Geschichte, als dem Richter und Retter sind alle Bereiche des Lebens untertan, einschließlich des Lebens des Weisen, dessen Frömmigkeit ein wichtiger Aspekt bei der Beschreibung Gottes ist. Dies kommt in zahlreichen Passagen verschiedener Gattungen zum Ausdruck: In Texten, die Ben Siras Schöpfungstheologie zusammenfassen, in Texten, die die Haltung des Autors zur Geschichte Israels wiederspiegeln, in Texten, in denen auf die erste Person bezuggenommen wird, oder in Texten, die kollektive oder individuelle Gebete und Klagen enthalten. Ihre übergreifende Botschaft—neben anderen—ist, dass das Gesellschaftsgefüge durch den Plan Gottes, des allmächtigen und allgegenwärtigen Schöpfers, zusammengehalten wird. Dort, wo Gott mit anthropomorphen Attributen beschrieben wird, entsprechen diese denen, die man auch für Menschen verwendet. Andererseits betont der Autor, dass Gott sich vom Menschen unterscheidet. Gott könne man vertrauen und sich allzeit auf ihn verlassen. Ben Siras Vielfalt an Ausdrucksmöglichkeiten macht deutlich, dass er auf zahlreiche literarische Stilmittel und auf eine kraftvolle Sprache zurückgreifen konnte, einerseits mit dem Ziel, den Schöpfer zu verherrlichen, der seine Lehren inspiriert hat, und andererseits, seine Schüler zu unterrichten, zu korrigieren und zu züchtigen, um sie auf dem Pfad des Lebens zu halten.

Introduction

The Greek term *anthropomorphism* refers in a broad sense to ideas or phrases that speak of a deity or nonhuman entities in analogy to a human being, attributing to them/it human traits, intentions, or emotions, or recognizing human qualities in these beings. In theology, it portrays the personal character of God by ascribing to him human characteristics or human feelings, identifies him and his actions with roles from human social life, and compares them to processes in the experience environment of the addressees. In biblical literature human body parts are attributed to God; among them the most common are face, hands, eyes, and nose, but we also find repeated references to ears, mouth, arm, right hand, throat, and foot. He is also conceived of as exhibiting physical actions such as laughing and smelling and having emotions or passions such as hatred, anger, vengeance, and sorrow (the latter are referred to as anthropopathism). Anthropomorphism appears in various ways in the Scriptures through the employment of metaphors or analogies and is widely distributed across various literary genres. It frequently appears in psalms, prophecy, narratives, apocalyptic literature, and more rarely in legal texts.[1]

Since it is a very broad term, upon examination of any biblical book one needs to make a selection of passages that are relevant. For this reason, most of the general statements such as God is merciful or mighty are left out of consideration.[2]

---

1. Jürgen van Oorschot, "Anthropomorphism," https://www.bibelwissenschaft. de/stichwort/13433/; Murray A. Rae, "Anthropomorphism," *Dictionary for Theological Interpretation of the Bible*, ed. Kevin J. Vanhoozer et al. (Grand Rapids: Baker Academic, 2005) 48–49. Recent works attempt to classify anthropomorphism in the Old Testament. Annette Schellenberg differentiates between verbal and metaphorical statements; see Schellenberg, *Der Mensch, das Bild Gottes? Zum Gedanken einer Sonderstellung des Menschen im Alten Testament und in weiteren altorientalischen Quellen*, ATANT 101 (Zürich: Theologischer Verlag, 2011), 253–54. Another way of categorizing forms of anthropomorphism is found in Esther J. Hamori, *"When Gods Were Men": The Embodied God in Biblical and Near Eastern Literature*, BZAW 384 (Berlin: de Gruyter, 2008), 65–103, who distinguishes between "concrete anthropomorphism" (concrete, physical embodiment), "envisioned anthropomorphism" (visions and dreams), "immanent anthropomorphism" (God is described in anthropomorphic terms but is not physically embodied), "transcendent anthropomorphism" (God is not concretely embodied, but speaks from heaven), and "figurative anthropomorphism" (using metaphors).

2. At times when the Hebrew and Greek texts are significantly different, the original text of both versions is provided; generally, only the English text is given with selected Hebrew and Greek terms inserted into it. Unless otherwise noted, the translation of the passages is mine.

Among others, three very distinctive characteristics appear for the readers of the book of Ben Sira, namely, a creation theology that has principles characteristic of especially Ben Sira, the concern with the history and the description of the historically significant persons in the *Laus Patrum*, and the strong emphasis placed on the relationship of the individual with God. While the work is in the tradition of other widom writings, it also departs from them—such as Proverbs—in terms of literary forms, for instance, in the use of autobiographical narratives (51:13–22), hymns of praise to God (39:12–35; 42:15–43:33), and prayer of petition (22:27–23:6). In contrast to the individual sayings of Proverbs, the book of Ben Sira consists of several short treatises.[3] The personal prayers betray a lot about Ben Sira's view of God and of the piety of the godly in general. Considering the ways anthropomorphism can be perceived in the book, we may assert that both metaphors and analogies appear. Employing metaphors is generally an important trait in Ben Sira. The relevant passages are organized in the following categories: (1) God's work in and plan for creation (nature, wisdom, human beings in general); (2) God's work in history (*Laus Patrum*); (3) God's work in the life of the individual and of society (God is righteous, exacting retribution as judge and savior); and (4) prayers.

1. God's Work in and Plan for Creation (Nature, Wisdom, Human Beings in General)

1.1. Wisdom as a Gift of God

1:8–10

[8] εἷς ἐστιν σοφός φοβερὸς σφόδρα καθήμενος ἐπὶ τοῦ θρόνου αὐτοῦ
[9] κύριος αὐτὸς ἔκτισεν αὐτὴν καὶ εἶδεν καὶ ἐξηρίθμησεν αὐτὴν καὶ ἐξέχεεν αὐτὴν ἐπὶ πάντα τὰ ἔργα αὐτοῦ
[10] μετὰ πάσης σαρκὸς κατὰ τὴν δόσιν αὐτοῦ καὶ ἐχορήγησεν αὐτὴν τοῖς ἀγαπῶσιν αὐτόν

[8] There is one wise, greatly feared, seated upon his throne.

---

3. John J. Collins, *Jewish Wisdom in the Hellenistic Age*, OTL (Louisville: Westminster John Knox, 1997), 44.

⁹ The Lord, he created her, and he saw and enumerated her, and poured
her out upon all his works,⁴
¹⁰ among all flesh according to his giving, and he furnished her abundantly to those who love him.⁵

The context of the passage is the book's first wisdom poem found in
Sir 1:1–10. The emphasis of Sir 1:8–10 is that only God can understand
wisdom, which is not distinct from creation but is poured upon all God's
works (1:9c). Sirach 1:10b ("he furnished her abundantly to those who
love him"), together with 1:26 (see below), suggests that Ben Sira's ideas on
wisdom are firmly embedded in the faith of his people.⁶ Sirach 1:9c–10b
provides the answer not only to the question in Job 28:12 but also to that in
Sir 1:6 ("The root of wisdom—to whom has it been revealed? Her subtle-
ties—who knows them?").⁷ Sirach 1:6–10 implies that wisdom and her
"great deeds" are revealed to the sage and to others like him.⁸ There is,

---

4. For 1:9, see Benjamin G. Wright, "Wisdom of Iesous Son of Sirach," in *A New
English Translation of the Septuagint and the Other Greek Translations Traditionally
Included under That Title*, ed. Albert Pietersma and Benjamin G. Wright (Oxford:
Oxford University Press, 2007), 720.

5. For 1:10 see Wright, "Wisdom of Iesous Son of Sirach," 720.

6. Helge Stadelmann, *Ben Sira als Schriftgelehrter: Eine Untersuchung zum Berufs-
bild des vor-makkabäischen Sōfēr unter Berücksichtigung seines Verhältnisses zu Pries-
ter-, Propheten- und Weisheitslehrertum*, WUNT 2/6 (Tübingen: Mohr, 1980), 299–
300. See also Sir 1:10cd (witnessed in GII), which repeats some of the ideas of 1:10ab
and adds that it is through wisdom that humans may see God; also see Sir 1:14, 16,
18, 20, 27; 19:20; 21:11; 32:14. Greg S. Goering, *Wisdom's Root Revealed: Ben Sira and
the Election of Israel*, JSJSupp 139 (Leiden: Brill, 2009), 21–24, 78–102 distinguishes
between two apportionments of wisdom. God "poured out" the first allocation of
wisdom upon all his creation, including all humans (in Goering's work Sir 1:9c–10a
appears as 1:9b–10a on pp. 21–24, while in appendix A on pp. 254–55, as 1:9c–10a).
The second allotment of wisdom is "lavished" upon a *"particular subset of humanity,"* those, who love God according to 1:10b (Goering, *Wisdom's Root Revealed*, 22,
emphasis original). The difference between the two apportionments is not qualitative,
but quantitative, the second portion is more abundant implying that those who love
God receive an extra measure of wisdom. The two sets of human beings are not portrayed as opposites. The first allotment, general wisdom is universally available, while
the second, special wisdom is revealed to Israel.

7. See the question of Sir 1:7 (GII).

8. See also Randal A. Argall, *1 Enoch and Sirach: A Comparative Literary and Conceptual Analysis of the Themes of Revelation, Creation and Judgment*, EJL 8 (Atlanta:
Scholars Press, 1995), 71, who argues that Sir 51:20d ("her secrets I came to know,"

however, a difference in allotting wisdom in verse 9 and verse 10: she is first given to all of creation and all humanity (Sir 1:9b–10a) and then to a select group ("those who love him," Sir 1:10b). Taken together with 1:8, these verses depict the Lord, on the one hand, as a wise and sovereign creator and, on the other, a ruler generously dispensing wisdom to whomever he chooses, in whatever amount he chooses.

1:26

ἐπιθυμήσας σοφίαν διατήρησον ἐντολάς καὶ κύριος χορηγήσει σοι αὐτήν

If you desire wisdom, keep the commandments, and the Lord will lavish her upon you.

Sirach 1:26 is a significant addition to the foregoing in declaring that attaining wisdom has a condition: to keep the commandments. As such, the verse is more specific than 1:8–10, and it also uses the term "lavish," an idea appearing in Sir 39:33 toward the end of one of the praises of creation for stressing that the Lord supplies every need in its time.[9]

4:12–14:

12 ὁ ἀγαπῶν αὐτὴν ἀγαπᾷ ζωήν καὶ οἱ ὀρθρίζοντες πρὸς αὐτὴν ἐμπλησθήσονται εὐφροσύνης
13 ὁ κρατῶν αὐτῆς κληρονομήσει δόξαν καὶ οὗ εἰσπορεύεται εὐλογεῖ κύριος
14 οἱ λατρεύοντες αὐτῇ λειτουργήσουσιν ἁγίῳ καὶ τοὺς ἀγαπῶντας αὐτὴν ἀγαπᾷ ὁ κύριος

11Q5/11QPs[a]) may be the answer to the question of Sir 1:6, forming an *inclusio* around the book (pp. 66–72). He also notes that the idea of the revelation of wisdom to humans is also present in Sir 42:18–19 in the context of 42:15–43:33 (pp. 71–72).

9. In Sir 25:22 the term "furnish," "provide," or "support" is used negatively: ὀργὴ καὶ ἀναίδεια καὶ αἰσχύνη μεγάλη γυνὴ ἐὰν ἐπιχορηγῇ τῷ ἀνδρὶ αὐτῆς ("It is anger and impudence and great disgrace when a wife supports her husband"). In MS C the text may be reconstructed as follows: "It is hard slavery and great shame, when a wife supports [lit., sustains, nourishes, maintains = כול] her husband." Since Sir 1:10 and 1:26 are not extant in Hebrew, we do not know which term is translated as χορηγέω.

¹² Whoever loves her loves life and whoever rises early for her will be filled with joy.
¹³ Whoever holds her fast will inherit glory, and wherever he enters, the Lord blesses.
¹⁴ Those who serve her will minister to the Holy One, and those who love her, the Lord loves.

Lines 4:13a and 4:14b conclude with the description of the rewards of the person's action for wisdom in both Hebrew and Greek: "will find glory from the Lord," 4:13a, "the Lord loves," 4:14b, MS A.[10] The Greek version differs from the Hebrew in the second half of verse 12. While in MS A it reads: "those who seek her out will win [lit. 'obtain' = פוק] the Lord's favor," 4:12b, the LXX translates: "whoever rises early for her will be filled with joy." The word "favor" or "goodwill" (רצון) is frequently used in wisdom literature. It is in the context of God (God's favor, pleasure, or goodwill) in Pss 5:13; 30:6, 8; 51:20; 89:18; 106:4; Prov 12:2; 18:22 as it is in Sir 4:12b. Together with glory (in both versions of Sir 4:13a), in Sir 4:12–13 the rewards probably include long life, prosperity, offspring, or status in society. The reading "will win the Lord's favor" in Hebrew, however, is more specific in terms of anthropomorphism than the Greek reading of the line ("will be filled with joy"), where God is not mentioned. Regarding divine love in Sir 4:14b we may note that the verb אהב is not often used with God as subject and individuals or a people as objects, and when it is, it may refer to Jacob, the patriarch, and his descendants as in Mal 1:3.[11] Ben Sira, however, boldly attests that those who love wisdom will be loved by the Lord.

1.2. The Elements of Nature/Creation and the Place of Humans in Society Are Decreed and Ordered by God

Ben Sira has long poems praising the wonders of creation and the wisdom of God in creating everything for a purpose. Within the created world the place and role of the individual are ordered. We may find it demonstrated in the long elaboration on respect for parents in 3:1–16. Verse 2 (ὁ γὰρ κύριος ἐδόξασεν πατέρα ἐπὶ τέκνοις καὶ κρίσιν μητρὸς ἐστερέωσεν ἐφ᾽ υἱοῖς: "For the

---

10. See also Prov 8:35b; 12:2a.

11. James L. Crenshaw, *Defending God: Biblical Responses to the Problem of Evil* (Oxford: Oxford University Press, 2005), 105.

Lord honored/glorified the father above the children, and made firm the right of the mother over the sons") implies that their authority is divinely decreed. In comparison with Exod 20:12 and Deut 5:16 the use of the verb "honored" or "glorified" is noteworthy. God rarely glorifies humans; one of them in Ben Sira is Moses (45:3), who has an elevated place in the history of Israel, and as Markus Witte points out, he is the mediator and teacher of the torah, which is vital for the contemporary existence of Israel.[12] The verb στερεόω appears—among others—regarding the establishing of creation in Isa 48:13, Ps 93:1 (LXX: 92:1), in a similar context in Sir 42:17 and regarding strengthening Aaron (Sir 45:8). This also shows the importance of parents and their special place and authority in God's plan to instruct their children.[13] In the final verse of Sir 3:1–16, we find a surprising verb used in connection with God: he can curse somebody (ὡς βλάσφημος ὁ ἐγκαταλιπὼν πατέρα καὶ κεκατηραμένος ὑπὸ κυρίου ὁ παροργίζων μητέρα αὐτοῦ: "Like a blasphemer is he who forsakes his father, and he is cursed by the Lord whoever angers his mother"). God curses somebody or something in the Bible in the most serious of circumstances (Gen 3:14, 17; 4:11; 5:29; 12:3; Jer 11:3; Mal 2:2; 3:9; Prov 3:33), and curse in the passage on parents also demonstrates the emphasis on respect toward them.

10:4–5

4 ביד אלהים ממשלת תבל ואיש לעת יעמד עליה

5 ביד אלהים ממשלת כל גבר ולפני מחוקק ישית הודו :MS A

4 Sovereignty/governance over the world is in the hand of God, who raises up on it the person for the time.
5 Sovereignty over everyone is in the hand of God, who imparts his splendor/majesty to the ruler.

4 ἐν χειρὶ κυρίου ἡ ἐξουσία τῆς γῆς καὶ τὸν χρήσιμον ἐγερεῖ εἰς καιρὸν ἐπ' αὐτῆς

---

12. Markus Witte, "'Mose, sein Andenken sei zum Segen' (Sir 45,1): Das Mosebild des Sirachbuchs," in Texte und Kontexte des Sirachbuchs: Gesammelte Studien zu Ben Sira und zur frühjüdischen Weisheit, ed. Markus Witte, FAT 98 (Tübingen: Mohr Siebeck, 2015), 137.

13. Exod 21:17; Lev 20:9; Prov 1:8; 6:20; 19:26; 20:20; 23:22, 25; 28:24; 30:17 (also cf. 30:11); Tob 4:3–4; 14:12–13; the commandment is referred to in Matt 15:3–6; Mark 7:9–13; Luke 18:20; Eph 6:2–3.

⁵ ἐν χειρὶ κυρίου εὐοδία ἀνδρός καὶ προσώπῳ γραμματέως ἐπιθήσει δόξαν αὐτοῦ

⁴ The governance of the earth is in the hand of the Lord, and he will raise up over it the useful person for the time.
⁵ Human success is in the hand of the Lord, and to a scribe's face he will add his glory/praise/reputation.

The Hebrew version of both verses expresses some of the most important notions of ancient Israelite royal ideology: the appointment, the power and majesty of the earthly ruler is from God, who is alone the true king of Israel. This thought fits into the context (Sir 9:17–10:18) dealing with rulers and the sins of arrogance, and is also in line with the statement of Prov 8:15–16 according to which it is the wisdom of God that enables kings to reign and rulers to decree justice or govern in righteousness. Sirach 10:4–5 in the context may refer to the arrogance of the Hellenistic rulers who considered themselves to be gods. This may be supported by Sir 13:17 where the image of a lamb may convey the concept of shepherds as Israel's rulers whom the prophets frequently accuse of apostasy. Instead of looking after and caring for their flock they devour them.[14] The expression "lamb" in Sir 13:17 may have such an underlying idea and can be understood as a warning against associating with the Tobiads.[15] The distrust exhibited in many of the passages about the wealthy or Israel's leaders is possibly due to the fact that some of them associated with the Hellenistic rulers. The corruption of some members of the Tobiad family, such as Joseph, is representative of the hardships the region had to endure during at least some periods of Hellenistic rule. If Ben Sira wrote around 180 BCE, then the burden of the taxes imposed by the Romans on the Seleucids at the peace treaty of Apamea (188 BCE) has also been felt by the Jews.[16] The Greek

---

14. For the image of sheep and shepherd; for sheep, see 2 Sam 24:17; Jer 23:1–3; 50:17; Ezek 34:2–6; Zech 11:17; Ps 74:1; 1 Chr 21:17; for shepherd, see 2 Sam 7:7; Jer 23:1–4; Ezek 34:2–10; Mic 5:4; Zech 11:16–17; 1 Chr 17:6.

15. Jeremy Corley, *Ben Sira's Teaching on Friendship*, BJS 316 (Providence: Brown Judaic Studies, 2002), 138.

16. Henk Jagersma, *Izráel története 2: Nagy Sándortól Bar Kochbáig* (Budapest: Református Zsinati Iroda Sajtóosztálya, 1991), 24–25, 30; Collins, *Jewish Wisdom*, 28–29; Martin Hengel, *Judaism and Hellenism: Studies in Their Encounter in Palestine during the Early Hellenistic Period*, trans. John Bowden (Philadelphia: Fortress, 1974), 27–28.

version of Sir 10:4 is not significantly different from its Hebrew original. In verse 5, however, it renders the Hebrew term מחוקק with γραμματεύς ("scribe"). The reason behind the rendering may be that the Hebrew term חקק in the *qal* stem carries the meaning "to cut," "inscribe," "decree" and in *poel* "to fix," "to determine," "to inscribe (as a law)," hence the meaning "prescriber of laws" or "sovereign authority" in the participle form. Since the arm or the hand of God is often connected with his power and sovereignty, Sir 10:4–5 in the Hebrew and 10:4 in the Greek contrast the power of God with the "power" of earthly rulers.[17] Along with passages such as Sir 17:17, Wis 6:1–3, and Prov 8:16, these verses imply that the authorities were established by God, and as mediators of divine wisdom *do they* or *should they* rule.[18] Even though the Greek text of Prov 8:15 has a word (γράφω) related to γραμματεύς for the Hebrew חקק (Hebrew: "By me kings reign, and rulers decree [from חקק] what is just"; Greek: "Through me kings rule, and rulers prescribe [from γράφω] justice"), its message is similar to that of Sir 10:4–5 (MS A) and 10:4 (Greek), while the Greek text of Sir 10:5 takes a different direction altogether when translating "Human success is in the hand of the Lord, and to a scribe's face he will add his glory/praise/reputation."[19] The word used for "success" or "advantage" (εὐοδία) is favored by wisdom literature for a variety of usages (Prov 25:15; Sir 10:5; 20:9; 38:13). By combining this noun with γραμματεύς, Sir 10:5 in Greek shifts the emphasis from rulers to scribes/sages on whose roles he elaborates at length in a number of maxims (e.g., Sir 38:24–39:11).[20] They all contain the following notions: it is the Lord who grants wisdom, authority in teaching, and reputation to the sages; their own role in imparting knowledge is significant and is described using a variety of literary devices.

---

17. For the arm/hand of God, see P. R. Ackroyd, "יָד," *TDOT* 5:393–426.

18. See also Dan 2:21, 37; 5:21; Rom 13:1.

19. See also Deut 33:21 Hebrew: "He chose the best for himself, for there a commander's [from חקק and ἄρχων] allotment was reserved; he came at the head of the people, he executed the justice of the LORD, and his ordinances for Israel."

20. See Jan Liesen, "Strategical Self-References in Ben Sira," in *Treasures of Wisdom: Studies in Ben Sira and the Book of Wisdom; Festschrift M. Gilbert*, ed. N. Calduch-Benages and J. Vermeylen (Leuven: Peeters, 1999), 63–74; Ibolya Balla, "Images of Imparting Wisdom in Ben Sira and Proverbs," in *Canonicity, Setting, Wisdom in the Deuterocanonicals: Papers of the Jubilee Meeting of the International Conference on the Deuterocanonical Books, 4–6 June, 2013, Budapest, Hungary*, ed. Géza G. Xeravits, József Zsengellér, and Xavér Szabó, DCLS 22 (Berlin: de Gruyter, 2014), 173–82.

Ibolya Balla

26:3

אשה [ובה]²¹ []²² מנה []²³ ובחלק ירא יי תנת[]²³ (MS C)

A [good]²⁴ wife—a []²⁵ portion, and [will be given]²⁶ in the portion to him who fears the Lord²⁷

γυνὴ ἀγαθὴ μερὶς ἀγαθή ἐν μερίδι φοβουμένων κύριον δοθήσεται

A good wife—a good portion, (she) will be allotted in the portion to those who fear the Lord

In the context of Sir 26:1–4, 13–18, verse 3 combines the fear of the Lord with the idea that the good wife is the gift of God. Similar notions occur in other passages with different attributes attached to the woman or wife. 26:23b (GII) is relevant in asserting that a pious woman will be given to the God-fearing man. Proverbs 19:14 has a similar comment, where the "sensible" wife is compared to an inheritance. While material assets such as inheritance are something a person may count on, a sensible wife is more difficult to obtain. It is not up to humans who will receive her since she is the gift of the Lord. The opposite is also true: "A godless wife is given as a portion to a lawless man" (Sir 26:23a, GII).

16:26–17:20²⁸

²⁶ In the Lord's creation [ἐν κτίσει κυρίου] are his works from the beginning, and, from the making of them, he defined [διέστειλεν] their portions [μερίδας αὐτῶν],

---

21. Read טובה ("good") as reconstructed. See Warren C. Trenchard, *Ben Sira's View of Women: A Literary Analysis*, BJS 38 (Chico, CA: Scholars Press, 1982), 188 n. 6 and the Greek text.

22. Reconstructed text, read טובה ("good"); see Trenchard, *Ben Sira's View*, 188 n. 6. The Greek text supports it.

23. Reconstructed by Trenchard, *Ben Sira's View*, 188 n. 7 as תנתן.

24. See the footnote on the text.

25. Read "good"; see the footnote on the text.

26. See the footnote on the text.

27. See also Trenchard, *Ben Sira's View*, 188 nn. 7–8.

28. The section is only extant in Greek except for 26:16.

²⁷ he put in order [ἐκόσμησεν] his tasks forever, and their dominion for all generations. They neither hungered nor did they grow weary, and they did not abandon their tasks.

²⁸ They do not crowd one another, and they never disobey his word.

²⁹ And after these things, the Lord looked upon [ἐπέβλεψεν] the earth, and filled [ἐνέπλησεν] it with his good things.

³⁰ With the soul of every living being he covered [ἐκάλυψεν] its surface, and into it is their return.

¹⁷:¹ The Lord created [ἔκτισεν] a human being out of earth, and he returned [ἀπέστρεψεν] him into it again.

² He gave [ἔδωκεν] them days in number and a fixed time, and granted [ἔδωκεν] them authority over the things upon it.

³ He endowed them with strength [ἐνέδυσεν αὐτούς] like his own, and made [ἐποίησεν] them in his own image.

⁴ He put [ἔθηκεν] the fear of him upon all flesh to have dominion over beasts and birds.

⁶ Deliberation and tongue and eyes, ears and a heart for thinking he gave [ἔδωκεν] them.

⁷ He filled [ἐνέπλησεν] them with knowledge of understanding, and showed [ὑπέδειξεν] them good and evil.

⁸ He put [ἔθηκεν] the fear of him upon their hearts to show them the majesty of his works.

¹⁰ And they will praise his holy name,

¹¹ He bestowed [προσέθηκεν] knowledge upon them, and allotted [ἐκληροδότησεν] to them the law of life.

¹² He established [ἔστησεν] with them an eternal covenant, and revealed [ὑπέδειξεν] to them his decrees.

¹³ Their eyes saw glorious majesty [μεγαλεῖον δόξης], and their ears heard the glory of his voice [δόξαν φωνῆς αὐτοῦ].

¹⁴ He said [εἶπεν] to them, "Beware of all evil." And he gave commandment [ἐνετείλατο] to each of them concerning the neighbor.

¹⁵ Their ways are always before him [ἐναντίον αὐτοῦ]; they will not be hidden from his eyes [οὐ κρυβήσονται ἀπὸ τῶν ὀφθαλμῶν αὐτοῦ].

¹⁷ He appointed [κατέστησεν] a ruler for every nation, and Israel is the Lord's own portion [μερὶς κυρίου].

¹⁹ All their works are before him [ἐναντίον αὐτοῦ] like the sun, and his eyes [οἱ ὀφθαλμοὶ αὐτοῦ] are ever upon their ways.

²⁰ Their iniquities were not hidden from him [οὐκ ἐκρύβησαν ... ἀπ' αὐτοῦ], and all their sins are before the Lord [ἔναντι κυρίου].

Ben Sira dedicates a lengthy passage to the creation of human beings, elaborating on the two creation stories, which he conflates. In comparison to

Gen 1–2, he refers to the task of human beings in great detail, emphasizes their ability to distinguish and includes the tradition of giving them commandments, which define their life as the law of life. Whatever they do is known to the Lord, including their departure from the commandments. These notions are augmented by the comment found in Sir 33:8–9, 11–13. In Sir 33:7–18 the author begins with a series of distinctions within creation where everything comes in pairs (see also v. 15). By divine ordering some days are more important than others (vv. 7–9), according to God's will people walk different paths even though they are formed from the same clay (vv. 10–11), some God blesses and exults, others he curses and brings low (v. 12). The section—using a series of dynamic verbs and anthropomorphic expressions—begins with the creation of nature and then moves to the creation of humans. Finally, 33:14 categorizes them as sinner and just/godly. Especially surprising are the concepts of God sanctifying and cursing humans, and turning them out of their place. Behind the latter we may suspect the tradition of God expelling the Canaanites as contained in Exod 33:1–3 and Deut 34:1–4, although without verbal correspondence:[29]

33:8–9, 11–13

[8] By the Lord's knowledge [ἐν γνώσει κυρίου] they were distinguished [διεχωρίσθησαν], and he made seasons and feasts different [ἠλλοίωσεν].
[9] Some of them he exalted [ἀνύψωσεν] and hallowed [ἡγίασεν], and some of them he established [ἔθηκεν] for a number of days.
[11] In fullness of knowledge [ἐν πλήθει ἐπιστήμης] the Lord distinguished [διεχώρισεν] them (humans) and made their ways different [ἠλλοίωσεν].
[12] Some of them he blessed [εὐλόγησεν] and exalted [ἀνύψωσεν], and some of them he hallowed [ἡγίασεν] and brought near to himself [πρὸς αὐτὸν ἤγγισεν]; some of them he cursed [κατηράσατο] and brought low [ἐταπείνωσεν], and turned [ἀνέστρεψεν] them out of their place.
[13] Like a potter's clay in his hand, to be molded according to his liking [κατὰ τὴν εὐδοκίαν αὐτοῦ οὕτως], so are human beings in the hand of him who made them [ἐν χειρὶ τοῦ ποιήσαντος αὐτούς], to be given according to his judgment [κατὰ τὴν κρίσιν αὐτοῦ].[30]

---

29. See Patrick W. Skehan and Alexander A. Di Lella, *The Wisdom of Ben Sira: A New Translation with Notes, Introduction and Commentary*, AB 39 (New York: Doubleday, 1987), 400; see also Ps 44:3–4 according to which God's right hand, arm, and the light of his countenance gave Israel victory over the Canaanites.
30. The text is reconstructed based on GI, GII, and the defective MS E.

Selected verses of 39:5–11, 16–35.

5 He sets his heart to rise early to seek the Lord who made him [τὸν ποιήσαντα αὐτόν], and to petition the Most High; he opens his mouth in prayer and asks pardon for his sins.

6 If the great Lord is willing [θελήσῃ], he will be filled with the spirit of understanding; he will pour forth words of wisdom of his own and give thanks to the Lord in prayer.

7 He will direct [κατευθυνεῖ] his counsel and knowledge, as he meditates on his mysteries [ἐν τοῖς ἀποκρύφοις αὐτοῦ].

16 All the works of the Lord are very good, and whatever he commands will be done at the appointed time. No one can say, 'What is this?' or 'Why is that?'—for at the appointed time everything will be sought out.

17 At his word [ἐν λόγῳ αὐτοῦ] the waters stood in a heap, and the reservoirs of water at the word of his mouth [פיו/ῥήματι στόματος αὐτου].

18 When he commands, his every purpose [רצונו/εὐδοκία] is fulfilled, and none can limit his saving power [תשועתו/τὸ σωτήριον αὐτοῦ].

19 The works of all are before him [נגדו/ἐνώπιον αὐτοῦ], and nothing can be hidden from his eyes [מנגד עיניו/ἀπὸ τῶν ὀφθαλμῶν αὐτοῦ].

20a From the beginning to the end of time he can see [יביט] [MS B, GI: watched, ἐπέβλεψεν] everything;

20b is there any counting what he achieves [תשועתו]? [MS B][31]

20c to him nothing is too small [MS B][32]

20d and nothing surprises or resists him [MS B]; nothing is a wonder before him [ἐναντίον αὐτοῦ; GI]

21 No one can say, 'What is this?' or 'Why is that?'—for everything is chosen for a need [MS B, GI: for their needs].[33]

22 Blessings [ברכות] overflow [הציפה] like the Nile [MS B]; GI: His blessing [ἡ εὐλογία αὐτοῦ] has covered [ἐπεκάλυψεν] over like a river, and like the Euphrates saturates the surface of the earth [MS B],[34] GI: like a flood it has drenched dry land.

23 But his wrath drives out [יוריש, inherits: κληρονομήσει] the nations, as when he turned [ויהפך, changed: μετέστρεψεν (Sir 39:23)] a watered land into salt [GI: salt water].

24 To the devout his ways [αἱ ὁδοὶ αὐτοῦ] are straight …

---

31. This line is not extant in Greek. For the reconstruction of the Hebrew, see Skehan and Di Lella, *Wisdom of Ben Sira*, 454, 457.

32. The line is not extant in Greek.

33. In MS B 39:34 follows 39:21.

34. See also Skehan and Di Lella, *Wisdom of Ben Sira*, 454.

> [25] From the beginning good things were created for the good, but for sinners good things and bad.
> [28] There are winds created for vengeance, and in his anger they made firm their scourges; at a time of consummation they will pour out strength and calm the anger of their Maker [τοῦ ποιήσαντος αὐτούς].
> [33] All the works of the Lord are good, and he will supply [χορηγήσει][35] every need in its time [MS B; GI: in its hour].

The context of these verses is significant. The first passage (39:1–11) concerns the scribe upon whose activity the sage places great emphasis. As noted before, for Ben Sira sages and scribes are counted among the godly, but their knowledge and authority come from God. In the fabric of society their role is ordered and allotted by the Lord. Sirach 39:12–13 functions as a transition between this section and the poem praising creation (39:16–35). 39:12 is one of Ben Sira's important self-references placed strategically at significant points, such as this; here it serves as an introduction to the praise of creation. Since 39:32 is another self-reference, together with verse 12 it provides a frame for all that the scribe can declare about the Lord's creation, in which everything is created and ordered for a purpose. Even though a person may never be able to discover God's wisdom behind it (Sir 42:17 and 43:27–31), the sage is able to declare that he has seen some of its wonders. This can also be found in a poem detailing the works of God (42:15–43:33). Some of its verses are especially noteworthy: 42:15 starts with another self-reference ("I will now call to mind the works of the Lord, and will declare what I have seen. By the word of the Lord his works are made; and he accepts the one who does his will [רצונו]."). [36] The final verse (43:33, GI) asserts that God has granted wisdom to the godly. These godly appear in the following verse (44:1) that starts the praise of Israel's ancestors (Sir 44–50). Along with Sir 15:9–10 (cf. Sir 51:22), which implies that the wise is able to praise the Lord—in contrast to the wicked who is excluded from it—the overall message of Sir 42:15–43:33 includes the claim underlined elsewhere that Ben Sira has counted himself among the godly.[37]

---

35. The Hebrew word is corrupt; the original was probably from שפק (= "to suffice," "to supply"). The Greek word supports this reading.

36. See also Skehan and Di Lella, *Wisdom of Ben Sira*, 484, 487.

37. Ben Sira's assertion to have seen some of God's works follows the very question of "who has seen him and will describe him" (43:31a), which uses the verbs generally referring to the sage himself: ὁράω and ἐκδιηγέομαι.

Selected verses of 42:15–43:33 are found below to demonstrate the richness of the language with which the author describes the creator and the creation:

42:17 Even God's holy ones are not empowered to recount the Lord's wonders [נפלאות/θαυμάσια αὐτοῦ], though God has given his hosts the strength to stand firm before his glory.
18 He searched [חקר/ἐξίχνευσεν] out the abyss and the heart; he understands [יתבונן, GI: considered: διενοήθη] their innermost secrets. For the Most High knew [38ידע/ἔγνω] all knowledge; and he saw [ἐνέβλεψεν] into the sign of the age.
19 He discloses/relates [מחוה/ἀπαγγέλλων] what has been and what is to be, and reveals [ומגלה/ἀποκαλύπτων] the traces of hidden things.
20 No thought escaped [נעדר, MS M/παρῆλθεν] him, and nothing is hidden [ἐκρύβη] from him.
21a He set in order [תכן/ἐκόσμησεν] the splendors of his wisdom.
24 All things come in pairs, one opposite the other, and he has made nothing incomplete.
43:12 It [the rainbow] ringed the sky in a circle of glory; the hands of the Most High have stretched it out [נטתה/ἐτάνυσαν].

2. God's Work in History (Laus Patrum)

In the Laus Patrum there are many comments that describe the Lord using anthropomorphic terms, often employing dynamic verbs. Their purpose is to demonstrate that these ancestors are special, elected people of God, endowed by him for specific tasks, such as leadership. This shows that for Ben Sira the history of Israel is important, and within it the election of the people and of the individual.[39] The purpose of the election of the individual, however, cannot be separated; the latter functions within the nation and has cultic or political significance. This is especially apparent in Sir 44–50. In the introduction to the section we find the following summary: "The Most High's portion great in glory, reserved to himself from ancient days."[40] (Sir 44:2; GI: "The Lord created much glory, his majesty

---

38. From MS M. MS B does not have 42:18cd.
39. See again Goering, Wisdom's Root Revealed.
40. For the corrected text of MS B, see Skehan and Di Lella, Wisdom of Ben Sira, 497, 498.

from eternity"). Following this general statement there are specific gifts apportioned to these people.

Abraham, Isaac, Jacob

44:21 Therefore the Lord assured him [הקים/ἔστησεν] with an oath that the nations would be blessed through his offspring; [only in GI: "that he would make him as numerous as the dust of the earth, and exalt his offspring like the stars"], and give them an inheritance from sea to sea and from the river to the ends [GI: end] of the earth.

22ab To Isaac also he gave the same assurance [הקים/ἔστησεν] for the sake of his father Abraham.

22cd MS B The covenant with all his forebears God fulfilled for him [נתון], and the blessing rested upon the head of Israel.

23 MS B God acknowledged him [ויכוננהו] as the firstborn, and gave [ויתן] him his inheritance; he fixed [ויציבהו] the boundaries for his tribes, and their division into twelve.

22c23 GI A blessing of all humankind and a covenant he made to rest on the head of Jacob; he acknowledged [ἐπέγνω] him with his blessings, and gave [ἔδωκεν] to him by an inheritance; he divided [διέστειλεν] his portions, and distributed them among twelve tribes.

Moses, Aaron

45:1 And he brought out [ἐξήγαγεν] of him a man of mercy (Moses) who found favor in the eyes of all and was beloved [ἠγαπημένον] by God and people, Moses, whose memory is blessed.

2 He made him equal [ὡμοίωσεν, MS B: strengthened him: ויאמצהו] in glory to the holy ones, and made him great, to the terror of his enemies.

5 He allowed him to hear [וישמיעהו/ἠκούτισεν] his voice, and led him [ויגישהו/εἰσήγαγεν] into the dark cloud, and gave into his hands the commandments [וישם/ἔδωκεν] [GI adds: "face to face"], the law of life and knowledge.

6 He exalted [וירם/ὕψωσεν] Aaron, a holy man like Moses who was his brother, of the tribe of Levi.

7 He made [וישימהו/ἔστησεν] an everlasting covenant[41] with him, [= 6b in MS B]

---

41. MS B has "statute."

^{GI} and gave [ἔδωκεν] him the priesthood of the people. He pronounced him happy [ἐμακάρισεν] with decorum, and he girded him with a cloak of glory.⁴²

8 ^{MS B} He clothed [וילבישהו] him in sublime splendor, and adorned [ויפאררהו] him with glorious vestments.

^{GI} He clothed [ἐνέδυσεν] him with perfection of boasting, and he crowned [ἐστερέωσεν] him with the implements of strength, breeches, and a full-length robe and shoulder strap.⁴³

²⁰ He added [προσέθηκεν] glory to Aaron and gave him [ויתן/ἔδωκεν] a heritage; he allotted [ἐμέρισεν] to him the best of the first fruits, and prepared [ἡτοίμασεν] bread of first fruits in abundance;

Joshua

^{46:5} He called upon the Most High, the Mighty One, when enemies pressed him on every side, and the great Lord answered [ויענהו/ἐπήκουσεν] him with hailstones of mighty power.

Caleb

⁹ The Lord gave [ויתן/ἔδωκεν] Caleb strength, which remained with him in his old age.

Samuel

¹³ Samuel was beloved [אהוב/ἠγαπημένος] by his Lord
¹⁷ And the Lord thundered [ἐβρόντησεν] from the sky, and made his voice heard [ἐποίησεν τὴν φωνὴν αὐτοῦ] with a mighty sound;
¹⁸ And he wiped out [ἐξέτριψεν] the leaders of the Tyrians and all the rulers of the Phylistiim.

David

^{47:5} For he called on the Lord, the Most High, and he gave [ויתן/ἔδωκεν] strength to his right arm to strike down a mighty warrior, and to exalt the power of his people.
¹¹ The Lord took away [העביר/ἀφεῖλεν] his sins, and exalted [וירם/ ἀνύψωσεν] his power forever; he gave [ἔδωκεν] him the rights of royalty

---

42. See Wright, "Wisdom of Iesous Son of Sirach," 756.
43. See Wright, "Wisdom of Iesous Son of Sirach," 756.

and established [הכין] his throne in Jerusalem. [v. 11cd GI: "he gave him a covenant of kings and a throune of glory in Israel"]

Solomon

⁴⁷:²² But the Lord will never give up [יטוש/καταλίπη] his mercy, or cause any of his words to fall to the ground [GI: and never caused any of his words to perish]; he will never blot out [ἐξαλείψη] the descendants of his chosen one, or destroy [ישמיד/ἐξάρη] the family line of him who loved him. So he gave a remnant to Jacob, and to David a root out of him.

Following the verses concerning the foolish nations (50:25–26), there is again an important self-reference in verse 27, which is also a postscript to the book in the context of verses 27–29. The reconstructed text of the Hebrew reads: "Instruction in wise conduct and smooth-running proverbs of … (name of sage) who poured (them) out from his understanding heart." In its Greek version the sage states in the first person that the teachings that are collected in his book for later generations include: instruction of understanding and knowledge. The ending of the sentence is only slightly different from the Hebrew: "who poured forth wisdom from his heart." The weight of such instructions is underlined by the verses that follow in verses 28–29, which imply that one not only has to meditate on his teachings but also to carry them, so one will be able to face all challenges, which may include the challenges of Hellenism, and remain faithful to Israel's religion and values. Taken together with the *Laus Patrum*, which concerns the history of Israel, their combined message may be that as the sage can save one through teaching in times of upheavals, so can the example of specific ancestors provide support and encouragement through strengthening identity. In addition, Sir 44–50 implies that wisdom is given to the nation, to ordinary people, and to extraordinary people who have special responsibilities.

3. God's Work in the Life of the Individual and Society (God Is Righteous, Exacting Retribution as Judge and Savior)

1:30

Do not exalt yourself, lest you may fall and bring dishonor to your soul. The Lord will reveal [ἀποκαλύψει] your secrets and overthrow [καταβαλεῖ] you in the midst of the congregation, because you did not come in the fear of the Lord, and your heart was full of deceit.

Revealing secrets is usually stated about humans in the book of Ben Sira. 27:16–21 is especially concerned with the topic and concludes that friendship cannot be repaired if one's confidence is betrayed. For the word "secret," however, there is no correspondence between the two passages. It is noteworthy, however, that 1:30 describes God and not people as revealing secrets. In the present context its meaning can be that persons who are haughty, double-hearted, and hypocrite, who lack the fear of the Lord, will inevitably bring shame to themselves; their outward actions will reflect their inward inclinations. Since the wider context contains the first wisdom poem (Sir 1:1–10), lacking wisdom and the fear of God are closely connected, having both would have prevented the person from ruination (see Prov 5:12–14). The assembly or a person's honor in the congregation is significant for Ben Sira (Sir 4:7; 7:7; 23:24; 41:18; 42:11).

2:11

> For the Lord is compassionate [οἰκτίρμων] and merciful [ἐλεήμων]; he forgives [ἀφίησιν] sins and saves [σῴζει] in a time of affliction.

In Joel 2:13 and Jonah 4:2 we find similar wording. These lines may represent the tradition behind Sir 2:11. The term "in a time of affliction" appears in passages on friendship. According to 6:8, 10, false friends will not remain with one in such times, while 22:23 instructs one to remain a friend even in such circumstances (see also 37:4). The maxim on divine justice in 35:24 (GI) emphasizes the contrast between God and humans. God can be trusted, whereas trustworthy friends are difficult to find.[44]

2:18

> Let us fall into the hands of the Lord [εἰς χεῖρας κυρίου] and not into the hands of human beings; for equal to his majesty is his mercy [τὸ ἔλεος].

The similar notion in 2 Sam 24:14 may have been paraphrased here by the author. In Ben Sira, the thoughts of divine justice, God as judge and God's mercy and wrath are frequently intertwined.[45] Apart from 2:18, Sir 5:6; 16:11–12; 18:11; 36:7–17; and 51:12a–o also underline the impor-

---

44. See Sir 40:24.
45. For the significance of the notion of God as judge and savior in Ben Sira's the-

tance of the connection between retribution, theodicy, and the mercy
and wrath of God. These sayings—along with the *Laus Patrum*—represent important examples of the concern with the (salvation-)history of
the individual and the nation that makes the work of Ben Sira distinctive
among the wisdom writings. They also demonstrate that the basis of the
compassion of humans is the mercy of God, and—in the context of the
entire book—that God's mercy is unlimited in contrast with the mercy
of humans.

4:10

> MS A: Be like a father to orphans and instead of a husband to widows,
> and God will call you [יקראך] son, and he will be kindly to you [ויחנך]
> and will deliver you [ויצילך] from the pit.
> Be like a father to orphans, and instead of a husband to their mother,
> and you will be like a son [ἔσῃ ὡς υἱός] of the Most High, and he will love
> [ἀγαπήσει] you more than does your mother.

Israel is called God's son in Hos 11:1, so is the king in 2 Sam 7:14. Here it
is reserved for those who show compassion to the marginalized. Whoever
follows the example of God as the protector of the weak (Ps 68:6) deserves
to be called God's son (Sir 4:10c).[46] This idea appears in both the Hebrew
and the Greek version. The Hebrew version of Sir 4:10d differs, however.
The Hebrew reads: "will deliver you from the pit" while the Greek renders
it as "and he will love you more than does your mother."[47] The former may
refer to a form of atonement. The restored relationship with God as deliverance from the pit may involve God's delayed punishment by blessing a
person with long life without afflictions, or saving them from anxiety over
the inevitable death. These are the probable meanings of deliverance from
the realm of not living. It is also significant that God loves an individual,
and his love is the model for motherly love.

---

ology, see also Markus Witte, "Theologien im Buch Jesus Sirach," in Witte, *Texte und
Kontexte des Sirachbuchs*, 59–82, esp. 69–79.

46. There are numerous examples in the Hebrew Bible for God as father and also
in the book of Ben Sira: Sir 23:1, 4; 51:10; Deut 32:6; Prov 3:12; Wis 2:13, 16; 14:3; Isa
63:16; 64:8; Jer 3:19; 31:9; Hos 11:1; Mal 1:6; 2:10.

47. Note the metaphor about God as mother in Isa 49:15; 66:13.

4:28

MS A: Even to death []⁴⁸ for truth/righteousness and the Lord will battle [נלחם] for you.
ἕως θανάτου ἀγώνισαι περὶ τῆς ἀληθείας καὶ κύριος ὁ θεὸς πολεμήσει ὑπὲρ σοῦ
Exert yourself⁴⁹ to the death for the truth, and the Lord God will battle [πολεμήσει] for you.

Both the Hebrew and the Greek word for "to battle" appear in the narrative about the crossing of the Red Sea (Exod 14:14), in the tradition that describes a particularly important event in the formation of the nation of Israel. In the summary of God's actions within Deuteronomy (3:22) we also find the notion—using the same Greek verb—that God fights for his people. In these instances the object of deliverance is the community, whereas in Ben Sira the individual is addressed and is assured that the reward of upholding righteousness is the protection and deliverance of God himself.

5:3–7

MS A: ³ Do not say, "Who can prevail against me?"⁵⁰ for the Lord will exact [מבקש; lit., pursues] the punishment.
⁴ Do not say, "I have sinned. What has befallen me?" for God is slow to anger [ארך אפים הוא]; do not say, "The Lord is compassionate [ארך אפים הוא] and all my sins he will forgive [lit. wipe/blot out: ימחה]."
⁵ Of forgiveness do not be overconfident, adding sin upon sin;
⁶ and saying, "Great is his mercy [רחמיו רבים], my many sins he will forgive [יסלח],"
for compassion and anger [רחמים ואף] are (with him), and upon the wicked he will alight his wrath [ינוח רגזו].
⁷ Do not delay turning to him, put it not off from day to day,
for suddenly his wrath [indignation: זעמו] comes forth [יצא] and on the day of vengeance you will be snatched away.

³ And do not say, "Who can have power over me?" for the Lord will surely punish [ἐκδικῶν ἐκδικήσει].

_____

48. The meaning of the word היעצה is uncertain.
49. See Wright, "Wisdom of Iesous Son of Sirach," 723.
50. Instead of כחו read כחי.

⁴ Do not say, "I sinned, yet what has happened to me?" for the Lord is slow to anger [μακρόθυμος].
⁵ Do not become fearless concerning atonement, to add sin upon sins;
⁶ And do not say, "His compassion is great [ὁ οἰκτιρμὸς αὐτοῦ πολύς]; it will atone for the multitude of my sins,"
for mercy and wrath [ἔλεος γὰρ καὶ ὀργή] are with him and upon sinners will his anger rest [καταπαύσει ὁ θυμὸς αὐτοῦ].
⁷ Do not wait to turn back to the Lord and do not postpone it day after day, for suddenly the wrath [ὀργή] of the Lord will go forth [ἐξελεύσεται] and in the time of punishment/vengeance you will perish.

The wider context of the text is 5:1–6:4. Within it Sir 5:1–8 deals with presumption and pride of sinners who presume on God's mercy and long-suffering.⁵¹ The so-called "do not say" formula—characteristic of wisdom literature—is an excellent instrument of not only arguing with opponents or simply contemporaries and of refuting their claims but also of teaching. They serve to correct bad practices, incorrect assumptions about God, his expectations from humans, about the workings of the world and the Israelite society at a religious-cultic and a social-moral level. Alexander Rofé points out that it has been a popular formula of wisdom literature in most of the ancient Near East and appears quite frequently in Ben Sira (5:1, 3, 4, 6; 7:9; 11:23, 24; 15:11, 12; 16:17; 31:12, 31) where it sometimes prefaces extensive theological sermons.⁵²

Selected Verses of 10:13–17

MS A: ¹³ᶜᵈ Because of it [pride] God sends⁵³ affliction [lit., "plague": נגע] and strikes him [ויכהו] with utter ruin.
¹⁴ The thrones of the arrogant God overturns [הפך], and enthrones [וישב] the humble in their stead.

---

51. For the term "slow to anger," see Exod 34:6, Num 14:18; Neh 9:17; Pss 86:15; 103:8; 145:8; Nah 1:3.

52. Alexander A. Rofé, "The Wisdom Formula 'Do Not Say...' and the Angel in Qohelet 5.5," in *Reading from Right to Left: Essays on the Hebrew Bible in Honour of David J. A. Clines*, ed. J. Cheryl Exum and H. G. M. Williamson, JSOTSup 373 (London: T&T Clark, 2003), 364–76, esp. 366–67. See also Job 32:13; Prov 20:22; 24:29; Qoh 7:10 (Qoh 5:6 is slightly different).

53. Behind MS A's corrupt text הפליא may be surmised here on the basis of the Greek word.

¹⁷ He removes them[54] from the earth and roots them out [ויתשם] and effaces [וישבת] the memory of them from the earth.

^{13cd} Therefore the Lord brought on incredible attacks [παρεδόξασεν κύριος τὰς ἐπαγωγάς], and ruined [κατέστρεψεν] them completely.
¹⁴ The Lord brought down [καθεῖλεν] the thrones of rulers, and enthroned [ἐκάθισεν] the lowly in their place.
¹⁵ The Lord plucked up [ἐξέτιλεν] the roots of the nations, and planted [ἐφύτευσεν] the humble in their place.
¹⁶ The Lord ruined [κατέστρεψεν] the lands of the nations, and destroyed [ἀπώλεσεν] them to the foundations of the earth.
¹⁷ He removed [ἐξῆρεν] some people and destroyed [ἀπώλεσεν] them, and he erased [κατέπαυσεν] their memorial from earth.[55]

In the long section of Sir 9:17–10:18 the teachings on rulers and leadership are intertwined with notions of pride and its punishment. In 10:13cd–17 the author sums up the judgment that pride entails. The Hebrew text of the extant verses does not mention nations as does the Greek. Taking into account Ben Sira's comments on leaders—some of which are veiled—it can be surmised that foreign, especially Hellenistic, rulers are in his view. Their greatest sin is arrogance since it excludes the fear of the Lord. For Ben Sira the root of wisdom is the fear of the Lord (1:20). Complete ruination is described by terms such as "plague" (Exod 11:1; 2 Sam 7:14; 1 Kgs 8:37), "roots" and "memory" (Deut 32:26). Without significant verbal correspondence, the thought of verse 15 may reflect the tradition of Ps 44:3 about the conquest of Israel, during which God has driven out the nations of Canaan and planted Israel in their stead.[56]

11:12

Another goes his way a broken-down drifter lacking strength[57] and abounding in weakness,
but the eye of the Lord looks kindly [צפתהו לטוב] upon him, and shakes him [ויניעריהו] free of the stinking mire.[58]

---

54. The probable reading comes from נסח ("to tear out") based on the emended text of MS A.
55. See also Wright, "Wisdom of Iesous Son of Sirach," 727.
56. Ps 44:3 has καταφυτεύω, "to plant."
57. Read כח for כל.
58. See Skehan and Di Lella, *Wisdom of Ben Sira*, 235, 237.

There are others who are sluggish and need help, who lack strength and
abound in poverty;
but the eyes of the Lord looked upon [ἐπέβλεψαν] him for good; and he
restored [ἀνώρθωσεν] him from his low estate.

The verse in the context of 11:7–28 attests that those in need of strength
and help may place their providence in God, but verse 22 underlines that
God blesses those who are just.

Selected Verses of 14:20–16:23

This extensive section consists of the fourth wisdom poem of the book
(14:20–15:10) and the author's observation of God's working within the
life of humans in terms of theodicy (16:6–23) and free will (15:11–20).
The topic of wisdom and folly, and the fear of the Lord are also overarch-
ing themes of the unit. The latter is summed up in the sayings on offspring
(16:1–4). As such, all subunits are closely connected with each other and
with the following unit (16:24–18:14) concerning God's wisdom and
mercy manifested in creation.

MS A: $^{15:9}$ Unseemly is praise on the lips of the impious, for it is not
apportioned [נחלקה] to him from God.
^{10} Praise is offered by [lit., in] the lips [lit., mouth] of the wise and the one
who has dominion/rule over it [ומשל בה] will teach it [ילמדנה].
^{11} Do not say, "It was God's doing that I fell away," for what he hates [שנא]
he does not do [עשה],
^{12} lest you say, "It was he who led me astray,"^{59} for he has no need [אין
צורך] for men of violence.
^{13} Wickedness and abomination the Lord hates [שנא], he does not let it
befall [יאננה] those who fear him.
^{14} God from the first created [ברא] humankind, and made/placed him
[וישיתהו]…,^{60} and made him [lit., gave him, ויתנהו] subject to his own
free choice.
^{18} Copious [ספקה]^{61} is the wisdom of the Lord, he is mighty [אמיץ] in
power and all-seeing [וחוזה כלם]
^{19} The eyes of God behold [יראו] his handiwork, he perceives [יכיר] a
person's every deed.

---

59. Based on the Greek ἐπλάνησεν.
60. "In the hand of his kidnapper" does not make sense here.
61. See also Skehan and Di Lella, *Wisdom of Ben Sira*, 267, 269.

^{20} No one did he command [צוה] to sin, nor will he be lenient [read: יחמל]^{62} with liars.

^{9} Praise is not proper in the mouth of a sinner, for it has not been apportioned [ἀπεστάλη] by the Lord.
^{10} For in wisdom praise will be uttered, and the Lord will make it prosper [εὐοδώσει].^{63}
^{11} Do not say, "It was the Lord's doing that I fell away [ἀπέστην]"; for he will not do [ποιήσει] what he hates [ἐμίσησεν].
^{12} Do not say, "It was he who led me astray [ἐπλάνησεν]"; for he has no need [οὐ γὰρ χρείαν] of the sinful.
^{13} The Lord hated [ἐμίσησεν] all abominations; such things are not loved by those who fear him.
^{14} It was he who created [ἐποίησεν] humankind from the beginning, and he left [ἀφῆκεν] him in the power of his deliberation.
^{16} He has placed [παρέθηκέν] before you fire and water; you shall stretch out your hand for whichever you choose.
^{18} For great is the wisdom [ἡ σοφία] of the Lord; he is mighty in power [ἰσχυρὸς ἐν δυναστείᾳ] and sees [βλέπων] everything;
^{19} his eyes [οἱ ὀφθαλμοί] are on those who fear him, and he will know [ἐπιγνώσεται] every human action.
^{20} He has not commanded [ἐνετείλατο] anyone to be wicked, and he has not given [ἔδωκεν] anyone permission to sin.

The context of the first part of the section is one of the wisdom poems (Sir 14:20–15:10), followed by a passage containing the "do not say" formula, commenting on free will and responsibility. The categorization of those that have wisdom and those that do not fits into the context of the teachings on free will and the choices one makes in life (15:11–20). The contrast between the pious and impious is an important characteristic of 15:1–10. Verses 7–8 with their reference to the worthless (fools in GI), the insolent (sinful in GI), the mockers (arrogance in GI) and the liars are a preparation for the theme of 15:9–10, since they attest that the impious are excluded even from the praise of God, which is the purpose of humans and the universe (see Ps 148). In contrast, those who are wise can pass on the instruction they received to others as "teachers" or "masters." The Hebrew text of 15:10b ("and the one who has dominion/rule over it will

---

62. MS A's verb does not make sense here, see also Skehan and Di Lella, *Wisdom of Ben Sira*, 267, 269–70.
63. See also Wright, "Wisdom of Iesous Son of Sirach," 731.

teach it") is somewhat puzzling. It may refer to a wisdom teacher who can master (rule) the instruction of others and is able to teach praise. It may also point to God himself who is the ultimate teacher of praise. These teachings have bearing on what the sage thinks about free will; the idea that one's actions always have consequences is frequently reflected in the book in a somewhat automatic action-consequence construct, similar to that found in the writings of the Deuteronomists. To this notion Sir 15:11–20 is an important addition by emphasizing that humans can choose between keeping the commandments and departing from them. These choices are placed before humans by God. In other words, the doctrine of the efficacy of works is apparent in Ben Sira's thoughts, combined with the notion that such works of humans are not hidden from the Lord, who repays every-one according to their deeds.[64] His appearance and visitation is sometimes described as mysterious. These are also attested in selected verses of chapters 16, 17, and 18:

16:12, 14

MS A: [12] Great as his mercy [רחמיו], so also is his chastisement [תוכחתו]; he judges [ישפט] a person according to one's deeds.
[14] Whoever does righteousness has his reward, and each receives before him according to his deeds.

[12] According to his great mercy [ἔλεος], so also is his chastisement [ἔλεγχος]; he will judge [κρινεῖ] a man according to his deeds.
[14] He will make a place [ποιήσει τόπον] for every act of mercy; everyone receives in accordance with one's deeds.

16:17a

MS A: [17a] Do not say, "I am hidden [נסתרתי] from God; in heaven who has me in mind [יזכרני]"?

[17a] Do not say, "I am hidden [κρυβήσομαι] from the Lord; and who from on high has me in mind [μνησθήσεται]?" Among so many people I am unknown, for what am I in a boundless creation?

---

64. It appears that Ben Sira is consistent on the theme of free will; only 33:13 is in contrast with his teachings.

16:19–20

^{18} Lo, heaven and the highest heaven, the abyss and the earth, tremble at
his visitation!
^{19} The very mountains and the foundations of the earth quiver and quake
when he looks [ἐπιβλέψαι] upon them.

17:22–24

^{22} One's charity is like a signet ring with him, and he will preserve
[συντηρήσει] a person's kindness like the apple of his eye.
^{23} After these things he will rise up [ἐξαναστήσεται] and repay [ἀνταποδώσει]
them, and he will bring [ἀποδώσει] their recompense on their heads.
^{24} Except to those who repented he granted a return [ἔδωκεν ἐπάνοδον],
and exhorted [παρεκάλεσεν] those who were losing hope.

23:18–21[65]

^{18} The person who leaves his (marriage) bed/strays from his bed says to
himself, "Who can see me?
Darkness surrounds me and the walls hide me, and no one sees me. Why
should I be afraid?
The Most High will never remember [μνησθήσεται] my sins."
^{19} And he fears the eyes of humans, and does not realize that the eyes
[ὀφθαλμοί] of the Lord
are ten thousand times brighter than the sun [μυριοπλασίως ἡλίου
φωτεινότεροι],
looking at [ἐπιβλέποντες] every way of men/humans and observing
[κατανοοῦντες] hidden parts.
^{20} Before all things were created they were known [ἔγνωσται] to him and
so it is since their completion.
^{21} This man will pay the penalty in the streets of the city, and when he
does not expect it, he will be apprehended.

Immoral conduct of men and adultery committed by a woman are the
themes of Sir 23:16–27, a passage that is surrounded by instructions
regarding self-control and various kinds of misconduct (22:27–23:27).
One of the sage's main themes, the fear of the Lord, closes the teachings
(23:27). In Sir 23:18c the adulterer claims that darkness and walls will hide

---

65. The text is only extant in Greek.

his acts.[66] The created elements seem to be his accomplices as he engages in adultery.[67] Sirach 16:21a ("If I sin, no eye will see me") resembles 23:18d ("And no one sees me: why should I be afraid").[68] While the adulterer in Sir 23:18–21 contemplates, "The Most High will never remember my sins" (23:18e), he acknowledges at the same time that what he is about to do is wrong in the eyes of the Lord. Adultery is a transgression against the divine pronouncements, against religious boundaries.[69] This is reflected in Sir 23:18a in a negation. While in Lev 18:20 a man who has sexual relations with his kinsman's wife will defile himself, this motif is missing from Sir 23:18–21.

Sirach 23:19a implies that the adulterer is aware that with his deeds he is about to cross communal boundaries as well ("and he fears the eyes of humans," 23:19a). This, however, does not keep him from sinning. Still, the author anticipates a divine intervention when he points out that even if the man is foolish enough to think that his actions will not be discovered, the Lord, who created everything and therefore knows everything, will see his actions (23:19b–20b). Therefore the adulterer should be afraid of his sins.[70] God's judgment is perhaps not immediate but operates according to its own timetable.[71] Proverbs 5:21–22 is similar but with only limited verbal correspondence ([21] "For the ways of a man are before the eyes [ὀφθαλμῶν] of God, and he observes/examines [σκοπεύει] all their paths. [22] Transgressions ensnare a man, and each one is bound by the rope of his own sin.").[72] The passage in Proverbs is shorter and more general, but attests that God is all-knowing. Ben Sira similarly confirms that God sees and knows everything and connects the idea with creation: "Before all things were created they were known to him and so it is since their completion" (v. 20). In sayings such as Sir 23:18–21 two important wisdom thoughts are combined: God is all-knowing since he is creator, and nobody will go unpunished by

---

66. See Job 24:15.
67. In Sir 16:17 it is the multitude of people and the immeasurable creation that hide the sinner; see Argall, 1 Enoch and Sirach, 233.
68. Argall, 1 Enoch and Sirach, 234.
69. Exod 20:14 in the context of 20:2–17; Deut 5:18 in the context of 5:6–21; within the Holiness Code: Lev 18:20 in the context of 18:6–23.
70. Argall, 1 Enoch and Sirach, 234.
71. Argall, 1 Enoch and Sirach, 234.
72. See also Prov 15:3: "The eyes of the LORD are in every place, keeping watch on the evil and the good."

him. As a result, two of Ben Sira's most important tenets appear here: the significance of creation theology and retribution.[73]

26:28

> At two things my heart is grieved, and because of a third anger came over me: a warrior in want through poverty, intelligent men when they are treated contemptuously, and a person brought from righteousness to sin—the Lord will prepare him for the sword [ἑτοιμάσει εἰς ῥομφαίαν αὐτόν]!

Ezekiel 18:24 treats the topic of individual retribution. Its verbal correspondence with the third element of the numerical saying in Sir 26:28 is limited to δικαιοσύνη ("righteousness") and ἁμαρτία ("sin," "sinful deed"); in addition, Ezek 18:24 uses the characteristic and general "will die" construct, whereas Sirach employs an image not used in the same form in the Hebrew Bible ("will prepare him for the sword"). The Sirach passage seems to depict a person who was righteous earlier but departed from righteousness and—as in Ezek 18:24—will not avoid punishment. It is a general statement that serves as a heading of sayings on concrete transgressions concerning a person's integrity (26:29–27:21), one of which is betraying a friend's confidence (27:16–21). Damages beyond human remedy are serious enough to deserve divine punishment.

34:19-20

> [19] The eyes [ὀφθαλμοί] of the Lord are on those who love him, a mighty shield and strong support, a shelter from the burning heat and shade from midday, a guard against stumbling and a help against falling;
> [20] one who uplifts [ἀνυψῶν] the soul and makes the eyes sparkle [φωτίζων]; gives [διδούς] health and life and blessing.

The providence of God is described by images widely attested in the Hebrew Bible.[74] These verses—and their context (34:1-20)—are note-

---

73. See Witte, "Theologien im Buch Jesus Sirach," 63–69.

74. "Shield," "support": Pss 3:4; 7:11; 18:2–3, 19, 36; 61:3–4; 91:1–4, but also in Gen 15:1; Deut 33:29, Prov 2:7; 30:5; "shelter": Isa 4:6; 25:4–5; Ps 121:5–6; "guard," "help": Pss 22:20; 91:11–12; 121:3; "health": Ps 30:3; "life": Pss 21:5; 36:10; "blessing": Ps 133:3.

worthy since the author intertwines the traditions depicting the blessings of God with the teaching on the fulfilment of the law and of wisdom (v. 8) and with a self-reference (vv. 12–13) that declares that the keeping of the precepts of the law and of the sage's teaching has saved him at the time of danger.

Selected Verses of 34:21–35:26

The topics of true worship and divine justice are combined in the long section that underlines that retribution is inevitable both in the life of the individual and that of the nation.[75] True worship includes offering unblemished sacrifices that are not ill-gotten, since God expects his creatures to be true to the stipulations of the commandments and to be righteous and charitable. Those who are oppressed by people who fall short of representing such a divine order and expectation can always rely on God's protection. Since God is just and righteous, he will respond to those who cry out for help, including the marginalized whose protector and defender he is (Sir 35:14–26).[76] Being poor, however, does not necessarily mean being righteous as well; poverty by and of itself is not a merit.

> GI: [34:23] The Most High is not pleased [εὐδοκεῖ] with the offerings of the ungodly, nor for a multitude of sacrifices does he forgive [ἐξιλάσκεται] sins.
> MS B: [35:14] Do not offer him a bribe, for he will not accept [יקח] it; do not trust in a sacrifice that is from oppression;
> [15] for he is the God of justice [משפט], and with him there is no partiality
> [16] He is not partial toward the poor, but the supplication of the distressed/oppressed he will hear [ישמע]
> [17] He does not reject [יטש] the cry of an orphan, nor the widow when she pours out (her) complaint:
> [18] Do not the tears go down (her) cheek and sigh against [].[77]
> [22bc] Indeed, God will not delay [יתמהמה], and like a warrior will not restrain [יתאפק] himself
> [23] until he crushes [ימחץ] the loins of the merciless, and repays vengeance [ישיב נקם] on the nations;

---

75. The wider context is Sir 34:21–36:22.

76. See also Ps 68:6.

77. Read "the one who causes them to fall"; see also Israel Lévi, *The Hebrew Text of the Book of Ecclesiasticus*, SSS 3 (Leiden: Brill, 1904), 36.

²³ until he destroys [יקם נקם] the scepter of the proud; and breaks off short [יגדע יגדע] the staff of the wicked;

²⁴ until he repays [ישיב] mortals according to their deeds, and the works of all according to their thoughts;

²⁵ until he judges the case of his people and makes them rejoice in his mercy [וישמחם בישועתו].

GI:⁷⁸ ¹¹ Do not offer him a bribe, for he will not accept [προσδέξεται] it, and do not be intent on a dishonest sacrifice;

¹² for the Lord is judge [κριτής], and with him there is no reputation of face.

¹³ He will not receive [λήμψεται] a person against a poor person; but he will listen [εἰσακούσεται] to the petition of one who is wronged.

¹⁴ He does not ignore [ὑπερίδῃ] the supplication of an orphan, nor a widow when she pours out (her) speech.

¹⁵ Do not a widow's tears go down on (her) cheek and is not (her) cry against the one who causes them to go down?

¹⁹ And the Lord will not delay [βραδύνῃ], nor will he be patient [μακροθυμήσῃ] regarding them

²⁰ until he crushes [συντρίψῃ] the loins of the unmerciful and will repay [ἀνταποδώσει] vengeance on the nations;

²¹ until he removes [ἐξάρῃ] the multitude of the insolent, and will shatter [συντρίψει] scepters of the unrighteous;

²² until he repays [ἀνταποδῷ] a person according to his deeds and the works of human beings according to their notions;

²⁵ until he judges [κρίνῃ] the case of his people and will gladden [εὐφρανεῖ] them with his mercy.

51:30

MS B: Work at your tasks in righteousness and he (God) will give [נותן] you your reward in his time.

Work at your task in due season and he (God) will give [δώσει] your reward in his time.

Following Ben Sira's prayer in Sir 51:1–12, 51:13–30 is his closing of the book in the form of an autobiographical poem on wisdom. In all of Ben Sir's wisdom poems the students are encouraged to search for wisdom in order to enjoy the rewards of the relationship with her. Those who attain

---

78. The numbering of the Greek text differs from that of the Hebrew.

her also win the Lord's favor. This thought is expressed in 51:30, where it is made clear that God is the ultimate source of rewards and he will repay the persons in his own time.

4. Prayers

4.1 National Prayer/Prayer for Israel or Jerusalem

Selected Verses of 36:1–22

[1] Come to our aid [הושיעֵנו], God of the universe,
[2] and put all the nations in fear of you [lit. put/cast your fear upon all the nations];
[3] Raise your hand [הניף] against the foreign people, that they may see your mighty deeds.
[6] Renew [הניף] signs and change [ושנה] wonder; show forth the splendor of your hand and right arm.[79]
[7] Rouse anger [העיר אף]; pour out wrath [ושפוך חמה]; humble [והכניע] [].
[8] Hasten [החיש] the ending; appoint the time [ופקוד מועד];
[10] Smash [השבת] the head of the temples of Moab,[80] who say, "There is no one besides me!"
[11] Gather [אסוף] all the tribes of Jacob, that they may inherit as in days of old.
[12] Show mercy [רחם] to the people called by your name, Israel, whom you named your firstborn.
[13] Take pity [רחם] on your holy city, Jerusalem, the foundation for your dwelling.
[14] Fill [מלא] Zion with your majesty; your temple with your glory.
[15] Give [תן] testimony of your deeds of old; fulfill [והקם] the prophecies spoken in your name.
[16] Reward [תן את פעלת] those who have hoped in you and let your prophets be proved true [יאמינו].

[1] Have mercy [ἐλέησον] upon us, O Master, the God of all, and cast [ἐπίβλεψον] the fear of you upon all the nations.

---

79. See Skehan and Di Lella, *Wisdom of Ben Sira*, 413, 415 for the reading of the text of MS B here.

80. Skehan and Di Lella, *Wisdom of Ben Sira*, 413, 416 change Moab to "enemy" and reads: "Smash the heads of the hostile rulers."

[2] Lift up [ἔπαρον] your hand [χεῖρα] against foreign nations and let them see your might [δυναστείαν].

[5] Renew [ἐγκαίνισον] signs, and change [ἀλλοίωσον] wonders; glorify [δόξασον] hand and right arm.

[6] Rouse [ἔγειρον] anger [θυμόν] and pour out [ἔκχεον] wrath [ὀργήν]; destroy [ἔξαρον] an adversary and crush [ἔκτριψον] an enemy.

[7] Hasten [σπεῦσον] the time, and remember [μνήσθητι] your determination, and let them recount [ἐκδιηγησάσθωσαν] your mighty deeds [μεγαλεῖα].

[8] In wrath of fire let him who survives be consumed, and may those who harm your people find destruction.

[9] Crush [σύντριψον] the heads of hostile rulers who say, "There is no one but ourselves."

[10] Gather [συνάγαγε] all the tribes of Jacob, and give them an inheritance [κατακληρονόμησον], as from the beginning.

[11] Have mercy [ἐλέησον], O Lord, on the people called by your name, and on Israel, whom you have likened to a firstborn,

[12] Have pity [οἰκτίρησον] on the city of your sanctuary, Jerusalem, the place of your rest [καταπαύματος].

[13] Fill [πλῆσον] Zion with the celebration of your mighty acts, and your shrine with your glory.

[20] Give [δός] testimony to your creations in the beginning, and raise up [ἔγειρον] prophecies that were in your name.

[21] Give [δός] a reward to those who wait for you, and let your prophets be found trustworthy [ἐμπιστευθήτωσαν].

As noted above, within 34:21–36:22 the author connects teachings on the true worship of God and the inevitable retribution for individuals and nations. In 35:14–22a it is the individuals who are oppressed, while in 35:22b–26 it is rather the nation, God's chosen people, whom he will save. These passages are followed by the prayer for Israel and Jerusalem (36:1–22). Some consider this section to be a late addition to the book. Bradley Gregory convincingly argues that the transition from the plight of the poor to the plight of Israel under foreign rule in Sir 35:14–16 suggests that Sir 36 with its prayer for deliverance from oppression is an integral part of the book.[81] In the prayer that is closely connected with 35:22b–26, and

81. Bradley C. Gregory, "The Relationship between the Poor in Judea and Israel under Foreign Rule: Sirach 35:14–26 among Second Temple Prayers and Hymns," *JSJ* 42 (2011): 311–27; see also Benjamin G. Wright, "'Put the Nations in Fear of You': Ben Sira and the Problem of Foreign Rule," in *Praise Israel for Wisdom and Instruction:*

that abounds with anthropomorphic terms—such as metaphorical expressions, dynamic verbs that provide a conceptual framework for depicting his actions or emotions—the author asks God to intervene in history. The petition for intervention may be a reference to foreign rulers, nations, and the afflictions Israel had to endure during the time of transition form Ptolemaic to Seleucid rule.[82] Ben Sira is concerned with what is happening around him, even though he is no fervent opponent of everything that is Greek. It appears that for the author it is possible to use some terms and ideology of Hellenism and oppose others. Compared with Proverbs, where the history of Israel is not in the forefront, Ben Sira asks God to do wonders on behalf of the elect people by demonstrating his power and his love for them and for the chosen city, Jerusalem. In Proverbs, there is no such wish.

4.2. Personal Prayer

Selected Verses of 22:27–23:6

> GI:[83] 23:1 O Lord, Father and Master of my life [κύριε πάτερ καὶ δέσποτα ζωῆς μου], do not abandon [ἐγκαταλίπῃς] me to their design, and do not let me fall [ἀφῇς] among them.
> 2 Who will set whips upon my thought and discipline of wisdom upon my heart so that they might not spare my faults of ignorance and he shall not let their sins go?
> 3 that my acts of ignorance may not be multiplied, and my sins may increase, and I will fall before my adversaries, and my enemy will rejoice over me.[84]
> 4 O Lord, Father and God of my life [κύριε πάτερ καὶ θεὲ ζωῆς μου], do not give [δῷς] me haughty eyes [lit. lifting up of eyes, μετεωρισμὸν ὀφθαλμῶν]
> 5 and turn [ἀπόστρεψον] desire/passion away from me,

Essays on Ben Sira and Wisdom, the Letter of Aristeas and the Septuagint, ed. Benjamin G. Wright, JSJSup 131 (Leiden: Brill, 2008), 127–46.

82. See Ibolya Balla, "Glimpses into Ben Sira's Society with a View to the Connection between Ben Sira and Amos," in *Figures who Shape Scriptures, Scriptures that Shape Figures: Essays in Honour of Benjamin G. Wright III,* ed. Géza G. Xeravits and Greg Schmidt Goering, DCLS 40 (Berlin: de Gruyter, 2018), 140–50; Wright, "Put the Nations in Fear of You," 134 notes that the series of petitions addressed to God have a "decidedly prophetic ring to them."

83. The text is not available in Hebrew.

84. See Wright, "Wisdom of Iesous Son of Sirach," 737.

⁶ let neither gluttony [lit. longing of the belly] nor sexual intercourse take
hold of me [καταλαβέτωσαν],
and do not surrender [παραδῷς] me to a shameless soul/life.

The wider context of these verses is 22:27–23:27, within which 22:27–23:6
consists of two prayers: to avoid the sins of the tongue (22:27–23:1) and
the sins of passion (23:2–6). 23:7–15 is again concerned with the hurts
one's lips can cause and 23:16–26 with sexual wrongdoing. Chapter 23
concludes with 23:27 with the call to fear the Lord and obey his commandments. The two prayers (22:27–23:1 and 23:2–6) have certain expressions
in common, such as "O Lord, Father" appearing in 23:1a and 23:4a. Sirach
23:4a within the prayer to avoid the sins of passion (23:4–6) is also the
answer to the distressing questions of 23:2–4, as 23:1a is the answer to
the question of 22:27. Sirach 6:1(2)–3(4) and Sir 18:30–19:3, together with
23:4–6, betray that desires and especially controlling them, were serious
issues for the author. 22:27–23:6 implies that the only way to avoid sin is
with the help of God: it is beyond the ability and control of the person.
This explains why Ben Sira addresses the Lord as Father in both 23:1a and
23:4a as an expression of confidence and trust.[85] The terms "Master of my
life" (23:1a) and "God of my life" (23:4a) seem to confirm this idea: only
God really knows the life and concerns of the author; only he can help.
The combination of the terms "Lord," "Father," "Master/God of my life"
contributes to a forceful language that indicates the greatness of the temp-
tations. The first and greatest concern in the prayer (Sir 23:4–6) and in its
context is the fear of falling into the control of desires, to be given over to
them. However, the source of anxiety for the sage is that his transgressons
may be observed by others as well (23:3). This thought is characteristic of
the writer. Becoming a byword or laughing-stock to others (especially to
the enemies) is also one of the sage's recurring fears.[86] Even though the
author seems to have found the answer to his concerns in the form of a
prayer in 23:6, in the following verses he calls the readers to be cautious in
order to avoid the sins of the lips (23:7–15) and again the danger of desires
(23:16–26).

---

85. God appears as father in Sir 51:10; Prov 3:12; Wis 2:13, 16; 14:3; Isa 63:16;
64:8; Jer 3:19; 31:9; Hos 11:1; Mal 1:6; 2:10.
86. See also Sir 6:4; 42:11bcd.

5. Conclusions

It is apparent that the theme of creation is very important for the author of the book. Some of its aspects can be found in other wisdom works; some are unique to Ben Sira. Related to this is the strong connection between the notion of creator and that of the governor of the universe and Lord of history. On the one hand, it is apparent that everything in creation (the elements of nature, days, festivals, the place of the individual in society) is divinely ordered and decreed. On the other, it can also be seen that God intervenes not only in the life of the individual, but also in the history of Israel and other nations. The depictions of the activities and emotions of God are intertwined with the sage's concern with God as creator, Lord of history, judge, and savior that will carry out retribution at a national and individual level. All aspects of life are under the dominion of the omnipotent and omnipresent God, including the life of the sage, whose personal piety is an important aspect in describing God. The reasons for the shaping of such a creation theology and for the forceful and anthropomorphic language are manifold but probably include the following. The composition of the unity of the book is different from Proverbs, which developed over a longer period of time. In the book of Ben Sira the voice of the speaker is very personal at times, especially when first-person references are included. It is an important intention of the author to stress that the fabric of society is held together by the plan of God for the nation and for individuals, for instance, leaders, parents, scribes. As noted above, in Ben Sira we find petition for a miraculous intervention in the life of the nation in the national prayer abounding in anthropomorphic expressions. In a number of passages God is described with the same attributes as humans; the author, however, emphasizes that God is also different from humans, he can be trusted, relied upon at all times. The immense number and variety of expressions, such as "creates," "looks at," "takes measure of," "pours out," "provides," "bestows knowledge," "gives dominion," "establishes covenant," "blesses," "curses," "raises up," "fills," "covers," "shows good and evil," "teaches," "punishes," "loves," "reveals secrets," "exalts," "brings low," "turns people out of their place," "drives out nations," "takes away sin," "does not give up mercy," "plucks up," "roots out," and "effaces memory," demonstrates that Ben Sira employed various literary devices and a forceful language in order to glorify the creator who inspired his teachings and also to instruct, correct, and chastise his students to keep them on the path of life.

Male and Female in Ben Sira:
What the Text Does and Does Not Say (Sir 25:13–26:18)

Anthony Forte

ZUSAMMENFASSUNG: Nur ein Drittel der 27 Verse in Sir 25,13–26,18 spricht von der „guten Frau" (26,1–4; 13–18), während sich die übrigen mit ihrem bösartigen Pendant auseinandersetzen (25,13–26; 26,9). Die unverhältnismäßig starke Betonung der bösen Frau hat dazu Anlass gegeben, Ben Sira eine Tendenz zur Frauenfeindlichkeit zuzuschreiben. Die Lehren selbst wurden als vermeintliches Zeugnis einer noch größeren frauenfeindlichen Stimmung verstanden, die sich schon in dem Material fand, das Ben Sira vorlag. In einem anderen Abschnitt des Sirachbuches (Sir 36,30) findet sich die Feststellung, der Mann, der keine Frau habe, sei hilflos: οὗ οὐκ ἔστιν φραγμός, διαρπαγήσεται κτῆμα· καὶ οὗ οὐκ ἔστιν γυνή, στενάξει πλανώμενος. „Wo kein Zaun ist, wird Hab und Gut geraubt, und wo keine Frau ist, wird er umherirren und seufzen". So ist es immer: Er will das eine haben und das andere nicht lassen.—Und das scheint unseren Autor nicht zu stören. In der Perikope, die wir dargestellt haben (Sir 25,13–26,18), ist die Beleglage im Großen und Ganzen klar: Ben Siras Frauenbild ist durch kulturell bedingte Vorurteile, die er gegen sie hegt, geringfügig verzerrt. Sollten sich jedoch die jungen Männer, für die diese Seiten geschrieben sind, in der Situation befinden, eine Frau wählen zu können, würde unser Autor sie ermutigen, eine gute Frau zu wählen und alles Menschenmögliche zu tun, keine schlechte zu heiraten.

Invited by Professor Roger Gryson to take over as editor of the second part of Ben Sira for the Vetus Latina Institute, I began my labors where Professor Walter Thiele left off: chapter 25.[1] This chapter is the halfway point of the book and, together with the chapter following, contains

---

1. Ben Sira was written in Jerusalem between 190–175 BCE. The grandson translated the Hebrew text into Greek in Egypt probably around 132 BCE. The prologue was added around 117 BCE.

some of the pivotal passages in which special prominence is accorded to women.[2] Yet only a third of these twenty-seven verses treat the "good wife" (26:1–4, 13–18), while the rest concern her bad counterpart (25:13–26; 26:5–9). The disproportionate emphasis on the bad wife has led some to suggest antiwoman bias on the part of Ben Sira, and the teachings themselves have been taken as purportedly illustrative of the larger antiwoman sentiment in the materials he had at his disposal. Richard Coggins, for example, comments: "Women are used as prime examples of all the evils envisaged."[3] I intend to show that this view is, perhaps, an exaggeration.

In the Latin Bible, our manuscripts often include "capitula," or summaries or divisions or rubrics written in the margins of a text.[4] Throughout they provide the reader with an indication of the argumenta found in the biblical text. The marginalia and capitula at Sir 25:17 (Vulg.), for example, announce explicitly what is to come, namely, reflections on the evil wife.[5] The Latin text of 26:1 is also preceded by capitula and/or notes in the margins. Here we encounter marginalia that signal explicitly a positive evaluation of women.[6] The question is: what does Ben Sira want the readers of this pericope, presumably young men learning how to live according to the law, to know about the relations between husband and wife here at the center of his opus? There is not an excess of explicit instructions as to how one is to live the married life, but the author, probably drawing from

---

2. Important texts that treat exclusively women are: 9:1–9; 23:22–27; 36:21–27; 42:9–11. The long pericope, 25:13–26:18, is the most genuine representation of Ben Sira's thinking about the "bad" wife.

3. Richard J. Coggins, *Sirach*, Guide to the Apocrypha and Pseudepigrapha 6 (Sheffield: Sheffield Academic, 1998), 87.

4. See Walter Thiele, ed., *Sirach (Ecclesiasticus)*, VLB 11.2.1 (Freiburg im Breisgau: Herder, 1987), 84–92. See also Donatien de Bruyne, *Sommaires, Divisions, et Rubriques de la Bible Latine* (Namur: Godenne, 1914).

5. + de nequitia mulieris BTSσ$^{R2?}$ Qx^V (nequitiae?) x^{P*} LM Φ^{TMZGRBV} EΓ^{BA} Π^L, Wien 1190 Paris lat. 11505 Reims 2 Milano B. 48 inf. Graz 167; KA A a, A b + de nequitia mulieris malae KA A^{br} + nequitia mulieris KA B + nequitiae mulieris KA B (Var) + de mulieribus mala KA C + de muliere mala K + in muliere mala AN s Et + in mulierem malam AN s Et (Var).

6. + de muliere bona X$^{2(mg)}$ Z^{2}BKSσ^{R*}QxΛ^L Λ^H (de mulier***) MΦ^{TMZGRB} EΓ^{BA}Π^{L}Ψ^D, Wien 1190 Paris lat. 11505 Reims 2 Milano B. 48 inf. Graz 167; KA A a; A b; A^{br} + de muliere***a L + de mulieris bona Φ^V + de mulier bona Σ^M (*cf.* KA A b).

other sources, informs the reader about good and not-so-good marriages *from a man's point of view*.[7]

Several years ago, during the 2013 summer school in Göttingen, the instructor of the workshop, Professor Benjamin Wright, a specialist in the book of Ben Sira, expressed his view that the author of the book was a misogynist and excessively androcentric. I am sure that Wright would be able to defend his position. My work on the Greek and Latin texts of the book, however, has inclined me to be somewhat more cautious in my evaluation of the antiwomen position. Ben Sira was a product of his culture, and his message echoed the signs of the times. Of course, there are not a few passages in the book of Ben Sira that strongly suggest that Ben Sira had a negative bias against women, at least to the modern reader's sensibilities.[8] But there are numerous passages where the woman is exalted, especially when Ben Sira gives instructions on relations between husband and wife. We can say the same about the teachings about women in Prov 31:10–31, which praise the ideal housewife.

In the introduction to her study of the book of Ben Sira, Ibolya Balla writes: "this thesis will seek to demonstrate that the author's view on sexuality is complex, subtle, and depends on the context of the individual sayings."[9] She corroborates my own view, that the evidence does not permit us to label Ben Sira a pure misogynist. We must not forget that Ben Sira never speaks about women in general terms, nor does he ever address them. When he speaks, he speaks as a teacher and father (Sir 3:1) (Ἐμοῦ τοῦ πατρὸς ἀκούσατε, τέκνα, καὶ οὕτως ποιήσατε, ἵνα σωθῆτε; "Listen to a father's reproof, children, and act accordingly so that you may be safe"), and it is our assumption, albeit one never explicitly articulated, that Ben Sira is addressing young men who are preparing themselves for marital life. The series of counsels that he gives is meant to assist young men to make the right decision to lead a happy life. Both the positive and negative are emphasized so as to help the young man decide wisely.

What about negative daughters

---

7. See Warren C. Trenchard, *Ben Sira's View of Women*, BJS 38 (Chico, CA: Scholars Press, 1982), 86. Trenchard divides the material on women in this book into five categories: "the woman as good wife; as mother and widow; as bad wife; as adulteress or prostitute (23:22–27); and as daughter (22:3–5)."

8. "In general, the feeling is never far distant that to be a woman is in itself a negative situation"; Coggins, *Sirach*, 87.

9. Ibolya Balla, *Ben Sira on Family, Gender, and Sexuality*, DCLS 8 (Berlin: de Gruyter, 2011), 10.

Before we look at Sir 25:13–26:18 (LXX)/25:18–26:23 (Vulg.), a long passage that reflects on married women, on both the good wife and the evil wife, it is to be noted that chapter 25 (both the LXX and Vulgate) mentions the relationships between husband and wife at the beginning of the chapter. Harmony, ὁμόνοια ἀδελφῶν (25:1), *concordia fratrum* (25:2), is the key for bringing joy to a person's heart. We read καὶ γυνὴ καὶ ἀνὴρ ἑαυτοῖς συμπεριφερόμενοι (25:1), translated by the Vulgate as *vir et mulier sibi consentientes* (25:1) or as *mulier et maritus sibi consentientes* at (25:2 J).[10] Balla is correct that the verb συμπεριφέρω can have a sexual connotation. This Greek word συμπεριφέρω and its Latin equivalent, *consentio*, are not insignificant. Bella wrote: "If the idea of sexual intercourse is accepted, the message behind Sir 25:1d may be either that intercourse between wife and husband, i.e., within a licit relationship, is pleasing to the Lord and to humans, or that it is only pleasing in the context of marriage."[11] Ben Sira is not teaching explicitly here but is telling his readers implicitly what a good marriage is and what a bad marriage is. The laudatory verse of the LXX (25:8), μακάριος ὁ συνοικῶν γυναικὶ συνετῇ, *beatus qui inhabitat cum muliere sensata* (25:11 Vulg.), is a reflection that sets the tone for the long and at times disconcerting pericope that follows. It is unclear what the author means by *sensata*. Earlier in the book (Sir 7:19 LXX), *sensata* (Sir 7:21 Vulg.) was employed to translate σοφῆς.[12] What is perhaps not sufficiently stressed in our verse (Sir 25:8 LXX/25:11 Vulg.) is that marriage to a *mulier sensata* or *prudente* renders the husband *beatus* (μακάριος). Again, it is all about the man. Note that type J (MS 171) renders συνετῇ as *prudente*. Balla wrote: "It seems that while one's wealth is something that

---

10. συμπεριφέρω here probably refers to sexual intercourse. See Balla, *Ben Sira on Family*, 59. See *consentio*, TLL 4, 397, line 9+. Thiele (*Sirach*, 140) notes that ἀνήρ is translated into Latin as *vir* (husband) for the most part; *maritus* is attested in the following passages: 22:4, 5; 25:2, 24, 32; 26:1.

11. Balla, *Ben Sira on Family*, 59.

12. According to Coggins, *Sirach*, 86, "there are several isolated sayings which can be grouped together as dealing with the good wife (7:19; 7:26a; 9:1; 25:8a; 28:15; 40:19, 23). Taken together they show that the good wife was regarded as a useful chattel." See Josephus (*B.J.* 1.421): ἀποσκευή = "furniture." Herod's second palace for the women, slaves, and children was translated as "furniture" by Thackeray (LCL). I render ἀποσκευή as "household" or *domus*. See Anthony J. Forte, "Translating Book I of Josephus' *Bellum Judaicum*: Some Critical Observations," in *Josephus and Jewish History in Flavian Rome and Beyond*, ed. Joseph Sievers and Gaia Lembi, JSJSup 104 (Leiden: Brill, 2005), 383–403.

in an ideal case one may count on, the selection of a prudent, sensible or discreet wife is not up to humans: it is a blessing of the Lord."[13] What is not said here is that sexuality is indeed an important part of marriage. It is not to be underestimated. Our author concerns himself only with the sensible wife. The same sentiment is found in Prov 19:14: οἶκον καὶ ὕπαρξιν μερίζουσι πατέρες παισί, παρὰ δὲ Κυρίου ἁρμόζεται γυνὴ ἀνδρί ("Fathers distribute house and substance to their children, but a woman is joined to a man by God").

The Hebrew MS C of Sir 25:8 reads as follows: "Happy the man who does not fumble with his tongue and does not serve someone inferior to himself. Blessed is the husband of a wise woman and one who does not plough with an ox and ass at the same time." The reference is to Deut 22:10: οὐκ ἀροτριάσεις ἐν μόσχῳ καὶ ὄνῳ ἐπὶ τὸ αὐτό. οὐκ ἀροτριάσεις ἐν μόσχῳ καὶ ὄνῳ ἐπὶ τὸ αὐτό ("You shall not plow with a calf and a donkey together"). This suggests that there should not be a significant difference of age between husband and wife. This metaphor comes from the agricultural world and is used to indicate marital incompatibility, that is, marriages that are totally unharmonious.

The first verse of this section (Sir 25:13–26:18 LXX/25:18–26:23 Vulg.) tells us that the wickedness of women is indeed a great evil; that women are responsible for "every wound" and "all wickedness" (Πᾶσαν πληγὴν ... καὶ πᾶσαν πονηρίαν; v. 13).[14] The Greek text of verse 13 is translated literally into Latin (vv. 18–19: et omnem plagam et non plagam videbit cordis [19] et omnem nequitiam et non nequitiam mulieris), but there is no Greek Vorlage for the Latin text of verse 17. For Sir 25:13 (LXX) we do have a Hebrew Vorlage: MS C: "Whatever wound except for the wound of the heart, whatever wickedness except for the wickedness of a woman." The trope of female wickedness is well known in classical Greek literature.[15] If what the woman does is in favor of or to the advantage of her husband, then she is a "good" wife. Otherwise, she is "evil."

The reader of Sirach is justifiably confused by the next two verses (vv. 14–15), which speak initially of the "vengeance of those who hate" (ἐπαγωγὴν μισούντων) and the "vengeance of the enemy" (ἐκδίκησιν ἐχθρῶν). We then read verse 15: "there is no worse poison than that of a

---

13. Balla, Ben Sira on the Family, 61.

14. The evil wives are treated in 25:13–26 and 26:5–12; the good wives are dealt with in 26:1–4 and 26:13–18.

15. See, e.g., Hesiod, Op. 704; Euripides, frag. 1059; Sophocles, Antigone.

serpent" (οὐκ ἔστι κεφαλὴ ὑπὲρ κεφαλὴν ὄφεως = "there is no head beyond a snake's head") and that "there is no anger beyond a woman's anger" (οὐκ ἔστι θυμὸς ὑπὲρ θυμὸν γυναικός). Some versions read θυμὸν ἐχθροῦ (e.g., Peshitta), which attribute anger to the woman and not to the enemy. It is to be noted that the Greek word κεφαλή is the usual translation of the Hebrew ראש "head." However, ראש is also the Hebrew word for "poison." Could this have led to an error on the part of the Greek translator? See Deut 32:33.[16]

The text is not immediately lucid, but Alexander A. Di Lella has offered a possible solution to the puzzle of its meaning. According to Di Lella, these two verses refer to the "evils of polygamy." Di Lella continues:

> If a man's wives did not get along with each other, they became "foes" to each other as well as to their husband, and all suffered the "worst of all afflictions" (v. 14a). The vengeance (v. 14b) refers to what the rival wives, who have become "enemies," try to wreak on one another. The "venom" (15b) of the feuding wives is said to be even greater than the dangerous "poison" of a serpent (15a). All the parties involved suffer due to this rivalry. As regards the problems, envy, and jealousy that arose in polygamous marriages, see Gen 29:31–30:24.[17]

The spiteful/wicked woman (πονηρία γυναικός) is the subject of the next two verses (25:16–18). The author specifically says that he would be "happy to live with a lion and a dragon rather than live with a wicked woman" (v. 16; συνοικῆσαι λέοντι καὶ δράκοντι εὐδοκήσω ἢ ἐνοικῆσαι μετὰ γυναικὸς πονηρᾶς). Di Lella calls this "a somewhat daring, if not preposterous, hyperbole."[18] He quotes two texts from Proverbs: Prov 21:19: "It is better to live in a desert land than with a contentious and fretful woman" and Prov 25:24: "It is better to live in a corner of the housetop than in a house shared with a contentious woman," which are equally hyperbolic. Verse 17 is extremely harsh: "A woman's wickedness alters her appearance

---

16. θυμὸς δρακόντων ὁ οἶνος αὐτῶν καὶ θυμὸς ἀσπίδων ἀνίατος = their wine is the wrath of dragons, and the wrath of asps beyond cure;

חמת תנינם יינם וראש פתנים אכזר = their wine is the poison of serpents, and the cruel venom of asps.

17. Patrick W. Skehan and Alexander A. Di Lella, *The Wisdom of Ben Sira: A New Translation with Notes, Introduction and Commentary*, AB 39 (New York: Doubleday, 1987), 347.

18. Skehan and Di Lella, *Wisdom of Ben Sira*, 347.

and it darkens her face like a bear." The meaning of 17a in Greek, πονηρία γυναικὸς ἀλλοιοῖ τὴν ὅρασιν αὐτῆς, according to Di Lella, is that "a woman's wickedness manifests itself in her appearance."[19] The Hebrew text (MS C) to 17a is extant and reads "the wickedness of a woman makes black the appearance of (her husband)."[20] More literally, according to the Greek: "and it [wickedness] darkens her face like a bear" (καὶ σκοτοῖ τὸ πρόσωπον αὐτῆς ὡς ἄρκος). It is interesting that Codex Vaticanus (B) and others read "like sackcloth" (ὡς σάκκον), while the Vulgate reads "like a bear and like sackcloth" (tamquam ursus et quasi saccum). Note that sackcloth is a penitential garment. Di Lella reminds us of the ferocity of the bear and makes reference to Sir 47:3: "he [David] played with lions as with young goats, and with bears as with lambs of the flock," where the bear is seen in parallel with lions.

As mentioned above, the Latin of verse 17 (omnis plaga tristitia cordis est et omnis malitia nequitia mulieris est) has no Greek Vorlage. This is picked up again in verses 18–19 of the Latin text, which is probably a Doublette.[21] The capitula and/or summaries in the margins referred to above are striking at this point in the text. They are all negative.

To the detriment of the wife, we are next told that "among his neighbors, her husband will recline [Syriac = "sits"] and involuntarily groans bitter things" (v. 18). Manuscript C reads: "her husband sits among the neighbors and groans nonstop." That is, the neighbors are onto the horrible state of the marriage: the man's bitter groaning lets all know that the marriage to a bad woman is indeed an unhappy one. Proverbs 31:23, 28 describes a good marriage to a good wife. In this section of the text, Ben Sira's interest is not the good wife but the evil woman who brings misery and misfortune to her husband.

Sirach 25:19–22 give us a good insight into the author's view of life with an evil woman. Verse 19a is overly harsh and with great exaggeration we are told that no evil is worse than a woman's evil (μικρά πᾶσα κακία πρός κακίαν γυναικός). Her evil brings on all sorts of woes and misfortune. Verse 19b continues the expressed desire that "a sinner's lot befall her" (κλῆρος ἁμαρτωλοῦ ἐπιπέσοι αὐτῇ) and that she become the wife of a sinner and not the wife of a man who is upright. The author insists that just as it is

---

19. Skehan and Di Lella, Wisdom of Ben Sira, 347.
20. ‏רע אשה ישחיר מראה איש ויקדיר פנ[י]ו.‏
21. My edition explains the problem as follows: omnis plaga … mulieris est V; DEF: cf 𝔖ᴾ; cf 25, 18–19 Doublette? interpres latinus alium textum graecum legisse videtur.

almost impossible for an old man to climb a hill that is covered with sand, so is it extremely difficult for a quiet husband to live with a garrulous wife (οὕτως γυνὴ γλωσσώδης ἀνδρὶ ἡσύχῳ). Verse 21 LXX (Vulg. v. 28) offers some sound advice: one should not marry a woman simply because she is attractive (μὴ προσπέσῃς ἐπὶ κάλλος γυναικὸς καὶ γυναῖκα μὴ ἐπιποθήσῃς; *ne respicias in mulieris speciem et non concupiscas mulierem in specie*), nor should she marry for wealth (22) in order to support her husband (ἐὰν ἐπιχορηγῇ τῷ ἀνδρὶ αὐτῆς). For this verse MS C reads: "because her company is dishonor, shameful is a woman who supports her husband." The same negative sentiment is expressed as follows by the Latin translator: *mulier si primatum habeat contraria est viro suo*. This is for Ben Sira disgraceful and very shameful (ἀναίδεια καὶ αἰσχύνη μεγάλη). What is not explicitly said is that honor plays an important role in Ben Sira's code of ethics. Also not explicitly said by the Greek version is that it is forbidden to lust after a woman: γυναῖκα μὴ ἐπιποθήσῃς. The Latin version transmits the following: *ne respicias in mulieris speciem et non concupiscas mulierem in specie*.

Verse 23 picks up the comments on the wife's appearance that had been earlier alluded to in verse 17a. Now the wicked wife, who does not make her husband happy (ἥτις οὐ μακαριεῖ τὸν ἄνδρα αὐτῆς), brings on a "dejected heart, a sullen face, slack hands, and weakened knees" (καρδία ταπεινὴ καὶ πρόσωπον σκυθρωπὸν καὶ πληγὴ καρδίας γυνὴ πονηρά· χεῖρες παρειμέναι καὶ γόνατα παραλελυμένα). Contrast this with Prov 31:10–12 that we have already discussed.[22]

Near the end of chapter 25, Ben Sira (v. 24) blames a woman for having brought sin into the world (arguably misogynistic; ἀπὸ γυναικὸς ἀρχὴ ἁμαρτίας), a clear reference to Gen 3:1–6. Manuscript C reads: "the beginning of sin is from a woman; because of her, we all die." What is not said is that if indeed wickedness comes from a woman, then it is she who is the cause of the destruction of the family. Verse 25 of chapter 25 contains some good advice to husbands of evil wives: "Do not give water an outlet and do not give freedom of speech to a wicked woman" (μὴ δῷς ὕδατι διέξοδον μηδὲ γυναικὶ πονηρᾷ ἐξουσίαν παρρησίαν). In order to keep water from leaking out of a cistern, there can be no cracks, or the cistern will be of no use. So, too, as the woman who is loose with her tongue and

---

22. Prov 31:10–12: [10] "Who can find a good wife? She is far more precious than jewels. [11] The heart of her husband trusts in her, and he will have no lack of gain. [12] She does him good, and not harm, all the days of her life."

is unscrupulous in her speech, is as harmful as a flood of running water. Ben Sira (v. 26) advises the husband to divorce her, "if she does not walk according to your hands, cut her off from your flesh" (εἰ μὴ πορεύεται κατὰ χεῖρά σου, ἀπὸ τῶν σαρκῶν σου ἀπότεμε αὐτήν). This seems to be a justification of the separation or estrangement of the wife, should she not obey her husband. It is all about the man and what he wants or needs. If he is displeased with her, he has the right to divorce (but she cannot do the same) especially if his wife proves to be evil and/or rebellious. As Coggins wrote, "the only remedy for the unfortunate male is divorce."[23] The Latin version, *a carnibus tuis abscide illa ne semper te abutatur* ("Cut her off from your flesh, lest she always abuse you") emphasizes the fact that the wife should be submissive to her husband.[24] Nuria Calduch-Benages wrote: "A spouse that 'does not walk by the hand' of the husband, is an independent spouse that does not want to be governed, directed or controlled in any circumstance or situation of life."[25]

Sirach 26:1–4 reopens the discussion about women, and the final section, 26:13–18, ends with positive comments about wives. What is not said is the reason for which Ben Sira wanted to include both positive (26:1–4; 26:13–18) and negative (25:13–26; 26:5–12) comments in this long pericope. The fifteen negative comments outweigh the four positive ones, but the fact that they are placed together in the same pericope is not without significance.

The first four verses of this chapter (26:1–4 LXX/Vulg.) briefly address the "good wife" (γυναικὸς ἀγαθῆς). One has to read the text carefully to understand what the text says and does not say. According to Coggins, "the 'good wife' is praised. But when this text is examined in greater detail, it quickly becomes apparent that a 'good' wife is seen as such entirely from her husband's point of view.... The wife is good because she is a desirable possession from her husband's viewpoint."[26] The various marginalia and/

---

23. Coggins, *Sirach*, 88. See Nuria Calduch-Benages, "'Cut Her Away from Your Flesh': Divorce in Ben Sira," in *Studies in the Book of Ben Sira: Papers of the Third International Conference on the Deuterocanonical Books, Shime'on Centre, Pápa, Hungary, 18–20 May, 2006*, ed. Géza G. Xeravits and József Zsengellér, JSJSup 127 (Leiden: Brill, 2008), 81–95.

24. See Gen 2:24 for a reflection on man and woman becoming "one flesh" and Deut 24:1 concerning divorce in Mosaic law.

25. Calduch-Benages, "Cut Her Away from Your Flesh," 90.

26. Coggins, *Sirach*, 86.

or divisions that are noted prepare us for something different.[27] We are informed in 26:1 that the wife is good and virtuous insofar as she takes care of and provides for her husband. What is not said but implied is that the good woman is not recognized and appreciated for herself. The text continues by saying that the good wife provides for her husband's spiritual well-being and she brings him happiness and joy. The implication here once again is that the good wife, in caring for her husband, likewise becomes a recipient of the same happiness and joy. The wife is good in that she doubles his days (ἀριθμὸς τῶν ἡμερῶν αὐτοῦ διπλάσιος).[28] Further, we read (in v. 2) that "a courageous wife gladdens her husband" (γυνὴ ἀνδρεία εὐφραίνει τὸν ἄνδρα αὐτῆς) so that "he will fulfill his years in peace" (καὶ τὰ ἔτη αὐτοῦ πληρώσει ἐν εἰρήνῃ).[29] The passage that is crucial for understanding Ben Sira's thinking about women is verse 3: "A good wife is a good portion (generous gift); she will be given as a portion to the one who fears the Lord" (γυνὴ ἀγαθὴ μερὶς ἀγαθή, ἐν μερίδι φοβουμένων Κύριον δοθήσεται). Fearing the Lord is the key to a happy marriage. The good wife/woman is a gift from God for all who fear him.

The verse that follows (v. 4) emphasizes that wealth is not essential, but the implication is that it can without a doubt help a marriage. Having a good, cheerful heart, endowed with a smile, being God-fearing, and in addition being a good wife, all these attributes of a wife make a happy and successful marriage (πλουσίου δὲ καὶ πτωχοῦ καρδία ἀγαθή, ἐν παντὶ καιρῷ πρόσωπον ἱλαρόν; "Whether rich or poor, a good heart, at every moment a cheerful face"). See Sir 7:24b where it is stated that a wife/mother should not show her children a smiling face, καὶ μὴ ἱλαρώσῃς πρὸς αὐτὰς τὸ πρόσωπόν σου. The implication is that should the wife not provide the necessary happiness and peace required for a happy marriage, she lacked the necessary characteristics of a good wife.

Sirach 26:5–12 is a return to a discussion about the bad wife. The author provides the reader with numerous details. Coggins describes the next five verses (5–9) as follows: "26:5–9 give a strongly negative picture.

---

27. See above, note 6: + de muliere bona X²(mg) Z²BKSσ^{R*}QxΛ^L ΛH (de mulier***) MΦ^{TMZGRB} ΕΓ^{BA}Π^LΨ^D, Wien 1190 Paris lat. 11505 Reims 2 Milano B. 48 inf. Graz 167; KA A a; A b; A^{br} + de muliere***a L + de mulieris bona Φ^v + de mulier bona Σ^M (cf. KA A b).

28. The doubling of one's days is a theme often repeated in Deuteronomy (5:16, 33; 6:2; 11:9; 22:7; 25:15).

29. See also Prov 31:10–12.

Having already listed evils that are 'worse than death', the text then suggests that the presence of a 'bad wife' is something even worse still, with drunkenness and unchastity only to be expected."[30] According to some scholars, verse 6 (ἄλγος καρδίας καὶ πένθος γυνὴ ἀντίζηλος ἐπὶ γυναικὶ καὶ μάστιξ γλώσσης πᾶσιν ἐπικοινωνοῦσα; "Heartbreak and sorrow is a woman who is a rival [jealous] to [of] a wife [woman], and this is the scourge of the tongue, the one who shares with everyone") is probably a reference to some of the problems associated with polygamy.

Ben Sira's language is quite graphic:

> [7] A chafing (badly fitting) ox-yoke is a wicked wife; he who holds her is like him who grasps a scorpion. [8] A great wrath is a drunken wife, and her shameful conduct she will not hide. [9] A wife's fornication (wantonness) is in her eyes' haughty looks, and it will be recognized in her eyelids.

Women are compared to an ox-yoke; she is like the scorpion that attacks whoever touches it; she is like a drunken wife that only angers her husband and in such a state acts promiscuously. In a word, the bad wife is jealous, a gossip, unbridled, prone to anger, and uncontrollable. The overwhelming sentiment is that the evil woman strikes again: more misery and more woes are brought upon the husband.

Verses 10–12 describe what a man must do to keep control over his problematic and unruly daughter[31]:

> ἐπὶ θυγατρὶ ἀδιατρέπτῳ στερέωσον φυλακήν, ἵνα μὴ εὑροῦσα ἄνεσιν ἑαυτῇ χρήσηται. ὀπίσω ἀναιδοῦς ὀφθαλμοῦ φύλαξαι, καὶ μὴ θαυμάσῃς ἐὰν εἰς σὲ πλημμελήσῃ· ὡς διψῶν ὁδοιπόρος τὸ στόμα ἀνοίξει, καὶ ἀπὸ παντὸς ὕδατος τοῦ σύνεγγυς πίεται, κατέναντι παντὸς πασσάλου καθήσεται καὶ ἔναντι βέλους ἀνοίξει φαρέτραν.

> [10] Over a wanton daughter keep strict watch, otherwise when she discovers release for herself, she will use it. [11] On her impudent eye watch out, and do not be surprised if she does wrong to you. [12] Like a traveler who is thirsty, she will open her mouth and will drink from any water

---

30. Coggins, *Sirach*, 87.

31. Some scholars interpret the θυγάτερ not as a daughter but as a young wife. See Maria Carmela Palmisano, *Siracide: Introduzione, traduzione e commento*, Nuova Versione della Bibbia dai Testi Antichi 34 (Milan: San Paolo, 2016), 249.

that is near; she will sit opposite every stake and she will open quiver to any arrow.

These three verses are highly euphemistic: should the daughter continue to live a "loose" life, the person who will have to pay the consequences, that is, suffer shame and humiliation, will be the father. Again, it is all about the male and his reputation and comfort. What is implicit here is an warning to the reader: stay away from this kind of imprudent or "easy" woman; she will only cause you more sorrow.

The next section (26:13–18) picks up once again the theme of the good wife. Now she is briefly exalted.

[13] χάρις γυναικὸς τέρψει τὸν ἄνδρα αὐτῆς, καὶ τὰ ὀστᾶ αὐτοῦ πιανεῖ ἡ ἐπιστήμη αὐτῆς. [14] δόσις Κυρίου γυνὴ σιγηρά, καὶ οὐκ ἔστιν ἀντάλλαγμα πεπαιδευμένης ψυχῆς. [15] χάρις ἐπὶ χάριτι γυνὴ αἰσχυντηρά, καὶ οὐκ ἔστι σταθμὸς πᾶς ἄξιος ἐγκρατοῦς ψυχῆς. [16] ἥλιος ἀνατέλλων ἐν ὑψίστοις Κυρίου καὶ κάλλος ἀγαθῆς γυναικὸς ἐν κόσμῳ οἰκίας αὐτῆς. [17] λύχνος ἐκλάμπων ἐπὶ λυχνίας ἁγίας καὶ κάλλος προσώπου ἐπὶ ἡλικίᾳ στασίμῃ. [18] στῦλοι χρύσεοι ἐπὶ βάσεως ἀργυρᾶς καὶ πόδες ὡραῖοι ἐπὶ στέρνοις εὐσταθοῦς.

[13] A wife's charm will delight her husband, and her skill will put fat on his bones. [14] A gift from the Lord is a silent wife, and there is no exchange for her disciplined soul. [15] Charm upon charm (A boon twice over) is a modest wife and there is no standard weight [= a chaste character cannot be overvalued] good enough for a self-controlled (chaste) soul. [16] When the sun rises over the heights (mountains) of the Lord, such is the beauty of a good wife, an ornament of her home. [17] Like a lamp shining forth upon a holy lampstand, such is a beautiful face on a well-proportioned body. [18] Like golden pillars upon a silver base—such are beautiful legs upon well-balanced feet (firm-set heels).

Verse 13 is no surprise. We are now accustomed to regard the actions of the good wife as important in so far as they are advantageous to the man. Here what she does both "charm[s]" and "delight[s]" her husband. It is as always all about the man. She fattens him and she knows her place: the good wife is silent and is a gift from God (v. 14) and her chaste soul is disciplined (v. 15). Ben Sira praises the good wife's natural beauty as an "ornament of her home" (v. 16). Her face is "beautiful" as is her "well-proportioned body" (v. 17). The good wife's beauty can even be compared to the temple (v. 18), and this could indicate that the author wants to emphasize equally that the wife's spiritual character plays a role here: her goodness is not seen only in so far as she is good for what she does for her husband, but for what she is for her own sake. It is my view that Ben Sira once again reminds us that the wife's physical appearance is essential because it is this, her sexually appealing appearance, that the husband wants. Everything has to be evaluated from the point of view of her husband. What the wife says or thinks is not important.

Conclusion

Later in the book (Sir 36:25) we are told that the man who does not have a wife is helpless: οὗ οὐκ ἔστι φραγμός, διαρπαγήσεται κτῆμα, καὶ οὗ οὐκ ἔστι γυνή, στενάξει πλανώμενος. The man, as always, wants it both ways: "Where there is no fence, property will be plundered, and where there is no wife, he will groan as he wanders." This does not seem to bother our author. In the pericope that we have presented, the evidence is on the whole clear: Ben Sira's view of women is slightly tainted by the cultural negative bias he had against them. However, should the young man for whom these pages of wisdom have been written be in the position of choosing a wife, our author would encourage him to choose a good wife and do everything possible to avoid marrying a bad one.

Jesus Sirach, Jesus von Nazareth und die Bösäugigkeit: Zu einem sozialpsychologischen Motiv in der jüdischen Weisheit

Jürgen Wehnert

ABSTRACT: Jesus Sirach and Jesus of Nazareth both use the phrases "evil eye" (*böses Auge*) and "good eye" (*gutes Auge*) in sapiential language. Both teachers take it for granted that their audience is acquainted with the semantic range of this terminology, so they do not give any explanation. In the case of Jesus of Nazareth, this causes misunderstandings. However, the frequent use of these metaphors in the text of Jesus Sirach enables the reader to deduce their correct meaning, which concerns a person's social-psychological approach to possession: greed and meanness (*Bösäugigkeit*), on the one hand, and unselfishness and generosity (*Gutäugigkeit*, also attributed to God), on the other. Presumably under the influence of the book of Sirach, Jesus of Nazareth has adopted this terminology in his sapiential-eschatological teaching without changing the semantics.

Eine auffällige Zahl von Berührungen zwischen den Weisheitsworten beider Lehrer wirft die Frage auf: Kannte Jesus von Nazareth das Buch des Jesus Sirach[1]? Auch wenn es darauf keine endgültige Antwort geben kann, lohnt es sich, diesem Verdacht nachzugehen. Falls Jesus von Nazareth, der Lehrer der eschatologischen Weisheit von der Königsherrschaft Gottes, außerbiblischer Literatur Beachtung geschenkt hat, dann vielleicht in besonderem Maße einem Werk, das die Weisheit der Väter und Mütter unter den Bedingungen der antiken Sozialverhältnisse neu ausformulierte.

---

1. Ich ziehe die Namensform Jesus Sirach dem üblich gewordenen Ben Sira vor. Der Name des Weisheitsdichters ist gut belegt (s. Prolog 7 des griechischen Übersetzers; Sir 50,27; 51,30LXX [subscriptio]) und muss nicht auf den seines Vorfahren reduziert werden.

Jedenfalls belegen die in Qumran und auf Masada gefundenen Reste von drei hebräischen Handschriften mit Sirach-Text, dass die Weisheit des Sirachen in den jüdischen Ländern des 1. Jahrhunderts gern gelesen wurde. Über die Hebräisch-Kenntnisse des aramäischsprachigen Jesus von Nazareth lässt sich freilich nichts Sicheres sagen, und ob es Targume des Sirach-Buches gegeben hat, muss offenbleiben. Das bedeutet jedoch wenig: Auch wenn dieses populäre jüdische Lehrbuch auf Hebräisch verfasst und weitergegeben wurde, ist, wie bei den später kanonisierten Büchern, mit einer begleitenden Rezeption in der Volkssprache zu rechnen. Dass der mündliche Vortrag prägnanter Stücke des Sirach-Buches das Denken des Nazareners beeinflusst haben kann, ist also eine zulässige Annahme. Erinnert sei in diesem Zusammenhang an die Sirach-Handschrift C, die eine recht willkürlich angeordnete Blütenlese der Sirach-Sentenzen bietet, oder an die Psalmen-Rolle 11QPsa (11Q5), die keine Sirach-Handschrift ist, sondern eine Liedersammlung, in der das Danklied an die Weisheit aus Sir 51,13–30 als selbständiger oder sekundär verselbständigter Text Aufnahme gefunden hat.

Die Weisheit des Jesus Sirach ist somit in Betracht zu ziehen, wenn man nach den traditionsgeschichtlichen Wurzeln der Weisheitsworte des Jesus von Nazareth fragt. Bei einigen Logien des Nazareners sind intertextuelle Bezüge zur Sirach-Überlieferung kaum von der Hand zu weisen. Das gilt z.B. für die Beispielerzählung vom reichen Kornbauern in Lk 12,16–21, die eine enge Parallele in Sir 11,16–17 hat, oder für den sogenannten Heilandsruf in Mt 11,28–29, der kaum unabhängig von Sir 51,23–26 entstanden ist,[2] von jenem Danklied des Jesus Sirach also, das, siehe 11Q5, auch selbständig in Umlauf war. Es gibt weitere bemerkenswerte Parallelen zwischen den Lehren beider Lehrer, die offenbar noch nie gründlich erfasst und ausgewertet worden sind.[3] Das ist bedauerlich, besteht doch aufgrund solcher intertextuellen Beziehungen die Möglich-

---

2. Vgl. ferner Sir 6,23–31; 24,19.

3. S. immerhin Henry Chadwick, *The Church in Ancient Society. From Galilee to Gregory the Great* (Oxford: Oxford University Press, 2001), 28; James K. Aitken, „Sanctus Matthaeus, Magister Sapientiae, Summa cum Laude", Pages 264–79 in *Intertextual Studies in Ben Sira and Tobit. Essays in Honor of Alexander A. Di Lella*, hrsg. von Jeremy Corley und Vincent Skemp, CBQMS 38 (Washington, DC: Catholic Biblical Association of America, 2005); David A. deSilva, *The Jewish Teachers of Jesus, James, and Jude. What Earliest Christianity Learned from the Apocrypha and Pseudepigrapha* (Oxford: Oxford University Press, 2012), bes. 68–82.

keit, die Semantik jener weisheitlichen Terminologie genauer zu erfassen, die von beiden Lehrern verwendet wird. Das soll dieser Beitrag exemplarisch zeigen.

1. Jesus von Nazareth und das „böse Auge", Teil I

Ein auffälliges Element dieser gemeinsamen Terminologie ist die Rede vom „bösen Auge". Dieser Ausdruck begegnet mehrfach in der Wortüberlieferung des Jesus von Nazareth (Mk 7,22; Mt 6,23 par. Lk 11,34; Mt 20,15) und stellt die Kommentatoren regelmäßig vor Erklärungsprobleme.

Der umstrittenste Beleg findet sich in Mt 6,22–23 und Lk 11,34–35 (mit wohl ursprünglicher Fortsetzung in 11,36[4]). Er stammt also aus der Logienquelle Q, die sich hier recht sicher rekonstruieren lässt:[5]

Mt 6,22–23	Q 11,34–35 (36?)	Lk 11,34–35 (36)
[22] Ὁ λύχνος τοῦ σώματός ἐστιν ὁ ὀφθαλμός. ἐὰν οὖν ᾖ ὁ ὀφθαλμός σου ἁπλοῦς, ὅλον τὸ σῶμά σου φωτεινὸν ἔσται· [23] ἐὰν δὲ ὁ ὀφθαλμός σου πονηρὸς ᾖ, ὅλον τὸ σῶμά σου σκοτεινὸν ἔσται. εἰ οὖν τὸ φῶς τὸ ἐν σοὶ σκότος ἐστίν, τὸ σκότος πόσον.	[34] Ὁ λύχνος τοῦ σώματός ἐστιν ὁ ὀφθαλμός. ὅταν ὁ ὀφθαλμός σου ἁπλοῦς ᾖ, ὅλον τὸ σῶμά σου φωτεινόν ἐστιν· ἐπὰν δὲ ὁ ὀφθαλμός σου πονηρὸς ᾖ, ὅλον τὸ σῶμά σου σκοτεινόν ἐστιν. [35] εἰ οὖν τὸ φῶς τὸ ἐν σοὶ σκότος ἐστίν, τὸ σκότος πόσον.	[34] Ὁ λύχνος τοῦ σώματός ἐστιν ὁ ὀφθαλμός σου. ὅταν ὁ ὀφθαλμός σου ἁπλοῦς ᾖ, καὶ ὅλον τὸ σῶμά σου φωτεινόν ἐστιν· ἐπὰν δὲ πονηρὸς ᾖ, καὶ τὸ σῶμά σου σκοτεινόν. [35] σκόπει οὖν μὴ τὸ φῶς τὸ ἐν σοὶ σκότος ἐστίν.

---

4. Nach James M. Robinson, Paul Hoffmann und John S. Kloppenborg, *The Critical Edition of Q* (Minneapolis: Fortress; Leuven: Peeters, 2000), 262–63, ist die Zugehörigkeit von Lk 11,36 zu Q fraglich. Aber woher soll der auf V. 34–35 bezogene, sprachlich weithin unlukanische Vers sonst stammen? Aus inhaltlichen Gründen erscheint es mir einzig sinnvoll, ihn dem Q-Stück zuzuschlagen: So, wie V. 35 eine Folgerung aus V. 34c zieht, so V. 36 aus V. 34b. Möglicherweise hat Mt V. 36 wegen seiner ihm unklaren Metaphorik weggelassen.—Dale C. Allison, „The Eye is the Lamp of the Body (Matthew 6,22–23 = Luke 11,34–36)", *NTS* 33 (1987): 80 rechnet Lk 11,36 zwar zu Q, möchte diesen Vers aber in einer wohl zu genauen Unterscheidung für „an ecclesiastical product" halten, um das die authentische Jesus-Überlieferung in Q 11,34f. ergänzt wurde.

5. Die Rekonstruktion des Q-Textes folgt Robinson, Hoffmann und Kloppenborg, *The Critical Edition of Q*, 258–61. Wo diese Ausgabe keine Entscheidung zwischen dem Wortlaut der Textfassungen trifft, schließe ich mich der Rekonstruktion von Allison, „The Eye is the Lamp of the Body", 72, an.

[36] εἰ οὖν τὸ σῶμά σου ὅλον   [36] εἰ οὖν τὸ σῶμά σου ὅλον
φωτεινόν, μὴ ἔχον μέρος τι   φωτεινόν, μὴ ἔχον μέρος τι
σκοτεινόν, ἔσται φωτεινὸν   σκοτεινόν, ἔσται φωτεινὸν
ὅλον ὡς ὅταν ὁ λύχνος τῇ   ὅλον ὡς ὅταν ὁ λύχνος τῇ
ἀστραπῇ φωτίζῃ σε.   ἀστραπῇ φωτίζῃ σε.

Neuere Auslegungen dieser schwierigen Verse[6] gehen weit auseinander
und flüchten sich angesichts ihrer ungewöhnlichen Bildhaftigkeit unter
anderem in existential-theologische[7] oder allegorische Deutungen[8], die
im Wesentlichen aus dem lukanischen bzw. matthäischen Kontext gewon-
nen werden.

Da die Q-Verse Lk 11,34–35+36 par. Mt 6,22–23 gegenüber ihren
Q-Rahmentexten 11,33 (Sprichwort vom Licht) und 11,39ff. (an Phari-
säer adressierte Weherufe) formgeschichtlich selbständig sind, muss eine
Erklärung der Rede vom Auge und von der Leuchte bzw. vom Licht in
Q 11,34–36 primär aus der Semantik dieser Jesus-Überlieferung gewon-

---

6. Diese Charakterisierung des Q-Stücks zieht sich seit Adolf Jülicher, *Die Gleich-
nisreden Jesu. Zweiter Teil: Auslegung der Gleichnisreden der drei ersten Evangelien*
(Tübingen: Mohr [Paul Siebeck], 1910), 98 als roter Faden durch die Literatur; s. zuletzt
Ulrich Luz, *Das Evangelium nach Matthäus. 1. Teilband. Mt 1–7*, EKK I/1 (Düsseldorf:
Benziger; Neukirchen-Vluyn: Neukirchener, 5. Auflage 2002), 465.—Symptomatisch
ist, dass Hans Dieter Betz, „Matthäus 6, 22–23 und die griechischen Sehtheorien", in
Studien zur Bergpredigt (Tübingen: Mohr Siebeck, 1985), 62–77, seine gründliche traditionsgeschichtliche Untersuchung des Stückes (s. E. eine der schwierigsten Passagen
der Evangelienüberlieferung, 62) mit der unbeantworteten Frage abschließt: „Wo liegt
… die paränetische Schärfe des Logions?" (77)
7. Conny Edlund, *Das Auge der Einfalt. Eine Untersuchung zu Matth. 6,22–23
und Luk. 11,34–35*, ASNU 19 (Kopenhagen: Munksgaard; Lund: Gleerups, 1952), 110,
möchte den Text vom Stichwort ἁπλοῦς her auslegen, das die „Ganzheitsforderung"
an den Menschen bezeichne. Der „totale Anspruch Gottes an den Menschen, der die
Auslegung des Gesetzes in der Bergpredigt beherrscht, bildet das zentrale Moment im
Logion vom Auge" (112).
8. Laut Marc Philonenko, „La parabole sur la lampe (Luc 11,33–36) et les horo-
scopes qoumrâniens", in *ZNW* 79 (1988): 151, könne die Leuchte nach lk. Vorstellung
„le Christ" und deren Blitzstrahl „l'éclair eschatologique" bedeuten.—Auch François
Bovon, *Das Evangelium nach Lukas. 2. Teilband. Lk 9,51–14,35*, EKK 3.2 (Zürich: Benziger; Neukirchen-Vluyn: Neukirchener 1996), 216, möchte den Text von Lk 11,33
her erschließen: „Christus ist das Licht der Welt (vgl. Joh 8,12)." Daraus folge: „Die
Christen und Christinnen ihrerseits sind das Licht der Welt (vgl. Mt 5,14), sie, deren
‚Auge' bzw. ‚Leuchte des Leibes' das Innere und das Äußere erleuchtet (VV 34–36)."

nen werden. Betrachten wir zunächst die Argumentationsstruktur des Q-Stückes:

Den Text eröffnet in V. 34a eine Sentenz zur Physiognomie des Menschen: „Die Leuchte des Leibes ist das Auge." Das Auge gilt also hier, wie seit Alkmaion, Parmenides und den Pythagoreern häufig angenommen wurde, als ein Organ, das Licht aussendet.[9] Die Teilverse Q 11,34b+c werten diese auch im Judentum breit rezipierte physikalische Vorstellung[10] in ethischer Hinsicht aus, indem sie das Auge als *pars pro toto* des Leibes verstehen und Schlüsse vom Zustand des Auges auf die Verfassung des mit ihm verbundenen Körpers, also der gesamten Person, ziehen: „Wenn dein Auge lauter (ἁπλοῦς) ist, ist dein ganzer Leib licht. Wenn aber dein Auge böse (πονηρός) ist, (ist) dein ganzer Leib finster." Die Verse 35 und 36 beschreiben aufgrund der beiden möglichen Zustände des Leibes in chiastischer Fortführung von V. 34a+b die Räume oder Sphären, in denen diese Leiber existieren: „Wenn nun das Licht in dir Finsternis ist, wie groß (ist dann) die Finsternis! Wenn nun dein Leib ganz licht ist und keinen finsteren Teil hat, wird er ganz licht sein, wie wenn die Leuchte mit dem Blitzstrahl dich erleuchtet."

Die Rede von Licht und Finsternis in V. 35–36 darf man als eschatologische Zuspitzung der einleitenden Betrachtung des menschlichen Auges verstehen und darin die jesuanische Pointe des Stückes erkennen: Je nach seinem „Auge" und seiner daraus zu erschließenden ethischen Verfasstheit gehört der Mensch in die Todessphäre tiefer Finsternis oder in die Lebenssphäre immensen Lichtes. Die Logien zeichnen sich in für den Nazarener charakteristischer Weise dadurch aus, dass sie nicht zeitlos gültige Klugheitsregeln formulieren, sondern den Adressaten die Augen dafür öffnen wollen, dass das Ethos des Menschen angesichts des gegenwärtigen Andrängens der göttlichen Herrschaft über sein endzeitliches Geschick zumindest mitentscheidet.[11] Unklar bleibt jedoch, welcher Zusammenhang zwischen dem endzeitlichen Status des Menschen und

---

9. Dazu Betz, „Matthäus 6, 22–23", 62–77; vgl. Allison, „The Eye is the Lamp of the Body", 63.

10. Belege bei Allison, „The Eye is the Lamp of the Body", 66–69.

11. Es ist daher zutreffend, das Q-Stück in den Zusammenhang jesuanischer Gerichtsrede zu stellen; vgl. Susan R. Garrett, „„Lest the Light in You Be Darkness'. Luke 11:33–36 and the Question of Commitment", *JBL* 110 (1991): 105. —Licht und Finsternis als stehende Metaphern für die Lebens- bzw. Todessphäre begegnen bei Jesus von Nazareth auch sonst gelegentlich (vgl. Mt 10,27 par. Lk 12,3 oder Lk 16,9).

dem dafür verantwortlichen Zustand seines Auges besteht: Was unter dem „lauteren" bzw. dem „bösen" Auge zu verstehen ist, bleibt hier wie in der sonstigen Jesus-Überlieferung unbeantwortet. Es handelt sich offenbar um geprägte weisheitliche Sprache, die der Nazarener als bekannt voraussetzt, und zwar um eine semitische Redeweise,[12] die in den indoeuropäischen Sprachen keine Entsprechung besitzt.

2. Jesus Sirach und das „böse Auge"

Bevor ich klärende Belege zum „lauteren" und zum „bösen" Auge aus dem Sirach-Buch anführe, möchte ich noch einen Zwischenschritt einlegen. Die auffällige Rede vom Auge in Q 11,34–36 ist nur *ein* Element des semantischen Netzes, das diese Rede des Jesus von Nazareth mit den Sprüchen des Jesus Sirach verbindet. An einem kurzen gleichnisartigen Sirach-Text möchte ich das verdeutlichen. Sir 23,18–19LXX (ähnlich die syrische Peschitta; ein hebräischer Textzeuge fehlt) lautet:

> Ein Mensch, der fern von seinem (Ehe-)Bett fremdgeht, sagt in seiner Seele: „Wer sieht mich? Finsternis umgibt mich, und die Mauern verbergen mich, und niemand sieht mich. Warum soll ich vorsichtig sein? Keinesfalls wird sich der Höchste an meine Sünden erinnern".[13] Ja, seine Furcht sind die Augen der Menschen, aber er hat nicht erkannt, dass die Augen des Herrn, (die) zehntausend Mal lichter (sind) als die Sonne, alle Wege der Menschen beobachten und in die verborgenen Bereiche hinein wahrnehmen.[14]

Trotz sachlicher Unterschiede—hier geht es um Ehebruch, dort um Gut- und Bösäugigkeit—findet sich in diesen beiden Sirach-Versen ein

---

12. Dass es um die weisheitliche Rede vom „guten" bzw. „bösen Auge" geht (dazu unten) wird bereits in der älteren Literatur häufig erwogen. Vgl. etwa Jülicher, *Die Gleichnisreden Jesu. Zweiter Teil*, 100–01; Wilhelm Michaelis, „ὀφθαλμός," *TWNT* 5:376–79, oder Edlund, *Das Auge der Einfalt*, 24, der diese traditionsgeschichtliche Herleitung S. 107 aufgrund der Einwände von Paul Billerbeck, *Kommentar zum Neuen Testament aus Talmud und Midrasch I: Das Evangelium nach Matthäus* (München: C.H. Beck, 9. Auflage 1986), 432 allerdings wieder in Frage stellt—zu Unrecht, denn Billerbeck dokumentiert, in merkwürdigem Selbstwiderspruch, 833–35 diesen Zusammenhang seinerseits anhand reicher Textbelege.

13. Vgl. Sir 16,15.18–19 (= 16,17.20–21LXX und Peschitta).

14. Vgl. Sir 17,15.19–20 (nur LXX und Peschitta); 39,19.

beträchtlicher Teil des semantischen Inventars der eben betrachteten Jesus-Überlieferung wieder: Der grundlegende Kontrast zwischen Licht und Finsternis, der Gegensatz zwischen dem sich unsichtbar wähnenden, nachtaktiven Ehebrecher und den von ihm gefürchteten Augen eventueller Zeugen sowie der Gegensatz zwischen dem Verbergen-Wollen der bösen Tat und den unendlich hellen Augen Gottes, die ins Verborgene dringen— all das gehört in unterschiedlich großen Anteilen zum semantischen Stoff, aus dem auch der Text des Nazareners gewebt ist. Besonders signifikant erscheint die Vorstellung von den göttlichen Augen, die zehntausend Mal lichter sind als die Sonne—eine Vorstellung, die exegetisch inspirierend wirkt: Jesu Bild von der Leuchte, die mit einem Blitzstrahl den Menschen in hellstes Licht taucht (Q 11,36), könnte an Sirachs Sprachbild von den unübertrefflich lichten göttlichen Augen anknüpfen, denn die „Leuchte" ist nach Q 11,34 eine Metapher für das „Auge".

Damit zurück zur Semantik der Augenmetaphorik in der Q-Überlieferung. Die Metaphern vom lichten, guten und vom finsteren, bösen Auge finden sich an zahlreichen Stellen des Sirach-Buches.[15] Es handelt sich tatsächlich um Metaphern, denn nirgends ist dort an ein gutes, gesundes Auge oder ein schlechtes, krankes Auge mit herabgesetzter Sehkraft gedacht. Auch auf die volkstümliche Vorstellung vom bösen Blick, der Schaden zufügt und vor dem man sich hüten muss, spielt Jesus Sirach mit dieser Redewendung nirgends an.[16] Worauf also verweist diese Metaphorik, die sogar in Bezug auf Gott verwendet wird, der allerdings, und das ist gewiss bedeutsam, bei Sirach nie böse, finstere, sondern stets gute, lichte Augen hat?

Besonders helles Licht auf die Semantik des Begriffs fällt aus einem Lehrstück des Jesus Sirach in 13,25–14,10. Es behandelt in typisch weisheitlicher Schwarz-weiß-Manier den Gegensatz zwischen dem „guten Auge" und dem „bösen Auge" und den Gegensatz zwischen ihren Besit-

---

15. Sir 14,3 (Hebr[B], Syr, ähnlich LXX); 14,8 (LXX); 14,10 (Hebr[B] [bis], LXX, Syr); 34,12[31,13aLXX] (Hebr[B]; LXX); 34,13a (Hebr[B], Syr); 34,13e[31,13bLXX] (Hebr[B]; LXX); 32,12[35,12(35,9)LXX] (Hebr[B]; LXX, Syr); 35,10[35,7] (LXX, Syr); 37,29 (Syr); vgl. ferner Sir 14,9[10] (Hebr[B], LXX, Syr); 20,14–15 (LXX, Syr); 30,19b–20a (Hebr[B], LXX, Syr). Für eine Liste der Belegstellen des Lexems „Auge" im syrischen Sirach-Buch danke ich meinem Freund und Kollegen Gabriel Rabo (Salzburg).

16. Gegen John H. Elliott, „The Evil Eye and the Sermon on the Mount", _BI_ 2 (1994): 51–84, der alle literarischen Belege für das „böse" Auge auf den in der antiken Kultur weitverbreiteten Glauben an die magische Kraft schädigender Blicke zurückführen möchte.

zern, dem „Gutäugigen" (טוב עין) und dem „Bösäugigen" (רע עין). Sir 13,25–14,10 lautet nach der hebräischen Handschrift A:

13,25

לב אנוש ישנא פניו / אם לטוב ואם לרע:

Das Trachten (wörtlich: Herz) des Menschen verändert sein Gesicht, / sei es zum Guten, sei es zum Bösen.

13,26

עקבת לב טוב פנים אורים / ושיג ישיח מחשבת עמל:

Die Spuren eines guten Trachtens (wörtlich: Herzens) sind ein leuchtendes Gesicht, / aber Kummer [?] klagt [?] über einen Gedanken von Mühsal [?].

14,1

אשרי אנוש לא עצבו פיהו / ולא אבה עליו דין לבו:

Glücklich ist ein Mensch, (wenn) sein Mund ihn nicht kränkt, / und (wenn) Kummer über sein Trachten (wörtlich: sein Herz)[17] nicht über ihn will.

14,2

אשרי איש לא חסרתו נפשו ולא שבתה תוחלתו:

Glücklich ist ein Mann, (wenn) ihn sein Ich (wörtlich: seine Seele) nicht Mangel leiden lässt, / und (wenn) seine Hoffnung nicht aufhört.

14,3

ללב קטן לא נאוה עושר / ולאיש רע עין לא נאוה חרוץ:

Für ein kindisches Trachten (wörtlich: kleines Herz) ist Reichtum nicht erfreulich, / und für einen bösäugigen Mann ist Gold nicht erfreulich.

14,4

מונע נפשו יקבץ לאחר / ובטובתו יתעבע זר:

Wer sich selbst vorenthält, sammelt für einen anderen, / und in seinem Glück wird ein Fremder schwelgen.

14,5

רע לנפשו למי ייטיב / ולא יקרה בטובתו:

Wer zu sich selbst böse ist: Wem wird er Gutes erweisen? / Und in seinem Glück wird er nicht angetroffen.

---

17. Die Constructus-Verbindung ist als Genitivus objectivus aufzulösen.

14,6

רע לנפשו אין רע ממנו / ועמו תשלומת רעתו:

Wer zu sich selbst böse ist: Es gibt keinen Böseren als ihn. / Und Vergeltung für seine Bosheit ist mit ihm.

14,7–8
[fehlt in Handschrift A]

14,9

בעין כושל מעט הוא חלקו / ולוקח חלק רעהו מאבד חלקו:

Im Auge eines Strauchelnden [?]) ist sein Besitzanteil zu klein. / Und wenn er den Besitzanteil seines Nachbarn nimmt, verliert er seinen Besitzanteil.

14,10

עין רע עין תעיט על לחם / ומהומה על שלחנו: / עין טובה מרבה הלחם / ומעין
יבש יזל מים על השלחן:

Das Auge des Bösäugigen stürzt sich aufs Brot,[18] / und Panik (herrscht) auf seinem Tisch. / Ein gutes Auge mehrt das Brot, / und aus einer trockenen Quelle (עין) strömt Wasser über den Tisch [?].[19]

Trotz einiger hebräischer Textprobleme, die hier auf sich beruhen können, sind die Oppositionen in diesem Lehrstück klar markiert. Scharf zugespitzte Verse charakterisieren zwei Menschentypen, die sich hinsichtlich ihrer ethischen Haltung zum Besitz grundsätzlich unterscheiden. Einleitend wird festgestellt, dass das Planen und Trachten, das hebräisches Denken im „Herzen" lokalisiert, die Physiognomie des Menschen prägt. Die Bedürfnisse, die ihn umtreiben, hinterlassen Spuren in seinem Aussehen—Spuren, die den Mitmenschen verraten, mit wem sie es zu tun haben. Das ist weisheitliche Psychologie vom Feinsten! Anschließend beschreibt Jesus Sirach die beiden Typen so anschaulich, dass seine Schülerschaft sie im Alltag zu erkennen und einzuschätzen lernt. Der vorbildliche Mensch ist der, dessen Planungsinstanz, das Herz, sich nichts vorwerfen lassen muss, der mit seinem Besitzanteil zufrieden ist, der seine טובה, das ihm geschenkte Gut und Glück, genießt, ohne sich in seinen Bedürfnissen künstlich einzuschränken. Der problematische Mensch ist der, der über

---

18. Vgl. Sir 37,29 (Syr).

19. Sir 14,10LXX: „Ein böses Auge ist neidisch über dem Brot / und Mangel ist auf seinem Tisch." Die Versteile 14,10c–d fehlen in LXX und Peschitta.

den ihm gewährten Besitzanteil hinaus nach Gütern strebt, dem fremder Reichtum unerträglich ist, der ansammelt, ohne das Angehäufte genießen oder teilen zu können, dessen Drang nach Mehrung seines Besitzes ihn niemals einen Zustand des Glücks finden lässt: Am Ende muss er seinen Erben hinterlassen, was er zusammengerafft hat.

Diesen zweiten Menschentypus nennt Jesus Sirach, in Aufnahme einer älteren weisheitlichen Terminologie, die seit den Proverbien (s. dort 22,9; 23,6) bezeugt ist,[20] den עין רע, den „Bösäugigen" (V. 10). Wie kein anderes Organ stellt das Auge die Verbindung zwischen dem Individuum und seiner Lebenswelt her. Was es sieht und dann begehrt, bestimmt wesentlich die Einstellungen und Handlungsstrategien, die der heranwachsende Mensch gegenüber seiner Umwelt entwickelt. Bestechend ist, dass Sirach die neurotische Disposition des bösäugigen Typus in ihrer Janusköpfigkeit erfasst: Der Bösäugige ist sowohl der nimmer satte Gierige, der nach dem Besitz seines Nächsten trachtet, als auch der unerbittlich Geizige, der niemandem Gutes erweist, unter dessen hungrigen Tischgenossen Panik herrscht, der sich selbst nichts gönnt und dadurch sein Lebensglück verspielt. Obwohl Gier und Geiz sozialpsychologisch eng zusammengehören, werden diese Phänomene in den indoeuropäischen Sprachen terminologisch unterschieden[21]: Weil es im Griechischen oder Lateinischen keinen zusammenfassenden Begriff für den Gier-Geiz gibt, begegnet die semitische Redeweise vom bösen Auge in den Sirach-Übersetzungen oft in wörtlicher Wiedergabe—auf die Gefahr hin, dass die Leser mit dem in den Zielsprachen semantisch dunklen Ausdruck nichts Rechtes anfangen können.

Das „gute Auge", von dem in 14,10 die Rede ist, erklärt sich nach dem Gesagten von selbst: Der Gutäugige weiß mit seinem Besitz angemessen umzugehen; er ist großzügig gegenüber sich selbst und gütig gegenüber anderen. An seinem Tisch werden die Hungrigen satt.[22] Das Ziel der Lehr-

---

20. Atl. und spätere Belege bei Franz Josef Stendebach, „עין", ThWAT 6:38; die Sir-Belege streift Stendebach nur oberflächlich (6:46–47). Vgl. ferner die in Anm. 12 genannte Literatur sowie Joseph Amstutz, ΑΠΛΟΤΗΣ. Eine begriffsgeschichtliche Studie zum jüdisch-christlichen Griechisch, Theoph. 19 (Bonn: Peter Hanstein, 1968), 99–101.—Von den rabbinischen Belegen verdient die sehr anschauliche Stelle mTer 4,3a (über geizige und großzügige Erstlingsgaben) besondere Beachtung; sie mag zudem von Sir 35,10(35,7) (LXX und Peschitta) mit inspiriert worden sein.

21. Im Griechischen etwa tritt neben die πλεονεξία (das Mehr-haben-Wollen) die φιλαργυρία (die Liebe zum Geld, die verhindert, es auszugeben).

22. Und am Altar ist Gott der Adressat reicher Opfer: „Gib ihm [Gott] ent-

rede ist klar: Sirach warnt seine vermutlich jugendlichen Schüler vor dem Bösäugigen und stellt ihnen das Ideal des Gutäugigen vor die noch lernfähigen Augen.

Jesus Sirach war gewiss ein ausgezeichneter Beobachter des Sozialverhaltens seiner Zeitgenossen, ein Psychologe im modernen Sinn war er nicht, denn er vermischt Beschreibung und Bewertung seiner idealtypischen Protagonisten. Wo man heute allenfalls von einer akzentuierten Persönlichkeit sprechen würde, redet er von einem Bösäugigen, qualifiziert also das Trachten des Betreffenden als negativ und folglich als ethisch verwerflich. Das Recht dazu gewinnt er aus der theologischen Perspektive, unter der er seine jüdischen Zeitgenossen, Mitglieder des Gottesvolkes wie er, betrachtet. Mögen die Heiden sich benehmen, wie sie wollen; unter dem jüdischen Volk zeltet die göttliche Weisheit (24,10–11) und offenbart ihm Regeln, deren Beachtung seinen Bestand und sein Wohlergehen sichert.

Diese theologische Dimension betont ein weiterer Lehrtext über die Bösäugigkeit, der sich in Sir 34[31LXX],12ff. findet. Seine Einleitung lautet in synoptischer Übersetzung der hebräischen Handschrift B, der Septuaginta und der Peschitta so:

LXX	Hebräischer Text (B)	Peschitta
12-tit. [in wenigen Kodizes]: Über (Gast-)Mahl und Speisen	12-tit.: Belehrung über Brot und Wein (= Mahl und Trinkgelage) zugleich	—
12a An einem großen Tisch sitzt du?	12a Mein Sohn, wenn du am Tisch eines Großen sitzt,	12a Mein Sohn, wenn du am Tisch eines reichen Mannes sitzt,
12b Öffne nicht über ihm deinen Rachen	12b öffne nicht über ihm deinen Rachen.	12b öffne nicht über ihm deinen Rachen
12c und sage nicht: Viel (ist) ja, was auf ihm (steht)!	12c Sage nicht: Reichlich ist auf ihm!	13 und sage nicht: Es ist nicht genug für mich!
13a Denke daran, dass ein böses Auge ein Übel ist.	12d Denke daran, dass ein böses Auge böse ist.	

sprechend seinem Geschenk an dich / in Gutäugigkeit (בטוב עין) und entsprechend (deinem) Vermögen." (Sir 32,12[35,9LXX])

Textvariante I: Langform
(HebrB + Syr)

13a Den Bösäugigen hasst   14 Denn ein böses Auge
Gott,   (Obj.) hasst Gott (Subj.),

13b und einen Böseren als   15a und (wisse), dass er
ihn hat er nicht erschaffen. Böseres als es nicht erschaf-
                            fen hat.

13c Ja, das (ist es): Ange- 15b Daher [?] erzittert das
sichts einer jeden Sache   Auge wegen allem,
zittert (sein) Auge,

13d und vom Angesicht her   15c und vom Gesicht her
weint es Tränen.   vergießt es Tränen.

Textvariante II: Kurzform
(HebrB + LXX)

13b Was ist Böseres als das   13e Böseres als *den Bösäu-*
Auge erschaffen worden?   *gigen*23 hat Gott nicht
                             zugeteilt (= erschaffen?).

13c Deshalb weint es von   13f Deshalb läuft seine (=
ganzem Angesicht.   des Auges) Feuchte ange-
                             sichts aller (Dinge) davon.

gemeinsame Fortsetzung

14a Wo er hinblickt, strecke 14a Wo er hinblickt, strecke 16 Strecke deine Hand nicht
nicht die Hand aus   die Hand nicht aus,   aus (zu dem), was du gese-
                                                         hen hast,

14b und stoße nicht mit   14b und nicht vereinige   17 und stecke deine Hand
ihm zusammen in der   sie sich24 mit ihm in der   nicht in eine Schüssel.
Schüssel.   Schüssel.

---

23. Der in Handschrift B überlieferte Text: „Böseres als das Auge", ist offensichtlich korrupt, obwohl er, wie die griechische Übersetzung zeigt, bereits der LXX vorlag.
Eine Marginalie der Handschrift B korrigiert einigermaßen verzweifelt ins Gegenteil: „Übleres als das Auge hat Gott erschaffen." Tatsächlich sind für Sirach die Augen
Teil der guten Schöpfung Gottes (Sir 17,5[6]). Der hebräische Wortlaut dürfte früh
durch Haplographie zweier Buchstaben entstellt worden sein: Die Parallelfassung in
V. 13a+b verlangt für V. 13e den Wortlaut: רע מרע עין.
   24. Verbesserung von B nach der dortigen Marginalie (Verschreibung von ת in
ד). Statt „nicht vereinige sie sich" auch möglich: „nicht vereinige dich".

Sirach erinnert zu Beginn seiner Rede über gutes Benehmen bei Gastmählern und Trinkgelagen an einen bekannten Sachverhalt. Die Hörerschaft weiß bereits, dass das „böse Auge", die Neigung zu Gier und Geiz, sozial schädlich ist: Das gilt nun speziell beim Symposium, dem herausragenden Ort sozialer Interaktion in der Antike. Um den Ernst seiner Mahnung einzuschärfen, begründet Sirach sie in V. 13 theologisch. Ein Blick in die Synopse zeigt, dass diese theologische Begründung im überlangen V. 13 des hebräischen Textes zweimal enthalten ist. Offenbar handelt es sich um zwei Varianten desselben Logions, eine längere in V. 13a–d und eine kürzere in V. 13e+f. Die längere Fassung hat der Syrer rezipiert, die kürzere liegt dem griechischen Text zugrunde. Der bedeutende anonyme Sirachphilologe des Mittelalters, dem das hebräische Manuskript B zu verdanken ist, hat in den ihm zugänglichen Handschriften beide Fassungen vorgefunden und sie in seinem Manuskript vermutlich selbst zu *einem* Text verbunden.

Beide Fassungen sind von Korruptelen nicht frei, aber erkennbar zweiteilig: Der erste Teil formuliert den göttlichen Abscheu, ja Hass, gegenüber dem Bösäugigen, der zweite führt als Begründung das jämmerliche Erscheinungsbild des Gierig-Geizigen an. Um die Objekte seiner unstillbaren Begierde zu erlangen, schämt sich der Bösäugige nicht, vor anderen kräftig auf die Tränendrüse zu drücken (vgl. Sir 12,16).

In dieser Karikatur fließt zusammen, was Jesus Sirach an zahlreichen Stellen seines Werkes über die Kumulation von Besitz in den Händen weniger und den Nahrungsmangel in den Mägen vieler zu sagen weiß. Zitiert seien exemplarisch die Sentenzen 34[31],21–22LXX: „Das Brot für die Bedürftigen ist der Lebensunterhalt der Armen, wer ihn zurückhält, ist ein Blutrünstiger (ἄνθρωπος αἱμάτων). Seinen Nächsten mordet, wer ihm den Lebensunterhalt wegnimmt, und Blut vergießt, wer den Lohn des Tagelöhners zurückhält." Jesus Sirach blickt auf eine entsolidarisierte Gesellschaft, in der die Besitzlosen täglich damit rechnen müssen, dass ihr Lebensfaden durch den Geiz der Vermögenden, durch deren fehlende soziale Empathie abgeschnitten wird. Dies ist der tiefere Grund für die theologische Kritik, die Sirach an den Bösäugigen übt. Der Maßstab für solche Kritik dürfte ein Verfassungsideal sein, nach dem alle Mitglieder des Gottesvolkes das Recht auf einen auskömmlichen Anteil an dem von Gott geschenkten Land und seinen Erträgen haben (vgl. oben Sir 14,9). Wo Geizige und Gierige sich den חלק des Ohnmächtigen aneignen, wird Gottesrecht gebrochen und die göttliche Weisheit, die in Jerusalem wohnt (24,11) und ein gelingendes Leben für alle Mitglieder des Gottesvolkes einfordert, *ad absurdum* geführt.

3. Jesus von Nazareth und das „böse Auge", Teil II

Es liegt nahe, dass die Rede des Jesus von Nazareth vom „lichten" und vom „bösen" Auge in der Tradition der Weisheitstheologie des Sirachen steht, zumal sie sich in dessen Buch häufiger findet als in jeder anderen antiken jüdischen Schrift. Eine Neucodierung dieser Terminologie findet bei dem Nazarener nicht statt. In der einleitend zitierten Q-Überlieferung 11,34–36 versteht er das Erscheinungsbild des Auges als Indikator für die sozialethische Grundhaltung eines Menschen—ganz im Sinne einer Variante zu Sir 16,21aLXX, die im Codex Sinaiticus als Marginalie festgehalten ist: „Und so, wie ein Mensch handelt, wird sein Auge blicken."[25]

Auch bei Jesus von Nazareth verweist die Rede vom guten und bösen Auge auf die soziale Kompetenz des Menschen—Uneigennützigkeit und Großzügigkeit auf der einen, Gier und Geiz auf der anderen Seite sind die psychischen Operatoren, die sein Sozialverhalten entscheidend prägen. Die theologische Qualifizierung des einen wie des anderen fällt bei Jesus von Nazareth noch deutlich schärfer aus als bei Jesus Sirach. Durch Gewährung oder Verweigerung von Solidarität gegenüber den Mittellosen positioniert sich der Mensch gegenüber dem parteiischen Gott: Gier und Geiz lassen ihn in die Finsternis der Gottesferne treten, Lauterkeit und Güte rücken ihn an die Seite des gutäugigen Gottes, so nah, dass der Blitzstrahl des göttlichen Auges ihn erleuchtet (Q 11,36).[26]

---

25. Die Textlesart von Sir 16,21aLXX enthält offenbar Korruptelen: „Der Windstoß, den ein Mensch nicht erblicken wird..." (Codex Sinaiticus beseitigt die Aposiopese durch den Zusatz: „..., wird auf ihn kommen.").

26. Dass es bei der Bösäugigkeit um das Verhältnis des Menschen zum Besitz geht, hat Mt noch gewusst, dessen Version der Q-Tradition in den besitzkritischen Abschnitt seiner Bergpredigt (6,19–34) unmittelbar vor dem Mammonswort (6,24) eingearbeitet ist. Zur Auslegung von Mt 6,22–23 s. Luz, *Das Evangelium nach Matthäus I*, 466–68, und Matthias Konrad, *Das Evangelium nach Matthäus*, NTD 1 (Göttingen: Vandenhoeck & Ruprecht, 2015), 112, die die Pointe der Tradition (Konradt ohne Hinweis auf Sir) im Ansatz zutreffend beschreiben.—Lk hat die Q-Überlieferung 11,34–36 mit dem Bildwort vom Licht 11,33 (par. Mt 5,15) verbunden (Stichwortanschluss). Die sozialpsychologische Bedeutung der Augenmetaphorik im antiken Judentum war ihm offenbar unbekannt; andernfalls hätte er das Stück, ähnlich wie Mt, womöglich im Zusammenhang von Lk 12,33–34 eingeordnet. Michael Wolter, *Das Lukasevangelium*. HNT 5 (Tübingen: Mohr Siebeck, 2008), 427, weist zu Lk 11,34 knapp auf den jüdischen Hintergrund der Rede vom „bösen" Auge hin, deren Semantik er mit dem gern assoziierten Begriffspaar „Neid und Missgunst" allerdings ungenau beschreibt.

Die gesellschaftliche Situation, in der beide Jesusse lebten, macht ihren theologisch begründeten Appell, übermäßigen individuellen Besitz zugunsten solidarischer Güte aufzugeben, ohne weiteres verständlich. Ohne die Gutäugigen, deren Zahl immer zu klein ist, bricht eine Gesellschaft auseinander. Davor warnen beide. Sie kennen die Triebstrukturen des Menschen und wissen, wie leicht er sich von seiner Gier fortreißen lässt.

Jesu Parabel von den Arbeitern im Weinberg (Mt 20,1–15) schließt mit einem denkwürdigen Dialog zwischen dem Anführer jener Arbeiter, die zwölf Stunden geschuftet haben, und dem Weinbergbesitzer, der jedem seiner Tagelöhner, für welche Arbeitszeit auch immer, denselben Lohn von einem Denar gibt. Dem Arbeiterführer, der gegen diese Praxis rebelliert, gibt er zur Antwort: „Freund, ich tue dir kein Unrecht. Bist du nicht um einen Denar mit mir übereingekommen? Nimm das Deine und geh! Ich will aber diesem letzten geben wie auch dir. Oder steht es mir nicht frei, mit dem Meinen zu tun, was ich will? Oder ist dein Auge böse, weil ich gütig bin?" (Mt 20,13b–15) Der rebellische Arbeiter ist nicht „neidisch" oder macht „ein böses Gesicht", wie es gängige Bibelübersetzungen wollen[27], sondern er ist „bösäugig", nämlich gierig, weil er meint, angesichts der Güte des Besitzers mehr für sich herausschlagen zu können als das, was für andere zum Leben reicht. Ob er begreift, dass es genügt, wenn er sein Auskommen hat, und dass es ein Segen ist, wenn jedes Mitglied der Gesellschaft bekommt, was es benötigt, lässt die Parabel offen. Es ist die Hörerschaft des jüngeren wie des älteren Jesus, die sich gegenüber der Zumutung solcher sozialfreundlichen Weisheit verhalten muss.

---

27. S. z.B. die *Gute Nachricht Bibel* („bist du neidisch...") oder die *Zürcher Bibel* („Machst du ein böses Gesicht...").

Trees of Wisdom: Visual Piety in Sir 24 and John 15

Elisa Uusimäki

ZUSAMMENFASSUNG: Dieser Artikel untersucht die Ausübung sichtbarer Frömmigkeit—die Kultivierung des Gesichtssinns—im alten Weisheitsdiskurs. Die Analyse konzentriert sich dabei auf die Anwendung eines bestimmten geistigen Bildes, nämlich dem der Weisheit als Weinstock in Sir 24 und Joh 15. Beide Texte laden ihre Adressaten ein, sich die Weisheit als Weinstock vorzustellen. Sie haben dabei eine gewisse „ekphrastische" Tendenz, wenn sie Analogien herstellen. Die Texte vermitteln ein geistiges Bild durch eine anschauliche literarische Beschreibung, mit der sie den Hörer oder Leser beeinflussen, um so bei der Zuhörerschaft eine emotionale Wirkung zu erzeugen. Diese Art der Analyse, bei der es um die Visualisierung von Weisheit geht, kann Gelehrten dabei helfen, einige der möglichen Funktionen alter Weisheitstexte zu bestimmen und zu erklären: Sir 24 und Joh 15 dokumentieren eine theologische Reflexion, aber solche Reflexionen haben die Funktion, Leben und Frömmigkeit der Adressaten zu gestalten und zu stärken, indem sie durch eine Bildsprache an ihre Herzen appellieren.

---

1. Introduction

How did ancient Jews and early Christians imagine wisdom? This paper focuses on the practice of visual piety—the cultivation of the sense of sight—in ancient wisdom discourse.[1] More specifically, it analyzes the application of one mental image, wisdom as a (vine) tree, in Sir 24 and

Logn paper

---

1. Jane Heath notes how biblical studies long tended to exclude "self-conscious visual interest," which resulted in neglecting many things visual. Some of the central factors that contributed to this state of affairs—especially in the context of study of early Christianity, where Paul's influence has been enormous—derive from the tradition of the dichotomy of the visible versus the invisible, the post-Reformation focus on the piety of the word and the related resistance of the piety of the image, and, finally, the intensification of such logocentricity in Enlightenment Europe; see Heath, *Paul's*

John 15.[2] As I aim to show, both texts invite the reader or listener to visualize wisdom, producing emotional effects in the audience. In so doing, they serve as invitations to pursue wisdom and to take part in wisdom's transformative power.

2. Image and Emotion in Ancient Literature

By focusing on visual piety, I hope to approach the study of wisdom discourse from a new angle. The term was first used by art historian David Morgan in his 1998 book, which explored the use of "popular religious imagery as part of a visual piety." The latter Morgan defined as "the visual formation and practice of religious belief."[3] One concrete example of visual piety is given in Morgan's treatment of Warner Sallman's *Head of Christ* (1940), one of the most popular mass-produced devotional images in North America. Morgan examines this image as a representative of contemporary visual piety, because visual practices related to it have shaped North American social and religious experiences on a communal level.[4]

Visual piety was introduced to the field of biblical studies by Jane Heath in her 2013 book on Paul's letters.[5] "Visual piety," Heath argues, "is not just

---

Visual Piety: The Metamorphosis of the Beholder (Oxford: Oxford University Press, 2013), 13–37.

2. The tree is not the only image associated with wisdom in ancient Jewish discourse. Wisdom is also commonly portrayed as a woman who both walks on the streets and resides in the heavenly realm, thus representing the right path to emulate; see esp. Prov 1–9; 4Q420 1; 4Q421 1 II; 4Q525 2 II, 1–5. Other wisdom-related images concern the essentials of life, such as water (see Prov 18:4; Sir 24:30–34; 4Q418 81+81a 1, 103 II, 6; 4Q525 21 7, 24 II, 8–9) and light (see Sir 24:32; Wis 6:12; 7:10, 26, 29; 1QS XI, 3b–5a; 1Q27 1 I, 5–6).

3. David Morgan, *Visual Piety: A History and Theory of Popular Religious Images* (Berkeley: University of California Press, 1998), 1.

4. Morgan, *Visual Piety*, 1–4, 17, 31–32, 56–57, 124–51. Morgan's research can be linked with wider developments in humanities over the late twentieth century. In academia, art has long been privileged within types of visual media, but the situation changed after the rise of visual studies in the 1970s and 1980s. This area of research has been characteristically interdisciplinary from the start, drawing on a range of fields such as anthropology, art history, gender studies, literature, and media studies. See Heath, *Paul's Visual Piety*, 40–41, 47.

5. Apart from Paul's letters, Heath makes valuable observations on the visual aspects of earlier biblical and Greco-Roman traditions—in the case of the former, paying particular attention to the Pentateuch and Hellenistic Jewish culture; see

a way of looking at art … but a way of using the sense of the sight in this world." Apart from having a material image, the object of practice may also have a mental one. In the context of ancient literary sources, the focus on visual piety means approaching them with a visual interest. In the words of Heath, "the words are read with a view to understanding the visual assumptions they make, or the visual practices they attempt to instill."[6]

In this essay, I analyze the image of wisdom as a (vine) tree to highlight that mental images constitute a significant aspect of visual matters in ancient texts.[7] Apart from offering visual commentary, both Sir 24 and John 15 produce an emotional effect in the audience. This is distinctive in that Hebrew wisdom discourse is dense with metaphors, but the link between images and emotions is rarely explicit.[8] Other sources from the ancient Mediterranean milieu, however, do discuss the emotional effect of literature, associating it rather with visualization. I turn now to a brief review of that evidence.

Beginning with the first century BCE, philosophical authors, rhetoricians, and poets became concerned with the visual effects of literature.[9] In addition to focusing on visualization, some authors from the first century

---

Heath, *Paul's Visual Piety*, 105–42. Recently, see also George J. Brooke, "The Visualisation of the Sacred at Qumran," in *Sibyls, Scriptures, and Scrolls: John Collins at Seventy*, ed. Joel Baden, Hindy Najman, and Eibert J. C. Tigchelaar, JSJSup 175 (Leiden: Brill, 2017), 225–40.

6. Heath, *Paul's Visual Piety*, 36.

7. On mental images, see Heath, *Paul's Visual Piety*, 52: "Material images are not necessarily more significant, more powerful, more vivid or put to work with more self-awareness in the construction of cultural relationships than those in the mind's eye. What matters more than materiality is how the image is used, or the role it plays in building and maintaining the community."

8. A major exception might be the description of wisdom and folly as women in Prov 1–9, as their portrayal is detailed, strongly visual, and at times sensual. Scholarly literature on these personified figures is vast. Recently, see, e.g., Matthew Goff, "The Personification of Wisdom and Folly in Ancient Judaism," in *Religion and Female Body in Ancient Judaism and Its Environments*, ed. Géza G. Xeravits, DCLS 28 (Berlin: de Gruyter, 2015), 128–54.

9. Heath, *Paul's Visual Piety*, 87. The anonymous author of Rhetorica ad Herennium (3.22.35–37), for example, discusses vivid speech and mentions how ordinary things are easily forgotten, "while the striking and novel stay longer in mind." This is not to say that earlier texts are not concerned with visualization. In particular, the detailed manner in which the Shield of Achilles is described in the *Iliad* (18.478–613) is seen as constituting "the touchstone for artistic admiration (and emulation) in word

CE explicitly consider appeals to emotion in their discussions on literary representation. According to Quintilian, the expression of emotions is best achieved when "the images of absent things are presented to the mind in such a way that we seem actually to see them with our eyes and have them physically present to us" (*Inst.* 6.2.28–30; see also 6.2.32).[10] Pseudo-Longinus stresses the speaker's personal involvement that is understood in both emotional and visual terms: "For the term *phantasia* [visualization] ... has now come to be used predominantly of passages where, inspired by strong emotion, you seem to see what you describe and bring it vividly before the eyes of your audience" (*Subl.* 15).[11]

Similarly, Plutarch, while quoting the Greek lyric poet Simonides of Ceos, reports that "painting is silent poetry, and poetry a speaking picture" (*Glor. Ath.* 3.346).[12] He then continues with the emotional impact of history writing, explaining that Thucydides pursues vividness (*enargeia*), "since it is his desire to make the reader a spectator, as it were, and to produce vividly in the minds of those who peruse his narrative the emotions of amazement and consternation which were experienced by those who beheld them" (*Glor. Ath.* 3.347). The same effect is evoked when Xenophon of Athens takes his readers into the battle of Cunaxa—the author thus makes his reader "a participant in the emotions of the perils of the struggle, as though it belonged, not to the past, but to the present" (Plutarch, *Art.* 8.1; see also Xenophon, *Anab.* 1).

In the first centuries CE, the actual literary technique of combining image and emotion was an established unit of study in the Greek schools of the Roman Empire. While the term *ekphrasis* now designates "the literary representation of visual art" in general,[13] it was then understood as a device that was employed in speech and in the training of orators.[14] Three particular properties were associated with *ekphrasis*: *enargeia* ("vividness"),

---

as in image." Thus Froma I. Zeitlin, "Figure: Ekphrasis," *Greece and Rome* 60.1 (2013): 17–31, esp. 18.

10. On Quintilian, see Heath, *Paul's Visual Piety*, 89–91. English translations of ancient Greek texts are from the Loeb Classical Library.

11. On Pseudo-Longinus, see Heath, *Paul's Visual Piety*, 88–89, 91.

12. See also the lyric poet Horace (65 BCE–8 CE): "A poem is like a picture [*ut pictura poesis*]" (*Ars* 361).

13. James A. W. Heffernan, *Museum of Words: The Poetics of Ekphrasis from Homer to Ashbery* (Chicago: University of Chicago Press, 1993), 1.

14. Zeitlin, "Figure: Ekphrasis," 17.

sapheneia ("clarity"), and *phantasia* ("mental image").[15] Several definitions of the technique originate from the first four centuries CE. They refer to *ekphrasis* as "descriptive speech," emphasizing its purpose of bringing the subject matter "before the eyes" through mental visualization.[16]

Hence, *ekphrasis* shapes one's mind by "sparking mental images." Apart from visualization, it encourages "emotional involvement." Pupils undertook the exercise to learn "how to expand the various elements of a narration" for the sake of creating an emotional effect and response: the listener or the reader was supposed to feel like a witness to the subject matter described.[17] In so doing, the technique aimed at producing "a viewing subject," while also transforming an exercise of reproduction from memory into one of literary composition.[18]

Ekphrasis is not limited to a single subject matter or genre, nor does every text about images count as *ekphrasis*.[19] The topics found in the Greek handbooks range from battles to landscapes and seasons, people and animals, festivals and objects.[20] This article does not analyze a physi-

---

15. Zeitlin, "Figure: Ekphrasis," 17–31, esp. 17. The quality of *enargeia* has been highlighted as the key to grasping the character of *ekphrasis*; it denotes "the vividness that makes absent things seem present by its appeal to the imagination." So Ruth Webb, *Ekphrasis, Imagination and Persuasion in Ancient Rhetorical Theory and Practice* (Abingdon: Ashgate, 2009), 193.

16. Webb, *Ekphrasis, Imagination and Persuasion*, 195. The earliest surviving evidence comes from Theon, who may have been active sometime in the late first century CE. Theon defines *ekphrasis* as "descriptive language, bringing what is portrayed clearly before the sight" (Theon, *Progymnasmata*, 118). Hermogenes of Tarsus (second century CE) maintains that "*ekphrasis* is descriptive speech, as they say, vivid and bringing what is being shown before the eyes" (Hermogenes, *Progymnasmata*, 22). Aphthonios the Sophist, a student of rhetoric from the second half of the fourth century CE, also states that "*ekphrasis* is descriptive language, bringing what is shown clearly before the eyes" (Aphthonios, *Progymnasmata* 36–37). Quotes from George A. Kennedy, *Progymnasmata: Greek Textbooks of Prose Compositions and Rhetoric*, WGRW 10 (Atlanta: Society of Biblical Literature, 2003), 1–2, 45–46, 71, 86, 89, 117. On the importance of setting the image before one's eyes, see Sandrine Dubel, "*Ekphrasis et energeia*: La description antique comme parcours," in *Dire l'évidence: Philosophie et rhétorique antiques*, ed. Carlos Levy and Laurent Pernot (Paris: L'Harmattan, 1997), 249–64, esp. 249.

17. Webb, *Ekphrasis, Imagination and Persuasion*, 193, 195.

18. Simon Goldhill, "What Is Ekphrasis For?," *CP* 102 (2007): 1–19, esp. 2. Dubel, "*Ekphrasis et energeia*," 264.

19. Webb, *Ekphrasis, Imagination and Persuasion*, 2, 4.

20. The idea of an *ekphrasis* as a description of a work of art is later; Zeitlin, "Figure: Ekphrasis," 18.

cal object but an abstract noun (wisdom) and the image in question (tree) draws on figurative wisdom discourse of the Hebrew tradition. Therefore, Sir 24 and John 15 are not argued to count as actual cases of ancient *ekphrasis*, but they can be read in light of the evidence suggesting that literary engagement was linked with visual and emotional involvement around the turn of the era. The term ekphrastic does not exhaustively explain the selected biblical evidence, but it does help one observe and explicate the mélange of striking visualization and its emotional effects in Sir 24 and John 15.

3. Plant Imagery in Ben Sira

In the ancient Near Eastern and Mediterranean cultures, a tree often served as a symbol of fertility, a symbol of the king's rule and power to bless, or a marker of a holy place.[21] In biblical literature, the motifs of wisdom, knowledge, and flora are intertwined specifically with the tree of life traditions that continued to grow in the Second Temple era and thereafter.[22] The very link between wisdom and a tree appears in Prov 3:18, for example, which depicts wisdom as a tree of life. Elsewhere, a wise and pious person is compared to a tree planted by a source of water (Ps 1:3) or one sprouting in the temple (Ps 91:13–15), whereas the godless person is compared to a tree that has lost its flowers (Job 15:32–33).[23]

Plant imagery is also frequently used in the book of Ben Sira. The first-person speaker invites the audience to listen so that they would thrive like

---

21. Michael Bauks, "Sacred Trees in the Garden of Eden and Their Ancient Near Eastern Precursors," *JAJ* 3 (2012): 267–301, esp. 270–82.

22. See, e.g., Peter Thacher Lanfer, *Remembering Eden: The Reception History of Genesis 3:22–24* (Oxford: Oxford University Press, 2012); Rachel Elior, "The Garden of Eden Is the Holy of Holies and the Dwelling of the Lord," *Studies in Spirituality* 24 (2014): 63–118. For a cross-cultural study of the tree of life motif, see E. O. James, *The Tree of Life: An Archaeological Study*, SHR 11 (Leiden: Brill, 1966).

23. A human being is also compared to a withering flower (Job 14:2), while plants in general symbolize hope (Job 14:7–9). See Richard S. Hess, "Floral Imagery," in *Dictionary of the Old Testament: Wisdom, Poetry and Writings*, ed. Tremper Longman III and Peter Enns (Downers Grove, IL: InterVarsity Press, 2008), 218–23. For the metaphorical use of plant imagery as referring to God's people, see Shozo Fujita, "The Metaphor of Plant in Jewish Literature of the Intertestamental Period," *JSJ* 7 (1976): 30–45; Paul Swarup, *The Self-Understanding of the Dead Sea Scrolls Community: An Eternal Planting, A House of Holiness*, LSTS 59 (London: T&T Clark, 2006).

roses by a stream and sprout like lilies (39:12–14).[24] A tree is further used as a metaphor for human life: its endless cycle of blooming and withering reminds one of the ever-changing generations of humankind (14:18).[25] Notably, wisdom herself is described in terms of flora. In Sir 51:14, the speaker describes his longing for wisdom, who came to him in "all her beauty," and the wisdom flower consequently developed into a mature grape (51:15). More often wisdom is depicted as a tree, as in Sir 1:20: "Wisdom's root is to fear the Lord, and her branches are length of days."[26] 14:20–27 also imagines wisdom as a green shelter. The seeker of understanding is depicted as wandering on the paths of wisdom, lurking into her gates, and peeking in through her windows (vv. 22–23). He sets camp beside wisdom's house (vv. 24–26), and wisdom's leafy branches offer a comfortable nest, as well as shade on scorching days (vv. 26–27).

All these cases illustrate the vitality of plant imagery in Ben Sira, but chapter 24, which starts the second part of the book, is most relevant for our present purposes, because it offers an extensive account on wisdom as a tree. This section survives only in Greek, perhaps suggesting that it should primarily be explored in the Egyptian Hellenistic context. An introduction in verses 1–2 is followed by wisdom's self-praise (24:3–17, 19–22), a passage equating wisdom with torah/law (24:23, 25–19), and another passage on the role of a wisdom teacher (24:30–33).[27] Wisdom, after telling how she served God in the holy tent and settled herself in Jerusalem (vv. 10–12), depicts herself through a series of plant imagery (vv. 12–17):[28]

---

24. The addressee is also encouraged to sow their seed in fertile land (26:20, see also 27:6).

25. Sir 14:18 probably contains a Homeric allusion; see James K. Aitken, "The Literary and Linguistic Subtlety of the Greek Version of Sirach," in *Texts and Contexts of the Book of Sirach / Texte und Kontexte des Sirachbuches*, ed. Gerhard Karner, Frank Ueberschaer, and Burkard Zapff, SCS 66 (Atlanta: Society of Biblical Literature, 2017), 115–40.

26. English translations of Sirach from NETS (trans. Benjamin G. Wright III).

27. On the structure of Sir 24, see Patrick W. Skehan and Alexander A. Di Lella, *The Wisdom of Ben Sira: A New Translation with Notes, Introduction and Commentary*, AB 39 (New York: Doubleday, 1987), 331–35. See also Maurice Gilbert, "L'éloge de la Sagesse (Siracide 24)," *RTL* 5 (1974): 326–48.

28. See Alain Fournier-Bidoz, "L'Arbre et la demeure: Siracide xxiv 10–17," *VT* 34 (1984): 1–10.

Like a cedar I was raised up in Lebanon, and like a cypress in the mountains of Haërmon. Like a palm I was raised up in Aiggada, and like rosebushes in Iericho, like a good-looking olive tree in a plain, and I was raised up like a plane tree. Like cinnamon and camel's thorn for spices, and like choice myrrh I gave forth a fragrance, like galbanum and onycha and stacte and like the vapor of frankincense in a tent. I, like a terebinth, spread out my branches, and my branches were branches of glory and grace. I, like a vine, budded forth favor, and my blossoms were the fruit of glory and wealth.

This comparison highlights wisdom's attractiveness: she is like a cedar, the symbol of strength and beauty (cf. Num 24:6; Ps 92:13); like a cypress known for its height (cf. Sir 50:10); like a palm producing dates (cf. 2 Chr 20:2); like a rosebush from the fertile garden of Jericho (cf. 2 Chr 28:15); or like an olive tree.[29] In verse 15, the imagery changes into one of fragrances; the spices mentioned allude to the sacred perfume prepared for the liturgical services of the meeting tent (Exod 30:23–38).[30] Wisdom compares herself to incense in the holy tent, underlining her sacredness and pleasantness to God. She also serves a liturgical and priestly function as mediator between humans and the divine. The flora analogy reappears in verses 16–17, where wisdom compares herself to a terebinth and a vine.[31]

The tree imagery carries with it echoes of the paradise of Eden, with its plethora of beautiful trees (cf. Gen 2:9).[32] Indeed, the vine and the tree of life seem to have become assimilated in Jewish imagination in the late Second Temple era.[33] Yet one subtext does not explain the exegetical creativity of the unit: the focus on gardens and spices also suggests an

---

29. For further discussions, see Skehan and Di Lella, *Wisdom of Ben Sira*, 334.

30. On the spices, see Skehan and Di Lella, *Wisdom of Ben Sira*, 334–35. See also Hess, "Floral Imagery," 221–22.

31. Skehan and Di Lella, *Wisdom of Ben Sira*, 335.

32. See, e.g., Matthew Goff, "Gardens of Knowledge: Teachers in Ben Sira, 4QInstruction, and the Hodayot," in *Pedagogy in Ancient Judaism and Early Christianity*, ed. Karina Martin Hogan, Matthew Goff, and Emma Wasserman, EJL 41 (Atlanta: SBL Press, 2017), 171–94, esp. 175.

33. Annie Jaubert, "L'image de la Vigne (Jean 15)," in *Oikonomia: Heilsgeschichte als Thema der Theologie; Oscar Cullmann zum 65. Geburtstag gewidmet*, ed. Felix Christ (Hamburg: Reich, 1967), 93–99, esp. 95. This was probably the result of depicting wisdom's life-giving power by symbolic means; Raymond E. Brown, *The Gospel according to John*, AB 29–29A (Garden City, NY: Doubleday, 1966–1970), 2:671.

influence from the imagery of the Song of Songs (esp. 4:12–5:1).[34] Apart from its literary echoes, the resulting "texture" produces an emotional effect in the audience. The content of Sir 24 goes beyond the sphere of the intellectual by introducing the senses of sight and smell.[35] Moreover, its visual content has an ekphrastic quality: the (male) addressee can see the subject matter (wisdom) in his mind's eye, to the extent that the wisdom-tree feels present and can be experienced with one's senses. The vivid description conveys an emphatic mental image of wisdom as a tree or, to be exact, as a series of trees.

Such an account expands the narration in chapter 24, which focuses on wisdom's dwelling and identification with torah/law. The section produces an emotional effect in that the addressee wants thereafter also to partake in the beauty of the tree: like a tree, wisdom spreads her fragrance (v. 15), reaches out with her branches (v. 16), and produces good fruit (v. 17). In the subsequent section (vv. 19–22), wisdom even invites her audience to take part in her. The sense of taste is further accentuated here:

> Come to me, you who desire me, and from my produce be filled. For the memory of me is sweet beyond honey, and the inheritance of me beyond a honeycomb of honey. Those who eat me will hunger for more, and those who drink me will thirst for more. He who obeys me will not be ashamed, and those who work with me will not sin.

Wisdom nourishes those who desire her. Her inheritance is reassociated with flora through the images of wisdom's products and honey. This invitation is followed by a section that celebrates the discovery of wisdom in torah/law through water-related analogies (24:23–29).[36] Finally, the focus

---

34. Martti Nissinen, "Wisdom as Mediatrix in Sirach 24: Ben Sira, Love Lyrics, and Prophecy," in *Of God(s), Trees, Kings, and Scholars: Neo-Assyrian and Related Studies in Honour of Simo Parpola*, ed. Mikko Luukko, Saana Svärd, and Raija Mattila, StOr 106 (Helsinki: Finnish Oriental Society, 2009), 377–90.

35. On senses in biblical and cognate literature, see, e.g., Deborah A. Green, *The Aroma of Righteousness: Scent and Seduction in Rabbinic Life and Literature* (University Park, PA: Penn State University Press, 2011); Greg Schmidt Goering, "Attentive Ears and Forward-Looking Eyes: Disciplining the Senses and Forming the Self in the Book of Proverbs," *JJS* 66 (2015): 242–64; Goering, "Honey and Wormwood: Taste and the Embodiment of Wisdom in the Book of Proverbs," *HBAI* 5 (2016): 23–41.

36. Thus, torah is presented as a fruit of the wisdom tree; see Goff, "Gardens of Knowledge," 174–77.

shifts back to Ben Sira as a wisdom teacher and a metaphorical gardener. The sage describes himself as a small river that waters its garden, but this river grows into a current and a sea, while the sage's teaching spreads out into distant lands and moves on like prophetic words (24:30–34). Hence, the teacher-gardener waters his saplings so that they may grow.[37] Or, as set out by Matthew Goff, the students can partake in Eden's fruit via Ben Sira.[38]

4. Jesus as the Tree of Wisdom in John 15

While the New Testament is rich with analogies linked to vegetation, our second source text specifically comes from Jesus's final speech including a section describing Jesus as a vine (John 15:1–17).[39] The latter part of the section, beginning with verse 7, involves themes that can be associated with other passages from the Farewell Discourse.[40] Our present discussion focuses on the vine motif, most explicit in verses 1–6 but echoed still in verses 7 ("remain in me"), 8 ("bearing much fruit"), and 16 ("bear fruit").[41]

Verses 1–6 contain allegorical features—the identification of the vine, the gardener, and the branches—but the stress remains on the relationship between Jesus and his disciples.[42] Remarkably, there are two "I am the real vine" statements in verses 1 and 5. Unlike other "I am" claims in John's Gospel, these statements are developed with an affirmation, "and my Father is the gardener" (v. 1) or "you are the branches" (v. 5). Yet the

---

37. On the motif of a gardener in wisdom and virtue discourse, see also Philo, *Prob.* 69–70; *Plant.* 35–37.

38. Goff, "Gardens of Knowledge," 176.

39. For analogies related to vegetation, see Petra von Gemünden, *Vegetationsmetaphorik im Neuen Testament und seiner Umwelt: Eine Bildfelduntersuchung*, NTOA 18 (Fribourg: Presses Universitaires; Göttingen: Vandenhoeck & Ruprecht, 1993). The unit in John 15:1–17 is separated from the following one by a change of subject between vv. 17 and 18; Brown, *Gospel according to John*, 2:665. Moreover, note that John 15–17 were regarded as later additions in earlier research, but contemporary research mostly approaches the text synchronically, the approach likewise undertaken in this article.

40. For an exposition of the parallels, see Brown, *Gospel according to John*, 2:666. On the vine as a possible eucharistic symbol, see 2:672–74.

41. As such, vv. 1–6 could be later insertions. See Brown, *Gospel according to John*, 2:666. The English translations of John 15 are from NRSV, slightly modified.

42. Brown, *Gospel according to John*, 2:668.

stress remains on Jesus as the real vine (esp. v. 1).[43] The adjective *alēthinos* is typical of John and "implies exclusivity in the sense of 'the only real,' as compared with the putative or would-be."[44] Jesus as the true vine supersedes, therefore, "anything else that might claim to be the source of a disciple's life."[45]

The parable maintains that the branch's sap comes from the vine—that is, "the disciple gets his life from Jesus." The branches remain on the vine as Jesus's disciples remain in him.[46] The question, then, is about a personal relationship in which "one cannot exist without the other."[47] This transforms John's unit into something more than a farewell discourse; as Ernst Haenchen observes, it grows into "a catechism for disciples or a bill of polity." Jesus expresses what is expected from his community.[48]

This section has many possible intertexts.[49] It may echo the ancient myth concerning the tree of life (cf. Rev 22:2) and/or the vineyard symbol, which in Hebrew literature often stands for Israel.[50] Yet the author identifies the vine with Jesus (not with a people) and stresses that the vine is

---

43. Brown, *Gospel according to John*, 2:659.

44. Brown, *Gospel according to John*, 1:500. For *alēthinos*, see also John 1:9; 6:32. Cf. John 4:23 and the remarks by Raimo Hakola, *Identity Matters: John, the Jews, and Jewishness*, NovTSup 118 (Leiden: Brill, 2005), 107–8.

45. Craig R. Koester, *Symbolism in the Fourth Gospel: Meaning, Mystery, Community* (Minneapolis: Fortress, 1995), 246.

46. Brown, *Gospel according to John*, 2:660–61.

47. Brown, *Gospel according to John*, 2:678.

48. Ernst Haenchen, *John: A Commentary on the Gospel of John; Chapters 7–21*, trans. Robert W. Funk, Hermeneia (Philadelphia: Fortress, 1984), 131.

49. See Brown, *Gospel according to John*, 2:672: "Certainly the tree of life figured in Johannine thought … and John's notion of the vine and the branches may stem from a combination of the imagery of Israel as the vine and the imagery of Wisdom as a life-giving tree or vine." Despite the possibly Semitic roots of the parable, in John's version, the Greek phrasing is itself "an essential vehicle," as is demonstrated, e.g., by the paronomasia with the verbs *airein* and *kathairein* in v. 2; Brown, *Gospel according to John*, 2:660.

50. See, e.g., Isa 27:2–6; Jer 5:10; 6:9; 12:10–11; Ezek 15:1–6; 17:5–10; 19:10–14; Hos 10:1; Ps 80:9–14; Brown, *Gospel according to John*, 2:669–70. On John 15 and the image of vineyard, see also Jean Zumstein, "Bildersprache und Relektüre am Beispiel von Joh 15,1–17," in *Imagery in the Gospel of John: Terms, Forms, Themes, and Theology of Johannine Figurative Language*, ed. Jörg Frey, Jan G. van der Watt, and Ruben Zimmermann, WUNT 200 (Tübingen: Mohr Siebeck, 2006), 139–56, esp. 153–55.

the source of life for its branches.[51] Accordingly, the figurative portrayal of wisdom as a tree seems to be a prominent source of influence.[52] Overall, such an interpretative act is typical of John's Gospel, since the author rehashes many traditional Jewish symbols by linking them with the figure of Jesus.[53]

Since Jesus is identified with wisdom in early Christian thought (e.g., John 1; 1 Cor 1:24, 30; Col 1:15–17; 2:2–3), this account, where Jesus depicts himself as a vine, fuses wisdom and vine imagery. The reader or listener is invited to meditate on a specific mental image. This image has a somewhat ekphrastic quality in that Jesus expands his narration by introducing this strikingly visual speech (comparing himself to a vine tree) that produces a specific emotional effect (inviting the audience to take part in the tree). The addressee sees the tree before his or her mind's eye, which shapes him or her as a viewing subject. As a result, the addressee is able to visualize Jesus as a tree even when he is physically absent. Yet the ekphrastic quality of the passage is less vivid than in Sir 24, since the mental image conveyed in John is more bare and focused.

As in Sir 24, the relationship between the vine and its branches is a generative one in John 15: Jesus's *philos* is supposed "to go and bear fruit" (vv. 15–16). Jesus imparts true life, that is, spiritual reality and existence that are to be lived in a concrete time and place.[54] Thus the visual image of a vine serves a formative purpose: the addressee should imagine his or her relationship to Jesus in the same way that a branch is associated with a tree. Such a relationship opens up a new reality that transforms a person and, presumably, enables him or her to achieve wisdom by participating in Jesus the embodiment of wisdom.

---

51. Brown, *Gospel according to John*, 2:670–71.

52. This suggestion is not entirely new; André Feuillet pointed out parallels between John 15 and Sir 24:17–21 in 1960; see Feuillet, "Les themes bibliques majeurs du discours sur le pain de vie (Jn 6)," *NRTh* 82 (1960): 803–22, 918–39, 1040–62, esp. 928.

53. R. Alan Culpepper, *Anatomy of the Fourth Gospel: A Study in Literary Design*, Foundations and Facets: New Testament (Philadelphia: Fortress, 1983), 180–98, esp. 184–85. On symbolism in John, see also Koester, *Symbolism in the Fourth Gospel*; Frey, *Imagery in the Gospel of John*.

54. Haenchen, *John*, 131.

5. Discussion

Both Sir 24 and John 15 present wisdom as a tree: Ben Sira imagines female wisdom through a variety of tree analogies, while Jesus the embodiment of wisdom is represented as a vine in John's visual piety. The reader is invited to visualize wisdom in a materialized form, with Ben Sira further evoking his or her sense of smell. While many scriptural traditions, from the paradise narrative to vineyard accounts, may lurk in the background, the representation of wisdom as a tree is especially prominent in these two accounts.

Both Sir 24 and John 15 build on the Hebrew tradition that compares wisdom to a tree. In so doing, these literary texts employ analogues to describe an abstract concept (wisdom) rather than a physical object. The accounts clearly do not count as actual cases of *ekphrasis* as the term was understood in the Greek schools of the first centuries CE, but the recognition of the somewhat ekphrastic quality of both texts, which is even more prominent in the case of Sir 24, highlights the connection between the visual and the emotional in these units.

The verbal and the visual are also closely intertwined, thus evoking the listener's or the reader's imagination and conveying a mental image in the wisdom discourses. The speech here is heavily descriptive: both sections create an image of wisdom as a tree before the eyes of the addressee.[55] Since the texts are literary documents, the image can be constantly reproduced. In this case, the flora imagery is dynamic, associated with constant growth and change. It is thus applied to wisdom not only as a literary embellishment but functions also as a powerful rhetorical tool and a prominent sign of visual piety.

In Sir 24, wisdom speaks in the first-person and compares herself to a variety of trees and spices. The vine appears in verse 18: "I, like a vine, budded forth favor, and my blossoms were the fruit of glory and wealth." Her fruit is meant to entice the audience, and the following section invites the audience to take part in wisdom's richness (24:19): "Come to me, you who desire me, and from my produce be filled." Those who hunger should eat her, while those who thirst should drink her (24:21).[56] The question is

---

55. See Dubel, "*Ekphrasis* et *energeia*," 249.

56. Cf. John 6:35, 48–51 on Jesus as the provider of nourishment; see Petrus Maritz and Gilbert Van Belle, "The Imagery of Eating and Drinking in John 6:35," in Frey, *Imagery in the Gospel of John*, 333–52, esp. 346–48.

not about observing wisdom from a distance but about desiring her, experiencing her through one's senses, and merging with her.

In John 15, Jesus the embodiment of wisdom speaks of himself as a true vine. While Ben Sira presents the wisdom teacher as a gardener, John reserves the role of pruning to God in heaven (15:1–2). Ben Sira encourages its audience to merge with wisdom, whereas John's audience is invited to take part in Jesus. Nevertheless, the relationship between wisdom and the disciples is perhaps more reciprocal, as is shown by Jesus's proclamations to "abide in me as I abide in you" (15:4; cf. 15:5). The focus here is on the result of such a relationship—that is, on the branches' capability to produce fruit because of their relationship with the vine: "Just as the branch cannot bear fruit by itself unless it abides in the vine, neither can you unless you abide in me" (15:4).

In both texts, the audience is invited to imagine flora, and this kind of visual piety then takes on a didactic quality: one should pursue wisdom and take part in her transformative power.[57] Even so, there are significant differences as well between the two texts.

The text of Sir 24 is much more dynamic, creating a sense of wonder with a wide cast of images.[58] The richness of the visual commentary is almost exhausting and culminates in the (male) gazer's amazement. The aspect of pleasure is explicitly present alongside the description of wisdom's physical beauty. The nature of John 15, on the other hand, is somewhat more static because of its focus on a particular tree; it is this very tree that deserves the gazer's attention, and the text is not concerned with the gender of the gazer. The portrayal of the tree is barer than in Ben Sira, but its emotional effect poignant. The addressee is invited to see himself or herself as a branch in the Jesus-tree—that is, to become a part of the image conveyed.

The imagery of Sir 24 and John 15 seems to have lived on in early Christian visual piety in the following centuries. The cross is imagined as a tree (of life) that produces fruit and whose branches are analogous to the parts of Christ's body in Ignatius's *Letter to the Trallians* (11:1–2). Pseudo-Hippolytus, an anonymous author from the fourth century CE,

---

57. Cf. the idea of an *ekphrasis* as a "guide book"; see Dubel, "*Ekphrasis et energeia*," 256–57.

58. Apart from trees, the water imagery is also rich in nuances, along with references to multiple rivers that can be associated with the Eden story; see Goff, "Gardens of Knowledge," 175–76.

also meditates on the cosmic significance of the cross. He combines the images of the tree and Jesus's cross, alluding in addition to the tree's pleasant fragrance.[59] Such an afterlife further testifies to the effectiveness of the wisdom–flora analogy.

6. Conclusions

The notion of visual piety offers one prospect for exploring wisdom discourses in Jewish and Christian antiquity. As I hope to have shown, both Sir 24 and John 15 invite their audiences to take part in visual piety by depicting wisdom as a tree and by sharing a somewhat ekphrastic tendency in constructing their analogues; the texts convey a mental image through a vivid literary description and affect the listener or the reader, shaping his or her imagination and emotions. This sort of analysis concerning wisdom's visualization may help in the recognition and explication of some of the possible functions of ancient wisdom texts. That is, such texts involved theological reflection, but such reflections themselves carried lived and experienced dimensions: they are meant to form, shape, and strengthen the addressee's life and piety through visual imagery and appeals to emotion.

---

59. For Pseudo-Hippolytus's Easter sermon, see Alister E. McGrath, *The Christian Theology Reader*, 2nd ed. (Oxford: Blackwell, 2001), 333–34.

Das Sirachbuch als Zusammenfassung der alttestamentlichen Theologie

Marko Marttila

ABSTRACT: Many scholars have approached the question of the theology of the Old Testament by proposing themes that could serve as its theological center. Among these themes one might mention concepts such as monotheism, election, covenant, righteousness, creation, dialogue, and encounter. It is characteristic of the book of Ben Sira that this famous sage referred in his teachings to several central theological concepts; he was quite familiar with the traditions that preceded him. In other words, Ben Sira created a kind of synthesis from various views related to Old Testament theology. At the end of this essay, attention is focused on the role of encounter in Ben Sira's work. It seems to be of the utmost importance for Ben Sira that the encounter between God and humans finds its manifestation in worship.

1. Einführung: Begriffsdefinition und Forschungsgeschichte

Der Titel dieses Aufsatzes ist bewusst provokant. Es fehlt nicht an Versuchen, das Konzept einer alttestamentlichen Theologie entweder nachzuweisen oder zu bestreiten. Manche Alttestamentler vertreten die Auffassung, es sei sinnvoller, statt von einer Theologie des Alten Testaments nachdrücklicher von einer Religionsgeschichte Israels zu sprechen.[1] Ein systematisch orientierter Umgang mit den Texten des Alten Testaments erscheint schon

---

1. Rainer Albertz, *Religionsgeschichte Israels in alttestamentlicher Zeit 1. Von den Anfängen bis zum Ende der Königszeit*, ATD Ergänzungsreihe 8/1, 2. durchgesehene Aufl. (Göttingen: Vandenhoeck & Ruprecht, 1996), 32–38, zählt mehrere Punkte auf, warum die Religionsgeschichte eine sinnvollere Zugangsweise zu den Texten des Alten Testaments biete als die Theologie des Alten Testaments. Er erwähnt u.a., dass die Religionsgeschichte der geschichtlichen Struktur des Alten Testaments besser entspreche und sie nicht gezwungen sei, die unterschiedlichen religiösen Aussagen auf einer gedanklichen Abstraktionsebene zu nivellieren.

deshalb unbefriedigend, weil sie keine einheitliche Theologie repräsentieren, sondern eine Vielfalt von Stimmen aus unterschiedlichen Zeiten. Wenn wir im Folgenden die alttestamentliche Theologie aus der Perspektive des Sirachbuches betrachten, dürfte dies weitere kritische Fragen hervorrufen. Ist es vernünftig, den Begriff „alttestamentliche Theologie" im Zusammenhang mit dem Sirachbuch zu verwenden? Gewiss kannte Ben Sira das Alte Testament nicht in dem Umfang oder der Form, wie es heute vorliegt. Die von den Vätern stammenden Schriften genossen noch kein kanonisches Ansehen, als Ben Sira im ersten Viertel des zweiten Jahrhunderts v. Chr. sein Weisheitswerk verfasste.[2] Die jüngsten Schriften oder Buchteile des späteren Alten Testaments waren zu seinen Lebzeiten noch nicht geschrieben, z.B. das Danielbuch und die spätesten Fortschreibungen des Jeremiabuches.[3]

Trotz der oben erwähnten kritischen Einwände möchte ich an der Bezeichnung „Theologie des Alten Testaments" festhalten. Obwohl dem Siraziden das Alte Testament nicht in der heutigen Form vorlag, hat er zweifelsohne den größten Teil davon gekannt.[4] Wortgetreue Zitate enthält das Sirachbuch nur wenige, aber der umfangreiche Abschnitt „Das Lob der Väter" (Sir 44–50) stellt ein unbestreitbares Zeugnis dafür dar, dass Ben Sira der Inhalt des Pentateuchs, der geschichtlichen und der prophetischen Bücher bekannt war. Sein Werk hat auch enge Berührungspunkte mit den Psalmen und Sprüchen. Ben Sira hat also die älteren Traditionen nicht nur gekannt, sondern sie auch ausgelegt und weiterentwickelt. Die Grenzen des hebräischen Kanons waren noch fließend, als Ben Sira wirkte, aber das Ergebnis der späteren Entwicklung wich wahrscheinlich nur wenig von der Bibel ab, die Ben Sira las und lehrte. So bewegte sich Ben Sira in einem damals noch nicht verbindlich abgegrenzten Bereich. Er schätzte das literarische Erbe der früheren Generationen, sah aber gleichzeitig sein eigenes Weisheitswerk als Kontinuum dieses Erbes an:

---

2. Zum Kanonisierungsprozess der hebräischen Bibel siehe die informative Übersicht bei Gunther Wanke, „Art. Bibel I," *TRE* 6 (1980): 1–8.

3. Die Literaturgeschichte der alttestamentlichen Bücher in ihrer chronologischen Reihenfolge hat zuletzt Konrad Schmid eingehend rekonstruiert. Zur Entstehung des Jeremia- und Danielbuches siehe Konrad Schmid, *Literaturgeschichte des Alten Testaments. Eine Einführung* (Darmstadt: Wissenschaftliche Buchgesellschaft, 2008), 166–70, 197–98, 200, 208–9.

4. J. L. Koole, „Die Bibel des Ben-Sira", *OtSt* 14 (1965): 374–96, hat schon in den 1960er Jahren über den Umfang der Bibel, die Ben Sira zugänglich war, nachgedacht.

Immerdar lasse ich Bildung leuchten wie den lichten Morgen und lasse
sie scheinen bis in die Ferne. / Immerdar schütte ich meine Lehre aus
wie eine Weissagung und hinterlasse sie künftigen Geschlechtern. / Seht,
dass ich mich nicht für mich allein gemüht habe, sondern für alle, die
Weisheit suchen. (Sir 24:32–34)[5]

Der Begriff „Theologie des Alten Testaments" ist zweideutig, denn er kann
entweder als *Genetivus subjectivus* oder als *Genetivus objectivus* verstanden werden. Im ersteren Fall handelt es sich um eine Theologie, die das
Alte Testament enthält, im zweiten Fall um eine Theologie, die das Alte
Testament zum Gegenstand hat. Natürlich ist unsere Ausdrucksweise in
diesem Zusammenhang leicht anachronistisch, weil der abstrakte Begriff
„Theologie" den biblischen Autoren fremd war. Unser wissenschaftlicher
Gebrauch des Wortes „Theologie" stammt aus der mittelalterlichen Scho-
lastik und ist von der Welt und Kultur des alten Israel weit entfernt. Die
alttestamentlichen Bücher enthalten jedoch zahlreiche Züge, die für die
spätere jüdische und christliche Theologie konstitutiv geworden sind.
Eine angemessene Definition wurde in den 1930er Jahren von Ludwig
Köhler gegeben: „Mit Theologie des Alten Testaments kann man ein
Buch bezeichnen, wenn es eine durch ihren Inhalt gerechtfertigte, in
den richtigen Zusammenhang gebrachte Zusammenstellung derjenigen
Anschauungen, Gedanken und Begriffe des AT bietet, welche theologisch
erheblich sind oder es sein können".[6] Mit anderen Worten: Angesichts der

---

5. Die deutschsprachigen Zitate aus dem Sirachbuch und aus den anderen biblischen Büchern sind hier und im Folgenden der revidierten Lutherbibel von 2017
entnommen.

6. Ludwig Köhler, *Theologie des Alten Testaments* (Tübingen: Mohr Siebeck,
1936), V. Später hat Claus Westermann die Aufgabe der Theologie des Alten Testaments folgendermaßen definiert: „Eine Theologie des Alten Testaments hat die Aufgabe, zusammenzufassen und zusammenzusehen, was das Alte Testament als ganzes,
in allen seinen Teilen von Gott sagt". Claus Westermann, *Theologie des Alten Testaments in Grundzügen*, ATD Ergänzungsreihe 6, 2. Aufl. (Göttingen: Vandenhoeck &
Ruprecht, 1985), 5. Gott mithilfe von philosophischen Denkkategorien und Begriffen
präziser zu bestimmen, wie es oft in der christlichen Dogmatik und in gewissem Grad
auch in Köhlers Werk geschieht, ist jedoch der alttestamentlichen Anschauung fremd.
Vielmehr wird Gott anhand seiner Taten beschrieben, insbesondere anhand seiner
Beziehung zu den Menschen. Deswegen ist es zutreffend, die göttliche Offenbarung
im Alten Testament als Dialog oder noch besser als Begegnung zwischen Gott und
Mensch zu verstehen, wie es z.B. Timo Veijola, „Offenbarung als Begegnung. Von der
Möglichkeit einer Theologie des Alten Testaments", in *Offenbarung und Anfechtung*.

Vielfalt der alttestamentlichen Theologien sollte man sich auf einige sinnvolle Grundlinien konzentrieren.

Dies hat dazu geführt, dass viele Forscher sich die Aufgabe gestellt haben, die Mitte der alttestamentlichen Theologie so präzis wie möglich zu bestimmen. Eine Fülle verschiedener Themen wurde im Laufe der Zeit in der Forschung als theologische Mitte vorgeschlagen, und die folgende Liste ist nicht einmal vollständig: Monotheismus, Erwählung, Erlösung, Bund, Bundesformel, Gott, Gerechtigkeit, Schöpfung, Tora und Begegnung.[7] Dies sind—ohne Zweifel—zentrale Aspekte der alttestamentlichen

---

Hermeneutisch-theologische Studien zum Alten Testament, hrsg. von Walter Dietrich in Zusammenarbeit mit Marko Marttila (Neukirchen-Vluyn: Neukirchener Verlag, 2007), 20–25 hervorgehoben hat. Siehe auch die Diskussion bei Horst Dietrich Preuß, *Theologie des Alten Testaments 1. JHWHs erwählendes und verpflichtendes Handeln* (Stuttgart: Kohlhammer, 1991), 1–30.

7. Monotheismus: Monotheismus wird üblicherweise im Judentum als das theologische Zentrum des AT angesehen. Auch einige moderne Forscher betonen diesen Aspekt, u.a. Werner H. Schmidt, der im ersten Gebot des Dekalogs das theologische Prinzip der ganzen hebräischen Bibel sieht; Werner H. Schmidt, *Das erste Gebot. Seine Bedeutung für das Alte Testament*, Theologische Existenz heute, N.F. 165 (München: Kaiser, 1970), 11.

Erwählung: Hans Wildberger, „Auf dem Wege zu einer biblischen Theologie", *EvT* 19 (1959): 77–78. Ausführlicher und detaillierter definiert Preuß die Mitte seiner Theologie des Alten Testaments unter dem Leitthema der Erwählung. Nach Preuß, *Theologie*, 29, sei „JHWHs erwählendes Geschichtshandeln an Israel zur Gemeinschaft mit seiner Welt", das zugleich ein dieses Volk (und die Völker) verpflichtendes Handeln ist, als Mitte des Alten Testaments zu bestimmen.

Erlösung: Heinrich Ewald, *Geschichte des Volkes Israel II*, 3. Aufl. (Leipzig: Hirzel, 1865), 156–57.

Bund: August Kayser, *Die Theologie des Alten Testaments in ihrer geschichtlichen Entwicklung dargestellt* (Straßburg: C.F. Schmidt, 1886), 74; Gustav Friedrich Oehler, *Theologie des Alten Testaments*, 2. Aufl. (Stuttgart: Steinkopf, 1882), 69; Walther Eichrodt, *Theologie des Alten Testaments I* (Leipzig: Hinrichs, 1933), 13–14.

Bundesformel: Rudolf Smend, *Die Mitte des Alten Testaments* (Tübingen: Mohr Siebeck, 2002), 1–29.

Gott: G. F. Hasel, „The Problem of the Center in the OT Theology Debate", *ZAW* 86 (1974): 65–82 (79–82); Magne Sæbø, „Hvem var Israels teologer?" *SEÅ* 41/42 (1977): 201–5; Henning Graf Reventlow, *Hauptprobleme der alttestamentlichen Theologie im 20. Jahrhundert*, EdF (Darmstadt: Wissenschaftliche Buchgesellschaft, 1982), 145–47. Neuerdings hat Markus Witte, *Vom Gott des Lebens. Predigten über Texte aus dem Alten Testament. Mit einer Einführung in seine Bedeutung für Glaube, Theologie und Kirche* (Neukirchen-Vluyn: Neukirchener Verlag, 2015), 17–18, vorgeschlagen,

Theologie, obwohl man sich vielleicht nie darüber einig wird, welcher die Mitte des Alten Testaments am treffendsten beschreibt.[8]

---

die Vorstellung von Gott als dem Gott des Lebens als einen roten Faden des Alten Testaments zu bestimmen.

Gerechtigkeit: Walter Dietrich, „Der rote Faden im Alten Testament", *EvT* 49/3 (1989): 232–50.

Schöpfung: Nicht als theologische Mitte des ganzen AT, aber als Mitte und Hintergrund der biblischen Weisheitsliteratur betrachtet Leo G. Perdue, *Wisdom Literature. A Theological History* (Louisville: Westminster, 2007), 17–36, die Schöpfung.

Tora: Otto Kaiser, *Der Gott des Alten Testaments. Teil I: Grundlegung*, UTB 1747 (Göttingen: Vandenhoeck & Ruprecht, 1993), 329–53. Nach Kaiser erreicht die theologische Entwicklung ihren Höhepunkt im Sirachbuch: „Durch dtr und nachdtr Redaktoren sind auch die Vorderen und Hinteren Propheten der Tora explizit als konkrete Auslegung ihrer Segensankündigungen und Fluchandrohungen zugeordnet. Spuren einer entsprechenden Zuordnung lassen sich auch in den Torapsalmen (Ps 1 und 119) und in den Weisheitsbüchern (Spr 28:4 und Koh 12:13) verfolgen. Die Identifikation der Weisheit mit der Tora bei Ben Sira vollendet diesen Prozeß" (329).

Begegnung: Zuerst hat man von einem dialogischen Prinzip oder von einem Wechselgeschehen zwischen Gott und Mensch gesprochen; vgl. Walther Zimmerli, „Das Alte Testament in der Verkündigung der christlichen Kirche", in *Das Alte Testament als Anrede*, BEvT 24 (München: Kaiser, 1956), 76; Zimmerli, „Art. Biblische Theologie: Altes Testament", *TRE* 6 (1980): 445–54; Zimmerli, *Grundriß der alttestamentlichen Theologie*, ThW 3, 4. Aufl. (Stuttgart: Kohlhammer, 1982), 11, 214; Westermann, *Theologie*, 7. Das Konzept von der ‚Mitte' darf man nicht zu statisch verstehen. Bernd Janowski, „Theologie des Alten Testaments. Plädoyer für eine integrative Perspektive", in *Congress Volume Basel*, hrsg. von André Lemaire, VTSup 92 (Leiden: Brill, 2002), 252, schreibt zutreffend: „Wenn es demnach die ‚Mitte' des Alten Testaments als Sinnmitte einer pluriformen Textsammlung nicht gibt und auch nicht geben kann, sondern Hauptthemen und Nebenthemen, Fragen, die immer wieder aufgegriffen und weitergeführt, aber auch solche, die nur angedeutet und abgebrochen werden, so bezeugen die Traditionen des Alten Testaments in ihrer sozialen, politischen und religiösen Vielfalt doch die Sach- und Wirkmitte eines Geschehens. Und zwar eines Geschehens, das es durchgängig mit JHWHs Wirken an Israel und der Welt zu tun hat". Weil dieses Wechselgeschehen nicht immer aus Worten und Reden besteht, hat Veijola vorgeschlagen, dass man eher von einer Begegnung zwischen Gott und Mensch sprechen sollte, die die sprachlose Kommunikation in sich einschließt (s.o. Anm. 6).

8. Neuerdings hat z.B. Jörg Jeremias, *Theologie des Alten Testaments*, ATD Ergänzungsreihe 6 (Göttingen: Vandenhoeck & Ruprecht, 2015), 5–7, es aufgegeben, von einer Mitte des Alten Testaments zu sprechen. Stattdessen bevorzugt er die Denkformen des Glaubens Israels, deren Entwicklung er von den frühen Anfängen bis zum Zeitalter der apokalyptischen Literatur verfolgen kann.

Bemerkenswert ist, dass das Sirachbuch viele dieser theologischen Kernthemen berücksichtigt. Ben Sira ist kein Systematiker nach heutigem Verständnis, aber er greift die Themen auf, die für ihn von Bedeutung waren. Wie es seine Nachfolger bis heute tun, versuchte schon Ben Sira, die früheren Überlieferungen zu aktualisieren. Im Folgenden will ich einige seiner theologischen Schlüsselbegriffe analysieren und zugleich meine Aufmerksamkeit darauf richten, wie Ben Sira die älteren Traditionen nutzte und sogar aktualisierte. Für eine nähere Betrachtung habe ich die folgenden Themen aus dem umfangreichen Material des Sirachbuches ausgewählt: Schöpfung, Bund, Kult, Gott, Erwählung und Begegnung.

2. Zentrale theologische Themen im Sirachbuch

2.1. Schöpfung

Die christlichen Glaubensbekenntnisse beginnen damit, dass sie Gott als Schöpfer ansprechen. Dieses Bekenntnis basiert auf dem, was man am Anfang der Bibel lesen kann. In den meisten alttestamentlichen Büchern fehlt der Gedanke von Gott als Schöpfer. Außer in den priester-schriftlichen und jahwistischen Schöpfungsgeschichten kommt der Gott Israels als Schöpfer des Himmels und der Erde vor allem in den poetischen Werken des Alten Testaments vor (Psalmen, Hiob). Wichtig ist die Schöpfungstätigkeit Jahwes auch bei Deuterojesaja. In gewisser Hinsicht ist die Rede von Jahwe als Schöpfer ein Spätling in der Religionsgeschichte Israels. Es handelt sich um einen Höhepunkt in der Entwicklung, die den ursprünglich auf dem Sinai beheimateten Berg- bzw. Wettergott Jahwe zu dem einzigen Gott des ganzen Erdkreises werden ließ.[9] Hand in Hand mit diesem Prozess verstärkte sich auch die Betonung des Monotheismus.[10]

---

9. Otto Kaiser, *Der Gott des Alten Testaments. Teil II: Wesen und Wirken*, UTB 2024 (Göttingen: Vandenhoeck & Ruprecht, 1998), 81–85; Kaiser, *Der Gott des Alten Testaments. Teil III: Jahwes Gerechtigkeit*, UTB 2392 (Göttingen: Vandenhoeck & Ruprecht, 2003), 360–89.

10. Juha Pakkala, „Die Entwicklung der Gotteskonzeptionen in den deuteronomistischen Redaktionen von polytheistischen zu monotheistischen Vorstellungen", in *Die deuteronomistischen Geschichtswerke. Redaktions- und religionsgeschichtliche Perspektiven zur „Deuteronomismus"-Diskussion in Tora und Vorderen Propheten*, hrsg. von Markus Witte et al., BZAW 365 (Berlin: De Gruyter, 2006), 239–48, hat die verschiedenen Etappen der Entwicklung analysiert, die von der rein polytheistischen vorexilischen Religion über die monolatrischen Züge der spätmonarchischen Zeit zu

Zu Lebzeiten Ben Siras waren sowohl der Monotheismus als auch die Aussagen über Jahwe als Schöpfergott tief in der Weltanschauung des jüdischen Volkes verwurzelt. Jedoch verwundert es, wie viel Ben Sira über die Schöpfung spricht. Die Annahme liegt nahe, dass er sich so sehr für sie interessiert, weil er die heidnischen Leser im Sinn hat, die er davon zu überzeugen versucht, dass Israels Gott der einzige Gott ist. Letzthin hat P. C. Beentjes stark dafür argumentiert, dass Ben Sira sich bewusst den außerisraelitischen Lesern habe zuwenden wollen.[11]

Zum ersten Mal begegnen wir dem Schöpfungsthema in Sir 15:14. Es gehört zu einem wichtigen Abschnitt (15:11–16:23), in dem Ben Sira die Problematik des freien Willens behandelt. Er warnt vor einem möglichen Missverständnis und lehrt, dass Gott nicht der Ursprung der Sünde sei (15:11), sondern dem Menschen schon am Anfang die Macht der eigenen Entscheidung überlassen habe (15:14). Diese Lehre enthält deutliche Anklänge an die Sündenfallgeschichte, auf die Ben Sira auch andernorts hinweist (z.B. 25:24). Freiheit und Verantwortung sind die immer spannungsgeladenen Pole, die Gott dem Menschen bei der Schöpfung zuwies.

Ben Sira erwähnt Gottes Schöpfungstaten ein weiteres Mal in 16:24–30. Der ganze Abschnitt unterstreicht, wie schön, regelmäßig und zweckmäßig die Schöpfung ist, weil sie auf dem göttlichen Plan basiert. Die systematisch geordnete Schöpfungsgeschichte der Priesterschrift, die bis zur Aufklärung und sogar später noch als wissenschaftliche Erklärung des Welturprungs allgemein anerkannt wurde, hat sicher eine

---

der intoleranten Monolatrie und in nachexilischer Zeit zum eigentlichen Monotheismus führte. Pakkala hat richtig beobachtet, dass der Begriff ‚Monotheismus' kein Monolith ist, sondern dass bei verschiedenen biblischen Autoren unterschiedliche Nuancen von Monotheismus vorkommen können. Deuterojesajas Monotheismus ist universal geprägt, was vor allem dadurch sichtbar wird, dass er den anderen Völkern die Möglichkeit eröffnet, Israels Jahwe zu verehren (Jes 45:18–23). Ein solcher universaler Monotheismus war allerdings für die deuteronomistischen Redaktoren undenkbar. Ihre Tradition blieb stark nationalistisch geprägt und hatte deswegen anderen Völkern nur wenig zu bieten.

11. „Since the author in vv.3–9 enumerates rather general categories of offices, he does not want to interest only Jewish readers, but also an hellenistic audience for the procession of Israel's heroes of the faith, which starts in Ben Sira 44:16". Pancratius C. Beentjes, „The ‚Praise of the Famous' and Its Prologue: Some Observations on Ben Sira 44:1–15 and the Question on Enoch in 44:16", in „Happy the One Who Meditates on Wisdom" (Sir 14,20). Collected Essays on the Book of Ben Sira, CBET 43 (Leuven: Peeters, 2006), 128.

signifikante Rolle bei der Entstehung dieses sirazidischen Abschnittes gespielt. Auch Ps 104 mit seinen bekannten Bildern von den Löwen, die nach ihrer Beute brüllen, oder von dem Menschen, der an sein Tagwerk geht, betont, wie gut und organisiert alles in der von Gott geschaffenen Welt geschieht.[12]

Sir 16:24–30 ist gewissermaßen eine Einführung zu dem folgenden Abschnitt (17:1–23), der eingehender die Schöpfung des Menschen behandelt. Leider ist diese Passage nicht im Hebräischen erhalten, weshalb es schwierig ist, die lexemischen Verbindungen zwischen Sir 17 und den beiden Schöpfungsgeschichten zu prüfen. Auf den ersten Blick fällt auf, dass nach Ben Sira „der Herr die Menschen aus Erde erschaffen hat" (17:1a), was eigentlich nur der jahwistischen Erzählung zufolge zutrifft. Die Fortsetzung „… und lässt sie wieder zu ihr (sc. der Erde) zurückkehren" (17:1b) sucht man in den Schöpfungsgeschichten vergeblich. Der Mensch war im Paradies vor dem Sündenfall sicher nicht unsterblich, aber das wird in Gen 1–2 nicht ausdrücklich festgestellt, sondern das Zurückkehren zum Staub kommt zum ersten Mal im Fluchwort Gen 3:19 vor.[13]

Sir 17:2–4 verweist auf den priesterschriftlichen Bericht in Gen 1:26–28.[14] Dass der Mensch die Macht über alles auf der Erde bekam (Sir 17:2), geht auf das Gotteswort in Gen 1:26–28 zurück. Dort wird erwähnt, dass die Herrschertätigkeit der Menschen die Fische des Meeres, die Vögel des Himmels, das Vieh, die ganze Erde und alle Kriechtiere umfasst. Ben Sira will in diesem Zusammenhang hervorheben, dass der Mensch nach dem Abbild Gottes erschaffen wurde (17:3), was den Wortlaut von Gen 1:27 voraussetzt. Tiere und Vögel als Untertanen der Menschen werden ein weiteres Mal in Sir 17:4b erwähnt. Was aber in 17:4a gesagt wird, ist überraschend. Diesem Satz zufolge hat Gott die Furcht vor dem Menschen auf alle Wesen gelegt. Ein entsprechender Gedanke kommt jedoch in den Schöpfungsgeschichten nicht vor. Stattdessen liegt die nächste Parallele in

---

12. Frank-Lothar Hossfeld, „Schöpfungsfrömmigkeit in Ps 104 und bei Jesus Sirach", in *Auf den Spuren der schriftgelehrten Weisen. Festschrift für Johannes Marböck anlässlich seiner Emeritierung*, hrsg. von Irmtraud Fischer et al., BZAW 331 (Berlin: De Gruyter, 2003), 131, 133.

13. Über die Anthropologie und die Sterblichkeit des Menschen bei Ben Sira siehe Hossfeld, „Schöpfungsfrömmigkeit", 134–36.

14. Die Feststellung in Sir 17:2a, dass den Lebenstagen der Menschen eine Grenze gesetzt ist, erinnert an das Thema der Kürze des Menschenlebens, das besonders in weisheitlichen Texten begegnet (vgl. Ps 90:10; Hi 14:1–2).

Gen 9:2 vor (wieder eine priesterschriftliche Passage), wo Gott an Noah fast die gleichen Worte richtet wie früher an Adam. Sie unterscheiden sich nur geringfügig, insofern nun der Aspekt der Furcht ergänzt ist: „Furcht und Schrecken vor euch soll sich auf alle Tiere der Erde legen, auf alle Vögel des Himmels, auf alles, was sich auf der Erde regt, und auf alle Fische des Meeres; euch sind sie übergeben". Es gibt aber noch eine andere Möglichkeit, die Erwähnung der Furcht in Sir 17:4a zu verstehen. Das Pronomen αὐτοῦ könnte auch auf Gott selbst verweisen—wie es im griechischen Text tatsächlich der Fall ist—und ohne Zweifel ist die Gottesfurcht eines der zentralen Themen im Sirachbuch. Sie wird ausdrücklich in Sir 17:8b erwähnt. Im Unterschied zu den Tieren erkennen die Menschen Gutes und Böses, weil Gott es sie gelehrt hat (Sir 17:7). Hier knüpft Ben Sira an die Ereignisse an, die dem Sündenfall vorangingen (Gen 2:17; 3:5) und ihm folgten (Gen 3:22). Von den Schöpfungsgeschichten weicht Ben Sira jedoch deutlich in 17:8–10 ab, wenn er schreibt:

> Er (Gott) richtete sein Auge auf ihre Herzen, ihnen die Größe seiner Werke zu zeigen, und trug ihnen auf, ewig den Ruhm seiner Wunder zu verkünden, damit sie seinen heiligen Namen loben und seine großen Taten erzählen sollten.

Das Gotteslob kommt in den biblischen Urgeschichten gar nicht vor, aber es ist ein häufiges Thema in den Psalmen. Insbesondere sei Ps 148:5,13 in diesem Zusammenhang erwähnt, denn dieses Loblied weist deutliche Berührungen mit Sir 17:9 auf.

Ben Sira setzt das Schöpfungsthema in 18:1 fort, wenn er Gott als souveränen Schöpfer näher beschreibt: Hier lehrt Ben Sira zuerst, dass Gott ewig sei. Gott habe alles geschaffen. Dies setzen die beiden Schöpfungsgeschichten, aber auch die deuterojesajanische Verkündigung als selbstverständlich voraus. In 18:2a heißt es, nur Gott sei gerecht, kein anderer. Die Allmacht Gottes wird in den zusätzlichen Versen 2a–3 noch stärker betont, weil aber diese Verse nur im GII-Text[15] überliefert sind, können sie nicht als ursprünglich gelten. Gottes Werke sind unermesslich (V.4–6), der Mensch kann sie nicht verstehen (V.7), und es besteht ein ungeheurer Unterschied zwischen dem ewigen Gott und dem sterblichen Menschen (V.8–10).

---

15. Was die komplizierte Textgeschichte des Sirachbuches betrifft, siehe z.B. die Erklärung bei Johannes Marböck, „Art. Sirach/Sirachbuch", *TRE* 31 (2000): 307–9.

Kapitel 24 gehört zu den berühmtesten und meistzitierten Texten des Sirachbuches. Die Schilderung der personifizierten Weisheit von ihrem vorweltlichen Ursprung her fügt einen neuen Zug zum Bild des Schöpfergottes hinzu, der den biblischen Schöpfungsgeschichten in Gen 1–2 noch völlig fremd und unbekannt war. Die Weisheit sagt laut Sir 24:9: „Vor der Welt, von Anbeginn hat er mich geschaffen, und ich werde ewig bleiben". Die personifizierte Weisheitsgestalt ist tatsächlich eine äußerst rätselhafte Figur. Zum ersten Mal wird sie im Hiobbuch vorgestellt wird (Hi 28), aber da bleibt ihr Wesen noch undefiniert.[16] Als eine Person mit präexistentem Ursprung taucht sie erst in Spr 8:22–31 auf. Für das Sirachbuch ist jedoch zu beobachten, dass sie, obgleich Frau Weisheit genannt, selbst keine schöpferische Macht neben Gott darstellt, sie ist und bleibt dem Gott Israels untergeordnet. Weisheit ist Gottes Schöpfungsgabe, sogar die höchste Krone der Schöpfung. Offensichtlich versucht Ben Sira zu zeigen, dass die universale Weisheit ihre vollständige Form und Manifestation in der Tora Israels gefunden hat.

Die Passage, in der Ben Sira das Thema „Schöpfung" am ausführlichsten behandelt, umfasst die Kapitel 42–43. Es ist kein Zufall, dass das Lob der Väter unmittelbar danach beginnt. Die Schöpfung stellt die Basis für alle späteren Begegnungen zwischen Gott und Mensch dar. Wie Ben Sira deutlich betont, hat ihn die Harmonie beeindruckt, die in der Natur spürbar ist. Als letztes Beispiel dafür erwähnt er vor dem Väterlob die Sterne, die den von Gott gesetzten Regeln tadellos folgen. Man darf zwischen den Zeilen lesen, dass ein ähnliches Verhalten auch in der Welt der Menschen angebracht gewesen wäre. Auffällig oft spricht Ben Sira vom Wort Gottes, wenn er die verschiedenen Schöpfungstaten schildert. Schon am Anfang des Abschnitts schreibt er, dass die Werke des Herrn durch seine Worte geschehen seien (Sir 42:15). Wenn er einige Verse später über die Sonne spricht, fasst er lobend zusammen: „Groß ist der Herr, der sie gemacht hat, auf seine Worte hin durcheilt sie ihre Bahn" (Sir 43:5). Daran schließt Ben Sira Ausführungen über den Mond an. Der Mond gibt der geschaffenen Welt die Ordnung, denn der Kalender und demzufolge das kultische Leben hängen vom Umlauf des Mondes ab. Der Mond vertritt tatsächlich die göttliche Ordnung in der Welt, aber auch in diesem Fall ist das eigentliche Prinzip im Hintergrund das Wort Gottes, das diese Ordnung

---

16. Martin Leuenberger, „Die personifizierte Weisheit vorweltlichen Ursprungs von Hi 28 bis Joh 1. Ein traditionsgeschichtlicher Strang zwischen den Testamenten", *ZAW* 120 (2008): 366–86.

bestimmt, wie Ben Sira feststellt; denn Gott wird nicht matt in seinem Wächteramt (Sir 43:10). Besonders die Verse Sir 43:13–20 haben enge Parallelen in Hiob 38 sowie in einigen Psalmen (z.B. Ps 147:16–17).

Dieser Überblick hat gezeigt, dass Ben Sira eng an frühere Traditionen anknüpft, wenn er über die Schöpfung spricht. Er verbindet Gedanken, deren Ursprung entweder in der Genesis, im Hiobbuch oder in den Psalmen zu finden ist. Aus den vielen Stimmen des Alten Testaments macht Ben Sira meisterhaft ein einheitliches Ganzes.

2.2. Bund

„Bund" ist ohne Zweifel ein Schlüsselbegriff im Alten Testament. Schon in der ersten Hälfte des Buches Genesis liest man, dass Gott einen Bund mit Noah schließt, und einige Kapitel später wird erzählt, dass Gott und Abraham Bundespartner sind. Auch für Ben Sira ist der Bund von großer Bedeutung. Seine „Bundestheologie" kommt in seinem Lob der Väter zum Ausdruck, aber man darf auch Sir 17:12 nicht außer Acht lassen, wo er mit dem Hinweis auf die Ereignisse auf dem Sinai sagt, dass Gott einen ewigen Bund geschlossen habe. Im Väterlob folgt Ben Sira den biblischen Überlieferungen ziemlich genau. Er hebt eine Reihe von sieben auf die Anfänge Israels konzentrierten Bundesschlüssen hervor, nämlich mit Noah, den Erzvätern (Abraham, Isaak und Jakob), Aaron, Pinhas und David.[17] In seiner Einführung in das Väterlob macht er darauf aufmerksam, dass der Bund nicht zwischen Gott und einem Individuum besteht, sondern auch deren Nachkommen mit einschließt (Sir 44:12).[18]

Am Ende der Sintflutgeschichte wird berichtet, wie Gott einen Bund mit Noah und seinen Nachkommen aufrichtet (Gen 9:8–9). Dieser Bund ist fast unbegrenzt, weil er alle lebendigen Wesen einschließt. Außer dem Menschen sind auch die Tiere Objekte dieses Bundes (Gen 9:10). Unbegrenzt ist auch die Dauer des Bundes, denn Gott sprach: „Darum soll mein

---

17. Johannes Marböck, „Die ‚Geschichte Israels' als 'Bundesgeschichte' nach dem Sirachbuch", in *Der Neue Bund im Alten. Studien zur Bundestheologie der beiden Testamente*, hrsg. von Erich Zenger, QD 146 (Freiburg: Herder, 1993), 193, 197.

18. Otto Kaiser, „Covenant and Law in Ben Sira", in *Covenant as Context. Essays in Honor of E. W. Nicholson*, hrsg. von A. D. H. Mayes and R. B. Salters (Oxford: Oxford University Press, 2003), 241, hat festgestellt: „Ben Sira had indeed already stated in the introduction to the praise of the fathers in 44:11–12 that later generations owed their existence to the fidelity towards the covenant of those men favoured by God".

Bogen in den Wolken sein, dass ich ihn ansehe und gedenke an den ewigen Bund zwischen Gott und allem lebendigen Getier unter allem Fleisch, das auf Erden ist" (Gen 9:16). Ben Sira weist auf die göttliche Verheißung hin und betont den ewigen Charakter des Noahbundes (Sir 44:18). Dieser Bund und der Regenbogen als dessen sichtbares Symbol sind eine Garantie dafür, dass Gott die Welt nicht mehr durch eine Flut zerstören lässt. Es ist kaum Zufall, dass Ben Sira den Regenbogen nochmals am Ende des Väterlobes erwähnt, wenn er den Glanz des Hohenpriesters Simon schildert (Sir 50:7b).[19]

Ben Sira folgt der Reihenfolge des Buches Genesis, wenn er nach Noah über Abraham berichtet. In dessen Darstellung spielt der Bund eine erhebliche Rolle. Abraham war Gottes Geboten gehorsam und hielt das Gesetz des Höchsten (Sir 44:20). Wieder ist es für Ben Sira wichtig, ein sichtbares Zeichen des Bundes hervorzuheben. Diesmal ist es nicht mehr der Regenbogen, sondern die Beschneidung. Es handelt sich nicht nur um das Bundeszeichen für Abraham allein, sondern auch für alle seine Nachkommen. Die Wirkungen des Abrahambundes reichen noch weiter, denn sogar die Völker (גוים) werden am Segen des Bundes beteiligt (Sir 44:21). Dies zeigt, dass Ben Sira die Tür für die Nicht-Juden offenhielt; auch für sie ist die Rettung möglich. Diesen theologischen Gedanken hat Ben Sira nicht selbst erfunden, sondern er ist hierin wieder seinen Quellen treu. Es ist zu beachten, dass Gen 17 von der Ewigkeit des Bundes zwischen Gott und Abraham bzw. Abrahams Nachkommen spricht (Gen 17:7), Ben Sira aber die ewige Dauer des Bundes nicht mit dem Wort עולם hat unterstreichen wollen, wie es oben beim Noahbund der Fall gewesen ist. Auf jeden Fall wird deutlich, dass der Abrahambund eine Kette von unzählbaren Generationen umspannt, wenn Ben Sira Abrahams Sohn und Enkelsohn als Beispiele dafür erwähnt, dass der Bund und der Segen immer gültig sind.

Als Gesetzgeber ist Mose eine der Hauptpersonen des gesamten Alten Testaments, und ihm widmet auch Ben Sira fünf Verse am Anfang des Kapitels 45, aber weder hier noch anderswo im Sirachbuch ist Mose ausdrücklich als Empfänger oder als Partner eines Bundes erwähnt.[20] Es wurde oft als überraschend empfunden, dass Aaron soviel mehr Beach-

---

19. Marböck, „Geschichte", 191, ist der Meinung, dass „[D]ie Erscheinung Simons wie der Bogen in den Wolken … geradezu kosmische Bezüge des Geschehens analog zum Noachbund" andeute.

20. Marböck, „Geschichte", 186.

tung geschenkt wurde als Mose: Die Ausführungen über ihn sind viermal so lang.[21] Den Terminus „Bund" gebraucht Ben Sira bewusst, wenn er Aaron als einen „Urvater" der Priester darstellt. Ben Sira interessierte sich sehr für den Kult, obwohl er selbst offensichtlich kein Priester war. Mit Aaron sieht er eine priesterliche Dynastie beginnen, die bis zu seiner eigenen Zeit reicht. Äußerst detailliert schildert er das priesterliche Gewand, in das Aaron gekleidet wurde (Sir 45:6–13). Sowohl das großartige Gewand als auch die Brandopfer und die Salbung mit dem heiligen Öl sind wiederum sichtbare Zeichen des Bundes, den Gott mit einem erwählten Menschen geschlossen hat. Ben Sira hebt in seiner Darstellung Aarons auch hervor, dass Gottes Bund mit ihm und seinen Söhnen ein ewiger Bund sei (Sir 45:15).

Ein beachtenswerter Vertreter dieses priesterlichen Bundes ist Aarons Enkelsohn Pinhas, der großen Eifer bewies und für den reinen Glauben kämpfte (Sir 45:23). Deswegen wurde ihm ein Bund des Friedens gegeben (ברית שלום). Dieser Bund enthält die Zusage, dass Pinhas' Nachkommen für immer im Priesteramt bleiben. Der Prätext ist natürlich Num 25:6–13. Es ist aber auffällig, wie zurückhaltend Ben Sira von den Einzelheiten der Heldentat Pinhas' erzählt. Sein Eifer ist zwar erwähnt, aber ein Leser, der Num 25 nicht kennt, wird sich kaum vorstellen können, dass Pinhas zwei Menschen getötet hat.[22] Ben Sira weist in seiner Darstellung auf den Tempel hin, der ebenfalls ein sichtbares Zeichen des Bundes darstellt. Durch ihn gehören Bund und Kult eng zusammen.

Die chronologische Darstellungsweise wird in Sir 45:25 gestört, wenn unvermittelt die Figur Davids auftaucht. Es war Ben Siras Absicht, den davidischen neben den priesterlichen Bund zu stellen. Leider ist der hebräische Text an dieser Stelle schwer zu verstehen. Der Aaron- bzw. Pinhasbund war, anders als der Davidbund, von ewiger Dauer. Auch die Zahl der Bundespartner war im priesterlichen Bund deutlich größer, weil die

---

21. Jeremy Corley, „Sirach Chapter 2 and the Temple", in *Various Aspects of Worship in Deuterocanonical and Cognate Literature*, hrsg. von Géza G. Xeravits, József Zsengellér and Ibolya Balla, DCLY 2016/17 (Berlin: de Gruyter, 2017), 81–82. Andererseits argumentiert Kaiser, „Covenant", 243, dass kein Bedarf bestand, ausführlicher über Mose zu sprechen, weil seine Bedeutung im zeitgenössischen Judentum alles übertraf.

22. Marko Marttila, *Foreign Nations in the Wisdom of Ben Sira. A Jewish Sage between Opposition and Assimilation*, DCLS 13 (Berlin: de Gruyter, 2012), 172–82, besonders 180.

göttlichen Verheißungen allen Nachkommen galten, während im David-
bund nur ein Sohn in der Thronnachfolge der legitimierte Empfänger der
Zusagen des Bundes war. Ben Sira hat in 47:1–11 mehr über David zu
sagen. Diese Darstellung enthält eine kurze Biographie Davids, in der Ben
Sira die negativen Züge des Lebens Davids fast völlig verschweigt. Vergeb-
lich sucht man explizite Hinweise auf den Ehebruch mit Batseba oder auf
Absaloms Aufstand. Ben Siras knappe Darstellung Davids folgt derselben
Linie wie die Chronikbücher. Das Hauptgewicht liegt auf Davids Rolle als
Kultbegründer.[23] Sein Bild als Psalmendichter war zur Zeit Ben Siras tief
eingeprägt. Im kultischen Zusammenhang erwähnt Ben Sira, dass Gott
David seine Sünden vergab (Sir 47:11). Ein Leser, der den biblischen
Hintergrund kennt, kann hier leicht eine Anspielung auf Davids Bezie-
hung mit Batseba erkennen, aber es ist bewundernswert, mit welchem
Feingefühl Ben Sira diese peinliche Angelegenheit bloß andeutet. Ohne
Kenntnis der Samuelbücher wäre nicht zu erahnen, was für eine Sünde
David begangen hatte. Ben Sira gibt keine detaillierte Beschreibung. Für
ihn ist David ein idealer König von Gottes Gnaden.

Was den Bund mit David anbelangt, so liegt der Ursprung in 2Sam 7,
wo Gott durch den Propheten Nathan David und seinem Geschlecht eine
ewige Dynastie verspricht. Diese Bundestheologie ist ein Lieblingsthema
der Deuteronomisten, die mehrere alttestamentliche Bücher redigiert und
ausgelegt haben. Auch Ben Sira vertritt in seiner Theologie deuteronomis-
tische Gedanken und Schwerpunkte, aber Gottes Verheißung an David
und der Bund mit Davids Haus stellten offensichtlich ein Problem für Ben
Sira dar. Zu seiner Zeit gab es keine davidische Monarchie mehr. Seit Jahr-
hunderten lebten die Israeliten ohne eigenen König. Eine Alternative war
die messianische Interpretation, nach der man am Ende der Zeit einen
neuen König wie David erwartete. Er würde die herausragende Stellung

---

23. Pancratius C. Beentjes, „Solomon's Temple and Israel's Earlier Cultic Traditions in 2 Chronicles 1–8", in *Various Aspects of Worship in Deuterocanonical and
Cognate Literature*, hrsg. von Géza G. Xeravits, József Zsengellér and Ibolya Balla,
DCLY 2016/17 (Berlin: de Gruyter, 2017), 64. Beentjes zitiert in diesem Zusammenhang einen Abschnitt aus Julius Wellhausens berühmten *Prolegomena zur Geschichte
Israels*, 5. Aufl. (Berlin: Reimer, 1899), wo Wellhausen zutreffend schreibt (181): „Was
hat die Chronik aus David gemacht! Der Gründer des Reichs ist zum Gründer des
Tempels und des Gottesdienstes geworden, der König und Held an der Spitze seiner
Waffengenossen zum Kantor und Liturgen an der Spitze eines Schwarmes von Priestern und Leviten, seine so scharf gezeichnete Figur zu einem matten Heiligenbilde,
umnebelt von einer Wolke von Weihrauch".

des Reiches und des Volkes wiederherstellen. Für Ben Sira war solche Ideologie nicht typisch, messianische Deutungen lassen sich in seinem Werk nur sporadisch finden. Auch eschatologische Züge sind selten. Doch sagt Ben Sira (Sir 47:11), dass Gott Davids Horn für alle Zeit erhöht habe. Der Bund garantierte das Königtum in Israel für Davids Dynastie, aber was war von diesem Bund in den Jahrzehnten, als Ben Sira lebte und Weisheit lehrte, sichtbar? Ben Sira gibt keine befriedigende Antwort. Gottes Bund mit David ist dahingefallen, und nichts ist an seine Stelle getreten.

Wenn man die oben erwähnten Bünde miteinander vergleicht, ist leicht festzustellen, dass der theologisch bedeutsamste Bund für Ben Sira der zwischen Gott und Aaron samt Aarons Geschlecht war. Man gewinnt den Eindruck, dass für Ben Sira alle Priester als Nachkommen Aarons galten und demzufolge als Bundesgenossen. Im Sirachbuch finden sich keine Anzeichen für eine Konkurrenz zwischen den Priesterfamilien Aarons und Zadoks.[24] Die sonst oft erwähnten Leviten sucht man im Sirachbuch vergeblich.

2.3. Kult

Oben haben wir schon einiges über Priester und ihre Rolle im Sirachbuch gesagt. Programmatisch drückt Ben Sira in Kapitel 7 seine Bewunderung für die Priester aus, wo er dazu mahnt, sie in allen Ehren zu halten (Sir 7:29). Diese Mahnung wird zwei Verse später wiederholt mit dem Befehl, dass man den Priestern ihren Anteil von den Erstlingsgaben und von verschiedenen Opfern geben solle. In diesen Satzungen lehnt Ben Sira sich an den Pentateuch an, wo an einigen Stellen ähnliche Mahnworte geäußert werden (Num 18:11–19; Dtn 6:5; 12:19).

Einige andere Passagen, die nicht nur von den Priestern, sondern allgemeiner vom Kult sprechen, möchte ich in diesem Zusammenhang noch hervorheben. In mancher Hinsicht ist Sir 24 ein wichtiges Kapitel

---

24. Marttila, *Nations*, 202–4. Heinz-Josef Fabry, „Jesus Sirach und das Priestertum", in *Auf den Spuren der schriftgelehrten Weisen. Festschrift für Johannes Marböck anlässlich seiner Emeritierung* hrsg. von Irmtraud Fischer et al,. BZAW 331 (Berlin: de Gruyter, 2003), 282 erwägt aufgrund von Sir 50, dass die Begriffe „aaronidisch" und „zadokidisch" in Ben Siras Zeit möglicherweise zwei verschiedene Kategorien bezeichneten. Das Label „aaronidisch" stehe für das Priestertum im Blick auf seine theologische Kompetenz (z.B. Reinheitsfragen, Opfertheologie, Kultkalender usw.), während das Label „zadokidisch" die politische Kompetenz des Priestertums betone.

des Buches, sogar ein theologisches und ideologisches Zentrum. Hier stellt Ben Sira die Weisheit personifiziert als „Frau Weisheit" dar, die ihr deutlichstes Vorbild in den Sprüchen hat. Die Weisheit fand ihre bleibende Wohnung in Israel (Sir 24:9). Das war ein besseres Schicksal als das, was der Frau Weisheit im Henochbuch widerfuhr; dort kehrte sie in den Himmel zurück, weil sich auf Erden keine angemessene Wohnstatt für sie fand (1 Hen. 42:1). Ben Siras Sprachgebrauch wird im Wortsinn liturgisch, wenn er die Tätigkeit der Weisheit in Jerusalem schildert. Er schreibt nämlich, dass sie im heiligen Zelt vor dem Herrn diente (ἐλειτουργήσα).[25] Man hat oft richtig gesehen, dass bei Ben Sira Weisheit und Gesetz eng zusammengehören, sogar in dem Maß, dass er das Gesetz Israels als die höchste Krone aller Weisheit betrachtet (vgl. Sir 24:23). Einen wichtigen Aspekt kann man all dem noch hinzufügen, nämlich den Kult. Die Weisheit hat ihren festen Platz im Gottesdienst. Nach Ben Sira kann man keine wahre Weisheit ohne kultisches Leben finden.

An anderer Stelle betont Ben Sira das enge Verhältnis zwischen Moral und Kult. In seinem Buch lehrt er durchaus auch, dass man sich um seine Nächsten kümmern soll. Besonders oft erwähnt er Hilfe für die Armen (z.B. Sir 4:1–10). Fast wie mit prophetischem Geist stellt er fest, dass es nichts nützt, wenn man Opfer darbringt, die widerrechtlich beschafft wurden. Ein Opfer von unrechtem Gut ist eine Lästerung (Sir 34:18). Kult ist keineswegs ein oberflächliches Phänomen, sondern das gerechte kultische Leben setzt voraus, dass man gesetzestreu handelt. Nach Ben Sira gefallen die Gaben der Gottlosen dem Höchsten nicht; auch vergäbe der Herr Sünden nicht, selbst wenn man viel opferte (Sir 34:19). Ben Sira fordert einen Wandel tief im Innersten des Menschen. Seine Überzeugung ähnelt den berühmten Worten aus dem Amosbuch:

Ich hasse und verachte eure Feste und mag eure Versammlungen nicht riechen—es sei denn, ihr bringt mir rechte Brandopfer dar—und an euren Speisopfern habe ich kein Gefallen, und euer fettes Schlachtopfer sehe ich nicht an. Tu weg von mir das Geplärr deiner Lieder; denn ich

---

25. Der zweimal erwähnte liturgische Dienst des Hohenpriesters Simon in Kapitel 50 entspricht dem Dienst der Weisheit im heiligen Zelt (Sir 24:10); Johannes Marböck, „Der Hohepriester Simon in Sir 50. Ein Beitrag zur Bedeutung von Priestertum und Kult im Sirachbuch," in *Weisheit und Frömmigkeit. Studien zur alttestamentlichen Literatur der Spätzeit*, ÖBS 29 (Frankfurt: Lang, 2006), 163.

mag dein Harfenspiel nicht hören! Es ströme aber das Recht wie Wasser und die Gerechtigkeit wie ein nie versiegender Bach. (Amos 5:21–24)

In seiner Lehre von den Opfern ist Ben Sira in mancher Hinsicht wieder vom Pentateuch abhängig. Einige Stellen aus dem Levitikus haben ihn deutlich beeinflusst (z.B. Lev 2:1–8; 3:1–10; 7:11–21; 22:17–25).

Das Lob der Väter darf man nicht außer Acht lassen, wenn man Ben Siras Stellung zum Kult analysiert. Die lange Vorstellung von Aaron konzentriert sich stark auf kultische Dinge. Detailliert schildert Ben Sira die priesterlichen Gewänder, die Aaron bei seinem kultischen Dienst trägt (Sir 45:6–13). Der Autor hat offensichtlich ein Auge für Schönheit, denn er spricht so hingebungsvoll von den ästhetischen Einzelheiten, die am Gewand Aarons zu finden sind. Die Prätexte, die Ben Sira an dieser Stelle offensichtlich inspiriert haben, sind Exodus 28 und 39. Nach der Beschreibung der Priestergewänder spricht Ben Sira auch über den Opferkult und erwähnt, dass Aarons Opfer täglich zweimal als Brandopfer dargebracht werden sollen. Aaron und allen Priestern nach ihm sei eine wichtige kultische Aufgabe anvertraut, wenn sie Brandopfer und Räucheropfer darbringen und dadurch dem Volk Sühne schaffen. Ben Sira fügt noch einen wichtigen Aspekt hinzu, wenn er erwähnt, dass Gott Aaron die Macht gab, Jakob die Satzungen zu lehren und Israel mit seinem Gesetz zu erleuchten (Sir 45:17). Das Priesteramt ist also ausdrücklich auch ein Lehramt. Für diesen Gedanken finden sich mühelos Beispiele im Alten Testament. In diesem Zusammenhang kann etwa auf das Maleachibuch hingewiesen werden:

Denn des Priesters Lippen sollen die Lehre bewahren, dass man aus seinem Munde Weisung suche; denn er ist ein Bote des Herrn Zebaoth. (Mal 2:7)

Wie oben schon festgestellt, konzentriert sich Ben Sira bei seiner Darstellung Davids im Väterlob auf den Kult. Zwar sind Davids Heldentaten erwähnt, aber von besonderer Bedeutung scheint er zu sein, weil er den Altardienst ordnete. Natürlich kennt Ben Sira David als großen Psalmendichter und -sänger. Im Judentum zu Ben Siras Zeit war die Vorstellung von David als Vater der israelitischen Psalmenpoesie schon tief verwurzelt. Ben Sira schreibt, dass David dem Heiligen und Höchsten mit herrlichen Worten dankte (Sir 47:8). Hier ist eine vortreffliche Antwort auf die Frage gegeben, was der Sinn des Lebens sei. Wie Bernd Janowski in seinen zahlreichen Psalmenstudien überzeugend gezeigt hat, ist nach den Psalmen der Sinn des Lebens das Gotteslob.[26] Loben ist tatsächlich ein wichtiger Aspekt alttestamentlicher Theologie, aber man darf nicht vergessen, dass Klagepsalmen den Psalter dominieren. Andererseits finden sich in den meisten Klagepsalmen wenigstens kurze Schlussdoxologien. Es besteht kein Zweifel daran, dass das Vorbild für Ben Sira in seiner Darstellung Davids 1Chr 16 gewesen ist.

Das letzte Beispiel für die Bedeutung des Kults im Sirachbuch stammt aus Kapitel 50, wo Ben Sira nicht mehr von den Ereignissen ferner Vergangenheit spricht, sondern seine eigene Zeit und Umgebung beschreibt. Sehr wahrscheinlich war Ben Sira selbst ein Augenzeuge des Gottesdienstes, den er in diesem Kapitel schildert. Man kann sich des Eindrucks nicht erwehren, dass er fasziniert war, wenn er an dem Gottesdienst teilnahm. Er schreibt voller Begeisterung über die Pracht des Hohenpriesters Simon, über die liturgischen Gewänder und die Musik. Uns liegt mit diesem Abschnitt ein wertvolles Zeugnis vom Gottesdienst im Judentum des hellenistischen Zeitalters vor. Schon in diesen frühen Zeiten steht der aaronidische Segen am Ende des Gottesdienstes (Sir 50:20). Ben Siras Schilderung ist eindrucksvoll: *„Die Psalmensänger lobten Gott mit ihren Stimmen, und alles war erfüllt von süßem Klang"* (Sir 50:18). Obwohl Ben Sira eschatologische Themen nur sehr zurückhaltend behandelt, muss man vielleicht eingestehen, dass Kapitel 50 etwas Eschatologisches enthält. Der vom Hohenpriester Simon geleitete Gottesdienst auf Erden hat Anteil am Himmel. Die Grenzen zwischen Diesseits und Jenseits scheinen zu verschmelzen. Ben Sira führt seine Leser Schritt für Schritt zu einer Stufe, wo das unendliche Gotteslob herrscht.

2.4. Gott

Selbstverständlich gehört zu jeder Theologie ein Gotteskonzept. Deswegen erstaunt es nicht, dass auch Ben Sira oft von Gott redet. Es gibt Aspekte, die er gern unterstreicht. Für ihn ist Gott vor allem Schöpfer. Er

---

26. Siehe z.B. Bernd Janowski, *Konfliktgespräche mit Gott. Eine Anthropologie der Psalmen* (Neukirchen-Vluyn: Neukirchener Verlag, 2003), 264–67. Ähnlich argumentiert auch Hermann Spieckermann, „Lob Gottes aus dem Staube. Psalm 103 als Quintessenz der Theologie des Gotteslobes", in *Lebenskunst und Gotteslob in Israel. Anregungen aus Psalter und Weisheit für die Theologie*, FAT 91 (Tübingen: Mohr Siebeck, 2014), 283–85.

betont Gottes Einzigkeit in klar monotheistischem Geist. Auffallend ist Ben Siras wiederholte Feststellung, dass Gott alles (הכל) ist. So fasst Ben Sira selbst seine Sicht der Schöpfungstheologie zusammen:

> Wenn wir auch viel sagen, so reicht es doch nicht aus; mit einem Wort:
> Er ist alles in allem. (Sir 43:27)

Gott ist nach Ben Siras Auffassung barmherzig. Diese Eigenschaft betont er schon zu Beginn seines Werkes. In Kapitel 2 mahnt er seine Zeitgenossen zur Geduld, weil Gott helfen und sich erbarmen wird. Er weist auch auf die Beispiele hin, die in den vergangenen Zeiten geschehen sind:

> Blickt auf die früheren Geschlechter und besinnt euch: Wer ist jemals zuschanden geworden, der auf den Herrn gehofft hat? Wer ist jemals verlassen worden, der in der Furcht des Herrn geblieben ist? Oder wer ist jemals von ihm verschmäht worden, der ihn angerufen hat? (Sir 2:10)

Dies sind offensichtlich rhetorische Fragen, die zu verneinen sind. Gott hat nach seinem Plan den Menschen den freien Willen gegeben (Sir 15:11–20). Mit der Hilfe des Gesetzes Gottes ist es den Menschen möglich, ein gerechtes Leben zu wählen. Wenn man nur will, kann man die Gebote halten. Das ist Ben Siras aufrichtige Überzeugung.

In Ben Siras Texten kommt sehr oft das Konzept der Gottesfurcht vor („die Furcht des Herrn").[27] Zu diesem Thema hat Josef Haspecker nunmehr vor fünfzig Jahren eine wichtige Untersuchung veröffentlicht,[28] auf die immer noch häufig verwiesen wird. In einer späteren Studie hat Renate Egger-Wenzel angemerkt, dass „Gottesfurcht" vielleicht nicht die bestmögliche Übersetzung für den hebräischen Ausdruck sei. Sie empfiehlt stattdessen, entweder vom Glauben an Gott oder vom Respekt vor Gott zu sprechen. Nicht ausgeschlossen wäre auch die Übersetzung „Liebe

---

27. Wenn man noch präziser sein will, spricht Ben Sira nie von der Gottesfurcht, sondern von der Furcht des Herrn. Dies haben zuletzt Friedrich Reiterer und Karin Schöpflin in ihrem Beitrag unterstrichen; siehe Schöpflin und Reiterer, „The Garland: A Sign of Worship and Acknowledgement. A Hellenistic Symbol in Late Old Testament Books", in *Various Aspects of Worship in Deuterocanonical and Cognate Literature*, hrsg. von Géza G. Xeravits, József Zsengellér and Ibolya Balla, DCLY 2016/17 (Berlin: de Gruyter, 2017), 18, 35.

28. Josef Haspecker, *Gottesfurcht bei Jesus Sirach. Ihre religiöse Struktur und ihre literarische und doktrinäre Bedeutung*, AnBib 30 (Rom: Pontificio Istituto Biblico, 1967).

zu Gott".[29] Alle diese Möglichkeiten erwecken positivere Gefühle. Dass die Gottesfurcht zu Ben Siras Lieblingsthemen gehört, ist schon am Anfang seines Buches offensichtlich. Im ersten Kapitel widmet Ben Sira diesem Thema mehrere Sätze. Sein Leitgedanke scheint zu sein, dass die Furcht des Herrn der Anfang der Weisheit ist (Sir 1:14). In dieser Formulierung hängt Ben Sira von seinen biblischen Vorgängern ab, was man daran erkennt, dass sie auch in anderen Weisheitsbüchern belegt ist (Ps 111:10; Hiob 28:28; Spr 1:7; 9:10; 15:33). Doch wieder einmal übernimmt Ben Sira eine Tradition nicht einfach mechanisch, sondern entwickelt sie weiter. Er bringt sie auf ein höheres Niveau, wenn er sogar schreibt, dass die Furcht des Herrn die Krone der Weisheit sei (Sir 1:18).[30] Aus dieser Furcht entspringt mancherlei Gutes, das sich beispielsweise in Frieden und Heil manifestiert. Zwar ist der hebräische Text des ersten Kapitels nicht erhalten, aber es liegt nahe anzunehmen, dass dem griechischen Terminus εἰρήνη das hebräische שלום entspricht, wie unter den Kommentatoren z.B. Georg Sauer festgestellt hat.[31] Dieses hebräische Wort umfasst ein umfangreiches semantisches Feld: Es bedeutet nicht nur Frieden als Gegensatz zum Krieg, sondern beinhaltet die ganze Existenz des Menschen im heilvollen Zustand. Ben Sira nennt weitere Früchte der Gottesfurcht, nämlich Ehre, Ruhm, Freude, Siegeskranz, Wonne und langes Leben (Sir 1:11–12). Ähnliches findet sich in Sir 15:1–6. Hinzuzufügen ist, dass die Gottesfurcht einen dynamischen Aspekt hat, insofern sie durch Zucht gekennzeichnet

---

29. Renate Egger-Wenzel, „„Faith in God' Rather ‚Than Fear of God' in Ben Sira and Job: A Necessary Adjustment in Terminology and Understanding", in *Intertextual Studies in Ben Sira and Tobit. Essays in Honor of Alexander A. Di Lella, O.F.M.*, hrsg. von Jeremy Corley und Vincent Skemp, CBQMS 38 (Washington, DC: The Catholic Biblical Association of America, 2005), 211–26. Das stellt tatsächlich eine Herausforderung für künftige Übersetzer des Sirachbuches dar: „Perhaps modern translators can dare—at least for the Book of Ben Sira—to make the step from ‚fear of God' (which does not cover the contents any more) to faith in God' or ‚respect for God', or even 'love of God'. After all, there is a big qualitative difference whether a person acts out of fear or out of love". Egger-Wenzel, "Faith", 226.

30. „In the Hellenistic world the garland is a sign of honour, acknowledgement and worship at the same time in any field where it occurs, whether as a symbol of victory for artists, in athletic or military contests, or in religious ceremonies. According to Greek conceptions religious and profane aspects were blended. On the level of wisdom, Sira does not oppose the garland, but he adopts its symbolic quality, subordinating it to his own ideas". Schöpflin und Reiterer, „Garland", 38.

31. Georg Sauer, *Jesus Sirach/Ben Sira*, ATD.A 1 (Göttingen: Vandenhoeck & Ruprecht, 2000), 50.

ist (Sir 1:27). Der Gottesfürchtige ist wie ein Schüler, der sich ständig weiterentwickelt, wenn er sich erziehen lässt. In Kapitel 19 kommt Ben Sira
ein weiteres Mal auf sein Lieblingsthema zu sprechen, wenn er die Gottesfurcht mit den göttlichen Geboten in Beziehung setzt. Eine Kernaussage
ist in Sir 19:20 zu finden:

> Alle Weisheit besteht in der Furcht des Herrn, und zu aller Weisheit
> gehört das Tun des Gesetzes.

Ben Sira ist kein Systematiker im modernen Sinn und zeichnet kein
lückenloses Bild von Gott. Daher müssen wir die verschiedenen Einzel-
aussagen zusammenstellen, um sein Verständnis von Gott zu erfassen.
Ein ergiebiges Kapitel ist in dieser Hinsicht Sir 18, wo Ben Sira Gott mit
mehreren Attributen beschreibt. Er beginnt den Abschnitt damit, dass
er Gottes ewiges Dasein, seine Schöpfungstaten und seine Gerechtigkeit
unterstreicht (Sir 18:1–2). Zusammenfassend kann man sagen, dass er
Gott als allmächtig ansieht. Gottes Taten und Pläne bleiben unerforsch-
lich. Niemand kann seine riesige Macht messen. Meisterhaft stellt Ben Sira
Gottes Größe der menschlichen Schwäche gegenüber. Der Unterschied
könnte kaum größer sein, Ben Sira schildert die schwindende Natur der
menschlichen Bestrebungen:

> Wenn der Mensch sein Bestes getan hat, steht er doch erst am Anfang;
> und wenn er zum Ende kommt, fehlt noch viel. (Sir 18:7)

Ben Sira zitiert den berühmten Satz aus Psalm 8 und stellt die rhetorische Frage: Was ist der Mensch? (vgl. Ps 8:5). Selbst wenn der Mensch
einhundert Jahre lang lebte, wäre dies nur wie ein Tropfen Wasser im
Meer, wenn man seine Jahre mit der Ewigkeit Gottes vergleicht. Neben
der Macht Gottes betont Ben Sira als wichtige Eigenschaft seine Barmherzigkeit. Gott erbarmt sich aller, die seine Ordnungen eifrig befolgen (Sir
18:14). Otto Mulder weist überdies darauf hin, dass Ben Siras Gottesbild
universalere Züge enthalte als die früheren Traditionen. Diese Eigenschaft
werde besonders in Sir 50 deutlich.[32]

---

32. Otto Mulder, „Two Approaches: Simon the High Priest and YHWH, God of
Israel/God of All in Sirach 50", in *Ben Sira's God. Proceedings of the International Ben
Sira Conference 1–4 July 2001 Durham-Ushaw College*, hrsg von Renate Egger-Wenzel,
BZAW 321 (Berlin: De Gruyter, 2002), 227.

2.5. Erwählung

Im Alten Testament gehören Bund und Erwählung oft eng zusammen.
Einige Exegeten, wie z.B. Horst Dietrich Preuß, haben das Konzept der
Erwählung so stark betont, dass sie gerade in diesem Begriff die theologische Mitte des gesamten Alten Testaments sehen.[33] Preuß betont zurecht,
dass eine Erwählung ohne Verpflichtung in der alttestamentlichen Theologie unvorstellbar ist. Meistens hat die Erwählung in der hebräischen Bibel
zweierlei Objekte. Es handelt sich entweder um die Erwählung des Gottesvolkes Israel oder um die Erwählung bestimmter Individuen. Gott ist das
souverän handelnde Subjekt in allen Erwählungsprozessen. Er ergreift die
Initiative und hat bekanntlich andere Maßstäbe als die Menschen. Nach
Dtn 7 ist die Begründung für die Erwählung Israels ausschließlich Gottes
Liebe. Man braucht keine anderen Motive. Gottes Liebe haben in den letzten Jahren besonders Hermann Spieckermann und Reinhard Feldmeier
als ein zentrales Thema der ganzen Bibel (also auch des Neuen Testaments) herausgestellt.[34] Eine eindrucksvolle Formulierung in Dtn 7:7–8
stützt diese theologische Ansicht:

> Nicht hat euch der Herr angenommen und euch erwählt, weil ihr größer
> wäret als alle Völker—denn du bist das kleinste unter allen Völkern—,
> sondern weil euch geliebt hat und damit er seinen Eid hielte, den er
> euren Vätern geschworen hat.

Ben Sira ist in mancher Hinsicht ein echter Nachfolger der vor ihm wirken-
den Deuteronomisten, wie z.B. Timo Veijola nachgewiesen hat.[35] Deswegen
ist es wahrscheinlich, dass Ben Sira die Aussagen von Dtn 7 bestens gekannt
hat. Er selbst gebraucht das Verb „erwählen" (בחר) nur relativ selten, aber
das Thema der Erwählung ist ihm keineswegs fremd.[36] Er spricht sowohl

---

33. Preuß, *Theologie*, 27–30.

34. Reinhard Feldmeier und Hermann Spieckermann, *Der Gott der Lebendigen.*
Eine biblische Gotteslehre, Topoi Biblischer Theologie 1 (Tübingen: Mohr Siebeck,
2011), 126–48.

35. Timo Veijola, „Law and Wisdom. The Deuteronomistic Heritage in Ben Sira's
Teaching of the Law", in *Leben nach der Weisung. Exegetisch-historische Studien zum
Alten Testament*, hrsg. von Walter Dietrich und Marko Marttila, FRLANT 224 (Göt-
tingen: Vandenhoeck & Ruprecht, 2008), 144–64.

36. Ein ähnliches Phänomen hat Preuß in den Büchern der hebräischen Bibel
beobachtet. Er weist zum Beispiel auf Gen 12:1–4 hin und stellt fest, dass dort die

von der speziellen Stellung des Gottesvolkes Israel (z.B. Sir 17:17) als auch von der besonderen Rolle einiger Individuen, die Gott beauftragt hat. Um sie geht es vor allem im Lob der Väter, wobei auffällt, dass es sich ausschließlich um Männer handelt. In Ben Siras Verständnis von Erwählung herrscht also kein Gleichgewicht zwischen den Geschlechtern.

Liest man das Sirachbuch systematisch von Anfang an, stößt man zum ersten Mal in Vers 17:17 auf den Namen „Israel". Der Inhalt des Verses lehnt sich deutlich an Dtn 32:8–9 an und legt Israels besondere Rolle fest. Israel unterscheidet sich von den anderen Völkern aufgrund seiner göttlichen Erwählung. Es ist aber nicht völlig sicher, dass Sir 17:17 ursprünglich von Ben Sira selbst stammt. Wie ich in meiner eingehenden Untersuchung gezeigt habe, ist dieser Vers in seinem Kontext isoliert und macht sowohl syntaktisch als auch inhaltlich einen sekundären Eindruck.[37] Auf jeden Fall unterstreicht Sir 17:17 im später etablierten Sirachbuch für seinen Teil die Erwählung Israels, ohne die spezifische Erwählungsterminologie zu verwenden.

Es verwundert zu Recht, dass Ben Sira so wenig über das Exodusgeschehen zu sagen hat.[38] In vielen anderen Büchern des Alten Testaments stellt die Flucht aus Ägypten ein heilsgeschichtliches Grundgeschehen dar, das wieder und wieder in Erinnerung gerufen wird. Der Exodus ist Gottes starke Antwort auf seine Erwählung. Er kann sein Eigentumsvolk nicht außer Acht lassen, sondern er nimmt dessen Bedrängnis wahr, befreit es und führt es ins gelobte Land. Unter dem Aspekt der Erwählung ist dies ein sehr wichtiges Geschehen, das sich nicht nur einmal in ferner Vergangenheit ereignet hat, sondern das sich in einer jeden Notlage aktualisiert. Gott kümmert sich um sein Volk in verschiedenen Phasen der Geschichte. Es ist aber rätselhaft, warum Ben Sira den Auszug aus Ägypten nur beiläufig erwähnt. Die Episode kommt nur ganz kurz in seiner Darstellung des Mose vor, wo er darauf hinweist, dass Gott Mose Zeichen tun ließ und ihn

---

Erwählung Abrams durch Jahwe zur Sprache komme, ohne dass die Vokabel בחר verwendet werde; Preuß, *Theologie*, 31.

37. Marttila, *Nations*, 65–66.

38. Wie Friedrich V. Reiterer, „The Influence of the Book of Exodus on Ben Sira", in *Intertextual Studies in Ben Sira and Tobit. Essays in Honor of Alexander A. Di Lella, O.F.M.*, hrsg. von Jeremy Corley und Vincent Skemp, CBQMS 38, (Washington, DC: The Catholic Biblical Association of America, 2005), 100–117, gezeigt hat, kennt Ben Sira das Exodusbuch und spielt geschickt auf einige Einzelheiten an, aber ein expliziter Hinweis auf den Auszug aus der Sklaverei von Ägypten fehlt im Sirachbuch.

vor Königen verherrlichte (Sir 45:3). In diesem Kontext verwendet Ben Sira Erwählungsterminologie und schreibt von Mose, dass Gott ihn um seiner Treue und Demut willen geheiligt und aus allen Menschen erwählt habe (V.4).

Vor dem Abschnitt über Mose erzählt Ben Sira von den Patriarchen und folgt dabei sorgfältig dem biblischen Vorbild. Obwohl er die Vokabel „erwählen" nicht im Zusammenhang mit Abraham verwendet, kann kein Zweifel daran bestehen, dass seine Erzählung über ihn nichts anderes als ein Erwählungsereignis beschreibt. Er beginnt seine Darstellung mit einem Gedanken, den er aus Gen 17:4–5 übernommen hat, nämlich dass Abraham der Vater vieler Völker war (Sir 44:19). Die Erwählung ist mit Verheißung und Segen verbunden, und dazu gehört auch, dass Abrahams Nachkommen so zahlreich wie der Staub der Erde werden sollen.

Hinsichtlich der Erwählung ist in Ben Siras Väterlob noch eine weitere Stelle bemerkenswert. Ben Sira geht von Aarons Enkel Pinhas zu Josua, dem Nachfolger Moses, über und schreibt, dass dieser Großes tat zur Rettung der Auserwählten des Herrn (Sir 46:1). Hier werden im hebräischen Text die Mitglieder des Volkes Israel ausdrücklich „die Auserwählten des Herrn" genannt. Das gesamte Lob der Väter zeigt verschiedene Schritte in Gottes Heilsgeschichte zugunsten seines Volkes auf. Gott hat entsprechend seinem Plan zwar auch einige Einzelpersonen ausdrücklich erwählt, um sein Volk zu führen, aber vor allem ist das Volk in seiner Gesamtheit das wesentliche Objekt der Erwählung.

Was die Erwählungstheologie im Sirachbuch angeht, scheint es mir die Annahme angebracht, dass für Ben Sira drei Kategorien das Verständnis der Erwählung bestimmen.[39] Zuerst gibt es eine Kategorie der Erwählten („elect"), die im biblischen Sinn fast ausschließlich das Volk Israel umfasst. Einen Gegensatz zu den Erwählten stellen die Anti-Erwählten dar („anti-elect"). Es handelt sich um die Völker, die wiederholt als Israels Feinde dargestellt werden. Im Alten Testament sind dies z.B. die Kanaanäer, die Philister und die Amalekiter. Nach Ben Siras Darstellung ist eine weitere Völkergruppe hinzuzufügen, nämlich die Samaritaner. Sie ist für Ben Sira tatsächlich ein Gräuel. Er hat gar nichts Positives über sie zu sagen. Neben diesem Gegensatzpaar gibt es noch eine dritte Partei, die Joel Kaminsky

---

39. Das Modell von drei Erwählungskategorien habe ich von Joel S. Kaminsky gelernt, der diese Auffassung in seinem Buch *Yet I Loved Jacob* detailliert und überzeugend vorstellt; siehe Joel S. Kaminsky, *Yet I Loved Jacob. Reclaiming the Biblical Concept of Election* (Nashville: Abingdon, 2007), 107–36.

Nicht-Erwählte („non-elect") nennt. Man kann sie mit gutem Grund als neutrale Gruppe definieren. Sie besteht aus Völkern, die mit Israel meist in Frieden leben und mit den Israeliten Handelsverkehr und Kulturaustausch haben. Für diese Völker gibt es noch Hoffnung,[40] nicht aber für die anti-erwählten Völker. Im Sirachbuch gehören meines Erachtens die Völker des hellenistischen Reiches zur Kategorie der Nicht-Erwählten. Ab und zu scheint Ben Sira Kultur und Sitten der Hellenen hochzuschätzen. Er gibt zu, dass die Weisheit auch unter anderen Völkern zu finden ist. Aber ihre höchste Krone hat die Weisheit nur in Israel erlangt, besonders im Gesetz. Jedoch steht Ben Sira den Völkern, die zu den Nicht-Erwählten gezählt werden, nicht feindlich gegenüber.

2.6. Begegnung

Wie ich in der Einführung anmerkte, wurde das Konzept der Begegnung bzw. des Wechselgeschehens zuerst und beinahe gleichzeitig von den bekannten und geschätzten Alttestamentlern Walther Zimmerli und Claus Westermann angeführt, die jedoch mehr von einem dialogischen Aspekt im Alten Testament sprachen. Mein Doktorvater Timo Veijola machte in einem wichtigen Beitrag darauf aufmerksam, dass statt von einem Dialog besser von einer Begegnung zu sprechen sei.[41] Gott begegnet einzelnen Menschen, den Völkern, dem erwählten Volk Israel und der ganzen Schöpfung im Alten Testament auf vielfache Weise. In einem Beitrag auf Finnisch hat Veijola ein Modell entworfen, wie sich die Begegnung in verschiedenen Textgattungen vollzieht.[42] Dieses ist nützlich, wenn man ausführlicher untersuchen will, wie Gott, Menschen und Welt einander im Sirachbuch begegnen.

Veijola weist beispielsweise auf den dialogischen Grundcharakter des Alten Testaments hin, der schon in der Schöpfungsgeschichte der Priesterschrift vorkommt. Nach dieser Schöpfungsgeschichte wurde

---

40. Kaminsky, *Jacob*, 125, schreibt über die Rolle der Nicht-Erwählten zutreffend: „A number of texts in the Hebrew Bible appear to be challenging Israel to recognize that the non-elect often have much to teach the elect about how one should act in the world and serve God".

41. Veijola, „Offenbarung", 20–29.

42. Timo Veijola, „Onko Vanhan testamentin teologiaa olemassa?" [= „Gibt es eine Theologie des Alten Testaments?"] in *Vanhan testamentin tutkimus ja teologia*, STKSJ 167 (Helsinki: Suomalainen Teologinen Kirjallisuusseura, 1990), 61–89.

der Mensch zum Abbild Gottes geschaffen (Gen 1:26–27). Es hat in der christlichen (und jüdischen) Theologie nicht an Versuchen gefehlt, dieses Abbildsein zu erklären. Veijola erwähnt sowohl Karl Barth und Claus Westermann als auch weitere Theologen, die den Sinn dieser Aussage richtig verstanden haben. Barth definierte das Konzept der ‚*imago Dei*‘ auf folgende Weise: „Sie besteht nicht in irgendetwas, was der Mensch ist oder tut. Sie besteht, indem der Mensch selber und als solcher als Gottes Geschöpf besteht. Er wäre nicht Mensch, wenn er nicht Gottes Ebenbild wäre. Er ist Gottes Ebenbild, indem er Mensch ist".[43] In seinem umfangreichen Genesis-Kommentar knüpft Westermann offensichtlich an Barths Gedanken an und führt das Thema der Begegnung zwischen Gott und Mensch ein: „Mit der Gottesebenbildlichkeit der menschlichen Existenz soll beschrieben werden der ‚besondere Charakter der menschlichen Existenz, kraft dessen der Mensch Gott gegenüber verhandlungsfähig wird‘, der ‚Charakter als ein von Gott anzuredendes Du und als ein vor Gott verantwortliches Ich‘."[44]

Der dialogische Aspekt ist nach Veijolas Auffassung auch im Exodusgeschehen evident, weil die unterdrückten Israeliten in Ägypten um Hilfe riefen und Jahwe ihren Notschrei hörte. Die Begegnung ist also sehr konkret, besonders in der Berufung des Mose. Es ist für die modernen Theologien des Alten Testaments oft kennzeichnend gewesen, dass sie zumindest einige Probleme haben, wenn sie die Verkündigung der Propheten einzuordnen versuchen.[45] Westermann hat zum Beispiel festgestellt, dass das Konzept vom Dialog bei den früheren Schriftpropheten nicht deutlich genug hervortritt.[46] Hier ist Veijola anderer Meinung und weist ausdrücklich darauf hin, wie die Berufungsgeschichten der Propheten ein dialogisches Muster vermitteln. Von nicht geringer Bedeutung ist auch die Rolle einiger Propheten als Fürbitter. Diese Funktion kommt u.a. im Amosbuch vor (Amos 7:2).

---

43. Karl Barth, *Die kirchliche Dogmatik 3,1: Die Lehre von der Schöpfung* (Zürich: Evangelischer Verlag, 1945), 206.

44. Claus Westermann, *Genesis 1–11*, BKAT 1.1 (Neukirchen-Vluyn: Neukirchener Verlag, 1974), 208. Siehe auch Westermann, *Theologie*, 8, 81, 83.

45. Gerhard von Rad, *Theologie des Alten Testaments I. Die Theologie der geschichtlichen Überlieferungen Israels*, 5. Aufl. (München: Kaiser, 1966), 172; Zimmerli, „Biblische Theologie", 444, sagt nachdrücklich: „Die Einordnung der Prophetie stellt auf jeden Fall einen Prüfstein für die Gestaltung jeder alttestamentlichen Theologie dar".

46. Westermann, *Theologie*, 109–20.

Die Überlegungen Veijolas zur Weisheitsliteratur und zur Apokalyptik sind für das Begegnungsthema im Sirachbuch besonders wichtig, weil das Sirachbuch ein echter Vertreter der jüdischen Weisheitsliteratur ist und weil es entstand, als die apokalyptischen Werke zu gedeihen begannen. Die alttestamentliche Weisheitsliteratur ist nicht aus einem Guss. Einerseits setzt der Dialog bzw. die Begegnung zwischen Gott und Mensch ziemlich klar in den Büchern Hiob und Kohelet ein, aber andererseits sind diese Aspekte in den älteren Teilen des Sprüchebuchs, die sich vor allem mit den profanen und auch mit ausländischen Weisheitstraditionen beschäftigen, nur schwer nachzuweisen. In Anlehnung an von Rad[47] stellt Veijola zu Recht fest, dass die jüdische Weisheitsliteratur besonders in Spr 1–9 und im Sirachbuch eine Theologisierung erfährt, und als Objekte begegnen mehr und mehr die Worte und Taten Jahwes. Somit hat man es wieder mit einem echten Dialog zu tun. Doch lehnt Veijola entschieden ab, dass Apokalyptik als eine Form des Dialogs zwischen Gott und Mensch verstanden werden könne. Diese Ansicht basiert auf seiner Deutung, dass sich die Ereignisse der Welt zu ihrem Ende hin unabhängig vom menschlichen Handeln entwickeln, weil alles nach dem souveränen Plan Gottes geschieht. Vor allem lehre uns die Apokalyptik, dass Gott das letzte Wort in dem langen Dialog mit den Menschen hat.

Ich selbst halte das Konzept der Begegnung für sehr fruchtbar, weil es als Thema flexibel ist. Will man einen roten Faden verfolgen, der die verschiedenen Bücher des Alten Testaments durchzieht, ist das Thema „Begegnung" ergiebiger als die anderen oben behandelten Kernbegriffe. Abschließend werde ich in gebotener Kürze prüfen, welche Erscheinungsformen die Begegnung im Sirachbuch aufweist.

Wie schon festgestellt, sind der Ursprung der Weisheit und die Gottesfurcht zentrale Themen im ersten Kapitel des Sirachbuches. Die Begegnung zwischen der ewigen göttlichen Weisheit und den sterblichen Menschen geschieht durch die Gebote Gottes (Sir 1:26). Dieser Sachverhalt wird im Sirachbuch wiederholt erwähnt. Gott hat seinen Willen im Gesetz bekanntgegeben. Er weist also den Weg und erwartet, dass der Mensch dieser Richtung folgt. Ein großer Teil der Lehre im Sirachbuch handelt vom ethischen Verhalten, wie man seinen Mitmenschen dienen soll. Dies ist ein konkretes Beispiel dafür, wie sich die Begegnung zwischen Gott und Mensch durch die Observanz der Tora in den menschlichen Beziehungen

---

47. Von Rad, *Theologie*, 454–67.

realisiert. Man darf auch Ben Siras Ausführung zum freien Willen nicht vergessen: Der Mensch steht immer vor einer Wahl. Es hängt von der Entscheidung eines jeden Individuums ab, ob es die von Gott angebotene Alternative wählt oder nicht:

> Er [Gott] hat im Anfang den Menschen geschaffen und ihm die Wahl gelassen: Wenn du willst, so kannst du die Gebote halten und in rechter Treue tun, was ihm gefällt. Er hat dich vor Feuer und Wasser gestellt: Wähle, was du willst! Der Mensch hat vor sich Leben und Tod; was er wählt, wird ihm gegeben werden. (Sir 15:14–17)

Die Begegnung beinhaltet die Möglichkeit, dass man sich wider den Willen Gottes verhält, und dafür gibt das Alte Testament zahlreiche Beispiele. Auf der anderen Seite ruft die personifizierte Weisheit Gottes die Menschen und lädt sie ein, sich an ihren Früchten zu sättigen (Sir 24:19). Es ist eine uferlose Aufgabe im positiven Sinn, weil es jeden, der von der Weisheit isst, nach immer mehr hungert.

Bitten sind ein deutliches Zeichen der Begegnung zwischen Gott und Mensch. In ihnen wird den tiefsten menschlichen Gefühlen, von der Klage bis zur großen Freude und Dankbarkeit, Ausdruck verliehen. Ben Sira verwendet in seinem Werk eine vielseitige Gebetsterminologie, und es kann kein Zweifel daran bestehen, dass ihm das Gebet sehr wichtig war. Wie Werner Urbanz in seiner Untersuchung festgestellt hat, sind es die Schüler Ben Siras, die am häufigsten mit dem Gebet in Zusammenhang gebracht werden.[48] Ben Sira gibt als Lehrer Ratschläge für das Gebetsleben, doch eigentliche Gebetstexte enthält das Sirachbuch nicht viele; in Frage kommen im Grunde nur Texte wie Sir 22:27–23:6; 36:1–17 und 51:1–12. Der dialogische Aspekt findet einen klaren Ausdruck z.B. in der Volksklage, die in Sir 36 zu finden ist. Hier wendet sich der Beter (oder das ganze Volk) an Jahwe und bittet um dessen Hilfe gegen die Feinde. Die göttliche Intervention soll auch dazu dienen, die fremden Völker zum Bekenntnis der Größe Gottes zu bewegen:

> Herr, Gott des Alls, erbarme dich unser, und wirf deinen Schrecken auf alle Völker! Erhebe deine Hand gegen die fremden Völker, dass sie deine Macht sehen.—Erhöre, Herr, das Gebet deiner Diener, da du Wohlgefal-

---

48. Werner Urbanz, *Gebet im Sirachbuch. Zur Terminologie von Klage und Lob in der griechischen Texttradition*, HBS 60 (Freiburg: Herder, 2009), 237.

len an deinem Volk hast, damit alle, die auf Erden wohnen, erkennen, dass du der Herr bist, der Gott der Ewigkeiten. (Sir 36:1–3, 19)

Auch einzelne Menschen werden ermahnt, sich zum Herrn zu bekehren und von den Sünden zu lassen (vgl. Sir 17:25). Die Bekehrung des verirrten Menschen zurück zu Gott ist eine Form der Begegnung.

Selbstverständlich sind auch die kurzen Erzählungen im Lob der Väter Zeugnisse für die Begegnung, die zwischen Gott und Menschen in verschiedenen Phasen der Geschichte stattgefunden hat. Wie bereits erwähnt, ist das kultische Leben von besonderer Bedeutung für Ben Sira. Im Kult begegnet Jahwe denen, die ihn verehren. Man geht kaum fehl, wenn man annimmt, dass der Tempel in Jerusalem einen Mittelpunkt in Ben Siras Weltanschauung darstellte. Der Tempel als konkretes Gebäude war wichtig, wie z.B. in Sir 50:1–3 zu lesen ist:

Simon, der Sohn des Onias, der Hohepriester—er besserte zu seiner Zeit das Haus des Herrn aus und befestigte den Tempel; er legte den Grundstein für die Stützmauern des Vorhofs, hohe Mauern, die das Heiligtum umschlossen. Zu seiner Zeit wurde ein Wasserbecken ausgehauen, ein Becken fast so groß wie ein Meer.

Viel wichtiger als das Gebäude war jedoch die kultische Funktion des Tempels. Im Kult ist der Gott Israels gegenwärtig und schenkt den Kultteilnehmern seinen Segen (Sir 50:20–21).

3. Fazit

Die Theologie des Alten Testaments hat sich als ein fruchtbares Forschungsfeld erwiesen. Mehrere Kernbegriffe und Modelle sind vorgeschlagen worden, die als theologische Mitte denkbar wären. Fast alle diese Themen sind auch im Sirachbuch vorhanden, denn Ben Sira kennt die vorangehenden Traditionen gut und fasst verschiedene Linien zusammen. Es ist deutlich geworden, dass Themen wie Schöpfung, Bund, Kult, Gott und Erwählung an zentralen Stellen im Sirachbuch vorkommen. Mir persönlich scheint jedoch das Thema Dialog bzw. Begegnung am wichtigsten, wie mein Lehrer Prof. Dr. Timo Veijola und vor ihm schon die deutschen Alttestamentler Claus Westermann und Walther Zimmerli ausgeführt haben.

In Ben Siras Weisheitswerk ist das Thema Begegnung häufig zu finden. Sie ist oft mit dem Gesetz verbunden und hat damit Einfluss auf die Beziehungen zu den Mitmenschen. Besonders wichtig scheint für Ben Sira zu

sein, dass die Begegnung sich im Kult manifestiert. Es spiegelt das Grund-
prinzip seiner Theologie wider, dass der umfangreiche Abschnitt „das Lob
der Väter" in einem langen und detaillierten Bild vom Gottesdienst kul-
miniert.

Die frühneuzeitliche Rezeption des Sirachbuches am Beispiel der Freien Reichsstadt Nürnberg. Neukontextualisierung, Textspektrum und Diskursrelevanz

Christine Ganslmayer

ABSTRACT: The reception of the book of Sirach in the early modern era focusing on the free imperial city of Nürnberg: new contextualization, different types of text, and discourse relevance.

The study concentrates on the recent history of the reception of the book of Sirach in the German-speaking territory in the early modern era. In the center there is the transfer of the text of Sirach into a socio-cultural context that differs significantly from the original historical location of the text in Jerusalem at the time of the Seleucid Empire. In the history of the reception of Sirach, the Reformation represents a clear break (§2): Martin Luther gives a new interpretation of the apocryphal book of Sirach as an educational tool for Christian lay people, especially for the Christian *pater familias*. The emphasis on the ethical-practical aspects of the Scripture causes an opening of the reception from the religious area to the daily area. The result of this popularization is a significant increase of the reception in the entire German-speaking area as the numerous special editions of the book of Sirach show, which are attested from Luther's time up to the end of the seventeenth century and verify the separate distribution of the text beyond the entire Bible. This intensification of the reception leads to the logical result that the discourse relevance of the book of Sirach has increased.

In my contribution I will show from the perspective of German studies what textual transformation processes the book was exposed to and how far the political, social, and cultural breaks of the time of the Reformation are reflected in the process of reception.

Using the example of the free imperial city of Nürnberg, which played an important role (§3) in the time of the Reformation, the relevance of the book of Sirach in the Protestant-influenced urban culture is reconstructed just as the scheme of its production and reception is elaborated. In conformity with the method of a historical discourse analysis, a Sirach text corpus from Nürnberg was gathered and the constellations of the reception were looked for and evaluated considering the different protagonists and texts. The analysis of the individual texts takes into account pragmatic factors such as the situational, medial, institutional, and historical context of the formation of the text and the intention of the authors or redactors (illocution), which often can be deduced from the paratexts. The following question is important: who redacts the text of Sirach, for whom, in what form, and for what purpose?

The Sirach text corpus from Nürnberg (§4 and in a chronological presentation, table 9) contains different groups of texts: (1) The Nürnberg Sirach editions of the Luther translation (§4.1); (2) Various redactions and transformations of the Sirach text, differentiated according to the groups that received them (adults vs. children and/or young adults) (§4.2); (3) A choice of Sirach citations on objects and in texts (§4.3).

The special editions of Luther's translation of Sirach are extant in Nürnberg, in a timeline of almost exactly one hundred years (1533–1632). During this time the Sirach text was frequently received and redacted in various ways. According to the number of copies, the most frequent one was the collection of homilies of Caspar Huberinus (sixteen Nürnberg editions between 1552 and 1588). Because of this collection the Sirach text became definitively part of the domestic literature of the *patres familias*. Here we can also add the poetic version of Hans Sachs, which is typical for Nürnberg. The fact that the book of Sirach additionally was exploited very early for the education of children and young people is shown with the book riddles by Behem, which has been documented in Nürnberg since 1535. In the seventeenth century, echoes of the book of Sirach are encountered, especially in the context of edifying literature used for preaching, in particular for funeral sermons, and have ended up in church music. As a long-term consequence of the literature of the *patres familias* the Sirach quotations, written on a single leaflet (1651), can be considered. A final transformation of the text exists in the last part of the eighteenth century in the form of children's books. The biblical quotations from the book of Sirach are likewise from the sixteenth and seventeenth centuries. They cover the presence of the text in everyday life, which goes beyond a limited ecclesial area.

All authors, respectively editors, with the exception of Georg Lauterbach and Hans Sachs, are Lutheran theologians or preachers; Lauterbach and Sachs likewise can be situated in the context of the literature of the Reformation. The texts can be put in order linguistically in the following manner: according to the communicative function of the text, we are mainly dealing with edifying texts that should strengthen the reader's faith, just as with didactic texts, which mediate the religious behavior to the recipients. There is in addition an entertaining function in the poetic editing, especially in the work of Hans Sachs, in which the text has been worked on artistically with aesthetic pretention. We are dealing also with texts in which the daily reality is interpreted and communicated. Sirach texts and their redaction belong to the religious world but also to everyday life and even to the world of poetry.

In summary: the transformational potential of the book of Sirach is immense, just as it is evident in the various texts of Nürnberg. Because Luther esteems it, the text acquired high authority. This text preserves as a matter of principle an enormous variety of interpretations in itself. That seems to be relevant for the Protestant-influenced civil society in the beginning of the modern era. As part of wisdom literature, the book of Sirach contains an extensive concept of education that is directed toward the ethical responsibility of the individual in the society: The teaching of Sirach mediates models of interpretation and action that guarantee a successful way of life in social relationships. According to the content it can be characterized as timeless and according to the mediated values it is to be seen as traditional, and according to today's standards it would be conservative. The position of the individuals is defined by their place in the hierarchic structures. Therefore it is not surprising that the book of Sirach has its place in the context of the Protestant discourse of education and culture. During the Reformation the individual responsibility for an ethically influenced way of life was emphasized, the house and the family as an area of living and working became the center of instruction for an ideal way of life. This may be one reason why ancient Jewish wisdom literature could realize its potential impact in the context of an urban culture in the early modern German era. The book of Sirach, similar to the catechism, inserts itself most positively into an ever more ecclesial daily life and a social discipline that influenced the era. We can observe that the precepts of values and norms of Sirach can be transferred easily to those of early modern urban culture. The text, especially single passages, soon became part of the collective knowledge of the young and old by means of sermons, reading at home and school, and memorization. Christian values were transported in a traditionally orientated form into general social contexts and extended to all areas of society. And also knowing that in the future development the reception of the Sirach text was increasingly separated from the person of Martin Luther, the models of reception were maintained for a long time.

For this reason the Sirach text, as a text of authority, could develop a power-oriented effect in the sociocultural surrounding of the free imperial city of Nürnberg: The text is instrumentalized in different discourses in such a form that social structures of order were fortified by referring to Christian norms, in order to guarantee the long-term continuity of the urban social culture.

1. Einleitung

Der vorliegende Beitrag widmet sich einem spezifischen Ausschnitt der jüngeren Rezeptionsgeschichte des Sirachbuches im deutschsprachigen Raum in der Frühen Neuzeit. Im Zentrum steht somit der Transfer des Sirachtextes in einen soziokulturellen Kontext, der von der historischen Verortung des Textes in Jerusalem zur Zeit der Seleukidenherrschaft stark abweicht.[1] Aus theologischer Perspektive haben bereits Ernst Koch und ergänzend Eve-Marie Becker aufgezeigt, dass die alttestamentliche Spruchweisheit für das Luthertum des 16. und 17. Jahrhunderts von großer Bedeutung war.[2] Für das Sirachbuch lässt sich im Anschluss an die Neudeutung der Schrift durch Martin Luther eine deutliche Zäsur in der Rezeption erkennen, die von einer starken Zunahme im deutschsprachigen Raum geprägt ist (vgl. Abschnitt 2). Dies erlaubt den Rückschluss auf eine gesteigerte Diskursrelevanz des Sirachbuches. Ziel des Beitrags ist es, aus germanistischer Perspektive exemplarisch aufzuzeigen,

---

1. Zum historischen Kontext des Sirachbuches im Überblick Folker Siegert, *Einleitung in die hellenistisch-jüdische Literatur: Apokrypha, Pseudepigrapha und Fragmente verlorener Autorenwerke* (Berlin: de Gruyter, 2016), 141–56, und zuletzt Siegfried Kreuzer, „Der soziokulturelle Hintergrund des Sirachbuches", in *Texts and Contexts of the Book of Sirach = Texte und Kontexte des Sirachbuches*, hrsg. Gerhard Karner, Frank Ueberschaer und Burkard M. Zapff, SCS 66 (Atlanta: SBL Press, 2017), 33–52. Aus Perspektive der Autorforschung vgl. Oda Wischmeyer, „Jesus ben Sira als erster frühjüdischer Autor", in *Autoren in religiösen Texten der späthellenistischen und frühkaiserlichen Welt: Zwölf Fallstudien = Authorial Voices in Religious Literary Texts*, hrsg. Eve-Marie Becker und Jörg Rüpke, CRPG 3 (Tübingen: Mohr Siebeck, 2018), 19–38. Zu Rekonstruktion bzw. Konstruktion von Kultur im Sirachbuch vgl. grundlegend Oda Wischmeyer, *Die Kultur des Buches Jesus Sirach*, BZNW 77 (Berlin: de Gruyter, 1995); Oda Wischmeyer, „Die Konstruktion von Kultur im Sirachbuch", in Karner, Ueberschaer und Zapff, *Texts and Contexts of the Book of Sirach*, 71–98.

2. Zur Wertschätzung des Sirachbuches im älteren Protestantismus siehe Ernst Koch, „Die ‚Himlische Philosophia des heiligen Geistes': Zur Bedeutung alttestamentlicher Spruchweisheit im Luthertum des 16. und 17. Jahrhunderts", TLZ 115.10 (1990): 705–20; Eve-Marie Becker, „Jesus Sirach und das Luthertum des 16. Jahrhunderts: Über Inhalt und Funktion eines schlesischen Katechismus von 1561", in *Ben Sira's God: Proceedings of the International Ben Sira Conference Durham—Ushaw College 2001*, hrsg. Renate Egger-Wenzel, BZAW 321 (Berlin: de Gruyter, 2002), 352–60.

welchen textuellen Transformationsprozessen das Buch infolge der Reformationsereignisse ausgesetzt war und inwieweit sich die politischen, gesellschaftlichen und kulturellen Umbrüche im Rezeptionsprozess widerspiegeln. Am Beispiel der Freien Reichsstadt Nürnberg, die „in der Reformation eine über den Durchschnitt der Städte herausgehobene Sonderrolle"[3] spielte (vgl. Abschnitt 3), wird die Relevanz des Sirachbuches im städtischen Kontext rekonstruiert.

In Anlehnung an die Methodik einer historischen Diskursanalyse[4] werden die Konstellationen der Rezeption anhand der beteiligten Akteure und Textzeugen ermittelt und ausgewertet. Konkret bedeutet dies, dass ein Sirach-Textkorpus mit Bezug zur Stadt Nürnberg ab der Frühen Neuzeit zusammengestellt wurde, das im Rahmen des Beitrags vorgestellt wird (vgl. Abschnitt 4). Bei der Einzeltextanalyse wird ein Schwerpunkt auf die Autoren bzw. Bearbeiter des Sirach-Textes gelegt; zentral ist die Frage nach den jeweiligen Intentionen der Textadaption (Textillokution): Wer bearbeitet den Sirach-Text für wen in welcher Form zu welchem Zweck? Die Textanalyse orientiert sich dabei am pragmatischen Paradigma, d.h. der situative, mediale, institutionelle und historische Kontext der Textentstehung wird einbezogen. Übergreifend soll so die Diskursrelevanz des Sirach-Textes in der städtischen Kultur ab der Frühen Neuzeit im deutschsprachigen Raum exemplifiziert werden. Folgende Fragestellungen sind leitend, um Rezeptionsmuster zu erarbeiten:

---

3. Berndt Hamm, „Die Reformation in Nürnberg", in *Deutschlands Auge & Ohr: Nürnberg als Medienzentrum der Reformationszeit*, hrsg. Thomas Schauerte, Schriftenreihe der Museen der Stadt Nürnberg 8 (Nürnberg: Tümmel, 2015), 13; Wiederabdruck aus *TLZ* 136 (2011). Zu Nürnberg als Ausgangspunkt exemplarischer Studien im Rahmen der Frühneuzeitforschung vgl. auch Klaus Garber, „Stadt und Literatur im alten deutschen Sprachraum: Umrisse der Forschung—Regionale Literaturgeschichte und kommunale Ikonologie—Nürnberg als Paradigma", in *Stadt und Literatur im deutschen Sprachraum der Frühen Neuzeit: Studien und Dokumente zur deutschen Literatur und Kultur im europäischen Kontext*, Bd. 1, hrsg. Klaus Garber, unter Mitwirkung von Stefan Anders und Thomas Elsmann (Tübingen: Niemeyer, 1998), 3–89.

4. Zur Methodik der historischen Diskursanalyse vgl. grundlegend Achim Landwehr, *Historische Diskursanalyse*, 2. Aufl., Historische Einführungen 4 (Frankfurt: Campus, 2009) sowie Jürgen Spitzmüller und Ingo H. Warnke, *Diskurslinguistik: Eine Einführung in Theorien und Methoden der transtextuellen Sprachanalyse*, de Gruyter Studium (Berlin: de Gruyter, 2011); Sylvia Bendel Larcher, *Linguistische Diskursanalyse: Ein Lehr- und Arbeitsbuch*, Narr Studienbücher (Tübingen: Narr, 2015).

1. Welche Akteure adaptieren in welchen institutionellen Kontexten den Sirach-Text in welchen Medien und Textformen?
2. Welche Faktoren beeinflussen die Produktion und Rezeption von Sirach-Texten im frühneuzeitlichen Nürnberg?
3. Welche Kategorisierungen, Kausalitäten und Wertehierarchien lassen die Aussagen der adaptierten Sirach-Texte erkennen? Welche Aussagen werden weniger stark fokussiert? Welches Menschenbild tritt in den frühneuzeitlichen Sirach-Texten hervor?
4. An welchen frühneuzeitlichen Diskursen hat das Sirachbuch Anteil bzw. inwiefern wird es im Kontext von Wissen und Macht funktionalisiert?

2. Rezeptionszunahme des Sirachbuches in der Frühen Neuzeit

Martin Luther weist den alttestamentlichen Apokryphen im Rahmen der Lutherbibel einen neuen Stellenwert zu.[5] Seine besondere Wertschätzung der Textgruppe als „nützlich und gut zu lesen"[6] bereitet, gestützt durch die mediale Erfolgsgeschichte der Lutherbibel, eine verstärkte Rezeption der Apokryphen-Bücher vor. Das Sirachbuch erfährt in diesem Zusammenhang durch Luther eine Neudeutung, die auch anhand einer bewussten Distanzierung von dem in der lateinischen Tradition verhafteten Titel *Ecclesiasticus* sichtbar wird: Die bislang übliche Verdeutschung des lateinischen Titels als „Die geistliche zucht" empfindet Luther als unpassend, schränkt dieser doch seiner Meinung nach den Kreis der Leser zu sehr ein und entspricht nicht der von Luther erkannten Intention der Weisheitsschrift.[7] Als neuen Subtitel prägt Luther „Ein Buch von der Hauszucht

---

5. Vgl. zum Stellenwert der Apokryphen in der Lutherbibel Hans Volz, „Luthers Stellung zu den Apokryphen des Alten Testaments", *Luther-Jahrbuch* 26 (1959): 93–108 und zuletzt Martin Rösel, „Die Apokryphen in der Lutherbibel und im Protestantismus", in *Die Apokryphen der Lutherbibel: Einführungen und Bibeltexte*, hrsg. Christfried Böttrich und Martin Rösel (Stuttgart: Deutsche Bibelgesellschaft; Leipzig: Evangelische Verlagsanstalt, 2017), 19–25.

6. So Martin Luther in der Einleitung des Inhaltsverzeichnisses zum Apokryphenteil der ersten Vollbibel: Martin Luther, „Apocrypha", in *Biblia / das ist / die gantze Heilige Schrifft Deudsch* (Wittenberg: Lufft, 1534), Ai[r]; ND Köln: Taschen, 2012.

7. Luther, „Apocrypha", E vj[r] (= p. XXX). Den Titel *Jesus Syrach* begründet Luther in der Vorrede damit, dass biblische Bücher und insbesondere Prophetenbücher in der Regel nach ihrem „meister" benannt seien.

/ odder von tugenden eines fromen haus herrn"[8] und deutet so die Weisheitsschrift neu als Bildungsschrift für den christlichen Laien. Den besonderen Wert des Sirachbuches sieht Luther in der möglichen Funktion als Richtschnur und Orientierungshilfe für den christlichen Hausvater bei sämtlichen relevanten Fragen zur Lebensführung, sei es im Verhältnis zu Gott und den Obrigkeiten, sei es im privaten und öffentlichen Bereich sowie zur individualethischen und sozialen Bildung:[9]

> Es ist ein nützlich Buch / fur den gemeinen man / Denn auch alle sein vleis ist / das er einen burger odder hausuater Gottfürchtig / from und klug mache / wie er sich gegen Gott / Gottes wort / Priestern / Eltern / weib / kindern / eigen leib / güter / knechten / nachbarn / freunden / feinden / Oberkeit vnd jederman / halten sol[10]

Im zeitlichen Umfeld der Arbeit am Sirach charakterisiert Luther das Buch wiederholt als „ökonomisches" Werk (Hervorhebungen durch die Autorin):

> Syrach manet tantum in **oeconomia**, non assurgit in res magnas, de quibus dicunt prophetae et euangelion.[11]

> Syrach est liber **politicus**.[12]

> Estque optimus liber (sc. Sir) et gratus propter praecepta **oeconomica**.[13]

> Et cum iste liber bonus quidem sit **iurista**, **legista** et **oeconomicus**, ideo placet mundo.[14]

---

8. Luther, „Apocrypha", E vj^r (= p. XXX).

9. Vgl. Christine Ganslmayer, Nina Irrgang, Gerhard Karner und Oda Wischmeyer, „Das Buch Jesus Sirach / Ben Sira", in Böttrich und Rösel, *Die Apokryphen der Lutherbibel*, 156–57.

10. Luther, „Apocrypha," E vj^r (= p. XXX).

11. *D. Martin Luthers Werke: Kritische Gesamtausgabe: Tischreden*, Bd. 1 (Weimar: Hermann Böhlaus Nachfolger, 1912), 247, Nr. 530 (VD. 188^b), 1533.

12. *D. Martin Luthers Werke: Kritische Gesamtausgabe: Tischreden*, Bd. 2 (Weimar: Hermann Böhlaus Nachfolger, 1913), 245, Nr. 1880 (Ror. Bos. q. 24^s, 97), 1533.

13. *D. Martin Luthers Werke: Kritische Gesamtausgabe: Tischreden*, Bd. 2, 653, Nr. 2776 b. (B. 2, 217), 1532.

14. *D. Martin Luthers Werke: Kritische Gesamtausgabe: Tischreden*, Bd. 3 (Weimar: Hermann Böhlaus Nachfolger, 1914), 254, Nr. 3294 a. (Cord. 1647; Zell. 595), 1533.

Quid est Hiesus Syrach? Quamvis optimus liber, ad apostolorum et Christi verba tantum est **legalis, juristisch** vnd **öconomisch** liber. Hoc miratur mundus ...[15]

Omnes homines legem Mosis et Hiesum Syrach diligunt et laudant, eo quod bona praecepta habeant.[16]

Damit stellt Luther einen Zusammenhang zwischen dem Sirachbuch und dem zeitgenössischen Bildungsdiskurs her, wie eine Profilierung des Ökonomie-Begriffs zu zeigen vermag: In der Reformationszeit erfuhr der Begriff „Oikonomia" im Rahmen der Unterweisung zur christlichen Haushaltung eine Neudeutung.[17] Diese manifestiert sich zuerst in der einflussreichen Schrift *Oeconomia Christiana* (1529)[18] des thüringischen Reformators Justus Menius, zu der Luther ein mehrseitiges Vorwort verfasst hat, in dem er die Schrift dem christlichen Hausvater zur Lektüre empfiehlt.[19] „Ökonomie" erscheint eingebettet in ein umfassendes (protestantisch) christliches Bildungskonzept, wobei dem Hauswesen als Mikrokosmos des Staatswesens der Status eines Ortes für Grundlagenerziehung zukommt:

Oeconomia / das ist haushaltung / vnd Politia / das ist landregierung / Jn der Oeconomia odder haushaltung ist verfasset / wie ein igliches haus Christlich vnd recht wol sol regiret werden / Wes sich darynnen ein igliches nach seinem stand vnd gebüre / Man / weib / kinder vnd gesinde gegen einander halten sollen / das es allenthalben nach Gottes befelh vnd ordenung / ym hause fein recht vnd wol zugehe.

---

15. *D. Martin Luthers Werke: Kritische Gesamtausgabe: Tischreden*, Bd. 3, 254–55, Nr. 3294 b. (B. 2, 217), 1533.

16. *D. Martin Luthers Werke: Kritische Gesamtausgabe: Tischreden*, Bd. 3, 255, Nr. 3295 b. (B. 1, 36), 1533.

17. Vgl. Gerhard Richter, *Oikonomia. Der Gebrauch des Wortes Oikonomia im Neuen Testament, bei den Kirchenvätern und in der theologischen Literatur bis ins 20. Jahrhundert*, Arbeiten zur Kirchengeschichte 90 (Berlin: de Gruyter, 2005), 615–27.

18. Eine kommentierte Edition mit Einleitung liegt vor: *Ehe und Familie im Geist des Luthertums: Die Oeconomia Christiana (1529) des Justus Menius*, hrsg. Ute Gause und Stephanie Scholz, Historisch-theologische Gender-Forschung 6 (Leipzig: Evangelische Verlagsanstalt, 2012).

19. Vgl. Martin Luther, „Vorrede" zu *Oeconomia Christiana* von Justus Menius (Wittenberg: Lufft, 1529), A iiij^v, zitiert nach dem Exemplar Bayerische Staatsbibliothek München, Mor. 1295 g, urn:nbn:de:bvb:12-bsb00038179-4.

Denn daran ist kein zweiffel / aus der Oeconomia odder haushaltung / mus die Politia odder landregierung / als aus einem brunnequel / entspringen vnd herkomen[20]

Im Kontext der Bildungsrevolution des 16. Jahrhunderts erfüllt der Hausvater als Vorstand des Hauswesens die Rolle, den Mitgliedern der Hausgemeinschaft die Grundlagen der christlichen Lebensführung zu vermitteln.[21] In „Familie und Haus" wurden bürgerliche „Primärtugenden wie Gehorsam und Fleiß, Arbeitsbereitschaft und Akzeptanz der Hierarchie eingeübt".[22]

Das Bildungskonzept des jüdischen Weisheitslehrers Ben Sira erscheint Luther offensichtlich adaptierbar für das soziokulturelle Umfeld des 16. Jahrhunderts. Durch seine Autorität wird das Sirachbuch längerfristig als Erziehungsschrift für weitere Kreise erschlossen. Diese Popularisierung und verstärkte Rezeption halten mindestens bis ins 18. Jahrhundert an. Dass das Sirachbuch zu einem „Lieblingsbuch jener Zeit"[23] avancieren konnte, zeigt sich nicht zuletzt an den zahlreichen Sondereditionen, die das Buch vor und nach Erscheinen der ersten Vollbibel 1534 erfahren hat:

Die Editio princeps *Jesus Syrach zu Wittemberg verdeudscht* (*42[24]; VD16 B 4071; vgl. Anhang, Abb. 1: Titelblatt) erschien in der Wittenberger Offizin von Hans Lufft rasch nach Abschluss der Übersetzung des Buches im Spätherbst 1532 durch Luther und seine Mitarbeiter Philipp Melanchthon und Caspar Cruciger zu einem vermarktungstechnisch günstigen

---

20. Menius, *Oeconomia Christiana* (Wittenberg: Lufft, 1529), B iij^v–B iiij^r.

21. Vgl. Walter Raitz, Werner Röcke und Dieter Seitz, „Konfessionalisierung der Reformation und Verkirchlichung des alltäglichen Lebens", in *Die Literatur im Übergang vom Mittelalter zur Neuzeit*, hrsg. Werner Röcke und Marina Münkler, Bd. 1 von *Hansers Sozialgeschichte der deutschen Literatur vom 16. Jahrhundert bis zur Gegenwart*, begründet von Rolf Grimminger (München: Hanser, 2004), 293–95; Werner Röcke, „Familie—Schule—Universität: Die ‚Bildungsrevolution' des 16. Jahrhunderts", in *Mit Milchbrei und Rute. Familie, Schule und Bildung in der Reformationszeit*, hrsg. Daniel Hess, Kulturgeschichtliche Spaziergänge im Germanischen Nationalmuseum 8 (Nürnberg: Verlag des Germanischen Nationalmuseums, 2005), 35–36; 41–45.

22. Röcke, „Familie—Schule—Universität", 35.

23. Koch, „Bedeutung alttestamentlicher Spruchweisheit", 715.

24. Vgl. „Bibliographie der Drucke der Lutherbibel 1522–1546", in *D. Martin Luthers Werke. Kritische Gesamtausgabe. Deutsche Bibel*, Bd. 2 (Weimar: Hermann Böhlaus Nachfolger, 1909), 528.

Zeitpunkt zur Leipziger Neujahrsmesse im Januar 1533.[25] Die Verbreitung der Schrift setzte also schon vor dem Erscheinen der ersten Vollbibel ein. Bemerkenswert ist, dass das Procedere der Sondereditionen auch nach 1534 beibehalten wurde, was Rückschlüsse auf eine weite Rezeption auch außerhalb des engeren kirchlichen Kontextes zulässt. Noch im Jahr 1533 folgten dem Erstdruck weitere ca. acht bislang identifizierte Sirach-Sonderdrucke innerhalb und außerhalb Wittenbergs, wodurch die überregionale Bekanntheit des lange erwarteten nächsten Teils der Lutherbibel schnell befördert wurde (vgl. Tab. 1).[26]

Tab. 1: Hoch- und niederdeutsche Sirach-Sondereditionen des Jahres 1533

Druckort	Offizin	VD16-Nummer	Titel nach VD16
Wittenberg	Hans Lufft	VD16 B 4071 (= ed. princeps)	Jesus Sy‖rach zu ‖ Wittemberg ‖ verdeudscht.‖ Mart. Luther.‖
Wittenberg	Georg Rhau	VD16 B 4072	Jesus Sy‖rach zu ‖ Wittemberg ‖ verdeudscht.‖ Mart. Luther.‖
Wittenberg	Georg Rhau	VD16 B 4073	Jesus Sy=‖rach zu ‖ Wittemberg ver=‖deudscht. ‖ Marti. Luther.‖
Erfurt	Melchior Sachse d.Ä.	VD16 B 4069	Jesus Sy=‖rach zu ‖ Wittemberg ver=‖deudscht.‖ Martinus Luth.‖
Magdeburg	Hans Walther	VD16 B 4123	Jesus Sy=‖rach tho ‖ Wittemberge ‖ Vordůdeschet.‖ Martinus Luther.‖ Welcker ym Latin Eccle=‖siasticus genŏmet wert.‖
Magdeburg	Hans Walther	VD16 B 4124	Jesus Sy=‖rach tho ‖ Wittemberge ‖ Vordůdeschet.‖ Martinus Luther.‖ Vp dat nye gecorrigeret ‖ vth der Biblien.‖
Nürnberg	Friedrich Peypus	VD16 ZV 16151	Jesus Sy=‖rach zu ‖ Wittemberg ver=‖deutsch.‖ Mart. Luther.‖

25. Vgl. Hans Volz, „Die Wittenberger Übersetzung des Apokryphenteils des Alten Testaments", in *D. Martin Luthers Werke. Kritische Gesamtausgabe. Deutsche Bibel*, Bd. 12 (Weimar: Hermann Böhlaus Nachfolger, 1961), XXXI.

26. Die Recherche der Sondereditionen erfolgte im September 2017 im *Verzeichnis der im deutschen Sprachbereich erschienenen Drucke des 16. Jahrhunderts (VD 16)*. Online: https://www.bsb-muenchen.de/ kompetenzzentren-und-landesweite-dienste/ kompetenzzentren/vd-16/ (Zugriff: 01.09.2018). Die Reihenfolge der Druckorte orientiert sich an der „Bibliographie der Drucke der Lutherbibel 1522–1546", in *WA DB* 2, 528–30; 534–41.

| Straßburg | Johann Albrecht | VD16 B 4070 | Jesus Sy=\|\|rach zů \|\| Wittemberg ver=\|\|teütscht. durch D.\|\| Mar. Luther.\|\| |
| s.l. | ? | VD16 B 4122 | Jesus Syrach/ to Wittemberge vordůde-sche. Mart. Luther/ vp dat nye gedruckt uth der Biblien. |

Allein in Wittenberg erfuhr das Sirachbuch zwischen 1533 und 1545 neben seinem Erscheinen im Rahmen der Vollbibel insgesamt mindestens elf separate Neuauflagen, dazu kommen weitere 21 Sondereditionen außerhalb Wittenbergs, die auf eine flächendeckende überregionale Verbreitung der Schrift schließen lassen (vgl. Tab. 2).

Tab. 2: Sirach-Sondereditionen außerhalb Wittenbergs (1533 bis 1545)

Anzahl	Sprachraum	Druckort (Anzahl)	Offizin: Jahr
5	mitteldeutsch	Erfurt (2)	Melchior Sachse d.Ä.: 1533, 1535
		Frankfurt a.M. (1)	Cyriacus Jacob: 1539
		Leipzig (2)	Valentin Schumann: 1542; Jakob Bärwald: 1545
7	oberdeutsch	Nürnberg (1)	Friedrich Peypus: 1533
			Johann Albrecht: 1533; Jakob
		Straßburg (2)	Frölich: 1537
			Silvan Otmar: 1537; Alexander
		Augsburg (3)	Weißenhorn I.: 1539, 1540
		Bern/Üechtland (1)	Matthias Apiarius: 1543
9	niederdeutsch		Hans Walther: 1533, um 1533, 1535, 1537, 1542; Wolfgang Mertz 1538; Michael Lotter 1539; Christian Rödinger d.Ä. 1545
		Magdeburg (8)	
		s.l. (1)	?: 1532

Diese erfolgreiche Druckgeschichte im gesamten mittel-, ober- und niederdeutschen Raum spricht für eine weite Verbreitung und hohe Popularität der Schrift. Abgesehen von den Psalmen sind jedenfalls zu keinem Buch der Lutherbibel mehr Sondereditionen nachgewiesen, wobei Ausgaben im Rahmen von Sammelwerken (z.B. in Verbindung mit *Weisheit Salomonis*) hier unberücksichtigt geblieben sind.

Auch nach Luthers Tod hält die Zahl der Sirach-Sondereditionen unvermindert an: Zwischen 1546 und 1698 konnten im deutschsprachigen Raum bislang 43 Ausgaben recherchiert werden. Festzuhalten ist,

dass die verstärkte Rezeption des Sirachbuches in der Frühen Neuzeit eindeutig eine reformationsbezogene Zäsur reflektiert und im Kontext des
protestantischen Erziehungskonzepts verortet werden kann. Die Neukon-
textualisierung des Sirachbuches als Erziehungsschrift spiegelt sich auch
darin, dass der Sirach in Sammelwerken gemeinsam mit dem Katechismus aufgenommen und ediert wurde.[27]

3. Frühneuzeitliche Rezeption des Sirachbuches am Beispiel der Freien Reichsstadt Nürnberg

Die Blütezeit der Freien Reichsstadt Nürnberg wird auf die Zeit zwischen
1438 und 1555 datiert.[28] Als Verwahrort der Reichskleinodien seit 1423
war Nürnberg nicht nur ein politisches Zentrum des Alten Reichs, sondern durch seine günstige Verkehrslage am Knotenpunkt der wichtigsten
Fernhandelsstraßen auch Handelszentrum. Durch seine Handwerkstradi-
tion und Teilhabe am weltweiten Exportgewerbe war Nürnberg zu einer
Wirtschaftsmetropole europäischen Rangs aufgestiegen.[29] Als Freie

---

27. Vgl. z.B. die beiden folgenden Sammeleditionen *Der Ander Theil/ Geistlichs
Kleinods /Darinnen fürnemlich begrieffen Christliche vnnd Gottselige Tagübung aus
dem Psalter Dauids. [v. Cyriacus Spangenberg] Catechismus D. Mart. Lutheri, sampt
nützlichen Fragstücken. Fest vnnd Sontags Episteln vnd Euangelien/ mit jhren zugehö-
rigen Gebetlein. Collecten aus der Kirchen Agenda. Hymni Patrum Deudsch/ auff den
gewönlichen Coral gerichtet. [Übers. v. (Ambros. Lobwasser)] Die Sprüche Salomonis.
[Übers. v. (Martin. Luther.)] Jtem/ Jesus Syrach ... (Jn ein newe vnd richtige Ordnung
gebracht. Durch Georgium Lauterbeck.)*, ohne Hrsg. (Leipzig: Zacharias Bärwald, 1592;
VD16 ZV 25264) und *Neues Testament Unsers Herrn Jesu Christi Nebst Psalter/ Syrach
und kleinen Catechismo D. Martini Lutheri; Auch Dessen Vorrede über dasselbe. Worin
der Inhalt dessen gezeiget; Welchem beygefüget sind Eines jeden Capitels kurze Summa-
rien/ viel nüzliche Parallelen, Und Eine Anweisung der Evangelien und Episteln durch
das gantze Jahr ...*, ohne Hrsg. (Wernigerode: Johann Wilhelm Mertens, 1698, VD17
14:675732N).

28. Vgl. zur Nürnberger Stadtgeschichte und der Bedeutung Nürnbergs im 15.
und 16. Jahrhundert: Gerhard Pfeiffer, Hrsg., *Nürnberg: Geschichte einer europäischen
Stadt* (München: Beck, 1971) und zusammenfassend Michael Diefenbacher, „Nürnberg, Reichsstadt: Politische und soziale Entwicklung", in Historisches Lexikon Bay-
erns (publiziert am 09.03.2010; Online: http://www.historisches-lexikon-bayerns.
de/Lexikon/Nürnberg,_Reichsstadt:_Politische_und_soziale_Entwicklung; Zugriff:
02.09.2018).

29. Vgl. Hermann Maué u.a., Hrsg., *Quasi Centrum Europae: Europa kauft in
Nürnberg 1400–1800* (Nürnberg: Verlag des Germanischen Nationalmuseums, 2002).

Reichsstadt genoss Nürnberg besondere Privilegien und war als selbst-verwalteter oligarchisch-patrizischer Stadtstaat unter der Ägide eines Rates organisiert. Die Bedeutung Nürnbergs ab dem Spätmittelalter spiegelt sich in der Entwicklung der Bevölkerungszahlen, die zwischen 1445 und 1500 immens anstiegen, so dass Nürnberg mit einer Einwoh-nerzahl von rund 40.000 Personen um 1500 neben Köln die größte Stadt im Reich darstellte.[30]

Als fortschrittlich ist auch das Nürnberger Bildungswesen der dama-ligen Zeit zu charakterisieren: Eine Nürnberger Schulreform um 1510 weitete den Schulbesuch auf breitere Kreise aus und passte die Inhalte bür-gerlichen Bedürfnissen an.[31] Das verhältnismäßig hohe Bildungsniveau schlägt sich in einer überdurchschnittlichen Alphabetisierungsquote von vermutlich mehr als 30 % nieder.[32] Dazu kommt Nürnbergs Bedeutung als ein Zentrum des neuen Mediums Buchdruck: Hier war nicht nur die euro-paweit führende Offizin von Anton Koberger ansässig, sondern für die 1. Hälfte des 16. Jahrhunderts sind darüber hinaus über 45 weitere Offizinen belegt, die mehrheitlich über viele Jahre agierten.[33]

Die Sonderstellung Nürnbergs am Vorabend der Reformation mani-festiert sich in einer „Verquickung von Reichtum, Frömmigkeit, sakraler Repräsentation, Lese- und Schreibfähigkeit, Gelehrsamkeit, Humanismus,

---

30. Vgl. Rudolf Endres, „Sozialstruktur Nürnbergs", in Pfeiffer, Nürnberg, 194; Rudolf Endres, „Zur Einwohnerzahl und Bevölkerungsstruktur Nürnbergs im 15./16. Jahrhundert", Mitteilungen des Vereins für Geschiche der Stadt Nürnberg 57 (1970): 242–71.

31. Rudolf Endres, „Nürnberger Bildungswesen zur Zeit der Reformation", Mit-teilungen des Vereins für Geschiche der Stadt Nürnberg 71 (1984): 112–14.

32. Endres, "Nürnberg Bildungswesen", 127–28; Rudolf Endres, „Das Schulwesen in Franken zur Zeit der Reformation", Zeitschrift für bayerische Kirchengeschichte 63 (1994): 28.

33. Vgl. Christoph Reske, Die Buchdrucker des 16. und 17. Jahrhunderts im deut-schen Sprachgebiet: Auf Grundlage des gleichnamigen Werkes von Josef Benzing, Bei-träge zum Buch- und Bibliothekswesen 51 (Wiesbaden: Harrassowitz, 2007), 655–82. Zu Nürnberg als Medienzentrum vgl. Lore Sporhan-Krempel, Nürnberg als Nachrich-tenzentrum zwischen 1400 und 1700, Nürnberger Forschungen 10 (Nürnberg: Verein für Geschichte der Stadt Nürnberg, 1968); Das Nürnberger Buchgewerbe: Buch- und Zeitungsdrucker, Verleger und Druckhändler vom 16. bis zum 18. Jahrhundert, hrsg. Michael Diefenbacher und Wiltrud Fischer-Pache, Quellen und Forschungen zur Geschichte und Kultur der Stadt Nürnberg 31 (Nürnberg: Selbstverlag des Stadtar-chivs Nürnberg), 2003; Deutschlands Auge & Ohr.

technologischem Innovationsvermögen und Kunstproduktion", wie der Kirchenhistoriker Berndt Hamm treffend zusammenfasst.[34]

Diese historischen Basisinformationen sollen helfen, die Vorreiterrolle Nürnbergs in der Reformation einzuordnen, war Nürnberg doch die erste Stadt, die 1525 die Reformation einführte. Materieller Reichtum und Fortschrittsgeist, zugleich eine für das Spätmittelalter typische Frömmigkeitskultur prägten das Klima und bildeten ideale Voraussetzungen für eine Aufgeschlossenheit gegenüber den reformatorischen Ideen.[35] Begünstigt wurde die Durchführung der Reformation in Nürnberg durch private Kontakte Martin Luthers zu einflussreichen Persönlichkeiten der Nürnberger Stadtgeschichte aus dem Umkreis der humanistischen Sodalitas Staupitziana, einem Anhängerkreis des Luther-Lehrers und -Beichtvaters Johannes von Staupitz, der als Gastprediger bereits ab 1504 mehrfach in der Stadt weilte.[36] Bereits ab 1520 besetzte der Nürnberger Rat leitende Stellen in der Kirchenverwaltung sowie Predigerstellen mit lutherisch gesinnten Theologen.[37] Die Wittenberger Reformation wurde jedenfalls in Nürnberg besonders rasch adaptiert, und der Stadt kommt eine Vorreiterrolle bei der Einführung der neuen Lehre zu.

Als typisches Beispiel für die Stadtreformation in Deutschland[38] und Medienzentrum der Reformationszeit scheint Nürnberg prädestiniert für eine exemplarische Untersuchung der Sirach-Rezeption ab dem 16. Jahrhundert.

---

34. Hamm, „Die Reformation in Nürnberg", 13.

35. Hamm, „Die Reformation in Nürnberg", 16–17.

36. Genannt seien hier nur der Nürnberger Ratsschreiber Lazarus Spengler, der Theologe Wenzeslaus Linck sowie die Patrizier Kaspar Nützel und Christoph Scheurl. Vgl. zur Lese- und Predigtbewegung als Ausgangspunkt der Nürnberger Reformation: Hamm, „Die Reformation in Nürnberg", 17–21. Vgl. auch Markus Wriedt, „Christliche Netzwerke in der Frühen Neuzeit", in *Europäische Geschichte Online (EGO)* (publiziert am 30.03.2011; Online: http://www.ieg-ego.eu/wriedtm-2011-de; urn:nbn:de:0159-2011020180; Zugriff: 02.09.2018).

37. Vgl. Hamm „Die Reformation in Nürnberg", 20.

38. Grundlegend hierzu Berndt Hamm, *Bürgertum und Glaube, Konturen der städtischen Reformation*, Sammlung Vandenhoeck (Göttingen: Vandenhoeck & Ruprecht), 1996.

4. „Jesus Sirach" in Nürnberg ab dem 16. Jahrhundert: Textspektrum

Der Aufbau eines Sirach-Textkorpus mit Bezug zur Stadt Nürnberg ab dem 16. Jahrhundert wurde vorwiegend durch umfangreiche Internetrecherchen in Bibliothekskatalogen und mittels des *Verzeichnis[ses] der im deutschen Sprachbereich erschienenen Drucke des 16. und 17. Jahrhunderts (VD 16/17)* geleistet. Das Korpus erhebt keinen Anspruch auf Vollständigkeit. Es umfasst verschiedene Textgruppen: Berücksichtigt sind nicht nur Nürnberger Sirach-Ausgaben der Luther-Übersetzung (vgl. Abschnitt 4.1), sondern auch vielfältige Bearbeitungen und Transformationen des Sirach-Textes (vgl. Abschnitt 4.2) sowie Sirach-Zitate auf Objekten und in Texten (vgl. Abschnitt 4.3).

Die folgende Vorstellung des Textkorpus versucht über eine Einbindung der Paratexte[39] die Autorenillokution zu fokussieren, um Handlungsmuster der Rezeption zu erarbeiten. Die Präsentation der zweiten Textgruppe orientiert sich an unterschiedlichen Rezipientengruppen, die nach Altersstufen (Erwachsenenalter vs. Kinder- und Jugendalter) differenziert werden (vgl. Abschnitte 4.2.1 und 4.2.2). Sirach-Zitate und ihre Funktion werden exemplarisch vorgestellt (vgl. Abschnitt 4.3).

4.1. Sirach-Sondereditionen in Nürnberg

Bereits im Jahr 1533, bald nach Erscheinen der Wittenberger Sonderedition der Luther-Übersetzung des Sirach im Januar, folgte als erster oberdeutscher Druck die Nürnberger Erstausgabe (Nr. 170[40]; vgl. Tab. 3 und Anhang, Abb. 2: Titelblatt). Diese besorgte mit Friedrich Peypus ein etablierter Nürnberger Drucker, der seit Einführung der Reformation zunehmend reformatorische Titel druckte und für Bibeldrucke in Nürnberg zu seiner Zeit als konkurrenzlos gilt.[41]

---

39. Vgl. Gérard Genette, *Paratexte: Das Buch vom Beiwerk des Buches*, übers. Dieter Hornig (Frankfurt am Main: Suhrkamp, 2001).

40. Vgl. „Bibliographie der Drucke der Lutherbibel 1522–1546", in *Weimarer Ausgabe: Abteilung Deutsche Bibel* 2:537–38.

41. Vgl. Reske, *Die Buchdrucker des 16. und 17. Jahrhunderts*, 665. Die Nürnberger Sirach-Ausgabe war der letzte Bibeldruck in der Luther-Übersetzung, den Peypus verlegte, vgl. Hans-Otto Keunecke, „Friedrich Peypus (1485–1535): Zu Leben und Werk des Nürnberger Buchdruckers und Buchhändlers", *Mitteilungen des Vereins für Geschichte der Stadt Nürnberg* 72 (1985): 43–44; 62.

Tab. 3: Sirach-Sondereditionen in Nürnberg

Jahr	Offizin	VD16-Nummer
1533	Friedrich Peypus	VD16 ZV 16151
1548	Johann Petreius	VD16 B 4083
1554	Johann vom Berg / Ulrich Neuber	VD16 ZV 1823
1584	Nikolaus Knorr	VD16 B 4114
1616	Georg Endter d.Ä. / Ludwig Lochner	VD17 12:122161B
1632	Wolff Endter	VD17 12:120879Y

Das Titelblatt unterscheidet sich inhaltlich nicht von demjenigen der Wittenberger Editio princeps (vgl. Abb. 1 und 2 im Anhang), lediglich das Kolophon weist auf Nürnberg als Druckort: „Gedruckt zů Nůrnberg bey Friderich Peypus. M. D. XXXIII."[42]

Wie häufig praktiziert, stellt der Nürnberger Erstdruck lediglich einen mitunter sprachlich leicht adaptierten, ansonsten jedoch unveränderten Nachdruck der Wittenberger Editio princeps dar, wie folgender Textvergleich ausgewählter Passagen erweisen kann. Das lautlich und graphisch modernere Deutsch aus heutiger Warte bietet die Nürnberger Ausgabe:

Textstelle	Wittenberg: Lufft, 1533	Nürnberg: Peypus, 1533
Vorrede (Luther)	DJß bůch ist bißher genant im latein / Ecclesiasticus / welchs sie habē verdeutscht / Die geystliche zucht / (A ij^r)	DJs buch ist bisher genant im latin Ecclesiasticus / welchs sie haben verdeudscht / Die geistliche zucht / (A ij^r)
Vorrede (Sirach)	ES haben vns vil vnd grosse leute / die weyßheyt / auß dem Gesetz / Propheten vnd andern / so den selbigen nach gefolget / dargethan / daher man můs Jsrael billich loben / vmb jre weyßheyt vnd lere / (A iij^r)	Es haben vns viel vnd grosse leute die weisheit / aus dem Gesetz / propheten vnd andern / so den selbigen nach gefolget / dargethan / Daher man mus Jsrael billich loben / vmb jre weisheit vnd lere / (A iiij^r)
Sir 1,1	ALle weyßheyt ist von Got dem HERREN / vnd ist bey jm ewigklich / (A iiij^r)	ALle weisheit ist von Gott dem HERRN / Vnd ist bey jm ewiglich / (A v^v)

42. Martin Luther, *Jesus Syrach zu Wittemberg verdeudscht* (Nürnberg: Peypus, 1533), G viij^v.

Sir 22,25	Wer vnter die vôgel wirfft / der scheucht sie wegk / Vnd wer seinen freundt schmehet / der zertrennet die freundtschafft. (D jʳ)	Wer vnter die vôgel wirfft / der scheucht sie weg / Vnd wer seinen freund schmehet / der zertrennet die freundschafft. (F jᵛ)
Sir 33,1	Wer den HERRN fôrcht / der lesst sich gern ziehen / Vnd wer sich frûe Darzů schickt / der wirdt gnaden finden. (E iijᵛ)	Wer den HERRN fûrcht / der lesst sich gern zihen / Vnd wer sich frue dazu schickt / der wird gnade finden. (H iijᵛ)
Sir 47,14	Nach jm ward Kônig / sein klûger sun Salomo / dem der vater gûte rûhe geschafft hette / das er jm fride regierte / (G iiijʳ)	Nach jm ward kônig / sein kluger son Salomo / dem der Vater gute ruge geschafft hatte / das er im friede regierte / (L vijʳ)

Das anhaltende Interesse an Sirach-Sondereditionen in der Luther-Übersetzung zeigt sich in den folgenden hundert Jahren an weiteren Nürnberger Ausgaben aus unterschiedlichen Offizinen, von denen im 16. Jahrhundert noch drei sowie im 17. Jahrhundert zwei folgen (vgl. Tab. 3). Erst mit dem Jahr 1632 ist die letzte Sirach-Sonderausgabe in Nürnberg belegt. Die deutschen Nürnberger Sirach-Ausgaben im handlichen Oktavformat stellen sicher, dass dieser Bibelteil über die gottesdienstliche Verbreitung hinaus seit den 1530er Jahren einen festen Bestandteil religiösen Wissens bildete.

Zusätzlich zu den deutschsprachigen Sirach-Ausgaben sind in Nürnberg auch lateinische erschienen. Dabei handelt es sich nicht um erneute Drucke der in der mittelalterlichen Überlieferungstradition stehenden Vulgata, sondern um mehrere Editionen der lateinischen Rückübersetzung der deutschen Luther-Übersetzung durch Justus Jonas: *Liber Iesu Syrach, ex Germanica translatione D. Mart. Lutheri, Latine redditus, per Iustum Ionam* (ed. princeps Wittenberg: Peter Seitz d.Ä., 1538).[43] Vermutlich entstand diese lateinische Ausgabe im Zusammenhang mit der Wittenberger Vulgata, die 1529 in Teilen erschienen war und zu der Justus Jonas 1538 diesen lateinischen Sirach ergänzte.[44] Die Intention der Wittenberger Vulgata bestand darin, den lateinischen Text nach dem

---

43. Titel zitiert nach dem Exemplar Bayerische Staatsbibliothek München, 1837167 Res/B.lat. 551 m, urn:nbn:de:bvb:12-bsb10205791-8.

44. Vgl. Volz, „Die Wittenberger Übersetzung", in *Weimarer Ausgabe: Abteilung Deutsche Bibel* 12:XXXIII–XLII.

Grundtext und nach Luthers deutschem Text zu revidieren und war für
den wissenschaftlichen Gebrauch in reformatorischen Kreisen gedacht.[45]
Im Widmungsschreiben der Wittenberger Erstausgabe charakterisiert
Justus Jonas das Sirachbuch wiederum als katechismusnahe Bildungsschrift mit hohem Aktualitätsanspruch und begründet damit unter
anderem seine Übersetzung:

> Ad eam piam externam conuersationem, ad honorandos ministros
> uerbi, ad conseruandam piam educationem iuuentutis, & ad reueren-
> ter tractandum cultum Dei, cum liber Iesu Syrach in primis diligenter
> adhortetur pios omnes, contineatque utilissimam catechesin, et tot exi-
> mias conciones, quibus Decalogus erudite explicatur, Illum ex Germanica
> translatione D. Mart. Lutheri transtuli in Latinum, ut et alijs nationibus
> usui esse possit in Ecclesia…. Multi loci sunt in Iesu Syrach, qui de qui-
> busdam rebus monere possunt, hoc tempore magnopere necessarijs.[46]

Für Nürnberg, wo der lateinische Sirach ohne das erwähnte Widmungsschreiben erschienen ist, sind insgesamt drei Ausgaben bezeugt,
die allesamt erst nach Luthers Tod datiert sind (vgl. Tab. 4; Titelblatt der
Nürnberger Erstausgabe als Abb. 3 im Anhang). Die Datierung auf ca.
1548 lässt darauf rückschließen, dass die Nürnberger Erstausgabe eventuell im Zusammenhang mit der zweiten deutschsprachigen Nürnberger
Ausgabe entstanden ist, die ebenfalls aus der Offizin von Johann Petreius
stammt, dem bedeutendsten Drucker nach Peypus' Tod.[47]

Tab. 4: Nürnberger Ausgaben der lateinischen Sirach-Übersetzung von Justus Jonas

Jahr	Offizin	VD-16-Nummer
um 1548	Johann Petreius	VD16 B 4050
1561	Valentin Neuber	VD16 ZV 28245
1566	Valentin Neuber	VD16 ZV 16150

---

45. Vgl. Erwin Nestle, „Einleitung", zu *D. Martin Luthers Werke: Kritische
Gesamtausgabe. Deutsche Bibel*, Bd. 5 (Weimar: Hermann Böhlaus Nachfolger, 1914),
XI, sowie entsprechende Hinweise im Widmungsbrief von Justus Jonas, *Liber Iesu
Syrach* (Wittenberg: Seitz, 1538), *2^r–*2^v.

46. Jonas, *Liber Iesu Syrach*, *6^v–*7^r.

47. Vgl. Reske, *Die Buchdrucker des 16. und 17. Jahrhunderts*, 667–68.

4.2.1. Bearbeitungen des Sirach-Textes in Nürnberg

Eine erste Bearbeitungsstufe des Sirach-Textes liegt mit der mehrfach gedruckten Ausgabe des Juristen und Pädagogen Georg Lauterbeck (ca. 1505–1570)[48] vor: *Jesus Syrach. Buch / Von der Hausszucht. Allen Hauß-vetern / Kindern / vnd Haußgesinde / notwendig vnd nützlich zu lesen / in Locos Communes, das ist / in richtige ordnung vnd Heubtartikel Christ-licher Lere vnd Zucht verfasset / Durch Georgium Lauterbeck* (VD16 B 4087).[49] Der erste aktuell nachweisbare Druck stammt aus der Wittenber-ger Offizin von Veit Kreuzer und ist auf 1555 (Kolophon: 1554) datiert; die enthaltene Vorrede datiert der Verfasser aber schon auf 26.12.1548,[50] und bereits 1555 ist der erste Nürnberger Druck belegt (vgl. Tab. 5; Titelblatt der Nürnberger Erstausgabe als Abb. 4 im Anhang).

Der Vorrede vorangestellt ist ein lateinisch und deutsch abgefasstes Dekatostichon des Theologen und Reformators Johann Spangenberg,[51] der Lauterbeck in die Reihe früherer Sirach-Autoren und -Bearbeiter ein-ordnet und damit die bisherige Textgenese rekapituliert: Genannt werden Sirach-Großvater und -Enkel ebenso wie Martin Luther als deutscher und Justus Jonas als lateinischer Übersetzer (vgl. Abschnitt 4.1).[52]

Lauterbecks Bearbeitung zeichnet sich dadurch aus, dass der Sirach-Text der Luther-Übersetzung in „locos communes" gebracht, also neu systema-

---

48. Zu Leben und Werk Georg Lauterbecks vgl. Michael Philipp, „Lauterbeck (Lauterbach), Georg", in *Frühe Neuzeit in Deutschland 1520–1620: Literaturwissen-schaftliches Verfasserlexikon*, hrsg. Wilhelm Kühlmann u.a., 6 Bände (Berlin: de Gruy-ter, 2015), 4:60–70. Die Sirach-Bearbeitung findet dort allerdings keine direkte Erwäh-nung. Sie lässt sich aber einer Lebensphase Lauterbecks zuordnen, in der er wohl vorwiegend publizistisch tätig war und sich als Verfasser von Werken „zur Rechts-wissenschaft, zur Erziehung und zum Unterrichtswesen" „einen Namen" machte, vgl. Philipp, „Lauterbeck (Lauterbach), Georg", 4:61.

49. Titel zitiert nach dem Exemplar Bayerische Staatsbibliothek München, Exeg. 219#Beibd.2, urn:nbn:de:bvb:12-bsb00037210-0.

50. Vgl. Lauterbeck, *Jesus Syrach* (Wittenberg: Kreutzer, 1555), A v[r]. Zur Datie-rung vgl. auch Volz, „Die Wittenberger Übersetzung", in *Weimarer Ausgabe: Abteilung Deutsche Bibel* 12:XXXVIII, Anm. 52.

51. Spangenberg ist 1550 verstorben, was ebenfalls für eine frühere Werkentste-hung spricht.

52. Vgl. Johann Spangenberg, „*Dekatostichon*" zu Jesus Syrach von Georg Lau-terbeck (Nürnberg: vom Berg & Neuber, 1555), A 2[r]–A 2[v], zitiert nach dem Exem-plar Wolfenbüttel, Herzog August Bibliothek, S: Alv.: Aa 163 (1), VD16 B 4090, urn:nbn:de:gbv:23-drucke/alv-aa-163-1s1.

tisiert wird. Dies bedeutet, dass der Text in neue Kapitel eingeteilt wird, zu deren Ordnung sich Lauterbeck in der Vorrede folgendermaßen äußert:

> Vnd habe diese Ordnung auff die beyde Tafeln gestellet / Nemlich / Wie man sich erstlich gegen Gott vnd seinem heiligen Wort / etc. Folgendt gegen dem Nehesten / Als Oberkeyt / Vatter / Mutter / Weyb / Kind / Gesinde / Freund / Feind / vnd jederman halten sol[53]

Als Motivation für seine Neuordnung führt Lauterbeck die unsystematische inhaltliche Konzeption des Sirach-Textes und den eklektischen Charakter an, wobei er mit dieser Kritik an Martin Luthers Vorrede anknüpft. Die pädagogisch wertvollen Inhalte des Buches, „darauß sich viel Leute bessern / vnd jre Haußzucht darnach anstellen kõnnen"[54] sollen mit der Bearbeitung systematisch erschlossen werden. Die Neubearbeitung zielt somit auf einen leichteren rezeptiven Zugang, der durch das beigefügte Register (vgl. Abb. 5 im Anhang) und gelegentliche, in den Text integrierte Verweise unterstützt wird. Lauterbeck unterscheidet 58 Kapitel, beginnend mit „Von Gõttlicher Weyßheit" und endend mit Sir 50,29–31 als „Beschluss". Unter den einzelnen Kapiteln sind jeweils sämtliche passende Verse aus Sirach im Wortlaut der Luther-Übersetzung subsumiert, die jeweilige Versnummer ist am Rand angegeben; auch die lutherischen Randglossen sind gegebenenfalls übernommen (vgl. Abb. 6 im Anhang). Diese Umgestaltung des Sirach-Textes zur Ratgeberliteratur, „das ein jetzlicher leichtlich beyeinander finden kann / was er bedarff / Welches man doch zuuorn auß vielen Capiteln hat müssen zusammen lesen",[55] führt auch zu Textverlusten. So sind beispielsweise weder das Lob der Väter noch Sirachs Gebet bei Lauterbeck integriert.

Für Nürnberg sind mit insgesamt vier Ausgaben der Lauterbeck-Bearbeitung die meisten Auflagen des Werks nachgewiesen. Die Drucküberlieferung hält bis in die erste Hälfte des 17. Jahrhunderts an (vgl. Tab. 5).

---

53. Lauterbeck, *Jesus Syrach* (Nürnberg: vom Berg & Neuber, 1555), A iij[v].
54. Lauterbeck, *Jesus Syrach*, A iij[r].
55. Lauterbeck, *Jesus Syrach*, A iij[v].

Tab. 5: Nürnberger Ausgaben der Sirach-Bearbeitung durch Georg Lauterbeck

Jahr	Offizin	VD-16-Nummer	Titel nach VD 16
1555	Johann vom Berg & Ulrich Neuber	VD16 B 4090	Jesus Syrach || zu Wittenberg ver=||deudscht.|| In eine newe vnd rich=||tige ordnung gebracht/|| Durch || Georgen Lauterbach.||
1571	?	VD16 ZV 16376	Jesus Syrach zu || Wittenberg ver=||deutscht.[v. Martin Luther] Jn eine newe vnd richti=||ge ord-nung gebracht/|| Durch || Georgen Lauterbach.||
1583	Valentin Neuber	VD16 ZV 1829	Jesus Sy=||rach Teutsch.|| Jm Latein/ Ecclesiasticus,|| genannt/ Von Bur-gerlichen || Thugenden/ vnd Ehrbar || Haußzucht.|| Jn ein newe vnd richtige || Ordnung gebracht.|| Durch || GEOR-GIVM LAV=||TERBACH.||
1620	Georg Endter d.Ä.	VD17 23:659295H	Jesus Syrach Teutsch: Im Latein Eccle-siasticus genanntVon Bürgerlichen Tugenden/ und Erbar Haußzucht

Eine entsprechende Systematisierung des Sirach-Textes, wie sie Georg Lauterbeck auf Basis der deutschen Luther-Übersetzung vorgenommen hat, existiert auch für die lateinische Rückübersetzung von Justus Jonas:[56] *Liber Iesv Syrach. Mvlto Quam Vvlgo Planiore Et Dexteriore versione latine redditus, & in Locos communes redactus. Cum indice locorum* (Titelblatt als Abb. 7 im Anhang).[57] Diese lateinische Ausgabe eines anonymen Bear-beiters ist m.W. nur in Nürnberg erschienen, und zwar 1563 ebenfalls in der Offizin von Johann vom Berg und Ulrich Neuber, allerdings bieten die Paratexte keinerlei Aufschluss über den Autor. Punktuelle Textvergleiche haben ergeben, dass Kapitelgliederung, Stellenzuordnung und Textum-fang nicht mit der Lauterbeck-Bearbeitung übereinstimmen, von dieser aber vermutlich angeregt sind.

---

56. Vgl. auch Volz, „Die Wittenberger Übersetzung", in *Weimarer Ausgabe: Abtei-lung Deutsche Bibel* 12:XLIII, Anm. 53.

57. Titel zitiert nach dem Exemplar Württembergische Landesbibliothek Stutt-gart, B lat.156304, VD16 B 4058, urn:nbn:de:bsz:24-digibib-bsz3532244489.

Eine vollständige Textedition des Sirach nach der Luther-Übersetzung inklusive Auslegung legte 1552 der Theologe und Erbauungsschriftsteller Caspar Huberinus (1500–1553)[58] vor: *Spiegel der haußucht / Jesus Syrach genant: Sampt eyner kurtzen Außlegung. Für die armen Haußvätter vnnd jhr Gesinde / Wie sie ein Gottselig leben gegen menigklich sollen erzeygen / Darinnen der Welt lauff begriffen / vnd wie sich ein jeglicher Christ / in seinem beruff / vnd in der Policey ehrlich vnnd löblich solle halten* (Titelblatt als Abb. 8 im Anhang).[59] Dieses umfangreiche Werk—die Editio princeps umfasst 623 Seiten—erschien erstmals in Nürnberg 1552 in der Offizin von Gabriel Hain.[60] Die insgesamt 16 belegten Nürnberger Ausgaben (vgl. Tab. 6) lassen auf eine hohe Popularität und Verbreitung der Schrift rückschließen. Auch ist bekannt, dass das Werk wie die Bibel als Familienchronik verwendet wurde.[61]

Tab. 6: Nürnberger Ausgaben von Caspar Huberinus, *Spiegel der Hauszucht*

Jahr	Offizin	VD16-Nummer
1552	Gabriel Hain	VD16 ZV 1816 (= ed. princeps)
1553	Hans Daubmann	VD16 B 4084
1553	Hans Daubmann	VD16 B 4085
1554	Ulrich Neuber & Johann vom Berg (Erben)	VD16 B 4086
1555	Johann vom Berg & Ulrich Neuber	VD16 B 4089
1556	Ulrich Neuber & Dietrich Gerlach	VD16 B 4091
1558	Ulrich Neuber & Johann vom Berg (Erben)	VD16 B 4093
1558	Ulrich Neuber & Johann vom Berg (Erben)	VD16 B 4094
1561	Ulrich Neuber & Johann vom Berg (Erben)	VD16 B 4096

58. Zu Leben und Werk Caspar Huberinus vgl. Claudia Resch, „Huberinus, Caspar", in *Frühe Neuzeit in Deutschland 1520–1620: Literaturwissenschaftliches Verfasserlexikon*, hrsg. Wilhelm Kühlmann u.a. (6 Bände, Berlin: de Gruyter, 2015), 3:415–22.

59. Titel zitiert nach dem Exemplar Bayerische Staatsbibliothek München, 2815005 Res/4 B.g.prot. 100 e, VD16 ZV 1816, urn:nbn:de:bvb:12-bsb10874482-5.

60. Über Nürnberg hinaus erschien der *Spiegel der Hauszucht* außerdem in Königsberg und Frankfurt am Main.

61. Vgl. Gunther Franz, „Huberinus, Caspar", in *Neue Deutsche Biographie*, hrsg. Historische Kommission bei der Bayerischen Akademie der Wissenschaften, 25 Bände (Berlin: Duncker & Humblot, 1972), 9:701.

1565	Ulrich Neuber & Johann vom Berg (Erben)	VD16 B 4098
1565	Ulrich Neuber & Johann vom Berg (Erben)	VD16 B 4099
1567	Ulrich Neuber & Dietrich Gerlach	VD16 B 4101
1567	Ulrich Neuber & Dietrich Gerlach	VD16 B 4102
1571	Dietrich Gerlach	VD16 B 4107
1580	Katharina Gerlach & Johann vom Berg (Erben)	VD16 B 4112
1588	Katharina Gerlach	VD16 B 4117

Der *Spiegel der Hauszucht* ist das letzte von Caspar Huberinus verfasste Werk und seiner Predigtliteratur zuzuordnen. Bereits früher hatte Huberinus Predigten publiziert, so nun auch die im Rahmen sonntäglicher Mittagspredigten über Sirach gehaltenen.[62] Inhaltlich ist der *Spiegel der Hauszucht* dergestalt konzipiert, dass in größerem Letterndruck vers- oder abschnittweise der vollständige Sirach-Text in der Luther-Übersetzung geboten wird, jeweils gefolgt von einer mehr oder weniger umfangreichen Auslegung in kleinerem Letterndruck (vgl. Beispielseite 359 als Abb. 9 im Anhang). Die Gliederung folgt kapitelweise der Luther-Übersetzung.

Den Vorreden können reflektierte Überlegungen des Autors entnommen werden, die zeigen, dass Caspar Huberinus auch ein bedeutender Theoretiker des lutherischen Erziehungssystems ist. Denn die Predigtsammlung soll nicht nur als Erbauungsschrift dienen, sondern wird theoretisch fundiert und didaktisch funktionalisiert. So differenziert Huberinus zwischen vier Typen des Theologen im privaten und öffentlichen Bereich, nämlich zwischen „Hauß Theologen", „Schul Theologen", „Policey Theologen" und „Kirchen Theologen", deren gesellschaftlich relevanter Auftrag ihrerseits darin besteht, in ihrem Wirken das Reich Gottes zu mehren:

> Nun sind dise viererley Theologen erfordert das Reych Christi / solle es anderst fruchtbarlich aufferbawet / vnd außgebreytet werden. Vnnd dise Christliche rechtschaffene viererley Theologen / muß einer dem andern die Hand bieten / vnd die jugent helffen pflantzen / vnd zum Gnadenreych Christi helffen weydnen.... Also wil gleichwol einem jegklichen diser vier Theologen gebüren / die weil er ein Christ ist / nach seinem beruff vnd ampt / das Reich Christi helffen erweytern / vnd die Kirchen Gottes helffen erbawen[63]

---

62. Vgl. Caspar Huberinus, *Spiegel der haußucht* (Nürnberg: Hain, 1552), Aiij^r.
63. Huberinus, *Spiegel der haußucht*, A ij^r–A ij^v.

Vor diesem Hintergrund kommt der Predigt und Predigtliteratur eine Schlüssel- und Multiplikatorfunktion für die religiöse Unterweisung zu. Huberinus selbst wendet sich insbesondere an die Hausväter als die „Hauß Theologen", „welche den ersten grund bey jrem gesinde legen sollen / mit dem Catechismo außwendig zu lernen / vnd ein Christliche Haußzucht bey den jren anrichten / inn steten brauch bringen / vnd helffen erhalten".[64]

In der Vorrede legt Huberinus weiterhin ausführlich dar, worin der spezifische Wert der Sirach-Lektüre und Auslegung besteht: „Allermeyst darumb / dieweil Syrach (gleych inn einer Summa auffs kûrtzest) fünfferley notwendige Puncten handlet / einem jegklichen Christen sehr nûtzlich vnd notwendig / nicht allein zu disem / sonder auch zu dem zukûnfftigen Leben erschießlich vnd dienstlich".[65] Mit einer detaillierten Ausführung dieser fünf Punkte stützt Huberinus seine positive Argumentation für den inhaltlichen Wert des Sirach-Textes:[66] (1) In der nach Sirach zu ergründenden himmlischen Weisheit spiegelt sich Christus selbst (christologische Argumentation). (2) Die Weisheitslehre des Sirach leitet zur Mäßigung der Affekte und zur Buße an (individualethische Argumentation). (3) Die Weisheitslehre des Sirach vermittelt Verhaltensregeln für den gesellschaftlichen Umgang (sozialethische Argumentation). (4) Durch den Lobpreis der Schöpfung erzieht Sirach zu Gottes Lob und Dank. (5) Sirach bietet lebenspraktische Regeln für ein gesundes, langes Leben und lehrt die ars moriendi. Die besondere Eignung des Sirachbuches besteht nach Huberinus demnach in der Ratgeberfunktion des Textes für alle Christen:

> Das dises Buch auch wol môchte ein Rathbuch genant werden / Denn darinnen findet ein jeglicher Christ einen trewen Rath vber den andern / wie er sich inn allen sachen vnd hendlen solle halten vnnd beweysen / das er mit gutem gewissen kônne bestehen / vor Gott vnnd allen menschen.[67]

Als Autor leistete Caspar Huberinus einen Beitrag zur häuslichen Sirach-Lektüre der christlichen Laien[68] und beförderte mittels seiner Aus-

---

64. Huberinus, *Spiegel der haußucht*, A ij[v].
65. Huberinus, *Spiegel der haußucht*, A iij[r].
66. Vgl. Huberinus, *Spiegel der haußucht*, Aiij[r]–Aiiij[r].
67. Huberinus, *Spiegel der haußucht*, Aiiij[r].
68. Zum „frommen (häuslichen) Lesen" in der Frühen Neuzeit vgl. Helmut Zedelmaier, „Lesetechniken: Die Praktiken der Lektüre in der Neuzeit", in *Die Prak-*

legungen das Niveau der katechetischen Grundlagenerziehung in den Familien. Eine katalysierende Wirkung der Huberinus-Auslegung für die Entfaltung der „theologia medicinalis" postuliert Johann Anselm Steiger.[69] Weitere Reflexe des Sirachbuches in der Nürnberger Predigtliteratur sind aus dem 17. Jahrhundert belegt. Der in Nürnberg geborene Theologe und Prediger Daniel Wülfer (1617–1685)[70] verfasste *Heilsame Cur=Gedanken: Die sich ein Christ selbst / bey Gebrauch Solcher nützlich machen kann / in Betrachtung seines Leibes Elendes. Dessen bewegliche Errinnerung Syrach gibt in XL. Cap. V. 1. 2. 3. 4* (Titelblatt als Abb. 10 im Anhang)[71], die 1658 in Nürnberg in der Offizin von Wolfgang Eberhard Felsecker einmalig erschienen sind. Dabei handelt es sich um Auslegungen von Sir 40,1, 2 und 5 in insgesamt drei Predigten, jeweils gegliedert in Predigttext (Bibeltext nach der Luther-Übersetzung), „Eingang" und „Abhandlung". Der Vorrede kann entnommen werden, dass Wülfer diese Predigten zur Lebens- und Sterbebewältigung abgefasst hat:

> Beydes mir und andern zum besten / hab ich Syrachs Wort etwas weitläuffiger überwogen. Mir / der ich meinen wenigen Kråfften zum besten / so GOTT will / des Sauerbrunnens zu gebrauchen gesonnen war. Andern / weil sie so wohl Menschen sind als ich / und mit mir / das gemeine Elend desto öffter betrachteten / uñ allezeit behutsamer gehen uñ stehen / gedultiger leiden und streiten / und wann das Stündlein kommt / frölicher und seliger abscheiden kônten.[72]

In Entsprechung zum Leitthema „Menschliches Elend auf Erden" können Wülfers Predigten als kontemplativ charakterisiert und als Beitrag zur Erbauungsliteratur eingestuft werden.

---

tiken der Gelehrsamkeit in der Frühen Neuzeit, hrsg. Helmut Zedelmaier und Martin Mulsow, Frühe Neuzeit 64 (Tübingen: Niemeyer, 2001), 15–19.

69. Johann Anselm Steiger, *Medizinische Theologie. Christus medicus und theologia medicinalis bei Martin Luther und im Luthertum der Barockzeit*, Studies in the History of Christian Traditions 121 (Leiden: Brill, 2005), 98–106, mit einer ausführlichen Analyse der Huberinus-Auslegung zu Sir 38.

70. Zu Leben und Werk Daniel Wülfers vgl. Paul Tschackert, „Wülfer, Daniel", in *Allgemeine Deutsche Biographie* 44 (1898): 562–63 (Online: https://www.deutsche-biographie.de/pnd117429740.html#adbcontent; Zugriff: 05.09.2018).

71. Titel zitiert nach dem Exemplar Herzog August Bibliothek Wolfenbüttel, M: Th 2871, VD17 23:668275U, urn:nbn:de:gbv:23-drucke/th-28719.

72. Daniel Wülfer, *Heilsame Cur=Gedanken* (Nürnberg: Felsecker, 1658), iiij^v–v^v.

Hier lässt sich unmittelbar anschließen, dass das Sirachbuch in der Frühen Neuzeit als Textus für Leichenpredigten sehr beliebt war. Bereits Ernst Koch hat verschiedene Leichenpredigtsammlungen gesichtet und festgestellt, dass anlässlich von Beerdigungen häufig Texte alttestamentlicher Spruchweisheit herangezogen wurden.[73] Eine aktuelle eigene Recherche im *Katalog der Leichenpredigten der HAB Wolfenbüttel*[74] hat ergeben, dass zwischen 1585 und 1735 insgesamt mind. 27 Leichenpredigten belegt sind, bei denen ein Sirach-Vers als Textus gewählt ist. Am häufigsten begegnet in diesem Kontext wiederum Sir 40 (fünfmal), gefolgt von Sir 7,40 (viermal) und Sir 41 (dreimal). Diese Stellenauswahl lässt erkennen, dass in den Leichenpredigten sowohl der zentrale Gedanke des geistlichen Trostes für die Angehörigen thematisiert wurde, aber auch die typischerweise vermittelte „Vorstellung eines Ideals christlicher Lebensführung"[75], wie besonders aus der Wahl von Sir 7,40 rückgeschlossen werden kann.

In diesen skizzierten Rahmen fügt sich die aus Nürnberg belegte Leichenpredigt *Sterbens Nohtwendigkeit Und Unterscheid/ Aus Sirachs/ C. XIV. 18.* von Conrad Feuerlein für den Altdorfer Theologieprofessor Johann Fabricius ein, die in der Nürnberger Rochuskapelle am 1. Mai 1676 gehalten wurde und im selben Jahr in der Offizin von Christoph Endters Erben[76] einmalig erschienen ist (Titelblatt als Abb. 11 im Anhang).[77] Die Leichenpredigt, gegliedert in „Eingang" (S. 7–8) und „Abhandlung" (S. 9–20), führt ausgehend von Sir 14,18 „Es ist der alte Bund ; Du must sterben!"[78] die menschliche Notwendigkeit zu sterben vor Augen und mündet in eine „Warnung vor Sicherheit / vnd Abhaltung von eitler Weltlieb und schnöder Uppigkeit"[79]. Der Verfasser Conrad Feuerlein (1629–1704)[80] war zur Zeit

---

73. Vgl. Koch, „Bedeutung alttestamentlicher Spruchweisheit", 708.

74. *Katalog der Leichenpredigten der Herzog August Bibliothek*, bearbeitet von Marina Arnold (2. erneuerte Aufl.; Wolfenbüttel: Herzog August Bibliothek, 2008). Online: http://diglib.hab.de/?db =leichenpredigten (Zugriff: 01.09.2018).

75. Mark Sven Hengerer, „Leichenpredigten", in *Höfe und Residenzen im spätmittelalterlichen Reich. Ein dynastisch-topographisches Handbuch. Hof und Schrift*, hrsg. Werner Paravicini, Residenzenforschung 15.3 (Ostfildern: Thorbecke, 2007), 497.

76. Vgl. Reske, *Die Buchdrucker des 16. und 17. Jahrhunderts*, 734–35.

77. Titel zitiert nach dem Exemplar Universitätsbibliothek Erlangen, H00/RAB 217, VD17 23:302848C, urn:nbn:de:bvb:29-bv012377278-6.

78. Conrad Feuerlein, *Sterbens Nohtwendigkeit Und Unterscheid/ Aus Sirachs/ C. XIV. 18* (Nürnberg: Endter, 1676), 12.

79. Feuerlein, *Sterbens Nohtwendigkeit Und Unterscheid*, 12.

80. Zu Leben und Werk von Conrad Feuerlein vgl. Matthias Wolfes, „Feuer-

des Begräbnisses noch Prediger in St. Jakob; zu seinen Werken zählen auch die Komposition und Dichtung von Kirchenliedern, und so findet sich in derselben Leichenpredigt ein Exempel für eine weitere Form der Sirachbearbeitung: Zu Sir 37,28 („Ein jeglicher hat eine bestimmte Zeit zu leben") hat Feuerlein den ersten der beiden Begräbnisgesänge gedichtet, zu singen auf die Melodie des bekannten Liedes „Freu dich sehr, o meine Seele". In der 3. Strophe wird der Textus der Leichenpredigt (Sir 14,18) wieder aufgegriffen und durch größere Drucktype (im Folgenden kursiv) hervorgehoben.

1. Freilich hat der Mensch auf Erden/
Eine zubestimmte Zeit/
Wieviel Jahr ihm sollen werden/
Hier in dieser Sterblichkeit.
Gott/ der alles mit Bedacht/
Wieget/ misset/ ordnet/ macht/
Pflegt/ wie weit sichs sol erstrecken/
Jeglichem sein Ziel zu stecken....
3. Da ist keiner ausgenommen/
keiner/ wer auch der mag seyn/
Reich und Armen/ Böß und Frommen/
Allen Menschen in gemein/
Steht bevor *der alte Bund*/
Den beschlossen Gottes Mund;
Mensch! du must/ wer kans dann meiden?
Sterben/ und den Tod erleiden....[81]

Insgesamt greift das 12-strophige Lied zentrale Gedanken der Leichenpredigt auf. Seine Entstehungsgeschichte wird ausführlich dargelegt, da ein unmittelbarer Zusammenhang zum Verstorbenen besteht: Der Text wurde aus dem „Concept" der letzten Leichenpredigt des Verstorbenen (zu Sir 37,28), während der er den tödlichen Schlaganfall erlitt, „Mehrentheils abgesehen / und kurtz zusammen gezogen".[82] Es liegt hier ein exemplarisches Beispiel indirekter Sirachrezeption vor, indem ein Predigttext über

---

lein, Konrad", in *Biographisch-Bibliographisches Kirchenlexikon*, hrsg. Traugott Bautz (Nordhausen: Bautz, 2001), 19:385–86.

81. Feuerlein, *Sterbens Nohtwendigkeit Und Unterscheid*, 36–39.

82. Feuerlein, *Sterbens Nohtwendigkeit Und Unterscheid*, 36, vgl. auch Titelblatt und 31–32.

Sirach Ausgangspunkt einer freien Nachdichtung wurde. Diese Art der Texttransformation ist in ihrer Wirkung mit Sicherheit nicht unerheblich, kann jedoch insgesamt nur schwer überblickt werden. Jedenfalls werden Bibeltext und zentrale Gedanken der Leichenpredigt hier in Summa volkssprachlich einprägsam gefasst. Durch das Singen des Liedes während des Begräbnisses wird die Lehre der Predigt in einem kollektiven performativen Akt synästhetisch erlebbar.

Auch außerhalb des unmittelbaren kirchlichen Umfeldes sind poetische Sirach-Bearbeitungen belegt, und zwar durch den Nürnberger Schuhmachermeister und hochproduktiven Schriftsteller Hans Sachs (1494–1576).[83] Bereits zwischen 1540 und 1544, im Rahmen seiner fünften Schaffensperiode, sind insgesamt zehn Meisterlieder entstanden, die Sirach-Einzelkapitel „ohne nennenswerte Abweichungen von der biblischen Vorlage"[84] versifizieren. Die Lieder sind nur über das handschriftliche Meistergesangbuch des Barthel Weber (1549) greifbar und bisher unveröffentlicht:[85] *Vermonung zur pues* (Sir 5), *Die waren freunt* (Sir 6,2–17), *Das weiber meiden* (Sir 9,1–13), *Die geselschaft* (Sir 13,1–29), *Das neunzehent Jesus Sirach* (Sir 18,30–33; 19,1–23), *Eprecher vnd eprecherin* (Sir 23,25–37), *Die 10 wolgefeligen stueck* (Sir 25, 9–16), *Das pôs weib* (Sir 25,21–34), *27 Jesw Sirach* (Sir 27,25; 28,1–4), *Das poes maẅl* (Sir 28,15–30).[86] Uta Dehnert weist darauf hin, dass Hans Sachs mit den ausgewählten Sirach-Kapiteln alltagsnahe Themen aufgreift. In inhaltlicher Hinsicht werden allgemeingültige Tugendkonzepte vermittelt, die ein „reibungslose[s] Zusammenleben einer städtisch-bürgerlichen Gemeinschaft garantier[en]".[87]

Die Poetisierung des Sirach-Textes beschäftigte Hans Sachs schließlich auch in seinen letzten Schaffensphasen: Systematisch wurde zwischen Februar 1562 und September 1565 der gesamte Sirach-Text in Knittelversen

---

83. Zu Leben und Werk von Hans Sachs vgl. Niklas Holzberg, „Sachs, Hans", in *Frühe Neuzeit in Deutschland 1520–1620: Literaturwissenschaftliches Verfasserlexikon*, hrsg. Wilhelm Kühlmann u.a., 6 Bände (Berlin: de Gruyter, 2016), 5:407–421.

84. Uta Dehnert, *Freiheit, Ordnung und Gemeinwohl, Spätmittelalter, Humanismus, Reformation* 102 (Tübingen: Mohr Siebeck, 2017), 216. Lediglich das Meisterlied *Die 10 wolgefeligen stueck* erweitert die Sirach-Vorlage, Dehnert, *Freiheit, Ordnung und Gemeinwohl*, 216, Anm. 124.

85. Dehnert, *Freiheit, Ordnung und Gemeinwohl*, 159–69.

86. Dehnert, *Freiheit, Ordnung und Gemeinwohl*, 215, Anm. 120; 216, Anm. 122–127.

87. Dehnert, *Freiheit, Ordnung und Gemeinwohl*, 216.

als Spruchgedichtsammlung ausgearbeitet. Seiner Gewohnheit entsprechend hat Hans Sachs jedes Kapitel mit dem Entstehungsdatum versehen. So lässt sich auch erkennen, dass er den Sirach im chronologischen Verlauf nicht fortlaufend bearbeitet hat. Diese Sirach-Spruchgedichtsammlung wurde 1579 in der Nürnberger Offizin von Leonhard Heußler postum veröffentlicht, und zwar unter dem Titel *Das Buch Jesu deß Sons Syrach* (Titelblatt als Abb. 12 im Anhang) im Rahmen des letzten Bandes der von Sachs selbst initiierten fünfbändigen Auswahlausgabe seiner Werke *Sehr Herrliche Schöne neuwe stück artlicher / gebundener / künstlicher Reimen / in drey vnterschidliche Bücher verfast*[88] unter anderem gemeinsam mit entsprechenden Bearbeitungen der *Psalmen* und *Weisheit Salomonis*. Als Herausgeber fungierte der Buchhändler Joachim Lochner, wie dessen Vorrede entnommen werden kann.

Makrostrukturell ist die zweispaltig gedruckte Bearbeitung nach den Kapiteln des Bibeltextes gegliedert. Der Kapitelzählung folgt jeweils eine Überschrift sowie der bearbeitete Bibeltext; jeder Abschnitt endet mit einem sog. „Beschluss", quasi einer Auslegung des jeweiligen Kapitels durch Hans Sachs (vgl. Beispielseite b ij^r mit dem Beschluss zu Kap. 29 und dem Anfang von Kap. 30 als Abb. 13 im Anhang).

Bei der Umarbeitung des Textes orientierte sich Hans Sachs sehr eng am zugrunde liegenden Bibeltext in der Luther-Übersetzung, wie folgender Textvergleich (Sir 30,1–6) zu demonstrieren vermag (von Hans Sachs übernommenes Wortmaterial der Lutherbibel hervorgehoben durch die Autorin):

Martin Luther, *Biblia*	Hans Sachs, *Jesus Syrach*
(Wittenberg: Lufft, 1545)	(Nürnberg: Heußler, 1579)
	Jesus Syrach vns klar bericht /
	Am dreissigsten Capitel spricht:
1 WEr **sein Kind lieb hat** /	Ein jeder / der **sein Kind lieb hat** /
der **helt es stet**s	**Der halt es stet** frü vnde spat
vnter der Ruten / **Das er hernach**	**Vnter der Rhutn** / **daß er hernach**
freude an jm erlebe.	**Freud an jm erleb** vnd empfach /

---

88. Titel zitiert nach dem Exemplar Bayerische Staatsbibliothek München, Rar. 2298-4/5, VD16 S 150, urn:nbn:de:bvb:12-bsb10149444-0.

2 WEr sein Kind in der Zucht helt /   Wer sein Kind helt in guter zucht /
der wird sich sein frewen /   Der wird sich frewen seiner frucht /
Vnd darff sich sein bey den Bekandten   Vnd darff sich darnach sein
nicht schemen.   nit schemen /
                                             Bey den bekanten schand einnemen /
3 WEnn einer sein Kind zeucht /   Welch man wol zeucht die Kinder sein /
das verdreusst seinen Feind /   Das verdreust seinen Feind allein /
vnd erfrewet seine Freunde /   Sein Freund darob groß freud erwirbet /
4 Denn wo sein Vater stirbt /   Denn wo hernach sein Vatter stirbet /
so ists / als were er nicht gestorben /   So ists / als wer er nit gestorben /
Denn er hat seines gleichen hinder sich   Weil er hat einen Son erworben /
gelassen.   Welchen er hinter jm hat glassen /
                                             Der jm geleichet aller massent /
5 Da er lebete / sahe er seine lust /   Da er lebt / lust an jm erwarb /
vnd hatte freude an jm. Da er starb /   Vnd hett freud an jm / da er starb /
dorfft er nicht sorgen /   Dorfft er nichts für in sorgn dermassen /
6 Denn er hat hinder sich gelassen   Wann er het hinder jm gelassen
einen Schutz wider seine Feinde /   Wider sein Feind ein starcken schutz /
vnd der den Freunden wider dienen kan.   Der auch sein Freunden thut alls guts /
                                             Vnd jn widerumb dienen kan.

In Entsprechung zu dem poetologischen Konzept „delectare et pro-
desse" motiviert Hans Sachs im „Zusatz" zur gereimten Vorrede des Sirach
die religiöse Spruchdichtung mit einer Begründung, die auf ethisch-
moralische Normenvermittlung und Werteerhalt abzielt. Das intendierte
Zielpublikum schließt alle Altersgruppen ein:

> Gleich die vrsach hat mich auch zwungen /
> Daß ich diß buch alten vñ jungen /
> Sprůchweis in Reimen hab gesetzt /
> Daß abgeschnitten würden zu letzt
> All schand / Laster vnd vbelthat /
> Vnd daß nach dises Buches rhat
> Lôblich zucht vnd tugend auffwachs /
> Dz wünschet der Dichter Hans Sachs.[89]

Die Rolle von Hans Sachs als dichterischer Wegbegleiter der Reformation in Nürnberg ist bekannt.[90] Dass nun der Sirach-Text im Rahmen
seiner religiösen Spruchdichtung einen hohen Stellenwert hat, überrascht

---

89. Hans Sachs, *Das Buch Jesu deß Sons Syrach* (Nürnberg: Heußler, 1579), e v[r].
90. Vgl. Holzberg, „Sachs, Hans", 408 und Gerald H. Seufert, „Nachwort" zu *Die*

letztlich nicht. Denn die überzeitliche Gültigkeit der altjüdischen Weisheitslehre des Sirach fügt sich gut zum volksnahen Charakter der (Lehr)
dichtung des Hans Sachs, der sich explizit an den „gemeinen Mann" wendet[91]
und auf dem Grund der lutherischen Theologie eigene Wertvorstellungen
entwickelt und in seinen Texten verbreitet. Gerade die lebenspraktisch
ausgerichteten Passagen des Sirach, die Oda Wischmeyer treffend als
„Lehrvorträge zu bestimmten Themen"[92] charakterisiert, schienen Hans
Sachs gut auf das eigene stadtbürgerliche Umfeld übertragbar, wie bereits
seine Kapitelauswahl im Zusammenhang mit der Sirach-Versifizierung in
den Meisterliedern gezeigt hat.

4.2.2. Bearbeitungen des Sirach-Textes für Kinder in Nürnberg

Einen hohen Stellenwert hatte der Sirach-Text auch im Rahmen der Kinder-
und Jugenderziehung, wie einige Beispiele verdeutlichen.

Zunächst ist zu erwähnen, dass das Sirachbuch im 16. Jahrhundert
als Schullektüre in Nürnberger Lateinschulen belegt ist. Dies kann einem
Schulgutachten (Datierung: 1541–1545) des Theologen Andreas Osiander
entnommen werden, in dem dieser Empfehlungen zur lateinischen Lektüre an der Schule von St. Lorenz ausspricht.[93] Der Sirach-Text wird dort
explizit nicht aus stilistischen, sondern aus inhaltlichen Gründen befür-
wortet:

> In der dritten classe liset man Jesum Syrach oder Parabolas Salomonis
> fur aine und fabulas Camerarii fur die andern lection. Un obwol Syrach
> und Salomon der lateinischen sprach zugut nicht vil dinstlich sein, so
> sollen sie doch von wegen der guten lehr auch bleyben.[94]

Wittenbergisch Nachtigall. Reformationsdichtung von Hans Sachs, RUB 9737 (Stuttgart: Reclam, 1974), 167–89.

91. Vgl. z.B. zum Zielpublikum des Meistergesangs Dehnert, *Freiheit, Ordnung
und Gemeinwohl*, 78.

92. Wischmeyer, „Jesus ben Sira als erster frühjüdischer Autor", 32.

93. Zum Kontext und der Datierung des Schulgutachtens vgl. Bernhard Schneider, „Einleitung" zu „Von schulen" von Andreas Osiander in *Schriften und Briefe April
1543 bis Ende 1548*, Bd. 8 von Andreas Osiander d. Ä., *Gesamtausgabe*, hrsg. Gottfried
Seebaß (Gütersloh: Gütersloher Verlagshaus Mohn, 1990), 370–73.

94. Andreas Osiander, „Von schulen", in *Gesamtausgabe*, 8:376.

Prinzipiell wurde im Schulunterricht Wert auf die Katechismuspflege gelegt.[95] Darüber hinaus sollten durch die biblische Schullektüre Sentenzen und Sprichwörter memoriert werden, was eine grundlegende Affinität zur alttestamentlichen Spruchweisheit erklärt.[96] Der Grundgedanke, dass durch die Memorierung christlicher Sentenzen christliche Lebenshaltung eingeübt werden kann, bedingt eine entsprechende Funktionalisierung des Sirach-Textes im Rahmen der Kinder- und Jugenderziehung. Bereits im 16. Jahrhundert entstanden Sirach-Katechismen in kindgerechter Aufbereitung: Äußerst erfolgreich war ein Rätselbuch des Johann Behem, dessen Editio princeps 1535 in Wittenberg erschienen ist. Als zweite Ausgabe erschien im selben Jahr auch der Nürnberger Erstdruck unter dem Titel *Ein Christlich Ratbüchlein/ für die Kinder/ Auß den büchern Salomonis vñ Jesu Syrach/ fleyssig zusamen bracht*[97] in der Offizin von Jobst Gutknecht (Titelblatt der zweiten Nürnberger Ausgabe als Abb. 14 im Anhang). Von den zwischen 1535 und 1606 insgesamt mind. 19 belegten hoch- und niederdeutschen Ausgaben sind vermutlich neun in Nürnberg erschienen (vgl. Tab. 7).[98] Der ansonsten unbekannte Autor[99] wirkte 1535 als protestantischer Prediger in Bayreuth, wie seiner Vorrede entnommen werden kann.

Tab. 7: Nürnberger Ausgaben von Johann Behem, *Ein Christlich Ratbüchlein*

Ort	Jahr	Offizin	VD16-Nummer	Bismark-Nr.
Nürnberg	1535	Jobst Gutknecht	VD16 B 1486	Bismark Nr. 194
Nürnberg [?]	1535	[Johann Petreius]	VD16 B 1488	Bismark Nr. 196
(†) Nürnberg	1535	[o. D.]		Bismark Nr. 197
Nürnberg	[1535]	Kunigunde Hergot	VD16 B 1487	Bismark Nr. 198
Nürnberg	1536	Jobst Gutknecht		Bismark Nr. 201
Nürnberg	1540	Jobst Gutknecht		Bismark Nr. 203

95. Vgl. Schneider, „Einleitung", 372.

96. Vgl. Georg Karl Mertz, *Das Schulwesen der deutschen Reformation im 16. Jahrhundert* (Heidelberg: Winter, 1902), 241 und Koch, „Bedeutung alttestamentlicher Spruchweisheit", 712.

97. Titel zitiert nach Heike Bismark, *Rätselbücher. Entstehung und Entwicklung eines frühneuzeitlichen Buchtyps im deutschsprachigen Raum. Mit einer Bibliographie der Rätselbücher bis 1800*, Frühe Neuzeit 122 (Tübingen: Niemeyer, 2007), 432 (Nr. 194).

98. Zur Editionsgeschichte und Beschreibung sämtlicher Drucke vgl. Bismark, *Rätselbücher*, 217–21; 431–43 (Nr. 193–212).

99. Vgl. Bismark, *Rätselbücher*, 212.

Nürnberg   [1539–47]   Georg Wachter   VD16 ZV 17350   Bismark Nr. 204

Nürnberg   1549   Kundigunde Wachter   Bismark Nr. 205

Nürnberg   [um 1550]   Valentin Neuber   Bismark Nr. 206

Das Ratbüchlein im handlichen Oktavformat ist so konzipiert, dass themenspezifisch bestimmte Bibelstellen ausgewählt und in Frage- und Antwortteil aufgelöst worden sind. Diese Bearbeitungstechnik beschreibt Johann Behem in seiner Vorrede folgendermaßen:

Hab auch ein Ratbůchlin zů gericht / Auß etlichen schönen bůchlin Gôtlicher schrifft / Sonderlich aber Solomonis des weisen Kônigs vnd auß Jesu Sirach gezogen. Dasselbig in etliche Tittel außgeteylet / vñ yede materien nach der kůrtz zůsamen bracht. Vnd wiewol man ein groß teyl der heyligē Bibel / also auff Frag oder Ratstück stellen môcht / so ist es doch vnnôtig. Darumb sol es nur ein klein Ratbůchlin / vñ fůr die kinder sein vnd heyssen.[100]

Wie die folgenden Beispiele zeigen (vgl. auch Beispielseite A vj^v als Abb. 15 im Anhang), sind die ausgewählten Bibelverse teils gekürzt, entsprechen jedoch nahezu wörtlich der Textform der Luther-Übersetzung. In der Frage ist entweder das Subjekt des Bibelverses ersetzt (vgl. Beispiele zu Sir 19,2. 20,31. 33,5), oder ein zugrunde liegender Vergleich wird zum Ausgangspunkt der Frage (vgl. Beispiel zu Sir 20,32):

Martin Luther, *Biblia* (Wittenberg: Lufft, 1545)		Johann Behem, *Ein Christlich Ratbüchlei* (Nürnberg: Hergot, 1535)	
Bibeltext	→	Frage	Antwort
WEin vnd Weiber bethören die Weisen / (Sir 19,2)		Was bethôret die weysen?	Wein vnd weyber.
GEschenck vnd Gaben verblenden die Weisen /Vnd legen jn einen Zaum ins maul / das sie nicht straffen können. (Sir 20,31)		Was verblendt die weysen vnd legt jn ein zaum ins maul?	Gaben vñ geschenck.

---

100. Johann Behem, „Vorrede" zu *Ein Christlich Ratbüchlein* (Nürnberg: Hergot, 1535), A ij^r, zitiert nach dem Exemplar Herzog August Bibliothek Wolfenbüttel, S: Alv.: Ab 236 (1), VD16 B 1487, urn:nbn:de:gbv:23-drucke/alv-ab-236-1s4.

EJn weiser Man / der sich nicht brauchen lesst /vnd ein vergrabener Schatz / Wo zu sind sie beide nütze? (Sir 20,32)	Ein weyser man der sich nicht brauchen leßt / wem ist er gleich?	Einem vergrabenen schatz.
DEs Narren hertz / ist wie ein Rad am wagen /Vnd seine gedancken lauffen vmb / wie die nabe. (Sir 33,5)	Was ist einem wagen rad gleich?	Des narren hertz / daṅ seine gedancken lauffen vmb / wie ein Nabe.

Am Rand findet sich jeweils ein Kurzverweis auf die entsprechende Bibelstelle. Die Stellenverweise löst Behem am Anfang des Registers für sein jugendliches Zielpublikum kindgemäß auf: „Erstlich sollen die kinderlin mercken / das das wŏrtlin.... Eccle. Bedeut das Capitel im Jhesu Sirach".[101] Anscheinend sollte durch den Gebrauch des Rätselbüchleins das Nachschlagen der Bibelverse eingeübt werden.[102]

Insgesamt beinhaltet das Rätselbuch 315 Fragen, die nach 66 inhaltlichen Rubriken gegliedert sind.[103] Den Fragen sind insgesamt 260 Bibelverweise aus den Büchern Spr, Pred, Sir und Weish zugeordnet. Aus Sirach begegnen rund 90 Verweise in 46 Rubriken.

Die thematische Ordnung orientiert sich in ihrer Grundanlage an der Hierarchie der Weltordnung, wie die Abfolge derjenigen Rubriken zeigt, die sich auf belebte Größen beziehen: *Von Got I.—Von glaubigen VII.—Heyligen X.—Menschen XI.—Torheyt. Narr XVI.—Oberkeyt XVIII.—Von Eltern XX.—Kinder XXI.—Von weybern XXII.—Von Armen XXXI.—Von Reichen XXXII.—Knecht LIIII.* Teils sind abstrakte Rubriken themenbezogen zugeordnet, vgl. z.B. *Von Got I.—Von Gottes weyßheit II.—Von Gottes wort III.—Von Gottes namen IIII.* Manche Serialisierungen evozieren durch gegenseitiges Framing bestimmte, vom Autor intendierte Sinnzusammenhänge, vgl. z.B. *Gottes wort hören V.—Glaub VI.—Von glaubigen VII.—Hoffnung VIII.—Liebe vnd barmhertzigkeyt VIIII.—Heyligen X.* oder *Oberkeyt XVIII.—Rath XIX.* oder *Torheyt. Narr XVI.—Gottloß XVII.* oder *Von weybern XXII.—Hŭrerey / Ehebruch XXIII.* Häufig sind für die Anordnung auch antithetische Überlegungen leitend, vgl. z.B. *Gŭt gewissen XIII.—Böß gewissen XIIII*; *Von Armen XXXI.—Von Reichen XXXII*; *Gesundtheyt XXXVI.—Krankheyt XXXVII.* Gegen Ende erscheint die

---

101. Johann Behem, „Register" zu *Ein Christlich Ratbüchlein*, C v^v.
102. Vgl. Bismark, *Rätselbücher*, 214.
103. Vgl. Bismark, *Rätselbücher*, 215.

Anordnung zunehmend willkürlich. Die drei umfangreichsten Rubriken sind *Reden LVII.* (12 zugeordnete Bibelverweise), *Oberkeyt XVIII.* und *Von weybern XXII.* (je 11 Bibelverweise).

Angeregt wurde Johann Behem zu seinem christlichen Rätselbuch durch ein beliebtes weltliches Straßburger Rätselbuch, das seiner Meinung nach aber im Widerspruch zu einer christlichen Elementarerziehung steht.[104] Entsprechend ist das Rätselbuch deutlich didaktisch motiviert. Johann Behem widmet es den Kindern seines Schwagers Hans Steger aus Freiberg, an den seine Vorrede gerichtet ist und der dazu aufgefordert wird, die Kinder zur Verwendung des Rätselbuches anzuleiten:

> Jch weiß mein gůter freundt wirds nit vnterlassen / Er wirds seinen kindern sagen vnd anzeygen. Wiewol jrs one das thut vnd gethan habt / ewre kindlin Got zů ehren dem nechsten zů gůt / aufferzogen.[105]

Hieraus lässt sich ableiten, dass das Rätselbuch nicht für den Gebrauch im Schulunterricht, sondern für die häusliche Lektüre unter Anleitung der Eltern gedacht war.[106] Dies kongruiert mit den in Abschnitt 2 skizzierten Vorstellungen zur Bildung, dass Haus und Familie als Raum für die christliche Elementarerziehung fungieren sollen.

Ein zweites Beispiel, wie der Sirach-Text im Rahmen der Kinder und Jugenderziehung funktionalisiert wurde, liegt erst aus dem 18. Jahrhundert vor: *Sittensprüche des Buchs Jesus Sirach für Kinder und junge Leute aus allen Stånden mit Bildern welche die vornehmsten Wôrter ausdrucken* (Nürnberg: Weigel & Schneider, [1784]) (Titelblatt als Abb. 16 im Anhang).[107] Dieses „kleine Lesebuch"[108] stammt von Jakob Friedrich Feddersen (1736–1788), der das Werk am Ende seiner Zeit als Domprediger in Braunschweig (1760–1787) verfasst hat.[109] Als erfolgreicher Jugendbuchautor trat der protestantische Pfarrer mit teils mehrfach verlegten

104. Vgl. Bismark, *Rätselbücher*, 211.

105. Behem, „Vorrede" zu *Ein Christlich Ratbüchlein*, A ij^v.

106. Bismark, *Rätselbücher*, 222.

107. Titel zitiert nach dem Exemplar Universitätsbibliothek Leipzig, PR 201.

108. Jakob Friedrich Feddersen, „Vorbericht" zu *Sittensprüche des Buchs Jesus Sirach* (Nürnberg: Weigel & Schneider, 1784), A 2^r, zitiert nach dem Exemplar Universitätsbibliothek Leipzig, PR 201.

109. Zu Leben und Werk Jakob Friedrich Feddersens vgl. Jakob Franck, „Feddersen, Jakob Friedrich", in *Allgemeine Deutsche Biographie* (1877), 6:594–595 (Online: https://www.deutsche-biographie.de/pnd116426012.html#adbcontent; Zugriff: 01.09.2018).

Werken bereits vorher in Erscheinung.[110] Im Vergleich dazu waren die *Sittensprüche des Buchs Jesus Sirach* mit m.W. nur einer Auflage weniger verbreitet. Dass sie abweichend zu den früheren Werken in Nürnberg bei Adam Gottlieb Schneider[111] verlegt wurden, hat eventuell mit den integrierten Kupfertafeln zu tun, auf die der Traditionsverlag spezialisiert war. Die undatiert erschienenen *Sittensprüche* sind vermutlich auf das Jahr 1784 zu datieren, wie Buchanzeigen vom Dezember 1784 entnommen werden kann.[112] Außerdem wurde das Buch in der *Allgemeinen Literatur-Zeitung* vom März 1785 rezensiert.[113]

Die Ausgabe beinhaltet eine Sammlung biblischer Sprüche aus Sirach für Kinder und ist aufwendig gestaltet: Einem ersten Teil (S. 5–30) mit thematisch orientierten Prosatexten, die essayartig sirachnahe Themen wie z.B. „Vorsichtigkeit im Reden", „Religion und Weisheit", „Gottseeligkeit, - und der Lohn derselben" – „Vertrauen zu Gott" – „Vom Gebet" behandeln, folgen 48 Sprüche aus Sirach (16 S.), die eine Auflösung zu Sirach-Bilderrätseln darstellen, die wiederum auf 28 Kupfertafeln im Anhang beigegeben sind. Die inhaltliche Konzeption kann anhand der ersten Kup-

---

110. Vgl. besonders *Das Leben Jesu für Kinder* (Halle: Hemmerde, 1775) mit mehreren Auflagen und Drucken bis 1827 und dessen Fortsetzung *Lehrreiche Erzählungen aus der biblischen Geschichte für Kinder* (Halle: Hemmerde, 1776; 2. Aufl. 1777). Vgl. zu Feddersen als Jugendschriftsteller der Aufklärung: Christine Reents und Christoph Melchior, *Die Geschichte der Kinder- und Schulbibel. Evangelisch—katholisch—jüdisch*, Arbeiten zur Religionspädagogik 48 (Göttingen: V&R unipress, 2011), 195–97.

111. August Gottlieb Schneider (1745–1815) führte den traditionsreichen Nürnberger Verlag des Kupferstechers und Kunsthändlers Johann Christoph Weigel (1661–1726) ab 1772 weiter. Vgl. Michael Bauer, „Christoph Weigel (1654–1725). Kupferstecher und Kunsthändler in Augsburg und Nürnberg", Archiv für Geschichte des Buchwesens 23 (1983), 794–804. Auch passen die Sittensprüche insofern zum Verlagsprogramm, da bei Weigel & Schneider weltliche Rätselbücher verlegt wurden: Bismark, *Rätselbücher*, 402–5 (Nr. 120–127), führt in ihrer Bibliographie acht weltliche Rätselbücher an, die bei Weigel & Schneider zwischen 1779 und 1828 erschienen sind.

112. Vgl. *Staats-Relation der neuesten europäischen Nachrichten und Begebenheiten 51* (17.12.1784) und *Regensburgisches Diarium oder wöchentliche Frag- und Anzeige-Nachrichten 51* (21.12.1784), 401.

113. Vgl. *Allgemeine Literatur-Zeitung* 1785, Bd. 1, Numero 60, 251 (März 1785). Kritik wird an den als „lächerlich" bezeichneten Bildern der Rätsel geübt, die in ihrer Qualität nicht dem Alter von Kindern gemäß seien, die die Lehren des Sirach erfassen können.

fertafel verdeutlicht werden, die zwei Bilderrätsel beinhaltet (vgl. Abb. 18 im Anhang): Am Anfang steht jeweils der Verweis auf eine Sirach-Stelle, die danach angeführt ist, wobei Schlüsselbegriffe durch Bilder ersetzt sind. Unter dem Bilderrätsel folgt abschließend in Kurrentschrift eine gereimte Ausführung des Verses, vgl. z.B. das erste Rätsel zu Sir 1,5:

Cap. I V. 5 (→ Sir 1,5)
Das Wort Bild 1 des Allerhöchsten
ist ein Bild 2 der Weißheit
und das ewige Bild 3 ist ihre Bild 4
Wie Brunn und Quelle kan . die Matten Lippen träncken
kan Weißheit und Gesetz . der Seel Erquickung schencken.

Im Textteil (S. X 1ʳ, vgl. Abb. 17 im Anhang) ist dieses Rätsel folgendermaßen aufgelöst, wobei eine Randnummerierung den unmittelbaren Bezug auf Kupfertafel 1 sicherstellt, die zu erratenden Begriffe im Sperrsatz erscheinen und der gereimte Vers in Fraktur gesetzt ist:

Cap. I V. 5 (→ Sir 1,5)
Das Wort G o t t e s des Allerhöchsten ist
ein B r u n n der Weißheit, und das ewige
G e b o t   i s t   i h r e   Q u e l l e.
Wie Brunn und Quelle kan die matten Lippen tränken,
Kan Weißheit und Gesetz, der Seel Erquickung schenken.

Während der Sirachvers wörtlich in der Textfassung der Luther-Übersetzung übernommen ist, besteht die Eigenleistung Feddersens in den gereimten Zusatzversen. Dies wird auf dem Titelblatt als „Neuübersetzung" beschrieben. Die Intention des Verfassers ist deutlich didaktisch motiviert und soll die Erziehung zur christlichen Tugend befördern, wie dem „Vorbericht" entnommen werden kann:

> Von dem großen Nutzen, welchen dieses kleine Lesebuch stiften kann, habe ich hier weiternichts zu sagen, als daß es aus dem biblischen Buch, das auf dem Titel genannt ist, gesammelt, und für die Jahre, Kenntnisse und Umstände junger Leute belehrend eingerichtet worden ist.
> Es sind die weisesten Sittensprüche für Menschen aus allen Ständen und Lebensaltern....
> Ueberhaupt giebt dieses Lesebuch Anlaß, das ganze Buch, und die

heilige Schrift selbst zu lesen, um dadurch heilsame Religionskennt-
niß, Frômmigkeit und Tugend unter Kindern und jungen Leuten zu
befôrdern[114]

Das Gesamtkonzept der Wissensvermittlung ist modern und pädago-
gisch-didaktisch dem Geist der Aufklärung verpflichtet. Die Aufmachung
wird differenziert begründet, wobei Sach- und Sprachwissen einheitlich
vermittelt werden: Zum einen werden die Kinder „zum Nachdenken
gewóhnt, wenn sie sich auf die Wôrter, deren Stelle die Figuren vertreten,
besinnen müssen".[115] Die Memoration wird durch die gereimten Sprüche
erleichtert, und durch die Teile in Kurrentschrift kann dieser Schrifttypus
eingeübt werden:

> Um die Sache so leicht als môglich zu machen, steht unter jedem Spruch
> ein Vers, welcher den ganzen Jnnhalt in sich fasset, und zum Aus-
> wendiglernen geschickt ist. Die Verse sind deshalb mit Currentschrift
> gestochen, um Kindern auch diese Art Schrift kennbar zu machen, und
> sie zur Uebung im Schreiben anzuhalten.[116]

Die Vertextungsstrategie in den Prosatexten des Lesebuchs ist der
Zeit der Entstehung entsprechend erwartungsgemäß appellativ ausgerichtet und vermittelt Handlungsnormen und Verhaltensanweisungen oft in
der Form des Imperativs: „Darum verlaß die Sünde, und kehre zu Gott
zurück".[117] „Verehre Gott nicht mit einem getheilten Herzen!"[118] Seine
Argumentation stützt Feddersen durch Verallgemeinerungen: „Denen, die
sich bessern, schenkt er den Wiedergenuß seiner Gnade".[119] „Wer weislich
heilsame Erinnerungen geben will, muß es ohne Erbitterung thun, und
zu rechter Zeit; sonst thut er besser, daß er schweigt".[120] Diese werden in
der Regel durch negative Kontraste verstärkt, in denen die Konsequenzen
des unerwünschten Fehlverhaltens drastisch hervortreten: „Ein Plauderer
wird verabscheut, und ein herrschsüchtiger, großpralerischer Mensch ist

---

114. Feddersen, „Vorbericht" zu *Sittensprüche des Buchs Jesus Sirach*, A 2ʳ–A 2ᵛ.
115. Feddersen, „Vorbericht" zu *Sittensprüche des Buchs Jesus Sirach*, A 2ʳ–A 2ᵛ.
116. Feddersen, „Vorbericht" zu *Sittensprüche des Buchs Jesus Sirach*, A 2ᵛ.
117. Feddersen, „Vorbericht" zu *Sittensprüche des Buchs Jesus Sirach*, 11.
118. Feddersen, „Vorbericht" zu *Sittensprüche des Buchs Jesus Sirach*, 12.
119. Feddersen, „Vorbericht" zu *Sittensprüche des Buchs Jesus Sirach*, 11.
120. Feddersen, „Vorbericht" zu *Sittensprüche des Buchs Jesus Sirach*, 19.

allen unleidlich".[121] Mitunter argumentiert Feddersen auch mit dem eigenen positiven Exempel: „Jn meiner Jugend ließ ich mich durch Verführer
nicht vom Guten abwendig machen. Jn Gegenwart meiner Eltern und
Lehrer; in der Kirche, und in der Einsamkeit, habe ich Gott um Weisheit
angerufen".[122]

Dahinter steht ein für die zweite Hälfte des 18. Jahrhunderts pä-
dagogisches Erziehungskonzept, das für die moralisch-belehrende
Jugendliteratur der Aufklärung als typisch gelten kann.[123] Dem Zeitgeist
der Aufklärung am Vorabend der französischen Revolution entspricht
auch, dass sich Feddersen an Kinder und Jugendliche „aus allen Ständen"
wendet, wie dem Titel entnommen werden kann. Feddersen vermittelt in
seinen Werken ein Erziehungsideal, in dem christlich-religiöse mit bür-
gerlichen Moralvorstellungen des 18. Jahrhunderts überblendet sind.

4.3. Sirach-Zitate in Texten und auf Objekten in Nürnberg

Dem Phänomen „Zitat" kann man sich aus formaler und/oder funktio-
naler Perspektive widmen; in einer ersten Annäherung können Zitate als
Redewiedergaben oder Reformulierungen mit direktem oder indirektem
Bezug auf einen Prätext definiert werden.[124] Die Diskursfunktion des
Zitats ist dabei eine mehrfache: Zitate können als Diskursreflexe verstanden werden; sie können aber auch als intertextuelle Bindeglieder Diskurse
miteinander verbinden, Diskurse verstärken bzw. weiterentwickeln und
somit in Diskursen funktionalisiert werden; zuletzt können sie neue Dis-
kurseffekte hervorrufen. Die Rekurrenz auf einen Text im Rahmen eines
Zitats eröffnet immer die Möglichkeit, die Intention der Zitatverwendung

---

121. Feddersen, „Vorbericht" zu *Sittensprüche des Buchs Jesus Sirach*, 19.

122. Feddersen, „Vorbericht" zu *Sittensprüche des Buchs Jesus Sirach*, 10.

123. Vgl. Reiner Wild, „Aufklärung," in *Geschichte der deutschen Kinder- und
Jugendliteratur*, hrsg. Reiner Wild, 3. Aufl. (Stuttgart: Metzler, 2008), 43–71 und 83–87.

124. Vgl. Mechthild Habermann, „Die Ethik des Zitierens aus linguistischer Sicht,"
in *Im Namen des anderen. Die Ethik des Zitierens*, hrsg. Joachim Jacob und Mathias
Mayer, Ethik—Text—Kultur 3 (München: Fink, 2010), 110–12; Elke Brendel, Jörg
Meibauer und Markus Steinbach, „Aspekte einer Theorie des Zitierens", in *Zitat und
Bedeutung*, hrsg. Elke Brendel, Jörg Meibauer und Markus Steinbach, Linguistische
Berichte Sonderheft 15 (Hamburg: Buske, 2007), 5–7; Wolfram Bublitz, „Introducing
Quoting as a Ubiquitous Meta-communicative Act", in *The Pragmatics of Quoting Now
and Then*, hrsg. Jenny Arendholz, Wolfram Bublitz und Monika Kirner-Ludwig, Topics
in English Linguistics 89 (Berlin: de Gruyter Mouton, 2015), 1–26.

zu hinterfragen. Auch hier sind verschiedene Möglichkeiten denkbar: Zitate können vom Autor für die Selbstinszenierung und zur Demonstration eigener Belesenheit eingesetzt werden; sie können als Ornatus des Textes dienen; sie können im Rahmen der Vertextung als argumentative Stütze und zur Steigerung der Glaubwürdigkeit verwendet werden; und sie können zur Vernetzung von Wissensbeständen, zum Abruf und zur Vergewisserung kollektiver Wissensbestände sowie zum Aufbau von Wissenstraditionen funktionalisiert werden. In allen genannten Fällen setzt die Verwendung eines Textes als Zitat voraus, dass diesem Text bereits eine gewisse Autorität zu eigen ist, was auf Rezipientenseite die Kenntnis des Textes oder seines Autors voraussetzt.

In Konsequenz zu dem in Abschnitt 4.1 und 4.2 vorgestellten Textspektrum und seiner Verbreitung sind in Nürnberg im 16. Jahrhundert Sirach-Zitate erwartungsgemäß umfangreich belegt. Im Alltagsleben sind sie sichtbar als Grabinschriften auf Epitaphien des Johannis- und Rochusfriedhofs. Sieht man von der an Sir 38,23 angelehnten Spruchvariante „Heut an mir, morgen an dir" bzw. „Hodie mihi cras tibi"[125] ab, sind im 16. Jahrhundert zwei Sirach-Zitate als Grabspruch belegt (vgl. Tab. 8 und Abb. 19 im Anhang).

Tab. 8: Sirach-Zitate auf Epitaphien in Nürnberg

Datum	Friedhof	Grabnr.	Inschrift (Zitat kursiv)
1570	Johannis	Grabnr. 987	Hans Hagers Felicitas seiner / Ehewirtin vnndt ihrer beder Erben Begrebnus Anno 1570 / *Alles was aus der erden kumpt / mus widerum zu erden werden* / Jesus Sirach am 4I Capittel. (Sir 41,13)

125. In der Lutherbibel 1545 lautet Sir 38,23: „Gedencke an jn / wie er gestorben / so mustu auch sterben / Gestern wars an mir / Heute ists an dir.", in der Vulgata „mihi heri et tibi hodie" (ed. Weber-Gryson, Editio quinta). Bei dieser Inschrift handelt es sich mit 34 Belegen um den insgesamt beliebtesten Grabspruch auf dem Johannisfriedhof, vgl. *Die Inschriften der Friedhöfe St. Johannis, St. Rochus und Wöhrd zu Nürnberg (1609 bis 1650)*, Teilband III von *Die Inschriften der Stadt Nürnberg*, hrsg. Peter Zahn, DI 90 (Wiesbaden: Reichert, 2013), 943. Infolge der Abwandlung und des allgemeinen Spruchcharakters ist der Sirach-Bezug aber nicht unmittelbar fassbar.

1595	Rochus	Grabnr. 524[126]	Heutt an mir, Morgen an dir. / Leonhard Binstocks gesaltzenen Fischers, Maria seiner Ehewürthin, Vnd Jhrer beeder Erben Begrebnuß. 1595 / *Gott hat den Menschen geschaffen auß der Erden, vnd macht Jhn wider Zur Erden, Vnd bestimbt Jhm die Zeit seines Lebens.* (Sir 17,1–3)

Beide Zitate greifen den Wortlaut der Luther-Übersetzung auf. Im ersten Fall ist sogar der Bibelstellenverweis angegeben, so dass das Zitat klar markiert ist. Die Tatsache, dass Sirachverse auf Gräbern zitiert werden, steht vermutlich im Zusammenhang mit der Tradition der Sirach-Zitate in Leichenpredigten und der Erbauungsliteratur (vgl. Abschnitt 4.2.2).

In einem anderen Fall begegnet ein themenverwandtes lateinisches Sirach-Zitat als Motto auf einem Notendruck der Nürnberger Offizin von Hieronymus Grapheus aus dem Jahr 1539: „IESVS SYRACH. Musica & Vinum lætificant cor hominis".[127] Auch hier ist die Quelle namentlich angeführt; das Zitat (Sir 40,20) steht in keinem inhaltlichen Zusammenhang mit den enthaltenen Kompositionen, so dass ihm eine schmückende, aufwertende Funktion auf dem Titelblatt zugesprochen werden kann. Zur besseren Anpassung an den Kontext des Notendrucks ist das Zitat leicht abgewandelt, indem im Unterschied zum Bibeltext die Musik („musica") vor dem Wein („vinum") genannt ist.

In beiden bislang angeführten Beispielen indizieren die Sirach-Zitate eine Bekanntheit der Sirachschrift und können als Diskursreflexe verstanden werden. Komplexer sind dagegen solche Fälle, in denen Sirach-Zitate in Texten argumentativ funktionalisiert werden.

Dies geschieht erwartungsgemäß im Rahmen des protestantischen Schrifttums, wo Bibelzitate bei der Textexegese durch Rückbindung an

---

126. Wegen Diebstahls (1746) Wiedergabe der Inschrift nach *Die Inschriften der Stadt Nürnberg II. Die Friedhöfe St. Johannis, St. Rochus und Wöhrd in Nürnberg (1581 bis 1608)*, Teilband II von *Die Inschriften der Stadt Nürnberg*, hrsg. Peter Zahn, DI 68 (Wiesbaden: Reichert, 2008), 301, Nr. 2202.

127. [o.V.], *Missae Tredecim quatuor vocum a praestantiss: artificib: compositae* ([Nürnberg]: [Grapheus], [1539]). Zitiert nach dem Exemplar Österreichische Nationalbibliothek, SA.76.C.14/2/1-4 MUS MAG, Online: http://data.onb.ac.at/rec/AC09196919 (Zugriff: 01.09.2018). Das Zitat erscheint wie der Supertitel auf dem Titelblatt der Tenorstimme.

die Schrift eine zentrale Rolle spielen. Eine Wirkung des reformatorischen sola-scriptura-Prinzips auf die argumentative Vertextungsstrategie wird hier direkt greifbar. Auch in Werken, die in Nürnberg entstanden bzw. rezipiert wurden, begegnen entsprechende Beispiele, wie anhand einer prominenten Leichenpredigt exemplifiziert werden soll: Am 22. September 1658 hielt der Nürnberger Prediger und Professor der Universität Jena Johann Michael Dilherr (1604–1669) in der Kapelle des Johannisfriedhofs für den bekannten Nürnberger Patrizier, Mitglied des Inneren Rats und Barockautor Georg Philipp Harsdörffer (1607–1658) die Leichenpredigt, die im selben Jahr in der Nürnberger Offizin von Wolfgang Endter dem Jüngeren einmalig im Druck erschien.[128] Den Textus der Predigt bildet Ps 31,16: „Meine Zeit stehet in deinen Händen".[129] Der üblichen Verweispraxis entsprechend sind die zitierten Bibelstellen als Marginalglossen am Rand des Textes angeführt. Diese wurden einer vollständigen Analyse unterzogen: Insgesamt beinhalten „Eingang" (S. 3–4) und „Erklärung" (S. 4–14) der Predigt über 50 deutschsprachige Bibelzitate, die sich wie folgt verteilen: Altes Testament 29 (davon Ps 13), Neues Testament 16 und Apokryphen 6. Zwei der Apokryphenzitate stammen dabei aus Sir:

Martin Luther, *Biblia*	→	Johann Michael Dilherr, *Der Menschen Stand in Gottes Hand*
(Wittenberg: Lufft, 1545)		(Nürnberg: Endter, 1658)
[17,1] GOtt hat den Menschen geschaffen / aus der Erden / [2] vnd macht jn wider zur Erden / [3] vnd bestimpt jnen die zeit jres Lebens / Vnd schuff sie beide / ein jglichs zu seiner Art / vnd macht sie nach seinem Bilde.		Denn *Gott bestimmet die Zeit ihres Lebens:* sagt Sirach / in dem 17. Cap. (S. 9, Zitat von Sir 17,3)

---

128. Gearbeitet wurde mit dem Exemplar der Herzog August Bibliothek Wolfenbüttel, M: Db 2253 (37), VD17 14:018717T, urn:nbn:de:gbv:23-drucke/db-2253-375 (Zugriff: 08.02.2011).

129. Johann Michael Dilherr, *Der Menschen Stand in Gottes Hand* (Nürnberg: Endter, 1658), 2.

[40,24] ALler Menschen werck sind
fur jm / vnd fur seinen Augen ist
nichts verborgen / [25] Er sihet alles
von anfang der Welt / bis ans ende
der welt / vnd fur jm ist kein ding
new

Aller Menschen Wercke sind für
Jhm ; und / für Seinen Augen / ist
nichts verborgen. Er siehet alles / von
Anfang der Welt / biß ans Ende der
Welt : aus dem Sir. im 40. Cap.
(S. 12, Zitat von Sir 40,24–25)

Beide Zitate finden sich im Auslegungsteil der Predigt. Dem Usus entsprechend sind sie im Text durch größeren Typendruck formal ausgezeichnet (in den Beispielen kursiv); in beiden Fällen ist die Zitateinbettung mit einer Nennung der Quelle verbunden, so dass der Verweis auf Sirach zusätzlich im Text erfolgt. Dabei wird Sirach bei Verweis auf Sir 40 als Text zitiert („aus dem Sir."), während der Verweis auf Sir 17,3 in personifizierter Form erfolgt („sagt Sirach"). Dieses Zitat wird so als wörtliche Wiedergabe des Weisheitslehrers gefasst und bezieht seine Autorität unmittelbar aus der auctoritas personae. Der Bibeltext wird in Form der Luther-Übersetzung wörtlich,[130] jedoch versbezogen nur in Ausschnitten übernommen. Durch einen Texteingriff bei Bezug auf Sir 17,3 wird die argumentative Einbindung in den eigenen Text besonders deutlich, indem die kopulative Konjunktion „Und" (Luther 1545) durch die kausale Konjunktion „Denn" (Dilherr) ersetzt ist. Dilherr nutzt das Sirach-Zitat zur Stützung im Rahmen seines fünften Arguments, weshalb der Menschen Zeit in Gottes Hand steht (Textus); er argumentiert hier „ratione determinationis" (S. 9) mit der „End- und Zielsetzung" des menschlichen Lebens durch Gott. Als Exempla werden mit Rebekka, Elias, Tobias, Simeon und Paulus biblische Gestalten namentlich genannt, deren Leben trotz diverser Schwierigkeiten nicht einfach geendet habe (gestützt durch Bibelverweise am Rand). Die Begründung erfolgt mit Sir 17,3: „Denn Gott bestimmt die Zeit ihres Lebens". Das zweite Sirach-Zitat Sir 40,24–25 findet sich im Rahmen einer Zitatreihe am Ende der Predigt, die die erste „Lehre von der Vorsorg und Fürsehung Gottes" (S. 11) stützt.

Dass Sirach-Zitate jedoch nicht nur in explizit religiösen Textsorten argumentativ funktionalisiert wurden, soll anhand eines letzten Textbeispiels dargestellt werden. Dabei handelt es sich um ein illustriertes

---

130. Zu sprachlichen Abweichungen vgl. Mechthild Habermann, „Leichenpredigten des 17. Jahrhunderts im konfessionellen Kontext", in *Konfession und Sprache in der Frühen Neuzeit. Interdisziplinäre Perspektiven*, hrsg. Jürgen Macha u.a., Studien und Texte zum Mittelalter und zur Frühen Neuzeit 18 (Münster: Waxmann, 2012), 73–77.

Flugblatt zum Thema Ehe mit dem Titel *Spiegel einer Christlichen und friedsamen Haußhaltung*[131], das 1651 von dem Nürnberger Kunsthändler Paul Fürst[132] (1608–1666) verlegt wurde (vgl. Abb. 20 im Anhang). Der Einblattdruck zeigt eine typische Text-Bild-Kombination[133], wobei die Textpassagen deutlich dominieren. Prominent erscheint bereits im Subtitel der Verweis auf Sirach: „Syrach am 25. vnd 26. Capitel". Als Mottotext folgen in 5,5 mittig gesetzten Zeilen ausgewählte Passagen aus den beiden genannten Kapiteln. Mit Sir 26,1.3.18.21 wird zuerst auf die „tugendsame" Ehefrau Bezug genommen, gefolgt von Sir 25,30.31.27.28.29.33 mit der Darstellung der „bösen" Ehefrau. Die kontrastive Gegenüberstellung wird durch einen Texteingriff verstärkt, indem Sir 25,30 mit adversativem „Aber" (Z. 4) angeschlossen ist. Ansonsten ist der Text wörtlich nach der Lutherbibel wiedergegeben. Der Haupttext selbst ist vierspaltig um die Abbildung angeordnet, wobei die Kolumnennummerierung der Leserlenkung dient: Die beiden äußeren Spalten beinhalten in Knittelversen Rede und Gegenrede der idealisierten Ehepartner, wobei zuerst die linke Spalte (1.) mit der Ansprache des „Mann[es] zu seiner Haußfrauen" zu lesen ist, danach die rechte Spalte (2.) mit der „Antwort der Frauen zu jhrem Haußwirth". Inhaltlich propagiert das Flugblatt die auch von Luther vertretene Hierarchisierung im Hausstand[134] mit der Vorrangstellung des

---

131. Titel zitiert nach dem Exemplar Wolfenbüttel, Herzog August Bibliothek, IE 30, VD17 23:674576D, URL: http://gateway-bayern.de/VD17+23%3A674576D (Zugriff: 01.09.2018).

132. Paul Fürst gilt als wichtigster Verleger von illustrierten Flugblättern des 17. Jahrhunderts. Vgl. Wolfgang Harms, „Einleitung" zu *Die Sammlung der Herzog-August-Bibliothek in Wolfenbüttel. Kommentierte Ausgabe. Teil 1: Ethica, Physica*, hrsg. Wolfgang Harms und Michael Schilling, Bd. I von *Deutsche illustrierte Flugblätter des 16. und 17. Jahrhunderts*, hrsg. Wolfgang Harms (Tübingen: Niemeyer, 1985), XXIII.

133. Zum „Zusammenspiel von Bild und Text" auf Flugblättern vgl. zusammenfassend Kerstin te Heesen, *Das illustrierte Flugblatt als Wissensmedium der Frühen Neuzeit* (Opladen, Farmington Hills, MI: Budrich UniPress, 2011), 114–23. Eine ausführliche Analyse der Graphik bietet Kristina Bake, *Spiegel einer Christlichen vnd friedsamen Haußhaltung. Die Ehe in der populären Druckgraphik des 16. und 17. Jahrhunderts*, Wolfenbütteler Arbeiten zur Barockforschung 49 (Wiesbaden: Harrassowitz, 2013), 99–100.

134. Zur Aufgabenverteilung in der Hausgemeinschaft sowie zu Familie und Haus als funktionale Einheit im Sinne der Oeconomia christiana vgl. Raitz, Röcke und Seitz, „Konfessionalisierung der Reformation", 293; Jörn Robert Westphal, *Die Darstellung von Unrecht in Flugblättern der Frühen Neuzeit*, Studien zur Kultur- und Rechtsgeschichte 4 (Mönchengladbach: Forum Verlag Godesberg, 2008), 48–49;

marriage Leaflet

Ehemanns als Hausvater, der seine Frau an ihre Pflichten und Tugenden im Hauswesen erinnert. Im Gegenzug erscheint die Ehefrau als sittsame, ihren Gatten unterstützende Hausmutter. Sprachlich spiegelt sich deren Unterordnung in der Hierarchisierung der Anredeformen: Während der Mann die Frau vertraulich duzt, ist in der Antwort der Frau die höflich-distanzierte Ihr-Form gewählt. Sekundär folgen in der Leseanordnung die beiden kürzeren Innenspalten (3. und 4.), die unter der Abbildung platziert sind. Diese beinhalten ausschließlich Bibelzitate, mit denen die vorangehenden Ausführungen der Eheleute argumentativ gestützt werden.[135] In der dritten, der Frau zugeordneten Spalte (4.), finden sich unter den insgesamt 15 angeführten Bibelstellen weitere vier Sirach-Zitate (Sir 4,35; 7,21; 7,28; 26,1–3).[136]

Kristina Bake hat überzeugend dargelegt, dass das Flugblatt ein konfessionsübergreifendes christliches Ehe- und Familienideal der Frühen Neuzeit vor Augen führt;[137] denn ein analoges Flugblatt mit gleichem Text und ähnlichem Bild wurde beispielsweise bereits 1615 im katholischen Köln vertrieben.[138] Bake weist dem „gemeinsame[n] Haushalten" der Ehepartner eine Schlüsselfunktion „für den häuslichen Frieden" zu, um „das Ansehen einer Familie in der Gemeinschaft" zu sichern.[139] Als Zielpublikum fungiert ein „städtische[r] Adressatenkreis, für den dieses Ehe-Ideal die Existenz sicherte: das zünftische Handwerk, bei dem Mann und Frau als Arbeitspaar gemeinsam agierten".[140]

In der Textsorte „Flugblatt" wurden durch den Rekurs auf die Bibel besonders adressatennah[141] christliche Wertvorstellungen propagiert und auf allgemeine gesellschaftliche Kontexte übertragen. Bezogen auf

---

Bake, *Spiegel einer Christlichen vnd friedsamen Haußhaltung*, 123–53, zusammenfassend 161.

135. Die argumentative Technik, Verhaltensnormen des Alltagslebens mit Bibelzitaten zu belegen, wird in die Tradition der sog. Haustafeln gestellt. Vgl. Harms, Schilling, *Deutsche illustrierte Flugblätter des 16. und 17. Jahrhunderts*, I:66 (I,27).

136. Diese Sirach-Zitate weichen vom Wortlaut der Lutherbibel 1545 stark ab; eine Vorlagenidentifizierung steht noch aus. Vermutlich aber ist von einer freien Paraphrase der Bibelstellen auszugehen.

137. Bake, *Spiegel einer Christlichen vnd friedsamen Haußhaltung*, 162.

138. Bake, *Spiegel einer Christlichen vnd friedsamen Haußhaltung*, 98–99.

139. Bake, *Spiegel einer Christlichen vnd friedsamen Haußhaltung*, 326–27.

140. Bake, *Spiegel einer Christlichen vnd friedsamen Haußhaltung*, 327.

141. Zur Verbreitung und dem Rezipientenkreis von Flugblättern vgl. te Heesen, *Das illustrierte Flugblatt als Wissensmedium der Frühen Neuzeit*, 97–99; 105–9.

Hauswesen, Familie und Ehe wird „das Ideal eine[r] patriarchalisch strukturierte[n] Gemeinschaft als Basis eines gottgefälligen Lebens"[142] gezeichnet. Die didaktische Funktion des Flugblattes lässt sich aus dem Titelbegriff „Spiegel" ableiten, der auf Handlungsreflexion vor der Folie der skizzierten Normen abzielt und der beispielsweise auch im Titel der Predigtsammlung von Caspar Huberinus erscheint. Generell kann dieses Flugblatt als Prototyp des ethischen Flugblattes mit moralisch-lehrhaftem Charakter gelten. Wolfgang Harms ordnet es ein „in den Umkreis der sozial-ethischen Katechismusexegese, wie sie durch die protestantischen Predigten über den christlichen Hausstand ausgeprägt wurde".[143]

5. Fazit

Das im vorliegenden Beitrag vorgestellte Textspektrum (vgl. Tab. 9) reicht von der ersten Sirach-Sonderedition der Luther-Übersetzung 1533 bis zu einem Sirach-Lesebuch für Kinder aus dem Jahr 1784.

Tab. 9: Textspektrum der Sirach-Überlieferung in Nürnberg
in chronologischer Reihenfolge

Text (Kurztitel)	Autor	Editio princeps	Nürnberger Ausgaben	Charakterisierung
Jesus Syrach	Martin Luther	Wittenberg: Lufft, 1533	6: 1533–1632	gesamter Text (dt.)
Ein Christlich Ratbüchlin	Johann Behem	Wittenberg: Rhau, 1535	9: 1535– ca. 1550	Rätselbuch für Kinder mit Sirach-Versen (Auswahl)
Zitat in Notendruck	anonym	[Nürnberg]: [Grapheus], [1539]	1: 1539	Sirach-Zitat (lat.) als Motto in Notendruck (Sir 40,20)

---

142. Westphal, *Die Darstellung von Unrecht in Flugblättern der Frühen Neuzeit*, 148.
143. Harms, Schilling, *Deutsche illustrierte Flugblätter des 16. und 17. Jahrhunderts*, I:66 (I,27).

10 Meisterlieder	Hans Sachs	—	(unveröf-fentlicht, Entstehung: 1540–1544)	Versifizierung zu Sir 5; 6,2–17; 9,1–13; 13,1–29; 18,30–33; 19,1–23; 23,25–37; 25, 9–16; 25,21–34; 27,25; 28,1–4; 28,15–30
Liber Iesu Syrach	Justus Jonas	Wittenberg: Seitz d.Ä., 1538	3: ca. 1548–1566	gesamter Text (lat.)
Spiegel der haußucht	Caspar Huberinus	Nürnberg: Hain, 1552	16: 1552–1588	gesamter Text (dt.), inkl. Auslegung (Predigtsammlung)
Jesus Syrach Teutsch	Georg Lauterbeck	Wittenberg: Kreutzer, 1554	4: 1555–1620	Luther-Text in Auszügen (dt.), neue Ordnung
Liber Iesu Syrach	anonym	Nürnberg: vom Berg & Neuber, 1563	1: 1563	Jonas-Text in Auszügen (lat.), neue Ordnung
Zitate auf Epitaphien	—	—	1569–1595	Sirach-Zitate in Grabinschriften (Sir 17, 1–3; 41,13)
Das Buch Jesu deß Sons Syrach	Hans Sachs	Nürnberg: Heußler, 1579	1: 1579	Spruchgedichtfassung des gesamten Sirach, inkl. „Beschlüsse"
Spiegel einer Christlichen vnd friedsamen Haußhaltung	anonym	(leicht variierend: Köln: Bussemacher, 1615)	1: 1651	Flugblatt mit Sirach-Zitaten (aus Sir 4, 7, 25, 26)
Heilsame Cur=Gedanken	Daniel Wülfer	Nürnberg: Felsecker, 1658	1: 1658	Auslegung (Predigt) zu Sir 40,1.2.5
Der Menschen Stand in Gottes Hand	Johann Michael Dilherr	Nürnberg: Endter, 1658	1: 1658	Sirach-Zitate in Leichenpredigt (Sir 17,3; 40,24–25)
Sterbens Nohtwendigkeit Und Unterscheid	Conrad Feuerlein	Nürnberg: Endter, [1676]	1: 1676	Leichenpredigt mit Sir 14,18 als Textus

Freilich hat der	Conrad	Nürnberg:	1:	Kirchenlied ausgehend
Mensch auf	Feuerlein	Endter,	1676	von Sir 37,28
Erden		[1676]		
Sittensprüche	Jakob	Nürnberg:	1:	Lesebuch für
des Buchs Jesus	Friedrich	Weigel &	1784	Kinder, u.a. mit
Sirach	Feddersen	Schneider,		Sirach-Bilderrätseln
		[1784]		

Über einen Zeitraum von fast genau hundert Jahren (1533–1632) sind die Sondereditionen der Luther-Übersetzung des Sirach in Nürnberg präsent. In diesem zeitlichen Rahmen wird der Sirach-Text am stärksten rezipiert und erfährt darüber hinaus vielfältige Bearbeitungen: Nach der Auflagenzahl am weitesten verbreitet war die Predigtsammlung des Caspar Huberinus (16 Nürnberger Drucke zwischen 1552 und 1588), durch die der Sirach-Text endgültig Teil der Hausväterliteratur wurde. Hier anzuschließen sind auch die nürnbergspezifischen poetischen Bearbeitungen des Hans Sachs. Dass das Sirachbuch außerdem sehr früh in der Kinder- und Jugenderziehung instrumentalisiert wurde, zeigt Behems Rätselbuch, das in Nürnberg ab 1535 belegt ist. Im 17. Jahrhundert begegnen Reflexe des Sirachbuches vor allem im Kontext der erbaulichen Predigtliteratur, besonders der Leichenpredigt, davon ausgehend auch im Kirchenlied. Als längerfristige Nachwirkung der Hausväterliteratur können auch die Sirach-Zitate auf einem Flugblatt (1651) eingestuft werden. Eine letzte Transformation des Textes ist aus dem späten 18. Jahrhundert mit dem Kinder-Lesebuch greifbar. Die präsentierten Zitat-Beispiele aus dem Sirach-Buch stammen ebenfalls aus dem 16. und 17. Jahrhundert. Sie belegen eine Präsenz des Textes im Alltagsleben, die über den engeren kirchlichen Raum hinausreicht.

Bei sämtlichen bekannten Autoren bzw. Bearbeitern der Texte handelt es sich—mit Ausnahme von Georg Lauterbeck und Hans Sachs—um lutherische Theologen oder Prediger; Lauterbeck und Sachs können aber ebenfalls im Kontext reformatorischen Schrifttums verortet werden.

Die besprochenen Texte lassen sich bekannten linguistischen Text-klassifikationssystemen entsprechend wie folgt einordnen: Nach der kommunikativen Textfunktion (ausgehend von der Autorenillokution)[144]

---

144. Vgl. *Frühneuhochdeutsches Lesebuch*, hrsg. Oskar Reichmann und Klaus-Peter Wegera (Tübingen: Niemeyer, 1988), 72; 117; 147.

handelt es sich vorwiegend um erbauende Texte, die den Leser im Glauben stärken sollen, sowie um belehrende Texte, die den Rezipienten religiöse Verhaltensnormen vermitteln. Zusätzlich unterhaltende Funktion ist den poetischen Bearbeitungen, besonders durch Hans Sachs, zuzuweisen, in denen der Text mit ästhetischem Anspruch künstlerisch bearbeitet ist. Nach „Sinnwelten", „in denen Wirklichkeit interpretiert und in Texten mitgeteilt wird,"[145] sind die Sirach-Texte und -Bearbeitungen der religiösen Welt zuzuordnen, aber auch der alltäglichen und sogar dichterischen Welt.

Insgesamt ist das Transformationspotential des Sirachbuches, wie es am Textspektrum der Sirachrezeption in Nürnberg in der Frühen Neuzeit ersichtlich wird, immens.

Durch die Neudeutung und Wertschätzung des von Luther als apokryph eingestuften Sirachbuches (vgl. Abschnitt 2) eröffneten sich neue Perspektiven für seine Rezeption, und es wird deutlich, dass die Rezeption des Sirachtextes in der Frühen Neuzeit einerseits zunimmt und andererseits unter einem neuartigen Fokus erfolgt: Die Betonung der ethisch-lebenspraktischen Aspekte der Schrift bedingt eine Ausdehnung ihrer Rezeption von der religiösen Lebenswelt auf die alltägliche. Diese Öffnung erschließt den Sirachtext für eine breitere Öffentlichkeit, woraus die Zunahme der Rezeption unmittelbar resultiert. Diese Rezeptionsverdichtung kann als Indiz für eine erhöhte Diskursrelevanz des Textes gewertet werden. Zeitlich steht diese Entwicklung eindeutig im Zusammenhang mit den Ereignissen der Reformation, so dass eine reformationsbezogene Zäsur in der Rezeptionsgeschichte des Sirachbuches konstatiert werden kann. Erinnert sei auch daran, dass die Rezeptionszunahme grundsätzlich erst durch die zeitgleiche Medienrevolution des Buchdrucks ermöglicht wurde, wodurch die Menge schriftlicher Erzeugnisse explosionsartig zunahm und Texte für breitere Schichten überhaupt erst finanziell erschwinglich wurden.

Paradox mutet an, dass die Neueinstufung des Sirachbuches als apokryphe bzw. deuterokanonische Schrift mit einer verstärkten Rezeption in Form der Lutherübersetzung einhergeht: Die Autorität Martin Luthers

---

145. Hannes Kästner, Eva Schütz und Johannes Schwitalla, „Die Textsorten des Frühneuhochdeutschen", in *Sprachgeschichte. Ein Handbuch zur Geschichte der deutschen Sprache und ihrer Erforschung*, 2. Teilbd., hrsg. Werner Besch u.a., Handbücher zur Sprach- und Kommunikationswissenschaft 2.2, 2. Aufl. (Berlin: de Gruyter, 2000), 1606.

überträgt sich auf einen Text, der aber zugleich ein Deutungspotential in sich birgt, das für die protestantisch geprägte Stadtgesellschaft in der Frühen Neuzeit relevant erscheint. Als Weisheitsschrift beinhaltet das Sirachbuch ein umfassendes Bildungskonzept, das auf die ethische Verantwortung des Einzelnen im gesellschaftlichen Kollektiv ausgerichtet ist: Die Lehre des Sirach vermittelt Deutungs- und Handlungsmuster, deren Umsetzung eine erfolgreiche Lebensführung im Sozialgefüge garantiert. Inhaltlich kann sie dabei als überzeitlich und hinsichtlich der vermittelten Werte als traditionell, aus heutiger Perspektive als konservativ charakterisiert werden.[146] Die Position des Einzelnen wird aus seiner Einfügung in hierarchische Strukturen heraus definiert.

Das Sirachbuch wurde stark im Rahmen des protestantischen Erziehungs- und Bildungsdiskurses funktionalisiert. Dies verwundert nicht, denn im Zuge der reformatorischen Ereignisse wurde die Selbstverantwortung des Einzelnen für eine ethisch geprägte Lebensführung betont. Haus und Familie rückten als Lebens- und Arbeitsraum in den Fokus der Unterweisung zur idealen Lebensführung. Hierin mag nun ein Grund zu sehen sein, dass eine altjüdische Weisheitsschrift im Rahmen einer frühneuzeitlichen deutschen städtischen Kultur ein derartiges Wirkungspotential entfalten konnte. In die konstatierte „Verkirchlichung des alltäglichen Lebens"[147] und epochenprägende „Sozialdisziplinierung"[148] fügt sich das Sirachbuch, ähnlich wie die Katechismen, jedenfalls bestens ein. Es lässt sich erkennen, dass die Wert- und Normvorstellungen des Sirach gut auf diejenigen der frühneuzeitlichen Stadtkultur übertragbar sind. Der Text bzw. Einzelpassagen daraus wurde durch Predigten, durch häusliche und schulische Lektüre und Memoration rasch Bestandteil des kollektiven Wissens von Jung und Alt. Christliche Wertvorstellungen wurden so in einer traditionell orientierten Form in allgemeine gesellschaftliche Kontexte transportiert und auf sämtliche Gesellschaftsschichten ausgedehnt. Sirach wurde quasi zum persönlichen Ratgeber des christlichen Hausvaters. Auch wenn in der weiteren zeitlichen Entwicklung die Rezeption des Sirach-Textes zunehmend von der Person Martin Luthers losgelöst wurde, blieben die etablierten Rezeptionsmuster für lange Zeit erhalten.

---

146. Vgl. Siegert, *Einleitung in die hellenistisch-jüdische Literatur*, 156; Wischmeyer, „Jesus ben Sira als erster frühjüdischer Autor", 21.

147. Raitz, Röcke und Seitz, „Konfessionalisierung der Reformation".

148. te Heesen, *Das illustrierte Flugblatt als Wissensmedium der Frühen Neuzeit*, 23–24.

Dadurch aber vermag der Sirach-Text im soziokulturellen Umfeld der Freien Reichsstadt Nürnberg als Autoritätstext eine machtorientierte Wirkung zu entfalten: Er ist in unterschiedlichen Diskursen dergestalt instrumentalisiert, dass soziale Ordnungsstrukturen durch christlichen Normbezug stabilisiert wurden, um die Kontinuität der städtischen Soziokultur längerfristig sicherzustellen.[149] Die Etablierung der Normen erfolgte in den skizzierten Textbeispielen häufig kontrastorientiert. Dies wiederum fügt sich zur antithetischen Grundkonzeption altjüdischer Spruchweisheit, wie sie auch im Sirachbuch sowohl kapitel- als auch versbezogen durch das Prinzip des parallelismus membrorum gegeben ist. Eine entsprechende argumentative Funktionalisierung des Sirachtextes wird somit bereits durch die Grundanlage des Ausgangstextes unterstützt.

Den soziokulturellen Transformationsprozessen, denen das Sirachbuch im Laufe seiner Rezeptionsgeschichte ausgesetzt war, sollte jedenfalls als ein Teilaspekt seine jüngere Rezeption in Form der Lutherübersetzung hinzugefügt werden. Dies ins Bewusstsein zu rufen, war das Anliegen des vorliegenden Beitrags.

Abbildungen

Abb. 1: Titelblatt der Wittenberger Sirach-Erstausgabe (Ed. princeps) (Hans Lufft, 1533). (Staatliche Bibliothek Regensburg, 999/Theol.syst.1437(12, urn:nbn :de:bvb:12-bsb11119611-8)

Abb. 2: Titelblatt der Nürnberger Sirach-Erstausgabe (Friedrich Peypus, 1533). (Universitäts- und Landesbibliothek Sachsen-Anhalt, urn:nbn:de:gbv:3:1-109489)

Abb. 3: Titelblatt der lateinischen Nürnberger Sirach-Erstausgabe (Johann Petreius, um 1548). (Württembergische Landesbibliothek Stuttgart, B lat.154806, urn:nbn:de:bsz:24-digibib-bsz50551723X9)

---

149. Dass christliche Normen, wie sie in der Ratgeber- und Hausväterliteratur aufscheinen, im Nürnberg des 16. Jahrhunderts zur familiären Identitätsstiftung, Stabilisierung und Kontinuitätssicherung generationsübergreifend funktionalisiert wurden, hat z.B. Christian Kuhn in einer Studie zur Nürnberger Patrizier- und Kaufmannsfamilie Tucher anhand der im Tucherschen Familienarchiv überlieferten Mahn- und Erziehungsbriefe dargelegt. Vgl. Christian Kuhn, *Generation als Grundbegriff einer historischen Geschichtskultur. Die Nürnberger Tucher im langen 16. Jahrhundert*, Formen der Erinnerung 45 (Göttingen: V&R unipress, 2010), 109–85. Für diesen Hinweis danke ich Franz Böhmisch herzlich.

Abb. 4: Titelblatt der Sirach-Bearbeitung durch Georg Lauterbeck (Nürnberg: vom Berg & Neuber, 1555). (Herzog August Bibliothek Wolfenbüttel, S: Alv.: Aa 163 (1), VD16 B 4090, urn:nbn:de:gbv:23-drucke /alv-aa-163-1s1)

Abb. 5: Register zur Sirach-Bearbeitung durch Georg Lauterbeck (Nürnberg: vom Berg & Neuber, 1555). (Herzog August Bibliothek Wolfenbüttel, S: Alv.: Aa 163 (1), VD16 B 4090, urn:nbn:de:gbv:23-drucke /alv-aa-163-1s1)

Abb. 6: Beispielseite G v^r zur Sirach-Bearbeitung durch Georg Lauterbeck (Nürnberg: vom Berg & Neuber, 1555). (Herzog August Bibliothek Wolfenbüttel, S: Alv.: Aa 163 (1), VD16 B 4090, urn:nbn:de:gbv:23-drucke /alv-aa-163-1s1)

Abb. 7: Titelblatt der anonymen lateinischen Sirach-Bearbeitung (Nürnberg: vom Berg & Neuber, 1563). (Württembergische Landesbibliothek Stuttgart, B lat.156304, VD16 B 4058, urn:nbn:de:bsz:24-digibib-bsz3532244489)

Abb. 8: Titelblatt der Nürnberger Erstausgabe (ed. princeps) von Caspar Huberinus, *Spiegel der haußucht* (Nürnberg: Hain, 1552). (Bayerische Staatsbibliothek München, 2815005 Res/4 B.g.prot. 100 e, VD16 ZV 1816, urn:nbn:de:bvb:12-bsb10874482-5)

Abb. 9: Beispielseite (S. 359) zu Caspar Huberinus, *Spiegel der haußucht* (Nürnberg: Hain, 1552). (Bayerische Staatsbibliothek München, 2815005 Res/4 B.g.prot. 100 e, VD16 ZV 1816, urn:nbn:de:bvb:12-bsb10874482-5)

Abb. 10: Titelblatt von Daniel Wülfer, *Heilsame Cur=Gedanken* (Nürnberg: Felsecker, 1658). (Herzog August Bibliothek Wolfenbüttel, M: Th 2871, VD17 23:668275U, urn:nbn:de:gbv:23-drucke/th-28719)

Abb. 11: Titelblatt von Conrad Feuerlein, *Sterbens Nohtwendigkeit Und Unterscheid* (Nürnberg: Endter, [1676]). (Universitätsbibliothek Erlangen, H00/RAB 217, VD17 23:302848C, urn:nbn:de:bvb:29-bv012377278-6)

Abb. 12: Titelblatt von Hans Sachs, *Das Buch Jesu deß Sons Syrach* (Nürnberg: Heußler, 1579). (Bayerische Staatsbibliothek München, Rar. 2298-4/5, VD16 S 150, urn:nbn:de:bvb:12-bsb10149444-0)

Abb. 13: Beispielseite b ij^r zu Hans Sachs, *Das Buch Jesu deß Sons Syrach* (Nürnberg: Heußler, 1579). (Bayerische Staatsbibliothek München, Rar. 2298-4/5, VD16 S 150, urn:nbn:de:bvb:12-bsb10149444-0)

Abb. 14: Titelblatt von Johann Behem, *Ein Christlich Ratbüchlein* (Nürnberg: Hergot, 1535). (Herzog August Bibliothek Wolfenbüttel, S: Alv.: Ab 236 (1), VD16 B 1487, urn:nbn:de:gbv:23-drucke/alv-ab-236-1s4)

Abb. 15: Beispielseite A vj^v zu Johann Behem, *Ein Christlich Ratbüchlein* (Nürnberg: Hergot, 1535). (Herzog August Bibliothek Wolfenbüttel, S: Alv.: Ab 236 (1), VD16 B 1487, urn:nbn:de:gbv:23-drucke/alv-ab-236-1s4)

Abb. 16: Titelblatt von Jakob Friedrich Feddersen, *Sittensprüche des Buchs Jesus Sirach* (Nürnberg: Weigel & Schneider, [1784]). (Universitätsbibliothek Leipzig, PR 201, eigenes Bild)

Abb. 17: Beispielseite X 1ʳ zu Jakob Friedrich Feddersen, *Sittensprüche des Buchs Jesus Sirach* (Nürnberg: Weigel & Schneider, [1784]). (Universitätsbibliothek Leipzig, PR 201, eigenes Bild)

Abb. 18: Beispielseite 1 (Anhang) zu Jakob Friedrich Feddersen, *Sittensprüche des Buchs Jesus Sirach* (Nürnberg: Weigel & Schneider, [1784]). (Universitätsbibliothek Leipzig, PR 201, eigenes Bild)

Abb. 19: Epitaph Nürnberg, Johannisfriedhof (Grabnr. 987), 1570 (eigenes Bild)

Abb. 20: Flugblatt: anonym, *Spiegel einer Christlichen und friedsamen Haushaltung*. Nürnberg: Fürst, 1651. (Wolfenbüttel, Herzog August Bibliothek, IE 30, VD17 23:674576D, URL: http://gateway-bayern.de/VD17+23%3A674576D, Zugriff: 01.09.2018)

Abb. 1

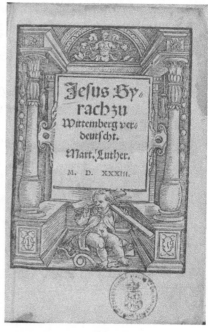

Abb. 2

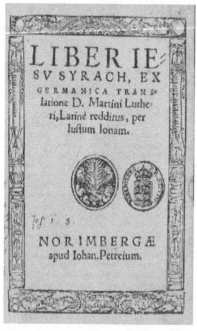

Abb. 3

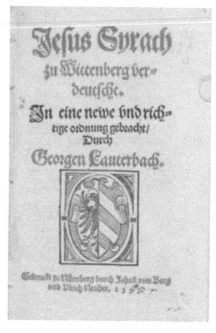

Abb. 4

Register.

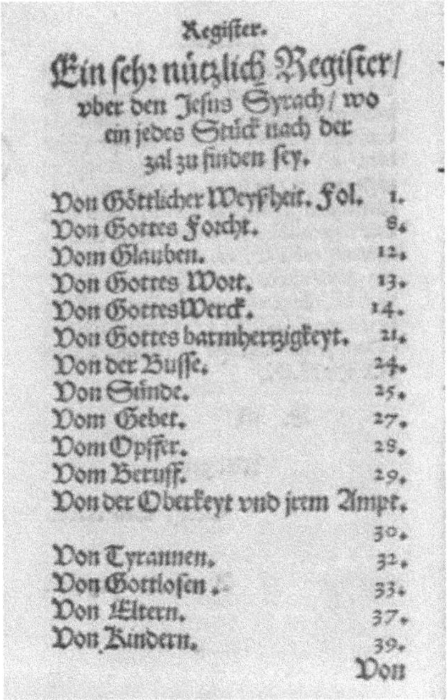

Ein sehr nützlich Register/ vber den Jesus Syrach/ wo ein jedes Stück nach der zal zu finden sey.

Von Göttlicher Weyßheit. Fol. 1.
Von Gottes Forcht. 8.
Vom Glauben. 12.
Von Gottes Wort. 13.
Von Gottes Werck. 14.
Von Gottes barmhertzigkeyt. 21.
Von der Busse. 24.
Von Sünde. 25.
Vom Gebet. 27.
Vom Opffer. 28.
Vom Beruff. 29.
Von der Oberkeyt vnd jrem Ampt. 30.
Von Tyrannen. 32.
Von Gottlosen. 33.
Von Eltern. 37.
Von Kindern. 39.
Von

Abb. 5

Jesus Syrach. 45

Ein Hürisch Weyb/erkennet man bey jrem vnzüchtigen gesicht/ vnd an jren Augen. 26.

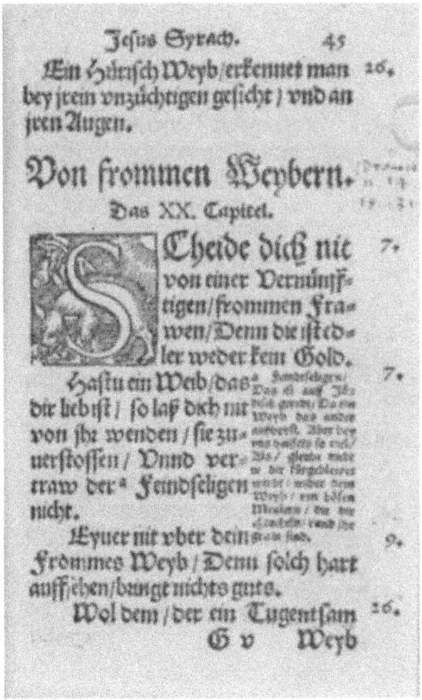

Von frommen Weybern.

Das XX. Capitel.

SCheide dich nit von einer Vernünfftigen/frommen Frawen/Denn die ist edler weder kein Gold. 7.

Hastu ein Weib/das dir liebist/ so laß dich nit von jhr wenden/ sie zuuerstossen/ Vnnd vertraw der a Feindseligen nicht. 7.

Eyuer nit vber dein Frommes Weyb/ Denn solch hart auffsehen/bringt nichts guts. 9.

Wol dem/der ein Tugentsam 26.

G v Weyb

Abb. 6

LIBER IESV SYRACH. MVLTO QVAM VVLGO PLANIORE ET DEXTERIore versione latine redditus. & in Locos communes redactus.

Cum indice locorum

LXXXIX.

Beatus populus qui scit iubilationem.

M. D. LXIII.

Abb. 7

Spiegel der haußzucht,

Jesus Syrach genant: Sampt eyner kurtzen Außlegung.

Für die armen Haußvätter vnnd jhr Gesinde/ Wie sie ein Gottselig leben gegen menigklich sollen erzeygen.

Darinnen der Welt lauff begriffen/ vnd wie sich ein jeglicher Christ in seinem beruff/ vnd in der Pollicey/ ehrlich vnnd löblich solle halten.

Caspar Huberinus.

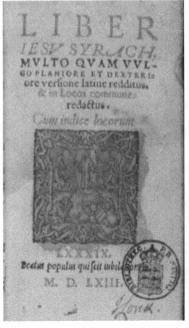

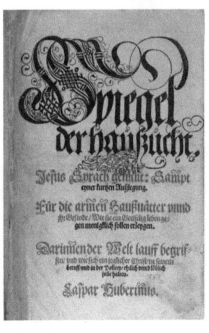

Abb. 8

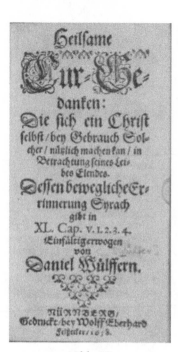

Abb. 9   Abb. 10

Abb. 11   Abb. 12

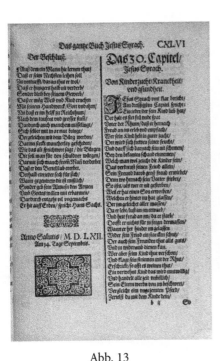
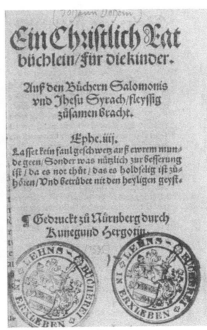

Abb. 13

Abb. 14

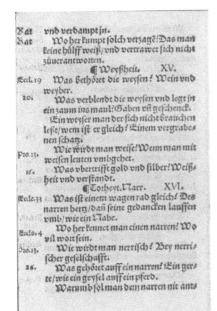

Abb. 15

Abb. 16

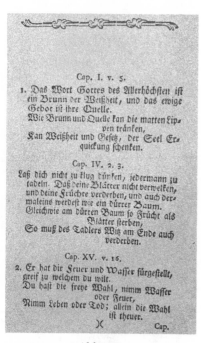

Cap. I. v. 5.

1. Das Wort Gottes des Allerhöchsten ist
ein Brunn der Weißheit, und das ewige
Gebot ist ihre Quelle.
Wie Brunn und Quelle kan die matten Lippen tränken,
Kan Weißheit und Gesetz, der Seel Erquickung schenken.

Cap. IV. 2. 3.

Laß dich nicht zu klug dünken, jedermann zu
tadeln. Daß deine Blätter nicht verwelken,
und deine Früchte verderben, und auch der-
maleins werdest wie ein dürrer Baum.
Gleichwie am dürren Baum so Frücht als
Blätter sterben,
So muß des Tadlers Witz am Ende auch
verderben.

Cap. XV. v. 16.

2. Er hat dir Feuer und Wasser fürgestellt,
greif zu welchem du wilt.
Du hast die freye Wahl, nimm Wasser
oder Feuer,
Nimm Leben oder Tod; allein die Wahl
ist theuer.
)(Cap.

Abb. 17

Abb. 18

Abb. 19

Abb. 20

Ancient Sources Index

CPSIA information can be obtained
at www.ICGtesting.com
Printed in the USA
FSHW011546081020
74538FS